THE INVASION of America

BY FRANCIS JENNINGS

THE INVASION OF AMERICA: *Indians, Colonialism, and the Cant of Conquest*

THE AMBIGUOUS IROQUOIS EMPIRE: *The Covenant Chain Confederation of Indian Tribes with English Colonies from Its Beginnings to the Lancaster Treaty of 1744*

EMPIRE OF FORTUNE: *Crowns, Colonies, and Tribes in the Seven Years War in America*

THE INVASION of America

INDIANS, COLONIALISM, AND THE CANT OF CONQUEST

꽃꽃꽃꽃 *by* FRANCIS JENNINGS

W · W · NORTON & COMPANY

New York · London

Published for the
Institute of Early American History and Culture
at Williamsburg, Virginia

W. W. Norton & Company, Inc., 500 Fifth Avenue, New York, N.Y. 10110
W. W. Norton & Company Ltd., 10 Coptic Street, London, WC1A 1PU

Books That Live
The Norton imprint on a book means that in the publisher's
estimation it is a book not for a single season but for the years.
W. W. Norton & Company, Inc.

Library of Congress Cataloging in Publication Data

Jennings, Francis, 1918-
    The invasion of America.
    (Norton Library paperback series)
    Bibliography: p.
    Includes index.
    1.   New England—History—Colonial period, ca. 1600-
1775.   2.   Indians of North America—New England.
3.   Indians, Treatment of—New England.   I.   Title.
F7.J46   1976   974'.02   76-25451

ISBN 0-393-00830-4

567890

PREFACE ❧

     This book got itself started, unknown to me, when I picked up a used set of Francis Parkman's works in 1956 (at ten cents the volume). Having acquired them, I did the uncharacteristic thing of reading them all the way through, fascinated by the flow of dramatic, if sometimes turgid, prose, and increasingly plagued by a sense of something terribly wrong. I had had an undergraduate course in anthropology under that good taskmaster George Simpson, and Parkman's Indians seemed impossible to reconcile with Simpson's. Growing curious, I began to investigate sources for comparison with Parkman's findings.

The casual inquiry led to a dissertation and a series of articles on matters of historical fact about which Parkman and others like him had been willfully and consistently misleading. (It is not enough to say merely that these historians were in error; in some instances there is evidence of deliberate deception.[1]) I saw little point in being only a negative Boswell; so I set myself the task of unearthing the history that Parkman *et al.* had buried under an ideology—the history of relationships between Europeans and Indians in what ordinarily is called the colonial period of United States history. From the Indian viewpoint, however, it is the period of invasion of Indian society by Europeans.

The Indian attitude seemed normal enough to contemporary Europeans, who armed themselves in anticipation. The invaders also anticipated, correctly, that other Europeans would question the morality of their enterprise. They therefore made preparations of two sorts: guns and munitions to overpower Indian resistance and quantities of propaganda to overpower their own countrymen's scruples. The propaganda gradually took standard form as an ideology with conventional assumptions and semantics. We live with it still.

One of the purposes of this book is to examine the origins of that ideology. Another is to demonstrate its fallaciousness. Both purposes require comparison of the rapidly changing cultures of Europeans and Indians during the period of invasion.

1. For a detailed analysis of text in one instance, see Francis Jennings, "A Vanishing Indian: Francis Parkman versus His Sources," *Pennsylvania Magazine of History and Biography*, LXXXVII (1963), 306–323.

The comparison has posed many problems, one being the sheer quantity of available evidence. While the documents are often tantalizingly scant for particular incidents at particular places, their mass for the whole continent over centuries of tumult is overwhelming. As I write, the Smithsonian Institution is preparing a twenty-volume revision of its encyclopedic *Handbook of American Indians North of Mexico*, calling upon the services of hundreds of scholar specialists. My one-man book must be on a one-man scale. By necessity I have been selective in my use of evidence, partly because of the inability of a single individual to master all the sources. Partly, however, the selectivity is based on my purposes. I am arguing theses that have emerged from far more research than can be presented in a tidy, readable volume. The manuscripts for sequel volumes have been drafted and will be offered for publication in due course. Here it has seemed advisable to hold this book within bounds by drawing mostly upon the evidence of a single region for illustration. For reasons that are discussed at some length in chapter 11, the region chosen is New England. There the phases of development of Amerindian-Euramerican acculturation went through a full cycle very rapidly, culminating in "King Philip's War" in 1675, and the sources of information are copious.

The book's two sections are organized and documented on different principles. In Part I organization is topical and analytical, and references are cited from a variety of sources as convenient for illustration. In Part II a short narrative history of southern New England is presented in which the references are intended more substantially to make the stated case stand up in court. The study nowhere aspires to be definitive. It aims instead to suggest redefinition of issues and to stimulate discussion and research along new approaches.

About the book's ethnohistorical method and terminology, something is said in chapter 1. One pair of terms is important enough to deserve special mention here—Amerindian and Euramerican. I do not ordinarily refer to white men and red, for reasons other than squeamishness. Such terms are extrapolations of modern conceptions into the past. Although invading Europeans perceived quite clearly that Indians had complexions different from their own, their dominant ideas regarding the "Americans" were long formed around conceptions other than race. The transition to racial stereotypes was a historical process that developed erratically at different eras in different regions. Regrettably, since Europeans of the second generation became native Americans distinct from those other Americans, clarity of reference has required names with extra syllables.

The longer names also seem to fit one of the book's theses; to wit, that modern American society is the product not only of interaction between colonists and natives but of contributions from both. Traditionally historians have conceived of our present culture as a transplantation of European culture to American soil. In this interpretation the Indians have been assigned the role of a mere foil, an opposing and distinct element whose only contribution was to stimulate the energy and ingenuity of European dispossessors. This interpretation seems fallacious to me because of the symbiotic interdependence that prevailed between the two societies in America for well over two centuries. Modern American society evolved from that web of interrelationship, and if much of the Indian contribution is not immediately visible nowadays, neither is very much of the Anglo-Saxon. We are not less the offspring of our ancestors because their bodies have been buried. Our society, like all others, is the product of its entire antecedent history, with all the human generators thereof. This thesis implies that formative processes in one society can be compared with those in others, and a tentative effort is made, in the Appendix, to summarize the analysis of the "colonial" formative period of modern American society in order to compare it with the "medieval" formative period of modern European society.

When assumptions are changed, phenomena appear in new aspects. The facts affirmed in this book will seem strange to students grounded in traditional lore. Some persons may find it incredible that the righteous, god-fearing folk who were their ancestors could have engaged in such practices as are here described, especially the pervasive calculated deception of the official records. Indians will not share in such incredulity; they have long known that pens could be as forked as tongues. I am writing this preface in the midst of the Watergate revelations. There is no need to dwell on them; I shall only remark that the Watergate deceits do not seem to be a very new thing in history. Persons and groups reaching for illicit power customarily assume attitudes of great moral rectitude to divert attention from the abandonment of their own moral standards of behavior. Deception of the multitude becomes necessary to sustain power, and deception of others rapidly progresses to deception of self. All conquest aristocracies have followed such paths. It would be incredible if ours had not.

Recognizing this reality should not be confused with condoning it. Despite the real pitfalls of historical moralizing, the logic seems plain that what we approve in past conduct will be repeated in the future. Realism that degenerates into cynicism becomes in the end a form of justification of immoral conduct. Determinist theories about past evil reveal themselves as exculpation of present transgressions. Call it predestination and the innate depravity of all men, or inevitability and the inequality of races—it all comes out to the same thing in practice. What is past is irrevocable, of course, but the relevance of inevitability doctrine is to the present and future. The issue is not whether something had to happen, but whether it has to happen again. I have made the assumption that human persons do have some power of choice over their own conduct and that their adherence to moral standards, whatever those standards may be, is a matter of historical concern.

This book ranges widely in subject matter and research disciplines, and it offers more than the ordinary number of opportunities for error; that I have inadvertently taken advantage of some of those opportunities may be the one certainty of the whole process. I have tried, of course, to minimize mistakes through standard research routines, and I have experimentally exposed parts of the study in journal articles and papers read to meetings of scholars. Let me thank the colleagues who have so patiently and sympathetically shared their knowledge. I am responsible for the mistakes they did not catch.

My acknowledgments offer the opportunity to observe that there is more than one tradition and more than one establishment in our huge society. Without the traditions of dedicated scholarship and freedom of discussion, and their preservation by certain great institutions, my work, for whatever it may be worth, would not have been possible. Let me first express gratitude to the American Philosophical Society, Philadelphia, for its valuable research library, its editorial hospitality, and the assistance of a research grant from its Penrose Fund. The staffs of many institutions have ungrudgingly given time and service, more especially in the libraries of the Historical Society of Pennsylvania, the Library Company of Philadelphia, and the University of Pennsylvania, all in Philadelphia; the New York State Library, Albany; the Public Record Office, London; and the libraries of Lehigh University, Bethlehem, Pa., and Cedar Crest College, Allentown, Pa. James D. Mack, Librarian of Lehigh University, has helped me on many occasions, and Jerry Rauch, Librarian of the Medical School of the University of Pennsylvania, has sifted and provided materials for me from the exotic literature of medicine.

The long catalog of my debts continues in extension through the reference notes where space is available for due appreciation. Here let me thank Professors Richard S. Dunn, Anthony F. C. Wallace, and Murray Murphey for early criticism and continued encouragement; Dr. Gordon M. Day for introducing me to the company of ethnohistorians and for his sustained friendly interest; Dr. William N. Fenton for pathbreaking scholarship and amiable cautions; Dr. Wilcomb E. Washburn for demonstrating the value of comparison of texts from different sources; Professor C. A. Weslager for a large correspondence of criticism, badinage, and shared learning; and Miss Maretta Quick for invaluable help of another sort. Thanks are due also to Deans Henry F. Pommer and Charles Peterson of Cedar Crest College for moral support, travel grants, and precious free time.

Last, and always first, to deserve full gratitude is my beloved and enduring partner, Joan Woollcott Jennings—an editorial critic of no mean abilities.

TECHNICAL NOTE 🐦

With one class of exceptions, all dates are given as in sources without adjustment from the Old Style, Julian calendar to the present New Style, Gregorian calendar. The exceptions are dates in January, February, and early March. These are removed from the end of the Old Style year and put at the beginning of the following year in conformity with present practice. Thus March 10, 1674, Old Style, becomes March 10, 1675. The distinction between the two calendars is critical in the interpretation of a number of documents.

Quotations generally follow the original in spelling, capitalization, and interior punctuation; in some instances spelling and punctuation have been sparingly modernized to clarify sense. Abbreviations have been spelled out, the ampersand has been expanded to "and," and "ye" and "yt" have been transliterated into "the" and "that." Typography conforms to modern usage. No words are omitted except where indicated by an ellipsis, and none are added except in square brackets. With these exceptions, quotations are as they appear in the cited sources.

CONTENTS ❧

ILLUSTRATIONS ↝

Part One 🐦 MYTHS
OF THE MARCHLANDS

> The particular conception of ideology ... signi-
> fies a phenomenon intermediate between a simple
> lie at one pole, and an error, which is the result
> of a distorted and faulty conceptual apparatus,
> at the other.

KARL MANNHEIM

Chapter 1 ❧ CRUSADER IDEOLOGY
—and an ALTERNATIVE

When Europe burst its bounds in the late fif-
teenth century, it was a continent of mixed attainments. Italy knew the
Renaissance, but Italy was not the base of the Reconnaissance. The
Atlantic coast countries destined for overseas empire had little of Italy's
artistic splendor or intellectual boldness. Spain and Portugal were deeply
steeped in feudal institutions and customs. France's kings had only just
won their long, debilitating contests with the kings of England and
the dukes of Burgundy, and in England the Tudors had just begun to
salvage what remained from the Wars of the Roses. However much
may now be seen of germs and origins of modern times, the peoples
of the springboard societies of western Europe knew only what they
had grown up with, and that was still feudal in conception, in conduct,
and in expectation. When Europeans began their astounding voyages
to dazzling "new" worlds, they could carry only the freight they possessed; the ideas and institutions with which they conquered and
colonized were the same they knew at home. On a thousand frontiers
Europeans used the technology of superior ships and guns to gain beachheads; they then imposed on top of indigenous societies the devices
best understood by the conquerors.[1]

The conception of feudalism, as the term is thus employed, cannot
be sharply limited to the single institution of lordship and vassalage.
Feudal times knew more complexity than one rigid pattern. Rather,
what is here meant is a whole society emerging from centuries of
struggle, during which Europe had been the invaded land. The pro-
logue to the feudal era was the destruction wrought by whole peoples

Under the title "The Legacy of Conquest," this chapter was delivered as the
presidential address to the American Society for Ethnohistory at its 21st annual
meeting, Oct. 26, 1973.

1. Two excellent introductions to the era are J. H. Parry, *The Age of Reconnaissance* (Cleveland, Ohio, 1963), and Boies Penrose, *Travel and Discovery in
the Renaissance, 1420–1620* (Cambridge, Mass., 1952). While much of their material necessarily overlaps, Parry has an especially good discussion on the era's
technology, and Penrose has excellent chapters on cartography and geographical
literature.

marching in arms. From each conflict more fragments were struck off until Europe became merely a name for a bewildering multiplicity of autonomous and semiautonomous communities—manorial, urban, ecclesiastical, commercial, and military. Feudal process was the incessant wrestling within and between these communities to establish relations of dominance and dependency. In such a world the ordering restraints of religion and law often became mere instruments for conquest, petty or grand.[2]

Medieval theologians taught that the fruits of any conquest could only be legitimate if the war that won them had been just. For ambitious warrior lords it was sometimes awkward to arrange the conditions of a just war at opportune moments, but they preferred not to give their enemies advantage by violating the doctrine too blatantly. Difficulties increased when the prospective candidates for subjection lived halfway round the world; it was hard to proclaim a righteously defensive war against an enemy who had never ventured within a thousand miles of one's domain. Happily there was a saving precedent: the Crusades had well established the principle that war conducted in the interests of Holy Church was automatically just.[3]

That principle stayed very much alive at the extremes of Europe where Islam held power. When the Ottoman conquest of Constantinople in 1453 opened all of the Balkans to Moslem invasion and gave the Turks naval power to threaten all of Mediterranean Christendom, Portugal and then Spain took the counteroffensive. Within two years after Constantinople's fall Pope Nicholas V empowered Portugal's king to enslave the persons and seize the lands and property of "all Saracens and pagans whatsoever, and all other enemies of Christ wheresoever placed."[4] The Portuguese used Nicholas's instruction to sanction their raids on Moslems of the African coast of the Mediterranean, but Portugal had also become interested in Africa's Atlantic coast, and the papal bull's "whatsoever" and "wheresoever" legitimized slaving expeditions anywhere. Persons and kingdoms who had never threatened Portugal—who had been unknown to all Europe—became just prey. Doctrine that had originated to sanctify conquest of the Holy Lands expanded to justify conquest of the world.[5]

2. I have adopted the orientation of Marc Bloch, *Feudal Society*, trans. L. A. Manyon (Chicago, 1961).

3. See Henry Osborn Taylor, *The Mediaeval Mind: A History of the Development of Thought and Emotion in the Middle Ages*, 4th ed. (London, 1925), I, 332–335.

4. The Bull Romanus Pontifex, Jan. 8, 1455, Frances Gardiner Davenport, ed., *European Treaties Bearing on the History of the United States and Its Dependencies*, Carnegie Institution of Washington Publication 254, I (Washington, D.C., 1917), 23.

5. Parry, *Age of Reconnaissance*, 36.

The Portuguese were soon joined in their sacred mission by other claimants to piety and plunder. In 1493 Rodrigo Borgia, in his capacity as Pope Alexander VI, granted to the rulers of Spain all the world not already possessed by Christian states, so that the abandoned heathen could be drawn "to embrace the Catholic faith and be trained in good morals." Borgia did this "of our own sole largesse and certain knowledge and out of the fullness of our apostolic power, by the authority of Almighty God." To remove all possible doubt of his intent, he characterized his document as "our exhortation, requisition, gift, grant, assignment, investiture, deed, constitution, deputation, mandate, inhibition, indult, extension, enlargement, will, and decree," threatening violators of all that with "the wrath of Almighty God" as well as, rather anticlimactically, the additional wrath of Saints Peter and Paul.[6]

Portugal's and Spain's willingness to undertake the sacrifice and toil of saving heathen souls failed to wring gratitude from other European powers. Henry VII of England, as orthodox in the Catholic faith as the rulers of Spain and Portugal, eschewed talk of morals or conversion to concentrate bluntly upon the real issue. In 1496 he commissioned John Cabot to "conquer, occupy and possess" the lands of "heathens and infidels." Henry's expressed motive was simply to acquire the "dominion, title and jurisdiction of the same."[7]

The emerging nation-states of Europe had centralized new military power in their kings' hands, but had held to old habit in warranting the use of power. Conquest as the extension of the Crusades was unarguably feudal in its conception. It was also not Christian in any sense taught by the master prophet of Christianity. The crusading mentality was formed by the feudal warlords' urge to conquest; in its turn it formed the rationalization for conquest and imprinted itself on everything the conquerors would do or become. The invaders of strange continents assumed an innate and absolute superiority over all other peoples because of divine endowment; their descendants would eventually secularize the endowment to claim it from nature instead of God, but would leave its absolute and innate qualities unchanged. Reconnaissance Europeans were both mostly Christian by profession and mostly Caucasian by heredity. When racism later emerged as the dominant principle of

6. The Bull Inter Caetera, May 3, 1493, Davenport, ed., *European Treaties*, I, 61–63.

7. The Cabot patent was simultaneously an affirmation of Christian right and a denial of papal sovereignty. The patent: James A. Williamson, ed., *The Cabot Voyages and Bristol Discovery under Henry VII*, Hakluyt Society Publications, 2d Ser., CXX (Cambridge, 1962), 49–53, 204–205. Papal sovereignty: H. Vander Linden, "Alexander VI. and the Demarcation of the Maritime and Colonial Domains of Spain and Portugal, 1493–1494," *American Historical Review*, XXII (1916–1917), 11, 15.

European conquest, it grew naturally by easy stages out of feudal religiosity.

The overwhelming importance of this fact can be seen in a single glance at the behavior and rationalizations of the Crusaders. Their enemies were also the enemies of the Crusaders' god and therefore outside the protection of the moral law applicable to that god's devotees. No slaughter was impermissible, no lie dishonorable, no breach of trust shameful, if it advantaged the champions of true religion. In the gradual transition from religious conceptions to racial conceptions, the gulf between persons calling themselves Christian and the other persons, whom they called heathen, translated smoothly into a chasm between whites and coloreds. The law of moral obligation sanctioned behavior on only one side of that chasm.[8]

The conquerors of America glorified the devastation they wrought in visions of righteousness, and their descendants have been reluctant to peer through the aura. Decent men with pigmentless skins no longer overtly espouse delusions of peculiar grandeur, but the myths created by the cant of conquest endure in many forms to mask the terrible tragedy that was Europe's glory. Although the ideologists of conquest can no longer evoke admiration for holy wars or pseudobiology, they have yet one great and powerful system of myth among their resources. In it the Christian Caucasians of Europe are not only holy and white but also *civilized*, while the pigmented heathens of distant lands are not only idolatrous and dark but *savage*. Thus the absolutes of predator and prey have been preserved, and the grandeur of invasion and massacre has kept its sanguinary radiance.

From very ancient times self-consciously "civilized" people have favorably compared themselves with their neighbors. The Greeks invented the term *barbarian* to apply to outsiders—even such as Egyptians and Persians—and the Romans were not slow to adopt the idea. As W. R. Jones has remarked, "The antithesis which opposed civilization

---

8. Despite his manifest virtues, I cannot agree with Winthrop D. Jordan's heavy emphasis on color as a dominant factor in racism. Gary B. Nash seems nearer right: "The image of the Indian was molded by the nature of colonization and the inner requirements of adventuring Englishmen. . . . [English attitudes] were closely linked to intentions and desires." Jordan argues that color dominated attitudes toward Africans, because Englishmen saw Africans in their homeland as free men, but this was surely not true in America, where Englishmen met Africans only in conditions of enforced servitude. In contrast, Indians preserved a degree of self-government here that compelled some personal respect. Cf. Winthrop D. Jordan, *White over Black: American Attitudes toward the Negro, 1550–1812* (Chapel Hill, N.C., 1968), 91–98; Gary B. Nash, "The Image of the Indian in the Southern Colonial Mind," *William and Mary Quarterly*, 3d Ser., XXIX (1972), 197, 217–218, 222–225. See also Nash's pertinent comments in *Red, White, and Black: The Peoples of Early America*, History of the American People Series (Englewood Cliffs, N.J., 1974), 164–165.

to barbarism was a highly useful cliché, and one which served equally well as a means of self-congratulation and as a rationalization for aggression."[9] Barbarism's definition varied from century to century, sometimes stressing linguistic or cultural differences, sometimes denoting little more than heathenism in religion, but always retaining a core meaning of inferiority in moral worth. In Jones's words, "The image of the 'barbarian,' whatever its specific historical context and to whomever applied, was the invention of civilized man who thereby expressed his own strong sense of cultural and moral superiority."[10]

Sometimes the factual difference between civilization and savagery was very slight indeed. In 1395 Richard II of England excoriated the "wild" Irish who maintained independence of his rule. "Wild Irishman" is a humorous phrase nowadays, but Richard was not making jokes, and neither were his officials in Ireland who used the term repeatedly and who hanged those Irishmen when they caught them. "Wild Irish" is really a translation from the Norman-French used by the conquest aristocracy. The words actually written by Richard were *"irrois savages, nos enemis"*—literally "savage Irish, our enemies." In an era of linguistic mixing, the words "wild" and "savage" were used interchangeably not only to identify Irish people but also to describe the Scots of the highlands and the islands, contrasting them with the anglicized inhabitants of the lowlands.[11] Ironically, Richard was attacking the Irish as savages at just the moment that England was plunging into the Wars of the Roses.

It may be worth our trouble to examine how fine a line actually distinguished the societies of England and Ireland at that time. Both countries were Christian and Catholic, although the independence of the Irish monastic movement kept rankling the bureaucratic hierarchy of the bishops and thus influenced the papacy to give its support to England. Both countries were fully agricultural, with flocks and herds as well as tillage. Both were haphazardly literate, and the Irish had their own alphabet as well as literature. Both had metals and masonry and weaving. Both had towns and ships and commerce with other countries; the Irish were, on the whole, a more rural people than the English, but England was by no means an urbanized country even by the standards of that day. A contemporary Italian would have laughed at the thought.

The difference was political and no more. What made Irishmen morally inferior to Englishmen, and thus imposed a duty on England's

9. W. R. Jones, "The Image of the Barbarian in Medieval Europe," *Comparative Studies in Society and History*, XIII (1971), 377. Thanks to Professor Edward Peters for calling this valuable article to my attention.

10. *Ibid.*, 405.

11. J. F. Lydon, *The Lordship of Ireland in the Middle Ages* (Toronto, 1972), 232, 283–285.

kings to conquer the "other island," was the government of most of Ireland by independent tribes and clans instead of subject vassal lords. One might say that Ireland was fit to be conquered simply because it was there, but wars require more elaborate justification than mountain climbing. With no substantial difference between the two societies except tribal government on the one hand and a feudal state on the other, the Norman-French kings of England set themselves up as carriers of civilization to a savage people.

At other times and on other occasions powers bent on conquest have been able to point to more substantial differences between their own cultures, always deemed as civilization, and the uncivilized societies of their opponents. Most frequently, perhaps, the difference has been one of religion. At other times it might have been nomadic instead of sedentary habitation or one mode of subsistence versus another: communities without agriculture—or those possessing horticulture but lacking animal husbandry—were barbarous or savage. Some social scientists have tried to bring validity and precision to these conceptions by making literacy the criterion of civilization. All of these floundering attempts at explanation only serve to obscure the essential fact that the civilized-uncivilized distinction is a moral sanction rather than any given combination of social traits susceptible to objective definition. It is a weapon of attack rather than a standard of measurement. There are other ways of using these terms, to be sure, although the taint of historical usage makes difficult any attempt to purify them.

The myth's moral antithesis has survived superficial changes in terminology. Toward the end of the Middle Ages, Europeans became aware of high cultures other than their own, and it was not easy for the rude mountaineers of Christian Castile to hurl "barbarian" at the cultivated Moors of Granada. But Europe expanded against simple societies also, and the tribes of Africa and America could readily be identified as social structures radically different from the forms of civilization reluctantly conceded to parts of Islam. The distant heathen were savage, and savagery imperceptibly displaced barbarism as civilization's antithesis.[12]

The ancient myth cast a heavy shadow over the nineteenth-century social scientists who attempted to structure the evolution of societies in *three* stages of savagery, barbarism, and civilization. A pioneer in this effort was the American lawyer-ethnologist Lewis Henry Morgan, whose work on the Iroquois Indians is often said to have founded the science of anthropology in the United States.[13] Torn between his

---

12. Jordan, *White over Black*, 24–28.
13. Lewis Henry Morgan, *League of the Ho-De-No-Sau-Nee, Iroquois* (Rochester, N.Y., 1851).

sympathy for the Indians and his contempt for their condition, Morgan recognized that they were not the savages of crude popular myth, but he was equally certain of the inferiority of their culture to his own. Thus he put them in between the bottom and the top and gave their intermediate position the name of barbarism, which had earlier been synonymous with savagery as a term for debasement. Searching for empirical criteria with which to distinguish one stage from the other, Morgan fixed upon literacy as the invention that had created civilization. The highest stage of human development, he wrote, had begun with the phonetic alphabet.[14]

Despite all goodwill toward his Iroquois friends and neighbors, Morgan could not suppress ethnocentric pride. His major theoretical work ended with an overt declaration of racial elitism: "It must be regarded as a marvelous fact that a portion of mankind five thousand years ago, less or more, attained to civilization. In strictness but two families, the Semitic and the Aryan, accomplished the work through unassisted self-development. The Aryan family represents the central stream of human progress, because it produced the highest type of mankind, and because it has proved its intrinsic superiority by gradually assuming the control of the earth."[15]

Morgan's ideas achieved great influence, partly directly and partly indirectly, through adoption by the founders of Marxism. Marx's colleague Friedrich Engels accepted the intermediate category of barbarism for the Indians of eastern North America and, like Morgan, found much to admire in this sort of barbarism. Also like Morgan, Engels believed in "the superior development of Aryans and Semites," though he generally avoided racial comparisons. He diverged from Morgan, however, in identifying the line of distinction between barbarism and civilization. In his extremely influential work, *The Origin of the Family, Private Property, and the State*, Engels concluded that "exploitation of one class by another" was "the basis of civilization" and that the characteristic institution of civilization was the territorial state with coercive power.[16] The difference between Engels's state power and Morgan's phonetic alphabet is not slight when one is to be considered as *the* measure of civilization, and the difference has never been bridged over.

Whatever efforts are made to objectify its definition, *civilization* necessarily implies not only technical but moral superiority over the stages assumed to be lower on the evolutionary scale. Civilization is

14. Lewis Henry Morgan, *Ancient Society, or Researches in the Lines of Human Progress from Savagery through Barbarism to Civilization* (1877), ed. Eleanor Burke Leacock (Cleveland, Ohio, 1963), 11–12.

15. *Ibid.*, 562–563.

16. Engels, *The Origin of the Family, Private Property, and the State* (1884), trans. Ernest Untermann (Chicago, 1902), 132, 175, 206, 216.

rarely conceived of in terms of empirical data, and although its phenomena might vary as widely as those of ancient Sparta and Victorian England, its essence is always its status on the top of the evolutionary ladder. That constant can be preserved through an infinity of empirical transformations.

There are, of course, many meanings that can be given to the word *civilization*. In its mythical sense it is an absolute quality that cannot be grammatically pluralized. This sense must be distinguished from the relative use of the term, as when Greek civilization is compared to medieval European civilization or Chinese civilization or even North American Indian civilization. In modern usage one may refer to different sorts of civilization in a way that makes the term interchangeable with the anthropological term *culture*. The ambiguity between absolute and relative meanings for the same term has created great confusion. The absolute meaning is the one under discussion here.

Civilization as an absolute quality is omnipresent in American history and literature. Roy Harvey Pearce has shown how our writers have developed a myth of social structure in which civilization and savagery stood as reciprocals, each defined as what the other was not, and both independent of any necessary correlation with empirical reality. Pearce found that the conjoined myth so greatly distorted Americans' perceptions of reality that they met constant frustration in dealing with the issues raised by the presence of Indians. "Even philanthropy and humanitarianism would not work. He on whom it was to work was in fact no Indian but an image which the civilized conscience had created just for the protecting, which the civilized intellect and the civilized imagination had earlier created just for the destroying. Civilization had created a savage, so to kill him. Idea had begotten image, so to kill it. The need was to go beyond image and idea to the man." [17]

In modern historical literature the civilization-savagery myth is most firmly fixed in the writings of the "frontier thesis" school. Although we customarily attribute the founding of this school to Frederick Jackson Turner, only a particular formulation of the frontier idea belongs to him, and some writers who have become dubious about Turner's sweeping rhetoric continue to use the more general civilization-savagery conception without reference to his special contribution.

As long ago as the 1620s Captain John Smith and the Reverend Samuel Purchas laid the foundation for that general conception, and the Puritan historians of "King Philip's War," most notably the Reverend William Hubbard, built upon it. [18] (It is significant, I think, that men trained in

17. Roy Harvey Pearce, *The Savages of America: A Study of the Indian and the Idea of Civilization*, rev. ed. (Baltimore, 1965), 3, 242.
18. See chaps. 5, 13, and 16 below.

theology were so prominent in the myth's origins.) In Hubbard's variant, civilization was the property of the divinely chosen people of
New England. The nineteenth-century historian Francis Parkman
maintained New England's primacy, but he secularized the basic myth
by transforming the author of Election from divinity to nature and
converting the triumph of the Chosen to the survival of the fittest.[19]
Frederick Jackson Turner, extending the scope of the myth to carry
it through the nineteenth century and across the continent, found a
good name for the survival of the fittest—he called it democracy.[20] In
the twentieth century Walter Prescott Webb suggested that the myth
should be expanded further to include the history of Europe and the
world.[21]

The twentieth century has also seen a determined movement among
historians to reexamine the realities of America's frontiers. Traditionalists have shown great flexibility in adapting the substance of the old
myth to new findings and new terminology. Turner's most forthright
disciple, Ray Allen Billington, has devoted his career to adapting the
frontier thesis to the facts disclosed by new research.[22] Douglas Edward
Leach and Alden T. Vaughan have taken different roads back to seventeenth-century New England to translate Puritan self-conceptions into
terms acceptable today; Leach overtly equated civilization versus savagery with white man versus red, while Vaughan preferred to type it
as Christianity versus heathenism, both authors taking pains to justify
the Puritan conquests.[23] Vaughan avoided the term *savage*, but introduced its substance under other names by dwelling upon the reciprocal
of civilization. Francis Paul Prucha has avoided direct dicta as author

19. Francis Parkman, *The Old Regime in Canada* (1874), New Library ed.
(Boston, 1908), 464-465, and *The Book of Roses* (Boston, 1866), 95, 98, 100, 105.
20. Frederick Jackson Turner, "Social Forces in American History," in *The
Frontier in American History* (New York, 1920), 320.
21. Walter Prescott Webb, *The Great Frontier* (1952), rpt. ed. (Austin, Tex.,
1964).
22. Billington's major work is *Westward Expansion: A History of the American Frontier*, 2d ed. with the collaboration of James Blaine Hedges (New York,
1960).
23. Douglas Edward Leach, *Flintlock and Tomahawk: New England in King
Philip's War* (New York, 1958), 1, 6, 249-250. In *The Northern Colonial Frontier,
1607-1763*, Histories of the American Frontier Series (New York, 1966), Leach
remarked that "this book is constructed frankly within the perspective of the
Anglo-American settlers ... and not within that of the Indians. It is the author's
sincere belief that this has been done without the sacrifice of justice or truth,
which would be a price too great to pay" (p. xiii). The logic of this remark
seems to define justice and truth as things limited by the settlers' perspective. For
Vaughan see his *New England Frontier: Puritans and Indians, 1620-1675* (Boston,
1965). See also the comments of Neal Emerson Salisbury, "Conquest of the 'Savage':
Puritans, Puritan Missionaries, and Indians, 1620-1680" (Ph.D. diss., University of
California, Los Angeles, 1972), 5-7.

while aligning himself unmistakably with the views he ascribes to conquest mythologists of times past.[24] In a review of writings in the field of Euramerican-Amerindian relations, Bernard W. Sheehan has explicitly accepted the civilization-savagery dichotomy.[25]

Such views are not confined to Americans or to narrow specialists. The noted English historian Hugh Trevor-Roper dismisses as merely amusing the study of "the unrewarding gyrations of barbarous tribes in picturesque but irrelevant corners of the globe: tribes whose chief function in history, in my opinion, is to show to the present an image of the past from which, by history, it has escaped."[26]

Reason must struggle to break the bonds of ideology so long established and so firmly fixed. National and racial religions of the present day are no less powerful than the crusader religions of days past in their grip on men's minds. The very words used to express thought give it shape and direction as well as symbolic substance,[27] and the words evolved from centuries of conquest have been created for the purposes of conquest rather than the purposes of knowledge. To call a man savage is to warrant his death and to leave him unknown and unmourned. To understand the processes called the history of America, it is necessary to employ semantic instruments designed for measurement rather than attack.

The designs and use of such tools are still experimental, for they have been created only within my own lifetime. We are indebted for them to the emerging social sciences, more particularly the discipline of anthropology. Regrettably, despite the urging of the Social Science Research Council and of past president Roy F. Nichols of the American Historical Association, the conceptual tools of anthropologists are only beginning to be used by historians—but that beginning has picked up momentum and holds great promise.[28]

24. Francis Paul Prucha, *American Indian Policy in the Formative Years: The Indian Trade and Intercourse Acts, 1790–1834* (Cambridge, Mass., 1962), 5, and *passim*.

25. Bernard W. Sheehan, "Indian-White Relations in Early America: A Review Essay," *WMQ*, 3d Ser., XXVI (1969), 283. For a review of the same field by a scholar who eschews the savagery mythology, see Wilcomb E. Washburn, "The Writing of American Indian History: A Status Report," *Pacific Historical Review*, XL (1971), 261–281; Washburn's comment on Sheehan is on pp. 267–268.

26. Hugh Trevor-Roper, *The Rise of Christian Europe* (New York, 1965), 9. Thanks to my colleague Henry Way, Jr., for showing me this.

27. See Edward Sapir, *Language: An Introduction to the Study of Speech* (New York, 1921), chap 11.

28. Jeannette P. Nichols, "Introduction," and Thomas C. Cochran, "The Social Sciences and the Problem of Historical Synthesis," in *The Social Sciences in Historical Study: A Report of the Committee on Historiography*, Social Science Research Council, Bulletin 64 (New York, 1954), 16, 164; Roy F. Nichols, "History in a Self-Governing Culture," *AHR*, LXXII (1966–1967), 411–424.

The alternative to the historian of frontier semantics and mythology is the ethnohistorian. In the lexicon of the ethnohistorian the opposing absolutes of evil savagery and good civilization become morally neutral and relatively comparable as "societies" and "cultures." Instead of assuming an impassable chasm between societies, the ethnohistorian postulates their capacity to exchange cultural traits in processes of cooperation as well as conflict, and he sets himself the task of describing those processes, to which he gives the inclusive neutral name of *acculturation*.[29] The word's equality of application must be noted carefully. "Acculturation" has been used improperly by some writers to mean merely something that happened to natives to make them more like Europeans; thus used, it becomes merely a synonym for "civilizing."

As the ethnohistorian holds the anthropologist's respect for theory, he analyzes events for their demonstration of known cultural processes; as he holds the historian's methodological respect for fact, he tests the theory of abstract processes by their fit on unique and unalterable events.[30] Thus, in examining the American past, an ethnohistorian finds, not the triumph of civilization over savagery, but an acculturation of Europeans and Indians that was marked by the interchange or diffusion of cultural traits and the emergence of social and cultural dominance by the Europeans in a large society marked by a submerged Indian subculture. Cultural origination was encouraged in both of the interacting societies by the acculturation situation. Dramatic demographic changes in both quantity and location of populations took place. Ecological balance was crucially changed by social alteration of geographical environment, and symbiosis continued between Europeans and Indians for a long time during which a certain amount of social assimilation occurred. Cultural conflict induced episodic efforts for the extermination of one population by the other, and finally the dominant groups in both societies asserted cultural identities independent of each other in conception though not in reality, emphasizing their differences in nativistic or nationalistic movements. These movements influenced the development of mythologies in both cultures, antipodal in form but sprung from the same historical womb.

29. Acculturation has been much discussed by anthropologists. See, for example, Ralph Linton, ed., *Acculturation in Seven American Indian Tribes* (New York, 1940), especially chaps. 8, 9, 10, on theory, which he wrote himself. A textbook treatment is John J. Honigmann, *The World of Man* (New York, 1959), chap. 17.

30. Perhaps the finest example of ethnohistorical method in a large-scale study is Edward H. Spicer, *Cycles of Conquest: The Impact of Spain, Mexico, and the United States on the Indians of the Southwest, 1533–1960* (Tucson, Ariz., 1962); chap. 19, "The Processes of Acculturation," is a valuable distillation of historical data. For the study of an individual tribe see the model of Anthony F. C. Wallace, *The Death and Rebirth of the Seneca* (New York, 1970).

This is a different world of discourse from that of civilization versus savagery, and it leads to the discovery of a different world of facts. To affirm that European-Indian interaction has produced cultural origination and trait diffusion is to identify something different in form and substance from "the continuous rebirth of society" of the frontier historian.[31] The latter conception assumes the true existence, in ideal form, of only one society; it is properly to be compared, as a phenomenon of culture conflict, with the revelations of Indian nativist prophets. There is no need, however, to impose a specialized scientific terminology on every description of events; plain English will serve the same end if it avoids the specialized terminology, conceptions, and purposes of myth.

The historian cannot wholly free himself from the outlook of his own cultural tradition. In perceiving and reflecting upon the interaction of two cultures, he necessarily adopts a viewpoint somewhere in his own. The idea of a neutral ethnohistory is itself a product of the scientific tradition of European culture. Because of this inescapable bias of outlook, reinforced by the historian's dependence for source materials on the literate Europeans' corpus of documents, it seems desirable to make a special effort of imagination to see things as Indians might. A modern historian has remarked that he had not, "for the most part, attempted to account for the actions and reactions of the natives." He took this approach, he said, "by necessity, as well as by inclination."[32] An ethnohistorian, I think, should not accept such a necessity or share such an inclination. When "natives" are regarded as rational human beings rather than mythical creatures, their actions and reactions do not seem so difficult to infer from both circumstances and the available documentary evidence. The same statement, it may be added, holds true for persons whose ancestors were natives of Europe.

31. Billington, *Westward Expansion*, 2.
32. Vaughan, *New England Frontier*, vii.

Chapter 2 ❧ WIDOWED LAND

European explorers and invaders discovered an inhabited land. Had it been pristine wilderness then, it would possibly be so still today, for neither the technology nor the social organization of Europe in the sixteenth and seventeenth centuries had the capacity to maintain, of its own resources, outpost colonies thousands of miles from home. Incapable of conquering true wilderness, the Europeans were highly competent in the skill of conquering other people, and that is what they did. They did not settle a virgin land. They invaded and displaced a resident population.

This is so simple a fact that it seems self-evident. All historians of the European colonies in America begin by describing the natives' reception of the newcomers. Yet, paradoxically, most of the same historians also repeat identical mythical phrases purporting that the land-starved people of Europe had found magnificent opportunity to pioneer in a savage wilderness and to bring civilization to it. As rationalization for the invasion and conquest of unoffending peoples, such phrases function to smother retroactive moral scruples that have been dismissed as irrelevant to objective history. Unfortunately, however, the price of repressing scruples has been the suppression of facts.

The basic conquest myth postulates that America was virgin land, or wilderness, inhabited by nonpeople called savages; that these savages were creatures sometimes defined as demons, sometimes as beasts "in the shape of men"; that their mode of existence and cast of mind were such as to make them incapable of civilization and therefore of full humanity; that civilization was required by divine sanction or the imperative of progress to conquer the wilderness and make it a garden; that the savage creatures of the wilderness, being unable to adapt to any environment other than the wild, stubbornly and viciously resisted God or fate, and thereby incurred their suicidal extermination; that civilization and its bearers were refined and ennobled in their contest with the dark powers of the wilderness; and that it all was inevitable.

Allowing for reasonable qualification and modification, the grand myth is fallacious because there never were such absolutes as "savagery" and "civilization" (considered as savagery's antithesis) that play the myth's active roles; there was accordingly no triumph of civilization and no death of savagery; there was nothing in the product of the events to make their survivors inherently superior to mankind elsewhere; and only the events unwilled by human agency were inevitable. Historians have now begun to examine and analyze the origins of the myth. The present chapter exhibits still-current assumptions and arguments that contribute to its maintenance.

Henry F. Dobyns has remarked that "the idea that social scientists hold of the size of the aboriginal population of the Americas directly affects their interpretation of New World civilizations and cultures."[1] His statement holds equally true when reversed. The idea that scholars hold of New World cultures directly affects their interpretation of the size of aboriginal populations. Proponents of the concept of savagery stipulate, among other things, that large populations are impossible in savage societies. It follows that if aboriginal populations can be shown to have been large, they could not have been savage. A logical approach may thus be made into the whole question of the nature of aboriginal society and culture through the gate of numbers.[2]

Despite logic, nobody has ever compiled the data given in contemporary sources for America north of the Rio Grande, and nobody has ever subjected those data to reasoned analysis verifiable by standard principles of logic and criticism. There is not even a subject heading for "Indians of North America—Population" in the Library of Congress directory to subjects, although "Ponies" and "Portraits" are there.[3]

The lack of research on the subject will surprise students who have repeatedly seen assurances that the pre-Columbian Indians of North America, excluding Mexico, numbered approximately one million. This has been the standard authoritative estimate since its first publication in 1928 in a posthumous article by James M. Mooney. Mooney's work had been interrupted by his death in 1921, and his editor carefully explained that the published article was composed of "provisional detailed estimates." The estimates were listed in tabular form, by region and tribe, without specific documentation. Discussion of the figures

1. Dobyns, "Estimating Aboriginal American Population: An Appraisal of Techniques with a New Hemispheric Estimate," *Current Anthropology*, VII (1966), 395 (a seminal work). See Wilbur R. Jacobs, "The Tip of an Iceberg: Pre-Columbian Indian Demography and Some Implications for Revisionism," *WMQ*, 3d Ser., XXXI (1974), 123–132.

2. See Robert L. Carneiro, "On the Relationship between Size of Population and Complexity of Social Organization," *Southwestern Journal of Anthropology*, XXIII (1967), 234–243.

3. *Subject Headings Used in the Dictionary Catalogs of the Library of Congress*, 7th ed. (Washington, D.C., 1966) and supplements (1967, 1968).

was general, and authority rested on a rather sketchy bibliography.[4]

A hint of Mooney's method appears in a remark about the estimates for New England. Mooney wrote that "the original Indian population of New England was probably about 25,000 or about one-half what the historian [John Gorham] Palfrey makes it."[5] Apparently Mooney had followed the tradition of Palfrey's own acceptance; that is, he took the estimate of a predecessor and discounted it. The same sort of procedure had been used by every generation of scholars since the original data were recorded in the seventeenth century, and by Mooney's time discount upon discount had reduced the accepted figures to a small fraction of what was mentioned in the sources. It is as if one were to estimate the population of white Americans in 1790 by successive slashes of the census data of that year on the grounds that the census takers were probably exaggerating their numbers for undisclosed reasons. Mooney's procedure is even less defensible because of a factor of strong ethnocentric bias. In acknowledging John Gorham Palfrey as an authority superior to the sources, Mooney accepted the implications of Palfrey's own biased interpretation of source data, and by halving Palfrey's population estimates, he extended Palfrey's spurious logic further than Palfrey himself had gone.[6]

It appears that Mooney applied the same sort of logic to his estimates for all of North America, and his total of 1,100,000 was immediately challenged. One component of the total was an estimate of 150,000 population for the Ohio Valley. Archaeologist H. J. Spinden appealed to the evidence of the multitude of burial mounds in that region and declared that the eastern agricultural area alone "must once have supported several millions." Anticipating what was to come, we may note that Spinden and Mooney agreed on one matter at least. Spinden called epidemic disease "the greatest factor in depopulation," and Mooney, according to his editor, "attached the greatest importance to it."[7]

It is strange therefore that Mooney's strongest supporter, upon entering the argument, ignored disease entirely in order to concentrate on "'social' factors of some sort," especially "warlike habits." This dictum by Alfred Louis Kroeber has received acceptance because of

4. J. M. Mooney, *The Aboriginal Population of America North of Mexico*, ed. John R. Swanton, Smithsonian Miscellaneous Collections, LXXX, no. 7 (Washington, D.C., 1928), hereafter cited as Mooney, *Aboriginal Population*.

5. *Ibid.*, 3.

6. John Gorham Palfrey, *History of New England* (Boston, 1858–1890), I, 24. Palfrey's virulent bias against Indians appears without disguise whenever he mentions them.

7. H. J. Spinden, "Population of Ancient America," Smithsonian Institution, *Annual Report* (Washington, D.C., 1929), 466; John R. Swanton, in Mooney, *Aboriginal Population*, 2.

Kroeber's tremendous authority as a scholar.[8] When he stated that a smaller density of population prevailed among East Coast horticulturalists than among California hunters and gatherers, his colleagues called the statement notable instead of incredible.[9] Kroeber adopted Mooney's conclusions almost without exception, and when a study of northwestern Mexico, based on original sources, conflicted with the Mooney-Kroeber estimates, Kroeber bridled. Though the region of that study is outside our present concern, the principles of criticism laid down by Kroeber are much to our point.

Referring to the methods of C. O. Sauer, the dissident scholar, Kroeber admitted, "It is difficult to meet Sauer's citations of seventeenth-century figures except with the generic supposition that the Spaniards counted or estimated excessively." Three pages later he decided that such difficulties did not really matter. "Where Sauer shaves sixteenth- and seventeenth-century statements, I am likely to reject most of them outright." Finally Kroeber decided to dismiss altogether the evidence that conflicted with Mooney's and his own speculative authority: "It is because Mooney was experienced in balancing and comparing, within his area, that most anthropologists will feel him a safer authority than Cortés or Las Casas, or registers of baptisms and deaths by priests knowing only some missions in one province."[10]

This is a fairly breathtaking claim, especially in view of Kroeber's admission in another part of the same book that all of his own estimates for America north of Mexico were "necessarily approximate and preliminary" and that all he had done with Mooney's figures was to convert them into terms of Kroeber's own tribal classifications.[11] The dispute with Sauer was therefore more complex than a mathematical disparity. It arose partly out of opposed methods of scholarship and partly out of antithetical conceptions of the quality and capacity of aboriginal cultures everywhere in the Americas. In this latter respect Kroeber was gratifyingly explicit. He emphatically rejected the notion that the natives of North America could be considered capable of so ordering their societies and technologies as to increase their populations beyond a

8. The major work in which Kroeber incorporated his responses could not be published until 1939. Preceding it, he published an "abstract of conclusions" called "Native American Population," in *American Anthropologist*, N.S., XXXVI (1934), 1–25. All my references are to Sec. 11, "Population," of the major work, *Cultural and Natural Areas of Native North America*, University of California Publications in American Archaeology and Ethnology, XXXVIII (Berkeley and Los Angeles, 1939). The "social factors" remark is at p. 148.

9. Kroeber, *Native North America*, 145; Harold E. Driver and William C. Massey, *Comparative Studies of North American Indians*, American Philosophical Society, *Transactions*, N.S., XLVII, pt. ii (1957), 214.

10. Kroeber, *Native North America*, 177, 180, 181.

11. *Ibid.*, 131.

static and sparsely distributed token representation. Kroeber's allotment of one million persons—a deduction of 10 percent from Mooney's—divides into the total area of Canada and the United States (including Alaska) in the ratio of one person per seven square miles. His explanation for this sparsity virtually blamed the condition of savagery, though he must be credited with avoidance of the term itself. He reasoned that Indian societies were characterized by "insane, unending, continuously attritional" warfare and by "the absence of all effective political organization, of the idea of the state."[12]

Although the political defect in Indian societies was all-important, technological backwardness also figured in Kroeber's assumptions. He knew well that the practice of agriculture had been the foundation of most large societies, and he knew also that many of the Indians of eastern North America were agriculturalists, but he rejected the obvious reasoning that agriculture should have had among Indians the same effects it had had among other peoples. Instead of concluding that he should revise his population figures upward to take account of agricultural surpluses, Kroeber held to his guessed numbers and deduced from them that the Indian "was not a farmer in our sense of the word." How so? "Agriculture, then, was not basic to life in the East; it was an auxiliary, in a sense a luxury."[13]

Pursuing this train of thought, Kroeber summarized:

We must think, then, of the East as agricultural indeed, but as inhabited by agricultural hunters, not by farmers, peasants, or peons. There were no economic classes, no peasantry to exploit nor rulers to profit from a peasantry. Every man, or his wife, grew food for his household. *The population remaining stationary, excess planting was not practiced, nor would it have led to anything in the way of economic or social benefit nor of increase of numbers.* Ninety-nine per cent or more of what might have been developed remained virgin, and was tolerated, or appreciated, as hunting ground, as waste intervening to the nearest enemy, or merely as something natural and inevitable.[14]

The error of this Olympian pronouncement is clearly evident in the historical sources that detail, for example, how the Jamestown colonists were kept from starving through gifts and purchases of surplus Indian corn. Another gauge of measurement is the strategy universally adopted by European troop commanders, who warred against Indians by destroying their crops, knowing that they thus destroyed the tribes' basic food supply.[15] These sources, as well as standard authorities on the methods

12. *Ibid.,* 148, 149.
13. *Ibid.,* 145, 147.
14. *Ibid.,* 150 (emphasis added).
15. E.g., Virginians destroyed Indian crops from 1622 to 1629. Capt. William Perse, "Relation," Aug. 1629, C.O. 1/5, Pt. 1, fol. 69, Public Record Office.

and productivity of Indian agriculture, were easily available to both Mooney and Kroeber. Mooney's bibliography indicates that he consulted many of them only to disregard their evidence, while Kroeber seems to have been content to rely on Mooney's reading of the sources without checking them himself. It appears that Kroeber blindly supported Mooney because Mooney's findings were what Kroeber thought ought to be found.

A careful distinction must be made between the two men. Though both avoided the terminology of savagery, Mooney let drop such phrases as "half-negro mongrels" and "fairly healthy blood" (in reference to a whole community).[16] Such language was typical of genteel racism in Mooney's time. Kroeber, however, used cleaner terminology, and indeed Kroeber was one of the early initiators of the movement toward acculturation concepts and terms. I am not able to account for his lapse in the population study from his frequently stressed standards of empirical foundations for theory. Perhaps it derived from a belief in a variable "progress" of cultures that implied inequality among them of a moral sort as well as other kinds.[17] The constant curiosity and immense erudition of Kroeber's mind makes it necessary to introduce such a suggestion with diffidence. Yet, in his work on population, the words are before us and the characterizations of Indian cultures are nonempirical and value laden, to the Indians' great prejudice.

However, enough has now been said of Kroeber's individual contribution to the aboriginal population fallacy. His writing provides a convenient target for criticism, and it has been enormously influential because of his prestige as a world leader in anthropology, but his greatest significance for present purposes is his faithful echo of an enduring tradition.

Among other factors maintaining that tradition is the subtle, pervasive influence of the idea of Progress. Since Europeans began to emerge from the endemic wars and epidemic diseases of medieval times, they have acquired an outlook in which the present seems better than the past and the future will be an improvement over the present. In this perspective, and against mountains of evidence, large-scale catastrophe becomes inconceivable. The fall of Rome was followed by an absolute decline in the population of all Europe, while plagues swept the

16. Mooney, *Aboriginal Population*, 3.
17. "Evolution, History and Culture," in A. L. Kroeber, *An Anthropologist Looks at History*, ed. Theodora Kroeber (Berkeley and Los Angeles, 1966), 197. In this essay Kroeber refers to controversy over his use of the idea of progress in an earlier book in which he also used the term *civilization* ambiguously and the term *primitive* as though it were equivalent to *savage*. See A. L. Kroeber, *Anthropology*, rev. ed. (New York, 1948), 296–304, esp. 301.

continent from end to end.[18] In the nineteenth century, over a period
of eighty years, the natives of Hawaii were observed to dwindle from
diseases and demoralization introduced by Europeans and Euramericans.[19] These were peoples remote in time or place, and their disappearance has not seemed to philosophers of Progress as more than a
temporary aberration in a grand advance.

Nonetheless there has been catastrophe, and the realization of its effects during European invasions of America is as essential to an understanding of aboriginal Indian societies as knowledge of the history of
catastrophe during Asian invasions of Europe is essential to comprehension of the last decades of the Roman Empire. To envision the
dimensions of what existed before the destruction, one must grasp the
scale of the destructive process.

Woodrow Borah and Sherburne F. Cook have provided an example
of the profundity that can be achieved by scholars with such a vista.
In a masterful summary of the history of Mexico from the Aztec Empire to today, they have written:

> To an already overextended population the Spanish conquest came as
> catastrophe. Destruction of war and the dislocation of productive and distributive systems were greatly compounded by the unwitting introduction
> within a few years and in rapid succession of the temperate and tropical
> diseases of the Old World. Within less than a century the population of
> central Mexico shrank from approximately twenty-five millions to under
> two millions; the tropical coasts became the disease-ridden wastes that they
> have remained until recent decades.
>
> Had the Spanish conquest taken place without catastrophic shrinkage of
> population, the history of Mexico might have been more nearly parallel
> to that of India or China, the superimposition of a numerically small ruling
> stratum that at a later date could be expelled by a reorganized native society.
> As events actually occurred in Mexico, the disappearance of the Indians
> made room for the addition of substantial contingents of Europeans and
> Negroes, who contributed the increasingly important and now numerically
> predominant group of mixed-bloods, mostly the Indian-European mixture
> known as mestizos. Culturally, the shrinkage of the Indian population permitted the entrance of European elements on a scale and with a thoroughness that would otherwise have been difficult, if not impossible.
>
> The reorganization of social and political structures paralleled the decline
> in native numbers.[20]

18. Bloch, *Feudal Society*, trans. Manyon, I, 60–61.

19. A systematic study indicates an observed decline of about 50% over 50
years, with further sharp reduction thereafter. Robert C. Schmitt, *Demographic
Statistics of Hawaii: 1778–1965* (Honolulu, 1968), table 6, p. 42. For reasons for
the decline, see pp. 158–159.

20. Woodrow Borah and Sherburne F. Cook, "Conquest and Population: A
Demographic Approach to Mexican History," *American Philosophical Society,
Proceedings*, CXIII (1969), 182. Borah and Cook have made a number of studies

Borah and Cook's rough ratio of 90 percent decline within a century after European contact has been confirmed by other researchers in Spanish America, where work in the field is advanced far beyond anything yet done for the region north of the Rio Grande.[21] That ratio cannot be ignored by historians of Anglo-America. It is true that Mexico is not the United States and that the Aztec Empire was certainly grander and more complex than Indian societies farther north; but smallpox was smallpox on the north bank of the Rio Grande as well as on the south, and the Indians on the north had as little biological immunity to this epidemic scourge as the Aztecs had. Indeed, if there is any truth to biological distinctions between the great racial stocks of mankind, the Europeans' capacity to resist certain diseases made them superior, in the pure Darwinian sense, to the Indians who succumbed. Is it not strange, then, that this genuine sort of superiority is never mentioned by philosophical racists? The reason is that racism demands a moral superiority, for which presumed (and invented) biological distinctions merely serve as talking points.

Even so, the European immunity was a matter of degree and historical experience rather than of absolute difference. Europeans had been through the plagues sooner and had succumbed earlier. The great folk migrations of Europe's Middle Ages, with their accompanying pestilences, had left survivors with a genetic inheritance of partial or complete immunity to many diseases that the isolated Indians of the Americas had never encountered until European invasion. The raging epidemics of Europe's most tragic centuries repeated themselves in America. Not even the most brutally depraved of the conquistadors was able purposely to slaughter Indians on the scale that the gentle priest unwittingly accomplished by going from his sickbed ministrations to lay his hands in blessing on his Indian converts. As the invaders were descendants of the toughened survivors of the Middle Ages, so the Indians of today descend from those who could live through the trauma of a European handshake. Even the genuine racial distinction turns out to be a historical product. Europe's superiority was an earlier catastrophe.

If we are to gain a reasonable impression of the dimensions of North American catastrophe, we must search in an era long antedating James-

---

pointing to the same conclusions. See their use of detailed sources in individual local communities in a comparatively small area: Sherburne F. Cook and Woodrow Borah, *The Population of the Mixteca Alta, 1520–1960*, Ibero-Americana, L (Berkeley and Los Angeles, 1968), estimates on pp. 32, 38, and descriptions of source documents on pp. 22–24.

21. J. H. Parry, *The Spanish Seaborne Empire*, The History of Human Society (New York, 1966), chap. 11, esp. 215; Carl Ortwin Sauer, *The Early Spanish Main* (Berkeley and Los Angeles, 1966), 65–69.

town. Permanent colonies are not a prerequisite for disease transmission; mere transient contact will do, and large numbers of contacts have been recorded for the sixteenth century. There were the well-known Spaniards on the Gulf coast: Coronado, de Soto, de Leon, and their expeditionary forces, and the founding of Saint Augustine in 1565. A Jesuit mission was attempted on the Chesapeake Bay in 1570. French colonies were attempted on what is now the coast of South Carolina from 1562 to 1565. Sir Walter Ralegh planted the first English colony in "Virginia" in 1585. Farther north John and Sebastian Cabot sailed along the coasts before the fifteenth century had ended, to be followed by Thomas Aubert and Jacques Cartier. Many more might be mentioned. Besides these men with known names, the anonymous crews of thousands of fishing boats frequented the Grand Banks and traded with the natives on shore: their numbers had grown to something like five hundred ships each year by the end of the sixteenth century and continued to increase.[22] Even without recorded instances of disease, the laws of statistics would require a certain proportion of these visitors to be sick men.

The consequences were observable on a large scale. When Englishmen began to attempt permanent colonization toward the end of the sixteenth century, some of them noted that Indian populations had already dropped off sharply. The reason was not always clear to European observers. Attributing decline to war and "civill dissentions," Arthur Barlowe found the Carolina Algonquians in 1585 to be "marvelously wasted, and in some places, the Countrey left desolate." But scientist Thomas Hariot noticed in 1588 that "the people began to die very fast" after Englishmen's visits to Indian towns, "and many in short space; in some townes about twentie, in some fourtie, in some sixtie, and in one sixe score, which in trueth was very manie in respect of their numbers." In 1608 another "strange mortalitie" was reported by Jamestown colonists to have smitten "a great part of the people" of Accomacke on the Chesapeake Bay.[23]

It should be noted that Mooney signally failed to allow for these phenomena. In treating the South Atlantic region, for example, he specifically put "out of account" the contacts of the sixteenth century,

22. Charles M. Andrews, *The Colonial Period of American History* (New Haven, Conn., 1934–1938), I, 17–26; W. J. Eccles, *The Canadian Frontier, 1534–1760*, Histories of the American Frontier (New York, 1969), 12–18.

23. "Arthur Barlowe's Discourse of the First Voyage" (1589), and Thomas Hariot, *A briefe and true report of the new found land of Virginia* (1588), in David Beers Quinn, ed., *The Roanoke Voyages, 1584–1590*, Hakluyt Society Publications, 2d Ser., CIV–CV (London, 1955), I, 113, 378; John Smith, *A Map of Virginia* (1612), in Philip L. Barbour, ed., *The Jamestown Voyages under the First Charter, 1606–1609*, Hakluyt Society Publications, CXXXVI–CXXXVII (Cambridge, 1969), II, 400.

remarking that "we may date the beginning of the decline [of Indian population] with the founding of the Virginia colony in 1607." Although Mooney fixed upon this date as the time of maximum Indian numbers, both the historical sources and archaeological evidence indicate unmistakably that depopulation was already far advanced by 1607. John R. Swanton's independent research in the South Atlantic region produced the finding that "at an earlier period . . . there are evidences of a great expansion of population." From the large populations signified by Swanton's archaeological evidence through the dwindling process reported by the earliest European observers, Indian numbers arrived at a low point in 1607 that Mooney arbitrarily designated as their highest point—a feat that he accomplished by simply ignoring the evidence.[24]

Swanton's findings for the Southeast have been confirmed generally by William H. Sears, and James B. Griffin has extended them to the Northeast. Associating growth specifically with the introduction into the Northeast of "the concept and practice of agriculture," Griffin has concluded from archaeological reports that the period after 800 A.D. showed "marked population increase throughout the area, in terms of both the size of individual villages and the number of contemporary villages."[25]

Reducing such generalities to tolerably reliable specific numbers is not easily done but not wholly impossible. Here and there in the historical sources are benchmark numbers. If the reality of catastrophic disease is accepted, the general ratio of decline established in Spanish America can be applied to the sparse northern benchmarks, and calculations can be extrapolated backward through the ratio to aboriginal times.

The ratio itself is confirmed, though vaguely, by northern observers. In 1656 Adriaen Van der Donck wrote from his experience in New Netherland that "the Indians . . . affirm, that before the arrival of the Christians, and before the small pox broke out amongst them, they were ten times as numerous as they now are, and that their population had been melted down by this disease, whereof nine-tenths of them have died."[26]

24. Mooney, *Aboriginal Population*, 5; John R. Swanton, *The Indians of the Southeastern United States*, Smithsonian Institution, Bureau of American Ethnology, Bulletin 137 (Washington, D.C., 1946), 11.

25. William H. Sears, "The Southeastern United States," in Jesse D. Jennings and Edward Norbeck, eds., *Prehistoric Man in the New World* (Chicago, 1964), 277; James B. Griffin, "The Northeast Woodlands Area," *ibid.*, 256.

26. Adriaen Van der Donck, *A Description of the New Netherlands* (2d ed., 1656), trans. Jeremiah Johnson, in New-York Historical Society, *Collections*, 2d Ser., I (New York, 1841), 183, hereafter cited as Van der Donck, *Description of New Netherlands*, in N.-Y. Hist. Soc., *Colls.*, 2d Ser., I.

Specific figures for the Huron Indians, confirmed in a variety of ways, show a decline from a minimum of 32,000 persons to about 10,000 in ten years, largely from the effects of epidemic, with further decline attributable to catastrophic war as well as disease. These data originate from Samuel de Champlain and Jesuit missionaries and are based largely on information provided by the Hurons, with some additional observations made personally by the Jesuits.[27]

Indian informants also provided the Jesuits with information about the Susquehannock tribe then occupying the central valley of modern Pennsylvania. From 1580 onward the Susquehannocks concentrated their people in one large community that occasionally moved from site to site.[28] In 1647 a Canadian missionary learned that "a single village"— it should be read as *the* single village—of the Susquehannocks had 1,300 warriors, which would conservatively imply a total population of 5,200 to 6,500.[29] War, as well as disease, reduced this number quickly.[30] A thorough archaeological examination of the site occupied by the Susque-

27. Samuel de Champlain, *Voyages and Discoveries in New France, from the year 1615 to the end of the year 1618* (1619), in Charles Pomeroy Otis, trans., and Edmund F. Slafter, ed., *Voyages of Samuel de Champlain*, Prince Society Publications, XI–XIII (Boston, 1880–1882), III, 160–161; Gabriel Sagard, *The Long Journey to the Country of the Hurons* (1632), ed. George M. Wrong, trans. H. H. Langton, Champlain Society Publications, XXV (Toronto, 1939), 91–92; Jerome Lalemant, "Relation of what occurred in the Mission of the Hurons, from the month of June in the year 1639, until the month of June in the year 1640," in Reuben Gold Thwaites, ed., *The Jesuit Relations and Allied Documents: Travels and Explorations of the Jesuit Missionaries in New France, 1610–1791* (Cleveland, Ohio, 1896–1901), XIX, 125–127. Bruce G. Trigger comments that the early estimates depend on whether the Hurons were able to estimate their population accurately—which I have assumed true—and whether Champlain understood them properly. I think Champlain heard aright, because Father Sagard confirmed him and Sagard was not merely parroting; he got a different count of villages than Champlain's. Both of them lived in the Huron country for extended periods of time. Bruce G. Trigger, *The Huron: Farmers of the North*, Case Studies in Cultural Anthropology (New York, 1969), 11–13. See also Trigger, "The Destruction of Huronia: A Study in Economic and Cultural Change, 1609–1650," Royal Canadian Institute, *Transactions*, XXXIII (1960), 16, 29–30.

28. John Witthoft, "Ancestry of the Susquehannocks," in John Witthoft and W. Fred Kinsey III, eds., *Susquehannock Miscellany* (Harrisburg, Pa., 1959), 29; Barry C. Kent, in an interview, Aug. 23, 1972, about unpublished findings of the Division of Archaeology, Pennsylvania Historical and Museum Commission, Harrisburg, Pa.

29. Paul Ragueneau, "Relation of what occurred in the Mission of the Fathers of the Society of Jesus in the Huron country, in New France, in the years 1647 and 1648," Apr. 16, 1648, Thwaites, ed., *Jesuit Relations*, XXXIII, 129.

30. The Susquehannocks suffered from the same smallpox epidemic that so terribly reduced the Hurons: François Joseph le Mercier, "Relation of what occurred in the mission of the Society of Jesus, in the land of the Hurons, in the Year 1637," June 21, 1637, *ibid.*, XIV, 9. For the Susquehannocks' subsequent woes see Francis Jennings, "Glory, Death, and Transfiguration: The Susquehannock Indians in the Seventeenth Century," Am. Phil. Soc., *Procs.*, CXII (1968), 21–45.

hannocks after 1652 indicates a population of 2,000 to 3,000.[31] By 1698 only "about fifty men"—some 200 to 250 people all told—were left.[32] It is true that an unguessable additional number may have assimilated by that time into the Iroquois Five Nations, but they also complained of being scourged by both smallpox and military casualties.

In 1674 Daniel Gookin, the supervisor of Massachusetts's mission reservations, queried old Indians of the tribes of lower New England. They told him that before the English coming the Pequots could "raise four thousand men, fit for war," but that only 300 men were left in 1674. The Narragansetts had declined from 5,000 warriors to barely 1,000. The Massachusets Indians had dropped from 3,000 to 300 men. The Wamesits (Gookin's "Pawtucketts") had fielded 3,000 men and were reduced to "not above two hundred and fifty men."[33]

Confirmation comes also from the easily observed space of two small islands, Martha's Vineyard and Block Island (see map 1, in Part II). When the English first settled in Martha's Vineyard in 1642, according to the best available estimate the island's Wampanoag Indians numbered about 3,000.[34] Possibly this figure represents the effects of sicknesses already acquired from Europeans, because the island had already been much visited by explorers before being colonized. However that may be, the Vineyard's Indians declined to about 800 in 1720 and further to 313 in 1764. In this instance no wars raged over the island's territory, so that the observed reduction in numbers can be confidently attributed to disease.[35]

31. Interview cited in n. 28 above.

32. Trader John Hans Tilman, in "Proceedings of the Council of Maryland," July 1, 1698, William Hand Browne et al., eds., Archives of Maryland (Baltimore, 1883-   ), XXIII, 444.

33. Daniel Gookin, "Historical Collections of the Indians in New England...," (1674), in Massachusetts Historical Society, Collections, 1st Ser., I (Boston, 1792), 147–149. That Gookin erred on the conservative side rather than the liberal is suggested by comparing his 1,000 Narragansett warriors in 1674 with William Hubbard's 2,000 "fighting men" among the Narragansetts at the same time. Gookin and Hubbard were contemporaries. Gookin's sources were missionaries and old Indians. Hubbard's sources were the interpreters Thomas and Robert Stanton. Hubbard, The Present State of New-England. Being a Narrative of the Troubles with the Indians in New-England, 2d ed. (London, 1677), "Postscript," 138, hereafter cited as Hubbard, Narrative.

34. Matthew Mayhew, A Brief Narrative of the Success which the Gospel hath had, among the Indians, of Martha's Vineyard (and the Places Adjacent) in New-England... (Boston, 1694), 24.

35. "A Description of Duke's County, Aug. 13th, 1807," Mass. Hist. Soc., Colls., 2d Ser., III (Boston, 1815), 92. Since this chapter was written, Sherburne F. Cook has published an article on the population of New England Indians in which he not only confirms my findings regarding Martha's Vineyard but also documents similar findings about Nantucket. Regrettably Cook's findings are flawed by his acceptance otherwise of the estimates of James Mooney for precontact population (reluctantly, as Cook says, for want of something better). As a result

About forty miles west and a little south of the Vineyard, Block Island had also been much visited and even warred against by the Massachusetts Puritans before 1662, the date of the first available estimate of Indian population. By then the English had established themselves as settlers and had confronted 300 unfriendly warriors, who with their families can be estimated to have represented a total Indian population of 1,200 to 1,500 persons.[36] It is certain that this figure showed a falling off from a greater predecessor, if only because of the effects of the "Pequot War" of 1636–1637, during which the English colonists had attacked the island; but the total of 300 warriors is the first specific figure we have to work with. It gains significance from subsequent decline. From 1662 to 1774 the Block Island Indians dropped from between 1,200 and 1,500 to a total of 51.[37]

As the figures for the islands indicate, general decline continued well into the eighteenth century. In 1709 John Lawson wrote of the Carolina Indians, "I do believe, there is not the sixth Savage living within two hundred Miles of all our Settlements, as there were fifty Years ago."[38] At mid-century the Swedish naturalist-traveler Peter Kalm observed that Indian communities seemed to "melt away."[39] Moravian missionary John Heckewelder commented on the Delaware Indians: "What the numbers of this nation were when the Europeans first came into this country is difficult to tell; all I can say is, that so early as 1760, their oldest men would say that they were not then as many hundreds as they had been thousands. They have considerably decreased since that period." (Heckewelder wrote in his old age, in 1817.)[40]

The reality of catastrophic decline is surely beyond doubt.[41] The ques-

the article presents what has to be called the absurdity of 6,000 Indians in the two small islands of Martha's Vineyard and Nantucket out of a total population of 36,500 Indians in the entire area of the present United States east of the Hudson River. Sherburne F. Cook, "The Significance of Disease in the Extinction of the New England Indians," *Human Biology*, XLV (1973), 485–508.

36. Samuel Niles, "A Summary Historical Narrative of the Wars in New-England with the French and Indians, in the Several Parts of the Country" (1760), Mass. Hist. Soc., *Colls.*, 3d Ser., VI (Boston, 1837), 194.

37. S. T. Livermore, *History of Block Island, Rhode Island* (1877), facsimile reprint (Forge Village, Mass., 1961), 63.

38. John Lawson, *A New Voyage to Carolina* (1709), March of America Facsimile Series, No. 35 (Ann Arbor, Mich., 1966), 224.

39. Adolph B. Benson, ed., *Peter Kalm's Travels in North America: The English Version of 1770* (New York, 1937), I, 258.

40. John Heckewelder, *An Account of the History, Manners, and Customs of the Indian Nations, Who Once Inhabited Pennsylvania and the Neighbouring States* (1819), ed. William C. Reichel, Historical Society of Pennsylvania, *Memoirs*, XII (Philadelphia, 1881), 85.

41. Two studies of the effects of epidemics are E. Wagner Stearn and Allen E. Stearn, *The Effect of Smallpox on the Destiny of the Amerindian* (Boston, 1945), and John Duffy, "Smallpox and the Indians in the American Colonies," *Bulletin*

tions at issue are its rate and extent. If decline was really as great as 90 percent within a century, then our understanding of what the population declined *from* must be very sharply revised upward from the limits given by Mooney and Kroeber. Such revision, of course, implies much greater densities of population than Kroeber allowed Indian cultures to be capable of maintaining. The historical sources show that agricultural Indians could indeed sustain those denser populations.

The Hurons lived in a territory of roughly 800 square miles.[42] If we assume that they knew how to count their own people, we have a minimum of 32,000 aboriginal Hurons in that area, giving a density of 40 Indians to the square mile. The 3,000 Indians of Martha's Vineyard lived in 109 square miles, in a density ratio of 27 persons to the square mile. Block Island has not more than 11 square miles, so its minimum population of 1,200 in 1662 must have been packed in at 109 persons to the square mile.[43] It is not surprising that the explorer Verrazano had commented that the island was "well-peopled, for we saw fires all along the coast."[44]

More vaguely, the extensive country of the Narragansetts was reported by Massachusetts's Governor John Winthrop in 1633 to be "full of Indians,"[45] and other sources described it as having been cleared of timber by those Indians for a distance of eight to ten miles from the

of the History of Medicine, XXV (1951), 324–341. Henry F. Dobyns gives an itemized listing of losses suffered by specific tribes in specific epidemics in the reply to commentators on "Estimating Aboriginal Population," *Current Anthro.*, VII (1966), 441–442. See also the pioneering study by Joseph Jones, "Explorations and Researches Concerning the Destruction of the Aboriginal Inhabitants of America by Various Diseases, as Syphilis, Matlazahuatl, Pestilence, Malarial Fever, and Small-pox," *New Orleans Medical and Surgical Journal*, V (1877–1878), 926–941.

42. Trigger, "Destruction of Huronia," Royal Can. Inst., *Trans.*, XXXIII (1960), 16.

43. These areas are National Geographic Society figures listed in *The World Almanac*, 1973 ed. (New York, 1972), 470.

44. Quoted in Livermore, *Block Island*, 9.

45. John Winthrop, *The History of New England from 1630 to 1649* (1690), ed. James Savage, 2d ed. (Boston, 1853), entry of Nov. 5, 1634, I, 146 (starred paging). Narragansett Bay was also called "full of inhabitants" by John White in *The Planters Plea* (1630), 17, in Peter Force, comp., *Tracts and Other Papers, Relating Principally to the Origin, Settlement, and Progress of the Colonies in North America, from the Discovery of the Country to the Year 1776* (Washington, D.C., 1836–1846), II.

A bibliographic note: The cited version of Winthrop's *History* is the second edited by James Savage, with more notes and appendixes than the first. The starred paging is identical in both. Either is more valuable than the filiopietistic edition by James K. Hosmer, which is more frequently cited and accessible because it is still in print. Hosmer reproduces Savage's text but suppresses his revealing commentary. James Kendall Hosmer, ed., *Winthrop's Journal, "History of New England,"* 1630–1649, Original Narratives of Early American History (New York, 1908).

coast—no small feat.[46] One of the earlier English settlers in the vicinity of the Narragansetts estimated, as of the 1630s or early 1640s, that he had 30,000 Indian neighbors.[47] The physical circumstances do not belie his credibility. To maintain so large an area as the Narragansett country free of the ever-encroaching bush would require a sizable number of people.[48]

Daniel Gookin's informants from the lower New England tribes gave accounts for populations before 1600 that add up to 18,000 warriors in five great confederacies. Allowing three or four dependents to each warrior, these data imply a range of 72,000 to 90,000 persons all told. It is possible to test these data by the 90 percent rule of decrease mentioned previously. As of 1674, when Gookin wrote, he had compiled population figures from English missionaries as well as Indian informants. As usual the figures given were for warriors, adding up to 2,150. Allowing for dependents, they imply a total of 8,600 to 10,750 Indians in 1674. According to Gookin's figures, then, there was a decline from 72,000 in 1600 A.D. to 8,600 in 1674 A.D., or if the larger dependency ratio is consistently allowed, the decline was from 90,000 Indians in 1600 A.D. to 10,750 in 1674 A.D. Such rates of decline harmonize well with the rule established in the research in Spanish America.[49]

In contrast, that rule is violated badly by Mooney's estimates, which allowed a total of only 25,000 New England Indians in 1600 A.D.[50] A decline from this aboriginal figure to Gookin's collected data of 8,600 to 10,750 in 1674 A.D. is much too small to reflect what we know of the effects of disease on populations lacking immunity. Such a slight decline could be explained only by assuming either that Gookin did not know how to count or that smallpox had slighter effect upon New England's Indians than among similarly susceptible Indians elsewhere. The latter notion, besides being inherently implausible, is belied by many woeful stories in the historical records. As for adding Gookin to the long list of people supposedly without mathematical ability, is

46. William Davis Miller, "The Narragansett Planters," American Antiquarian Society, *Proceedings*, N.S., XLIII (1933), 51.

47. Francis Brinley, "A Briefe Narrative of That Part of New England Called the Nanhiganset Countrey," Rhode Island Historical Society, *Publications*, N.S., VIII (1900), 74.

48. Two early sources comment on how the bush returned when untended. See White, *Planters Plea*, 14, in Force, comp., *Tracts*, II, and William Wood, *New Englands Prospect* (1634), Prince Society Publications, I (Boston, 1865), 17. Marc Bloch noted the same phenomenon in his "first feudal age" in Europe. Bloch, *Feudal Society*, trans. Manyon, I, 61.

49. Gookin, "Historical Collections," Mass. Hist. Soc., *Colls.*, 1st Ser., I, 147–149. Gookin omitted a figure as of 1674 for the Pokonokets, or Wampanoags, to whom I have arbitrarily assigned the same number as the Massachusets because their precontact estimates were equal.

50. Mooney, *Aboriginal Population*, 3.

it not time to suggest that the skills of simple arithmetic are not a monopoly of any one era, race, or ideological sect?

The American land was more like a widow than a virgin. Europeans did not find a wilderness here; rather, however involuntarily, they made one. Jamestown, Plymouth, Salem, Boston, Providence, New Amsterdam, Philadelphia—all grew upon sites previously occupied by Indian communities. So did Quebec and Montreal and Detroit and Chicago. The so-called settlement of America was a *re*settlement, a reoccupation of a land made waste by the diseases and demoralization introduced by the newcomers. Although the source data pertaining to populations have never been compiled, one careful scholar, Henry F. Dobyns, has provided a relatively conservative and meticulously reasoned estimate conforming to the known effects of conquest catastrophe. Dobyns has calculated a total aboriginal population for the western hemisphere within the range of 90 to 112 million, of which 10 to 12 million lived north of the Rio Grande.[51]

Another of the jobs waiting to be done is the calculation of the *total* population of North America—Amerindians, Euramericans, and Afro-Americans—at periodic intervals as European invasion progressed. Obviously a long time elapsed during which natives outnumbered immigrants even in the enclaves where the latter clustered most densely. European sources of the early seventeenth century speak unanimously of the multitudes of Indians surrounding each colony. Even in Massachusetts, where whole communities of Indians had been exterminated before Englishmen attempted to plant their villages—and where accordingly few Indians lived immediately adjacent—Puritan and heretic alike wrote often and without dissent of the many thousands of natives in surrounding tribes. Bostonians and Rhode Islanders agreed on few other matters as on this.

With the sources now available there is no possibility of precisely calculating the numbers of either Indians or immigrants, but absolute precision is not always necessary. For some purposes approximations and comparisons will do. Available data for New England, for example, suggest that the entire seventeenth century was consumed in restoring the same level of total population that had existed prior to European colonization. We must use Gookin's figures of 1674 A.D. as our benchmark once more. The United States Bureau of the Census's closest estimate for New England's Euramericans is pegged, as of 1670 A.D., at a figure of 52,000.[52] If we add Gookin's minimum of 8,600 Indians, we get

51. Dobyns, "Estimating Aboriginal Population," *Current Anthro.*, VII (1966), 414.

52. United States Bureau of the Census, *Historical Statistics of the United States, Colonial Times to 1957* (Washington, D.C., 1960), Ser. Z 1-19, p. 756.

a total of about 60,600 persons, English and Indian, as compared with the minimum of 72,000 Indians implied in Gookin's estimates for the period before English colonization. It may be noted that 1674 was a high watermark. Immediately afterwards the catastrophe called "King Philip's War" took great toll of life among both the English and the Indians, and the losses were not soon restored. With all their resources, and including both migration and natural increase, the English apparently required the full century to duplicate the populations that Indians alone had maintained in New England prior to invasion.

It is admitted here, as throughout, that much speculation has entered into the writing of this chapter; but, such as they are, the evidence and reasoning have been laid out in plain view. However unsatisfactory by ideal standards, this evidence and this reasoning seem to me to be superior to the arbitrary processes by which figures have often been produced, without sufficient regard to the available evidence and largely without justification except by the myths of savagery. Certainly some method is needed to break through the circular fallacy in which the supposed condition of Indian savagery establishes the limits of population estimates, and then, in turn, the numbers so produced are used to "prove" the condition of savagery.

Chapter 3 ❧ RECIPROCAL DISCOVERY

It is customary for our histories to dwell at some length on the immensity of the task of "settling" North America, mentioning the hazards of vast wilderness, the logistical problems of supplying colonists from faraway Europe, the strangeness of the flora and fauna, and the hostilities that the natives were sooner or later bound to display. The implications of this use of the word *settlement* are worth notice. First, it vaguely implies that preexisting populations did not classify as humanity, for it is not used to apply to Indians; only Europeans "settle." It also dismisses the Indians' ability to wrest a generally satisfactory living from the "wilderness" and to travel over established trails to known destinations. Most inaccurate is the word's bland misdirection about the Europeans' intentions, for their common purpose was to exploit rather than to settle. Among the early European visitors, residence was merely a means of increasing the efficiency of exploitation. A taste for permanent habitation came later. Regularly the first Europeans were welcomed by natives with gifts of food and tokens of honor until the moment came when the gifts were demanded as tribute and the honors were commanded as homage—a moment that sometimes came very rapidly. At the outset native hostility was never directed against European settlement as such; what made trouble was the European purpose of settling on top.[1]

To accomplish this end the Europeans did indeed face huge problems of logistics. The sheer size of their New World and its distance from home forestalled quick and easy occupation. There could be no massive, decisive, single crossing like that from France to England of William of Normandy. J. H. Parry's "roughest of rough guesses" puts something like a hundred thousand people in the class of permanent Spanish emigrants to the Americas during the whole sixteenth century.[2]

1. The "frontier of settlement" is the idea with which Frederick Jackson Turner began his famous essay "The Significance of the Frontier in American History," and it remains prominent throughout all his works. His disciple Ray Allen Billington properly stresses the idea as central to Turner's thought. Turner, *Frontier in American History*, 1; Billington, *Westward Expansion*, 1–3.
2. Parry, *Spanish Seaborne Empire*, 235.

The grim epics of Cortés and Pizarro, not to speak of Columbus himself, testify to the military abilities of Spanish soldiery, but these need to be compared as well with the great failures of Narvaez, Coronado, and de Soto. A decisive military victory was possible only where native populations lived under a centralized government that could be decapitated and put under Spanish direction. Scattered independent native communities simply could not be subjected and controlled with the available forces, or the effort was not worth the cost. And it must not be forgotten that the conquistadors, efficient killing machines though they were, did not conquer Mexico and Peru unaided. Native allies were indispensable. In a sense Spanish armed conquest was a judo trick by which Europeans, assisted by the pox and the plague, used the Indians' own strength to overthrow them.[3]

North of New Spain, invasion started later; so Frenchmen, Dutchmen, and Englishmen found native communities that had already been reduced by epidemic from base populations that had never approached the size of Mexico's. Yet the colonists of Jamestown, Quebec, and Plymouth immediately allied themselves to nearby natives to guarantee security.[4] Ralegh's colony at Roanoke, which had made no formal alliances and had antagonized every Indian in sight, simply disappeared.[5] The necessity for native alliance was not merely a matter of armed manpower; it was desirable and indeed indispensable because of massive European ignorance. To the European who lacked woodcraft, knew not the native trails, and imagined gothic horrors in every copse, the familiar hunting parks of the Indians were lethal wilderness. The European "settlers," who knew nothing of tillage methods in America and were often revolted at the labor of farming, depended on Indian gardens for subsistence between the deliveries of cargoes from overseas.[6] The Pilgrims despaired when their beer ran out and they had to fall back on that barbarous drink, water.[7]

What all this signifies is that technologies cannot properly be compared in absolute terms. In terms of direct management of America's

3. *Ibid.*, 96–97.

4. Edward Maria Wingfield, "Discourse" (1608), in Barbour, ed., *Jamestown Voyages*, I, 214–215; Otis, trans., and Slafter, ed., *Voyages of Samuel de Champlain*, II, 202–203; *Dictionary of Canadian Biography*, I (Toronto, 1966), s.v. "Champlain, Samuel de"; William Bradford, *Of Plymouth Plantation, 1620–1647*, ed. Samuel Eliot Morison (New York, 1952), 80–81.

5. Quinn, ed., *Roanoke Voyages*, I, 246–249.

6. Eccles, *Canadian Frontier*, 32, 34; Edmund S. Morgan, "The Labor Problem at Jamestown, 1607–18," *AHR*, LXXVI (1970–1971), 595–611. Ralph Lane at Roanoke accused the Indians of a plot for "starving us by their forbearing to sowe." "Discourse on the first colony" (1589), in Quinn, ed., *Roanoke Voyages*, I, 276, 281.

7. Bradford, *Of Plymouth Plantation*, ed. Morison, 78.

natural environment, Indians had developed a technology superior to that of Europe.[8] Europeans, of course, were certainly as adept in managing the European environment, but in America they were fish out of water. On the other hand, Europeans had developed techniques for managing other peoples. Despite their helplessness on strange land, they had become skillful on the seas, and they were technically capable of providing ample supplies to maintain beachhead colonies. They sometimes callously left their outpost colonists to make shift or die because other matters concerned them more.[9] In the sixteenth and seventeenth centuries Europeans had what we like to call an Oriental disregard for human life. Adventurers abroad paid their own way or were abandoned. Being unable to wrest a living for themselves from alien soil, they were often saved from death through "civilized" neglect only by native charity, tribute, and trade.

Europe's distractions were struggles over power and wealth, both within and between nations. Thrones were wobbly, wars endemic and chancy, and treasuries perpetually depleted. Christopher Columbus obtained no financing until Spain had conquered Granada. The tale of Queen Isabella's having pawned her jewels to back him is fanciful; more likely the Spanish crown invested part of its Moorish plunder.[10] Certainly the money was regarded as an investment, no matter where it came from. If religious mission figured as a motive of either Columbus or his royal sponsors, it does not appear in their agreements. The articles of April 17, 1492, speak of "merchandise" and "goods" and "merchants" and "traffic" and "business" and tenths and eighths to be apportioned. Nor was there mention of missionary obligation as a condition of Columbus's titles and powers granted two weeks later.[11] His function was to find wealth; salvation would be offered in exchange later when it could be debited to the account. Missionary Father Ascensión concisely summarized motivations in 1620: "If the Spaniard does not see any advantage he will not be moved to do good, and these souls will perish without remedy if it is understood that no profit will be drawn from going there."[12]

---

8. W. J. Eccles states it plainly: "The French were far more dependent on the Indians than the Indians were on them." *Canadian Frontier*, 24.

9. E.g., see Quinn, ed., *Roanoke Voyages*, II, 553–559.

10. C. O. Sauer states that "a major part" of the financing was done by "borrowing from the funds of the Santa Hermandad, the secret police of the time." *Early Spanish Main*, 17.

11. Samuel Eliot Morison, trans. and ed., *Journals and Other Documents on the Life and Voyages of Christopher Columbus* (New York, 1963), 26–30.

12. Fray Antonio de la Ascensión, "A Brief Report of the Discovery in the South Sea" (1602), in Herbert Eugene Bolton, trans. and ed., *Spanish Exploration*

The remark also applied validly to other nations interested in the Americas. Direct financial involvement of their crowns was minimal except for carefully stipulated provisions about royal benefits from colonizing ventures. By and large royalty resorted to a medieval device for making conquests at the risk of other people. As the marcher lords of Charlemagne had led their own men and lived off the country, the gentlemen and merchants adventurers of the Reconnaissance sailed to conquer with their own resources. Royalty's contribution was a charter.

Thus Francis I granted Canada to the seigneur de Roberval in 1541 in return for Roberval's undertaking to take and hold the place. After Roberval's failure the French crown took no further official notice of Canada for the rest of the century, although private enterprise brought thousands of ships there to fish and trade.[13] The second French effort at colonizing North America, just north of Florida in the period from 1562 to 1565, seems to have been intended as a base of operations against the Spaniards; it was financed by Huguenot Admiral Gaspard de Coligny and associates, and it ended disastrously.[14] England's Queen Elizabeth was as thrifty as any other monarch. She authorized court favorites to make colonizing conquests in Ireland at their own expense and gave patents to two of the same men, Sir Humphrey Gilbert and Sir Walter Ralegh, to conquer in America also, all at their own expense. Gilbert and Ralegh reduced the drain on their finances by looting and privateering, but ultimately failed in all their overseas ventures.[15]

The failures were succeeded by more durable enterprises at Jamestown, Quebec, New Plymouth, New Amsterdam, and Massachusetts Bay, for all of which the same rule held: sovereigns authorized, private enterprise organized. As in feudal times royalty's authority rose and fell proportionately to its distance from the scene of operations and its participation in them. While monarchs gradually consolidated their

---

in the Southwest, 1542–1706, Original Narratives of Early American History (New York, 1908), 131.

13. Gustave Lanctot, *A History of Canada,* trans. Josephine Hambleton and Margaret M. Cameron (Cambridge, Mass., 1963–1965), I, 64–68; Eccles, *Canadian Frontier,* 17–18.

14. Woodbury Lowery, *The Spanish Settlements within the Present Limits of the United States, 1513–1561* (New York, 1959 [orig. publ. New York, 1901–1902]), II, 204–207.

15. Gilbert's patent, June 11, 1578, in Richard Hakluyt, *The Principall Navigations Voiages and Discoveries of the English Nation* (1589), with an introduction by David Beers Quinn and Raleigh Ashlin Skelton, Hakluyt Society Extra Series, XXXIX (Cambridge, 1965), II, 677–679, hereafter cited as Hakluyt, *Principall Navigations*; Ralegh's patent, Mar. 25, 1584, Quinn, ed., *Roanoke Voyages,* I, 82–89.

nation-states at home, the substance of feudal lordship revived in the colonies, and for the same reasons that it had come into being originally. A crown could not enforce theoretical sovereignty until it could act through its own agency.

Still in the pattern of feudal times, this weakness of royal authority held terrible implications for the peoples indigenous to the territories being conquered. Centralized states may be indifferent to the welfare of particular persons, but they tend to be equally indifferent to all—a subject is a subject. Local lords strive ceaselessly for aggrandizement, and their extortions are refined by local knowledge.[16] Lacking better alternatives, Europe's feudal downtrodden had rallied to their kings for protection against local oppressors. This pattern, too, would be repeated in America as the crowns attempted, with erratic success, to enforce policies of ethnic accommodation against the heedless grasping and bellicosity of the colonials. The climax of English colonialism would come with a royal proclamation in 1763 to protect Indians in their territorial possessions, a colonial rebellion aimed in part at destroying the protecting boundary, and the fighting support of many Indians for their royal protector.[17]

One must remember, however, that royal concern was a function of royal interests and royal policy. The loyalist Iroquois of the American Revolution were abandoned without a qualm at the treaty table. It was not Indians as such that Louis XIV or William and Mary befriended; it was Indians claimed as subjects. The crowns restrained the petty greed of local lords in order to feed the grander though more diffuse appetites of the crowns. In the long run the Indians of North America were hurt as severely by the kings as by the colonists; distinctions of interests made small difference in outcome when the same Indians were required to effect both kinds of interest.[18] But schedules and processes varied according to the motives and choices of a multitude of persons. What must be seen is the enormous complexity of the struggles and conflicts hidden under the phrase "the conquest of America." To reduce the historical processes of centuries to the dimensions of a football game or a chess match—reds against whites—is an absurdity. Yet that fantasy has survived to proliferate offspring, among which the most pertinent at this point is the myth of the Indian Menace.

16. In New Spain the friars' partial protection of the Indians from local overlords was made possible by the crown's support. No other European power was able to establish in America such an extensive and centrally controlled royal bureaucracy as did Spain. Parry, *Spanish Seaborne Empire*, chap. 9.

17. Jack M. Sosin, *The Revolutionary Frontier, 1763–1783*, Histories of the American Frontier (New York, 1967), chaps. 5, 7.

18. See Barbara Graymont, *The Iroquois in the American Revolution* (Syracuse, N.Y., 1972), 2–3, 104–106.

This Indian Menace held small terror for the men of the Reconnaissance. The journals of the invaders speak cockily of easy triumphs by handfuls of European soldiers over great masses of Indian warriors.[19] Firearms, armor, horses, ships, and strong forts enabled the Europeans to hold any beachhead they chose to take, as long as provisions held out and ocean-borne communication was maintained. To be sure, there were some who sang a song of savage threats for reasons of their own. Thomas Morton has told us of the busy traders of New Plymouth: "And this as an article of the new creede of Canaan, would they have received of every new commer there to inhabit; that the Salvages are a dangerous people, subtill, secreat, and mischeivous, and that it is dangerous to live separated, but rather together, and so be under their Lee, that none might trade for Beaver, but [at] their pleasure ... but I have found the Massachussets Indian more full of humanity, then the Christians, and have had much better quarter with them." [20]

Undeniably there were times when Indians attacked European colonists, but such incidents give signs of prior provocation, of bullying and tyrannizing by the invaders, so that the attacks bear the character of reprisal and defense. The Indian Menace, in short, when there was substance to it, was a boomerang effect of the European Menace to the Indians. The greatest human obstacles to European colonization existed in Europe itself. The sixteenth century saw no successful imitation of Spain's conquests in America largely because of exhausting strife among the nations capable of mounting overseas expeditionary forces. Protestant and Catholic fought each other and the Turk. Dynastic convulsions in England and France combined with religious struggles to nullify exploitation of the voyages of the Cabots, Verrazano, and Cartier. Spain claimed the entire New World and threatened all rivals, and Spain's power could not be disregarded on land or sea. Colonization lacked allurement when the same amount of effort and risk might yield vast and instant fortune from privateering, so the greatest effort of rival nations went into raids upon the treasure already concentrated in Spain's fleets and ports.[21] Coligny's French colony was intended as a base for systematic attack upon Spain's shipping; Spain's Philip II prudently and ruthlessly exterminated it.[22]

19. E.g., Ralph Lane wrote, "Ten of us with our armes prepared, were a terrour to a hundred of the best sort of them." "Discourse on the First Colony," in Quinn, ed., *Roanoke Voyages*, I, 282. Miles Standish took 14 soldiers to attack the Indian town of Namasket. Bradford, *Of Plymouth Plantation*, ed. Morison, 87–89.
20. Thomas Morton, *New English Canaan; or, New Canaan* ... (1632), 77, in Force, comp., *Tracts*, II.
21. See Kenneth R. Andrews, ed., *English Privateering Voyages to the West Indies, 1588–1595*, Hakluyt Society Publications, 2d Ser., CXI (Cambridge, 1959), 34–35.
22. Lowery, *Spanish Settlements*, II, chap. 1, and 204–207.

A still more prudent queen of England avoided such direct challenges to the greatest power in Europe by restricting her westward-yearning gentlemen to clandestine hit-and-run adventures. The rich Netherlands across the North Sea could make no such choices. Subject to Philip II and possessed of more autonomy than he would tolerate, they reacted to his repressive measures by rebelling in 1568. Thus began the long, hard fighting that simultaneously drove Spain out of the Dutch Republic, made the Netherlands themselves an imperial power, and ended Spain's monopoly in North America. Alarmed by Spain's pretensions and omnipresence, Elizabeth allied England to the Netherlands in 1577. In 1578 she granted to Sir Humphrey Gilbert her first patent for colonization in America.[23] But Philip's menace could not be ignored even after the defeat of his mighty Armada in 1588. So long as he lived, no colonizing effort could be sustained by any of the nations he threatened. France, England, and the Netherlands had to wait for opportunity until Philip died in 1603. Then their migrations began in earnest.

The dates tell the story. Jamestown was founded in 1607, Quebec in 1608. Fort Nassau began the Dutch presence in 1614 where Albany subsequently grew. Plymouth began in 1620. More Dutch settled near Manhattan in 1624. The Massachusetts Bay grand fleet landed in 1630. Maryland's colonists arrived in 1634. These were the larger and more enduring colonies among an astonishing variety of initiatives. Even Sweden founded a short-lived colony on the Delaware River in 1638.

The nations that combined to end Spain's monopolistic regime had united against Spain rather than against monopoly. Each aspired to take Spain's place as the dominant or only power in America, and each employed all available devices. After the founding of Jamestown the Indians never succeeded in overwhelming the colonial presence of a single European power. New Sweden was conquered by the Dutch, the Dutch in turn by the English, and France and England contested for a century before England triumphed, only to be defeated after all by her own colonists. All these conquests were part of the conquest of America, and none of them was a conquest either of or by Indians alone. Wars of empire were more frequent and more dreaded than race wars. Indians did participate in the imperial conflicts, but always in combination, overtly or covertly, with European allies.

Yet it is transparently plain that after these wasting imperial wars the Europeans emerged stronger and more numerous while the Indians constantly declined in strength and numbers. Apart from the effects of disease, which have been noticed already, the simplistic notion of conquest by combat cannot explain either this phenomenon or the

23. J. B. Black, *The Reign of Elizabeth, 1558–1603*, The Oxford History of England (Oxford, 1936), 294–298, 205.

many decades of peaceful commerce and alliance between Indians of particular tribes and Europeans of particular colonies. The "conquest of America" was a mingling of conflict and cooperation, in which Indians generally became not merely weaker than Europeans generally but also dependent upon them. The process was further complicated because at particular times and places, and for specific purposes, particular Europeans were dependent in a variety of ways upon particular Indians.

That superb historian J. H. Parry opened a wide window with the comment that "Columbus did not discover a new world; he established contact between two worlds, both already old."[24] The word *contact* properly suggests the reciprocity of discovery that followed upon European initiatives of exploration; as surely as Europeans discovered Indians, Indians discovered Europeans. There are other subtleties of implication in *contact* that will be discussed a few pages farther on; its everyday meaning will do for present purposes. Initial contacts between Europeans and Indians were made in harbors or navigable rivers, and the circumstances sharpened each participant's consciousness of the differences between the two peoples. European technology boasted no more advanced product than oceangoing ships armed with cannon and furnished with charts and instruments of navigation.[25] We can hardly overestimate the shock of such an apparition to Indians gazing up at the wooden walls from their lowly canoes. Nor can we much exaggerate the contempt mixed with the curiosity of the seamen looking down. The contrast in power over material things increased when Indians saw the effect of firearms and compared steel implements with stone counterparts. Indians instantly felt themselves to be poor and craved a share of the vast wealth of their visitors. Reciprocally the Europeans envied the products of Indian specialized crafts. In the northern regions beyond Spain's control Europeans most coveted the fur pelts so casually tossed about by the natives. The simple basis for all trade existed from the first: each party had something expendable that was wanted by the other.

Prolonged contact between the two societies created interdependence and cultural change. Indian culture was revolutionized in at least six clearly identifiable ways. Because Indians preferred European implements and cloth to the products of their own neolithic crafts, they became involved in and dependent upon the European market economy. Competition for advantage in the market impelled them to unprecedented

---

24. Parry, *Spanish Seaborne Empire*, 65.
25. Parry, *Age of Reconnaissance*, chaps. 3, 4; Carlo M. Cipolla, *Guns, Sails and Empires: Technological Innovation and the Early Phases of European Expansion 1400–1700* (New York, 1965), 137–143.

large-scale warfare against each other and frequently to subservience toward their European trading partners. Firearms, obtainable only through trade and repairable only by the European smiths,[26] became the sine qua non of Indian existence, not only in warfare but in the commercial hunting that rose to dominance in Indian economy. Alcoholic drinks, introduced by the Europeans, created mass drunkenness and demoralization.[27] European diplomacy and religious missions worked schism and factionalism upon Indian institutions, and European expansion of colonization led to dispossession of Indians from their political territories and real property. The attritional long-term effects of these changes were magnified by the continuing ravages of epidemic disease through four centuries.

To Europeans intercultural contact was more benign. Indians fed the earliest colonizers and taught them how to grow strange crops under new conditions of soil and climate. Indians guided explorers and traders over established trails and routes through the wilderness that was otherwise so mysterious and frightening to the newcomers, and Indians gave instruction in transportation and survival techniques. They stimulated European industry to greater production, particularly the textile industry so critical to the developing Industrial Revolution, by paying for its products with furs and hides; and the exorbitant profits of the Indian trade concentrated capital among merchants on both sides of the Atlantic. Indians conveyed improved lands—Europeans were uninterested in forest and swamp—in the form both of subsistence hunting parklands that had been cleared by burning over and of croplands and townsites that had been cleared by girdling trees and grubbing up their roots.

There was a fundamental disparity in the exchanges between Euro-

26. The rule was general but not absolute. Patrick M. Malone has documented some Indians' ability to repair firearms by cannibalizing parts and has identified a forge and skilled blacksmith among the Narragansetts. "Changing Military Technology among the Indians of Southern New England, 1600–1677," *American Quarterly*, XXV (1973), 56–58.

27. The phenomena reported in early records must not be confused with behavior observable today. Nancy Oestreich Lurie's studies of contemporary drunkenness among Indians indicate that it has become "an old, patterned form of recreational behavior [that] is managed and probably no more hazardous to health than karate, mountain climbing, or mushroom hunting." "The World's Oldest On-Going Protest Demonstration: North American Indian Drinking Patterns," *Pac. Hist. Rev.*, XL (1971), 331.

Management of alcohol is not the same thing as susceptibility to it. Recent experimentation establishes that, when Europeans, Indians, and Eskimos are infused intravenously with alcohol, the Indians and Eskimos are "significantly slower at metabolizing the alcohol." The experimenters concluded that genetic differences were probably the cause. "Eskimos, Indians Are Found to Metabolize Alcohol Slowly," *Medical Tribune*, XIV, No. 36 (Sept. 26, 1973), 32.

peans and Indians. After the Europeans had been taught how to make and use canoes, moccasins, buckskin clothing, and backwoods shelters, they could dispense with further Indian guidance. When Indians granted or sold lands, the territory became European forever. In return the Indians received trade goods but not the means or skills of making and repairing such goods themselves. Becoming addicted to European products, the Indians soon lost their own neolithic skills through disuse; bowmakers found no apprentices where hunters and warriors knew the advantages of guns, and an artisan gap of a single generation can wipe out a craft in an illiterate society. In the trade that thus came to dominate their economy, the Indians had no choice but to supply the commodities demanded by the Europeans. Apart from personal and military services, the Indians' only commodities of value were food, peltry, and lands. When European farms and herds began to flourish, the demand for Indian-produced food dropped off. Commercial hunting and the sale of lands perpetually depleted the stocks of the very commodities on which the Indians depended. Military services destroyed their bodies as well.

Through such processes as these, the dependence of Europeans upon Indians declined, while the dependence of Indians upon Europeans increased. Social and political factors were involved as well, which will be noticed in due course, but underlying all others was European domination made possible by an exchange in which the Indian gifts were greater. Civilization was not brought from Europe to triumph over the Indians; rather the Indians paid a staggering price in lives, labor, goods, and lands as their part in the creation of modern American society and culture, and their influence upon today's Europe was not negligible.[28]

The one sure truth in this long process is that both Indian and European societies underwent constant transformation and evolution throughout the centuries of their interaction. Francis Parkman's savage "hewn out of a rock"—the Indian who would not change—never existed but in an ideological stereotype.[29] Indians, like Europeans, could make certain choices about direction of change, and individual Indians did choose a wide variety of adjustments and experiments in their behavior, but the one choice never within their power was to stay exactly the same.

To say this is to state both a principle and a problem. If the principle

28. See, for example, two articles by A. Irving Hallowell: "The Impact of the American Indian on American Culture," *Am. Anthro.*, N.S., LIX (1957), 201–217, and "The Backwash of the Frontier: The Impact of the Indian on American Culture," in *The Frontier in Perspective*, ed. Walker D. Wyman and Clifton B. Kroeber (Madison, Wis., 1957), 229–258.

29. Francis Parkman, *The Conspiracy of Pontiac* (1851), New Library ed. (Boston, 1909), I, 48.

be true, the problem is to uncover successive layers of acculturation in order to see the societies as they were at time of contact; and the effort to solve the problem reveals ambiguities in the significance of *contact*. In the larger sense contact occurred between the whole of European society and the whole of Indian society on October 12, 1492. In both societies there were immediate reverberations throughout their continents. Europeans were stimulated to launch more ships and men, while disease and trade goods raced among the Indians far ahead of European explorers. People of each society who had never seen representatives of the other became conscious of each other and of each other's ways of conduct. Because of the resonance of first contact, subsequent behavior was modified on both sides, so that one cannot speak of the establishment of Roanoke colony, much less of Jamestown, as a contact in the same sense as the original one. The Powhatan who greeted John Smith was perhaps as knowledgeable in the ways of Europeans as Smith was about Indians. Yet in a sense permanent colonization by Europeans at any given site did inaugurate a new era there and so may properly be conceived as a contact period.

For clarity it seems advisable to distinguish between macrocontact and microcontacts. Students of ethnology, who place great importance on the data associated with a contact period, will do well to remember that such data vary in every microcontact case, partly because of repercussions from previous contacts. The historian's maxim of the uniqueness of events must here stand as a warning to theorists for whom all contacts were created equal. What Was in the Beginning has never again been quite the same.

Chapter 4 ❧ SAVAGE HEATHEN

In early medieval Europe the greatest resistance to the powers of both church and state originated in the stubbornly maintained tribal customs of pagan or heathen countrymen. Etymologically the words *pagan* and *heathen* derive respectively from Latin and Anglo-Saxon terms for dwellers in the country or heath, and our modern word *peasant* is in the same line of descent as *pagan*.[1] These country people harbored ancient nature cults with their own deities and priests. For government they counseled among themselves, and their kings were merely chiefs of kindreds. The inheritors of what was left of ancient Rome knew that such materials would have to be remolded before Rome's glories could be recreated. As Henry Osborn Taylor has remarked, "With Charles Martel, with Pippin, and with Charlemagne, Latin Christianity is the symbol of civilized order, while heathendom and savagery are identical."[2]

Christian lords and bishops made no distinction between civilizing and converting the rural brutes and wild men. The alliance between church and state became a condition of thought as well as a necessity of action. Until yesterday, historically speaking, no cultured European could conceive of a society's being stable and enduring unless it was founded on the sanctions of the only true faith—whichever that happened to be. It followed logically that religion was too much the center of social concern to be left to the vagaries of individual choice. It followed also that societies came to be seen through their religions as through refracting lenses. A religion became much more than a set of doctrines and rituals; it was immanent in the total behavior of its adherents.[3]

When a religion was bad, its people were necessarily also bad. It did not matter that they had never done wrong to the Christian contemplating them; they were enemies to God. They were therefore also enemies to God's people. The Middle Ages bequeathed to the Renais-

1. *Oxford English Dictionary*, s.v. "heathen," "peasant." Thanks to Professor Daniel F. McCall for calling my attention to this.

2. Taylor, *Mediaeval Mind*, I, 169-170.

3. W. R. Jones, "Image of Barbarian," *Comp. Studies in Soc. and Hist.*, XIII (1971), 387, 390-391, 397-398.

sance and the Reconnaissance this unquestioned assumption. Not only was religion an acceptable sanction for conquest; it was the only unarguably proper one. Henry Osborn Taylor asks, "With whom should wars be waged if not with hostile aliens of different faith?" He continues: "When at the close of the eleventh century the heathen were not so close at hand in western Europe, the West began a series of distant holy wars. . . . The religious motive led, was indeed the torch which fired the whole train of feudal, economic, fanatical combustibles."[4]

This "religious motive," however, was a complex aggregate of doctrine and appetite. Its unresolved contradictions and confusions appear clearly in the detailed specifications of the Bull of Pope Nicholas V, previously noticed in chapter 1. Nicholas felt obliged to "bestow suitable favors and special graces on those Catholic kings and princes, who . . . not only restrain the savage excesses of the Saracens and of other infidels . . . but also for the defense and increase of the faith vanquish them and their kingdoms and habitations, though situated in the remotest parts unknown to us." For this great work of propagation of the faith even to persons who offered it no threat, Nicholas granted to King Alfonso of Portugal "free and ample faculty . . . to invade, search out, capture, vanquish, and subdue all Saracens and pagans whatsoever, and other enemies of Christ wheresoever placed, and the kingdoms, dukedoms, principalities, dominions, possessions, and all movable and immovable goods whatsoever held and possessed by them and to reduce their persons to perpetual slavery, and to apply and appropriate to himself and his successors the kingdoms, dukedoms, counties, principalities, dominions, possessions, and goods, and to convert them to his and their use and profit."[5]

With sanction like that Pope Nicholas's beneficiaries may perhaps be excused for some confusion in motives. Historians have had no less difficulty in sorting them out. For the moment, however, we need concern ourselves only with that quality of infidelity that justified its conquest. In an age of absolutist dogma one attribute was enough. Regardless of whatever apparent merits or virtues might be possessed by religions other than Christianity, their otherness was all that mattered. The religions of persons "situated in the remotest parts unknown" were nevertheless known to be evil.

The reforms of Protestantism did not extend to change of outlook toward non-Christians. The first fury of Spanish conquest became

---

4. Taylor, *Mediaeval Mind*, I, 332–333.
5. The Bull Romanus Pontifex, Jan. 8, 1455, Davenport, ed., *European Treaties*, I, 21, 23. The Latin *feritatem* is anachronistically mistranslated as "savage." *Ibid.,* 14, 21.

tempered by gropings toward a theory of natural rights to be recognized as belonging to even the most barbarous peoples, and the Dominican jurist Francisco de Vitoria argued in 1539 that idolatry probably was not cause in itself for a just war.[6] Perhaps this was merely the theoretical kind of justice that best serves the interests of the country that has already made its conquests. By depriving ambitious competitors of easy justification for new wars, such a theory could do little harm to Spain's empire in being, and it might be useful in diplomatic contention against climbers. Thus Spain's government, though initially resentful, gradually embodied much of the natural rights theory in law. However that may be, Protestant England ignored it in the sixteenth century. In 1578 Queen Elizabeth I authorized Sir Humphrey Gilbert to seize "remote heathen and barbarous lands,"[7] and again in 1584 she issued a patent to Sir Walter Ralegh in the same language.[8] Neither patent mentioned intent or obligation to convert the destined prey to Christianity. Both spoke at length of seizure of property and imposition of government.

The Protestant Reformation brought with it an increase rather than a decline in fear and hatred of infidels. Turkish conquests in eastern Europe alarmed the Protestant Germans, who poured out a copious propaganda of purported description of Turkish customs and religion, unrestrained by considerations of actuality. A recent study of this propaganda finds that the medieval Christian heritage of anti-Moslem prejudice "determined" the European image of the Turk "down to the last detail."[9] So also in America, what Europeans saw of Indian religion passed through refracting and filtering lenses of preconceptions formed and crystallized in the propaganda of aggressive expansion.

No effort will be made here to describe the many manifestations of Indian religions. Such descriptions have filled many large books, and it would be impossible to do justice to that subject without distracting from the purpose at hand. Present concerns are with European conceptions, their correspondence to the reality as it is now understood, and their implications for intersocietal relations.

Some part of the ideas of Elizabethan English colonizers were brought to America from their previous experience in Ireland. Nicholas

6. Parry, *Age of Reconnaissance*, 305–307; see also the discussion of Spanish reasoning in Wilcomb E. Washburn, *Red Man's Land/White Man's Law: A Study of the Past and Present Status of the American Indian* (New York, 1971), chap. 1.

7. Letters patent, June 11, 1578, David Beers Quinn, ed., *The Voyages and Colonising Enterprises of Sir Humphrey Gilbert*, Hakluyt Society Publications, 2d Ser., LXXXIII–LXXXIV (London, 1940), I, 188–194, quotation at 188.

8. Letters patent, Mar. 25, 1584, Quinn, ed., *Roanoke Voyages*, I, 82–89.

9. John W. Bohnstedt, *The Infidel Scourge of God: The Turkish Menace as Seen by German Pamphleteers of the Reformation Era*, Am. Phil. Soc., Trans., N.S., LVIII, pt. ix (1968), 18–19.

P. Canny suggests that "their years in Ireland were years of apprenticeship." These adventurers had gone to Ireland, he adds, with "a preconceived idea of a barbaric society and they merely tailored the Irishman to fit this ideological strait jacket." They and their successors carried the same preconceptions to America to fit onto Indians, "using the same pretexts for the extermination of the Indians as their counterparts had used in the 1560s and 1570s for the slaughter of numbers of the Irish." What is especially to the present point is that the English had convinced themselves that Irish religion varied so much from English orthodoxy that it was really not Christian at all. "Once it was established that the Irish were pagans, the first logical step had been taken toward declaring them barbarians." The Irish became a "savage nation" that lived "like beastes"—a lower order of humanity.[10]

The years of English expansion to America were simultaneously years of aggressive voyaging all over the world. Sir Thomas Smythe, who held the post of treasurer of the Virginia Company from 1609 to 1620, was simultaneously governor of the East India Company and had previously been a founder of the Levant Company.[11] In his Virginia Company's employ was that omnipresent adventurer Captain John Smith, who took the same eyes to the holy war against the Turks and the invasion of America. In Virginia, Smith unsurprisingly found native religion to be devil worship. With his preconceptions and utter lack of self-doubt, he described an initiation ceremony for adolescent boys by turning it into a "solemn sacrifice of children" and portrayed other Indian rituals with more contempt than confirmability.[12] Such aspersions on barbarians

10. Nicholas P. Canny, "The Ideology of English Colonization: From Ireland to America," *WMQ*, 3d Ser., XXX (1973), 595, 597, 596, 586, 588; Clarence Steinberg, "Atin, Pyrochles, Cymochles: On Irish Emblems in 'The Faerie Queene,'" *Neuphilologische Mitteilungen*, LXXII (Helsinki, 1971), 757–758.
Roger Williams caught a hint of the ideological implications of the word *heathen*. He described and denounced the distinctions it made both as between Englishman and Indian and as between Protestant and Catholic. *Christenings make not Christians, or A Briefe Discourse concerning that name Heathen, commonly given to the Indians. As also concerning that great point of their Conversion* (1645), in *Rhode Island Historical Tracts*, XIV (Providence, R.I., 1881), 2–3, 6–7.

11. *Dictionary of National Biography*, s.v. "Smith or Smythe, Sir Thomas"; George Masselman, *The Cradle of Colonialism* (New Haven, Conn., 1963), 279.

12. Smith, *Map of Virginia*, in Barbour, ed., *Jamestown Voyages*, II, 364–368. Regarding initiation, see Robert Beverley, *The History and Present State of Virginia* (1705), ed. Louis B. Wright (Chapel Hill, N.C., 1947), 205–208. Smith affirmed also, on the basis of Portuguese accounts, that in black Africa "the devill hath the greatest part of their devotions." John Smith, *The True Travels, Adventures, and Observations of Captain John Smith* (1630), in Edward Arber and A. G. Bradley, eds., *The Travels and Works of Captain John Smith, President of Virginia, and Admiral of New England, 1580-1631* (Edinburgh, 1910), II, 876.

echoed the practice, already common in Ireland, of accusing the natives of obscene behavior, even to calling them cannibals.[13]

Although John Smith's range of experience was wider than most men's, his perceptions of Indian religion were typical of travelers' literature on that subject. David Ingram gave circumstantial details in 1569 about the Indians' "Colluchio or Devil, who they do worship." Ingram claimed to have encountered this Colluchio in an Indian's house, "with very great eyes like a blacke Calfe." Ingram and his two companions, both conveniently dead at the time of this tale's telling, piously blessed themselves and defied the Evil One, who presently "shrancke away in a stealing maner forth of the doores, and was seene no more unto them." The rest of Ingram's yarn is demonstrably no better than this in some of its episodes, but he had influence on the gentlemen in the circle of Sir Humphrey Gilbert and the Hakluyts.[14]

Henry Hawkes, in 1572, wrote that the Indians of New Spain "use divers times to talke with the Devill, to whome they doe certaine sacrifices and oblations: many times they have bene taken with the same, and I have seene them most cruelly punished for that offence."[15] The London-based instigator of expeditions, Sir George Peckham, wrote in 1583 of winning the savages "from the devill to Christ, from hell to heaven."[16]

For various reasons there were exceptions to the chorus. The promotional literature of Sir Walter Ralegh and the Virginia Company soft-pedaled savage horrors, apparently in order to attract settlers to the colonies. William Penn probably had the same motive in 1683, but his remarks were notably more sympathetic and perceptive; he not only avoided devil language but also took pains to mention that the Indians he knew "believe a God and Immortality, without the help of Metaphysicks."[17]

These were indeed exceptions. In the sixteenth and early seventeenth centuries devil language was the rule. The Dutchman Adriaen Van der Donck, the Swede Peter Lindeström, and the Englishmen Samuel Purchas, Roger Williams, and Cotton Mather—all good Protestants—

13. Canny, "Ideology of English Colonization," *WMQ*, 3d Ser., XXX (1973), 587.

14. "The Relation of David Ingram," in Hakluyt, *Principall Navigations*, II, 561; *Dictionary of Canadian Biography*, I, s.v. "Ingram, David."

15. Henry Hawkes, "Relation" (1572), in Hakluyt, *Principall Navigations*, II, 548.

16. Humphrey Gilbert and George Peckham, "A true Report of the late discoveries . . . ," *ibid.*, 713.

17. "Letter from William Penn to the Committee of the Free Society of Traders, 1683," Albert Cook Myers, ed., *Narratives of Early Pennsylvania, West New Jersey, and Delaware, 1630–1707*, Original Narratives of Early American History (New York, 1912), 234.

separately and independently put the devil into the savages' religion, however much they differed in observed details.[18] In this respect they were members of a great company and in full agreement with the Jesuit missionaries of New France.[19]

It is impossible to say how much of their narrative output was tailored to serve the varied interests of church, state, or commerce. Certainly a large and perhaps preponderant share of misconception (and misperception) was caused by the inability of ethnocentric minds to transcend their own cultures. What the European saw in Indian villages offended his deepest sense of right conduct. It seemed irrational, "filthy," and it was certainly heathen. As Peter Lindeström remarked, "These wild people in New Sweden, they are not wild because we believe them to be mad and insane, but on account of their idolatry and error in religion."[20]

The Indians had no Scriptures or reasoned theology. When a European tried to inquire into their "metaphysicks," he was likely to hear traditional tales in which men turned into animals and vice versa, people journeyed into supernatural realms and returned, animals conversed with each other and humans, and the spirits of rocks and trees had to be placated. The European knew that such nonsense was rank superstition, and it never occurred to him that there might be historical events in it, disguised by alien metaphor.[21] Nor did he see any likeness between his own theologically certified miracles and mysteries of Christianity and the traditionally certified myths of the Indians. Then there were the wildly irrational antics of the Indian powwows—the priest-physicians who donned weird masks and costumes, cast spells, and howled and cavorted about their patients' bedsides.[22] (But there

18. Van der Donck, *Description of New Netherlands*, in N.-Y. Hist. Soc., *Colls.*, 2d Ser., I, 202–203, 213; Peter Lindeström, *Geographia Americae, with An Account of the Delaware Indians, Based on Surveys and Notes Made in 1654–1656*, trans. and ed. Amandus Johnson, (Philadelphia, 1925), 207–209; Samuel Purchas, *Hakluytus Posthumus or Purchas His Pilgrimes...* (London, 1625), IV, 1814, and Philip L. Barbour, *Pocahontas and Her World* (Boston, 1970), 169–173; Roger Williams, *A Key into the Language of America: Or, An help to the Language of the Natives in that part of America, called New-England...* (1643), ed. James Hammond Trumbull, Narragansett Club, *Publications*, I (Providence, R.I., 1866), 153; Cotton Mather, *The Life and Death of the Renown'd Mr. John Eliot, Who was the First Preacher of the Gospel to the Indians in America*, 2d ed. (London, 1691), 74.

19. Sagard, *Long Journey to the Hurons*, ed. Wrong, trans. Langton, 170–171.

20. Lindeström, *Geographia Americae*, ed. Johnson, 191.

21. Indian tradition has often been attacked as superstitious nonsense. Its source value, when properly used, is discussed in Bernard L. Fontana, "American Indian Oral History: An Anthropologist's Note," *History and Theory: Studies in the Philosophy of History*, VIII (1969), 366–370.

22. Beverley, *History of Virginia*, ed. Wright, 202–204. See "The Shaman and Primitive Psychopathology in General," in Erwin H. Ackerknecht, *Medicine and*

was plenty of superstition remaining in European medicine in the seventeenth century.[23])

Perhaps superstition could be ascribed simply to ignorance and childish minds, but "filthiness" was sin.[24] Every European knew that the Christian moral law was founded in the "laws of nature." Here were these natural people violating these supposedly natural laws without compunction. They showed small concern about covering their nakedness. They were happily loose about premarital sex.[25] Women were mistresses of their own bodies. They had no real marriage at all in the eyes of some Europeans. Divorce was easy, and—utterest abomination—male homosexuality was tolerated openly, even institutionalized.[26]

Indian rituals were often held outdoors, whether they involved a *cantico* community dance or the deeply private sojourning in a wild place of the individual seeking a dream or trance revelation. Although Europeans sometimes held processions on holy days, their worship

Ethnology: Select Essays, ed. H. H. Walser and H. M. Koelbing (Baltimore, 1971), 57–90.

23. Edward Eggleston, *The Transit of Civilization from England to America in the Seventeenth Century* (Boston, 1959 [orig. publ. New York, 1900]), chap. 2; Marc Bloch, *The Royal Touch: Sacred Monarchy and Scrofula in England and France*, trans. J. E. Anderson (London, 1973), 214–228.

24. Roger Williams especially has made an impression with his use of the word *filthy*. He meant it as we use the phrase "filthy language." Fires without flues made Indian lodges smoky, but the Indians were neat housekeepers. See Lawson, *New Voyages to Carolina*, 176–177; Nicholas N. Smith, "The Transition from Wigwams to Frame Houses by the Old Town, Maine, Penobscot and the Woodstock, New Brunswick, Malecite," a paper delivered at the Fourth Conference on Algonquian Studies, Big Moose Lake, N.Y., Sept. 24–26, 1971. The *Oxford English Dictionary* points out that *filthy* was used in a moral sense in Old English, and, as long ago as the 12th century, it was used by the English prelate Giraldus Cambrensis to attack the "barbarous" Irish as "a most filthy people, utterly enveloped in vices, most untutored of all peoples in the rudiments of faith." Lydon, *Lordship of Ireland*, 283. Finally, English colonists in America soon discovered the Indians had good reason to cover themselves with bear's grease, regardless of how unappetizing it made them look. The purpose was to protect against extremes of heat, cold, and mosquitoes, Salisbury, "Conquest of the 'Savage,'" 51.

25. See, e.g., Van der Donck, *Description of New Netherlands*, N.-Y. Hist. Soc., *Colls.*, 2d Ser., I, 198–200. Easy sex did not offend all Europeans, needless to say. John Lawson puffed it into one of the chief attractions of the New World. Lawson, *New Voyage to Carolina*, 183–184, 186–187.

26. See references to the literature in Henry Angelino and Charles L. Shedd, "A Note on Berdache," *Am. Anthro.*, N.S., LVII (1955), 121–126. In New England and New Netherland homosexuality and bestiality were punishable by death, and the executions embellished with sadistic refinements. Bradford, *Of Plymouth Plantation*, ed. Morison, 320–321, app. x, 404–408; New Netherland Council Minutes, June 25, 1646, New York Colonial Manuscripts, Dutch, IV, 262 (A. J. F. van Laer's translation, pp. 326–328), New York State Library, Albany; abstract of minutes, June 17, 1660, E. B. O'Callaghan, ed., *Calendar of Historical Manuscripts in the Office of the Secretary of State, Albany, N.Y.* (Albany, N.Y., 1865–1866), I, 213.

was mostly conducted indoors in specially constructed and consecrated places. Even their private searches for revelation were likely to happen in clerical studies or in solitary meditation in or near the church. To them outdoor rituals smacked of irreverence and shameless casualness or, worse, of devil worship.[27]

Then there was the Indians' astonishing, and surely superstitious, ritual of daily washing. We read so much about the dirty ways of demoralized and enculturated tribes that we are apt to overlook the early observers' reports of the cold plunges at dawn performed by villages en masse.[28] These were purification rites that happened also to accord with modern notions of hygiene, but the seventeenth-century European was neither so superstitious as to believe in the religious motivation nor so silly as to get himself wet all over on a chill November morn. The craze for daily bathing had to overcome tough resistance before it penetrated European culture. Perfume was more rational.

The social functions of religion in any society are to unify outlook and regulate conduct. Among Europeans and Indians alike, ruler and priest cooperated for mutual benefit. Religious sanctions supported the enforcing systems of custom, law, and individual morality. The two cultures did differ, as has been already noticed, in their notions of rationality, and it showed particularly in their conceptions of the natural as distinguished from the supernatural.[29] Oddly, though, the most rationalistic and literate of European faiths was also the most literal in its adherence to certain beliefs about the supernatural that accorded closely with Indian conceptions, even as it violently denounced Indian superstition. The demons who stalk through Cotton Mather's pages clank the chains of Puritan fundamentalist dogma—supported always, of course, by prodigiously reasoned argument.

There is often a curiously childlike quality about the reasoning of both Cotton Mather and his father, Increase. When Cotton got no response to his effort to exorcise a demon from a young woman by using Indian words for his incantation, he petulantly concluded that the Indian language was so hard and stupid that not even demons understood it. Increase Mather delighted in rain magic. He twice gave minute details of Puritan congregations praying up rain and gloated that they had succeeded after Indian powwowing had failed. The incidents shed

27. One of the reasons for persecuting Quakers in 17th-century England was their habit at that time of open-air worship. Their hostility to "steeple houses" antagonized the frequenters thereof. Godfrey Davies, *The Early Stuarts, 1603–1660*, Oxford History of England (Oxford, 1937), 194–195. There was also the ancient association of outdoors worship with nature worship and witchcraft.

28. Lawson, *New Voyage to Carolina*, 191; John Smith, *Map of Virginia*, in Barbour, ed., *Jamestown Voyages*, II, 356.

29. See Ackerknecht, *Medicine and Ethnology*, 167 and n. 4.

some light on what Puritans meant when they denounced Indian superstition. The Indians were not superstitious because they had a ritual for persuading divinity to make rain; their superstition lay in sending their prayers to the wrong address.[30]

Puritans as well as Indians believed in witches and punished them. Everyone knows of Salem's horrors, and Salem was exceptional only in quantity of victims. A scholar has at last performed the practical chore of tabulating witchcraft incidents in the seventeenth century. Frederick C. Drake counted 95 incidents involving colonials with witchcraft before 1692, in which twenty-two people were executed and others severely punished. Almost all of them occurred in Puritan New England. Aside from killings performed by sailors at sea, no witches were executed by colonials other than Puritans.[31] To pinpoint the issue specifically as a matter of religion rather than regionalism: no cases whatever of witchcraft occurred in Rhode Island, where scornful "Gortonoge" heretics defied the Puritans with the sacrilege that "there be no other witches upon earth, nor devils, but your own pastors and ministers and such as they are."[32]

The Indian's "priest" was also his physician. It followed that the Indian's conception of medicine was shaped in accordance with his conception of religion. The natural and supernatural cohabited comfortably under the same term, to the bewilderment and disdain of the European onlooker.[33] Prayer, fetishes, magic, witchcraft, surgery, and herbalism were all "medicine."[34] What made the mixture more confusing was its apparent efficacy. Even today Indians are apt to respond more positively to their own medicine men than to Euramerican physicians. As this chapter was being written, the United States National Institute of Health decided that the medicine man's efficiency was

30. Cotton Mather, *Life of Eliot*, 78; Increase Mather, *A Brief History of the War with the Indians in New-England*..., 2d ed. (London, 1676), 45, and *A Relation Of the Troubles which have hapned in New-England, By reason of the Indians there*... (1677), ed. Samuel G. Drake as *Early History of New England; Being a Relation of Hostile Passages between the Indians and European Voyagers and First Settlers*... (Albany, N.Y., 1864), 108-109.

31. Frederick C. Drake, "Witchcraft in the American Colonies, 1647-62," *Am. Qtly.*, XX (1968), 697-708, and see his comment on John Winthrop, Sr., p. 714.

32. William Arnold to the governor of Massachusetts, Sept. 1, 1651, in Thomas Hutchinson, comp., *Collection of Original Papers Relative to the History of the Colony of Massachusetts-Bay* (Boston, 1769), 238. The Gortonoges are discussed below, in chap. 15.

33. Frederick Webb Hodge, ed., *Handbook of American Indians North of Mexico*, Smithsonian Institution, Bureau of American Ethnology, Bulletin 30, pt. 2 (Washington, D.C., 1907-1910), s.v. "Religion"; Ackerknecht, *Medicine and Ethnology*, 21.

34. Virgil J. Vogel, *American Indian Medicine*, Civilization of the American Indian Series, XCV (Norman, Okla., 1970), chap. 2.

worth preserving and funded a training program for an enlarged new generation of these practitioners among the Navajos.[35]

In colonial times lowly practitioners of European folk medicine picked up the Indian herb lore, blended it with their own variants of superstition, and practiced in a shadowy region largely unexplored by scholars. The powwow of the "Pennsylvania Dutch" got his name as well as a bag of tricks from the powwow of his woodland neighbors.[36] But educated Europeans refused to learn the genuinely effective Indian remedies because of the powwow's hocus-pocus and the heathen superstition that tainted his medicine. They paid a heavy price in lives for their stubbornness.

Jacques Cartier learned and used an Indian cure for scurvy, but Europe forgot the lesson and continued to endure the disease until a British naval surgeon read Cartier's account two centuries later. Indians did the "pharmaceutical spadework" that led to the discovery of insulin, as acknowledged by the discoverer.[37] Modern obstetricians have learned—but only since World War II—of the superiority of Indian obstetrical practices to European (and childbirth was the great killer of Europe's women).[38] The Indians used American foxglove as a cardiac stimulant for centuries before digitalis was discovered in England.[39]

Their knowledge of the properties of plants has been summarized by Virgil J. Vogel in his recent study, *American Indian Medicine*. Vogel notes that more than two hundred indigenous drugs used by Indian tribes for curative purposes have been included at one time or another in *The Pharmacopeia of the United States of America* or in the *National Formulary*. Only a handful of indigenous vegetable drugs known to science today were not used by aboriginal Indians, and the Indian usages generally corresponded with modern approved practice. Vogel properly adds that, although Indian herbalism was not a science, seventeenth-century European medicine was not much of a science either.[40] The brevity of European life expectations in that era is confirmation enough.

As one of the strongest unifying factors in any Indian community, the Indian medicine man became the object of the most intense hatred

35. *New York Times*, July 7, 1972, p. 33.

36. Vogel, *American Indian Medicine*, chap. 5, esp. 126–128.

37. *Ibid.*, 3–4.

38. *Ibid.*, 231–236; Morris L. Rotstein, "Getting Patients Out of Bed Early in the Puerperium," *Journal of the American Medical Association*, CXXV (1944), 838–840; Benjamin W. Black, "Do Normal Maternity Cases Require Ten Days in the Hospital?" *Modern Hospital*, LX (1943), 52–53.

39. Vogel, *American Indian Medicine*, 10–11.

40. *Ibid.*, 6.

of Europeans striving to weaken and dominate his tribe. Vogel remarks that "all of the principal forces of European erosion of Indian society have been brought to bear in the assault against the medicine man. To the extent that his influence was weakened, white influence was able to penetrate."[41]

Europeans, for the most part, did not expect to learn anything from heathen religions. The professed goal of European colonization was to convert the heathen to doctrines of truth rather than to learn from them the errors of evil. These professions may be seen in several aspects, however. Undoubtedly Europeans of all ranks valued their faiths far higher than those of naked wild men, and undoubtedly also sincere, devout religionists among the Europeans were motivated by altruism to save the heathen for the heathen's sake. The Jesuit martyrs of New France were not cynics. But these were exceptions. The tough and callous men commanding colonies regarded the natives as mere objects for their own enrichment and advantage. For the colonists in general as well as their commanders the purpose of proselytizing was to create firm allies among the natives. Englishmen were not merely Christians; they were Protestants, and they converted Indians to Protestantism rather than just to Christianity. Frenchmen converted their Indians to Catholicism. The seventeenth century was an era of merciless war between Protestants and Catholics, and Englishmen instigated their Protestant Indians to attack Catholic Indians with at least as much energy as went into attacking heathens.

Englishmen quickly found that missions could be practical after another fashion. They discovered what may be most concisely termed the missionary racket. (Perhaps the English were not alone in this discovery, but only English missions have been researched for this study.) Both in Virginia and New England missions were organized to extract from pious Englishmen—Anglicans in the one case, Puritans in the other—donations that were diverted to ends other than pious. The Puritan missions are examined in detail in chapter 14 below. Here we may glance briefly at the earlier missionary project of the Virginia Company.[42]

The Virginia Company followed the standard pattern by stressing conversion of the Indians as one of the company's great objectives.[43] For this announced goal the crown ordered a general contribution in 1615 and again in 1617 in all the parishes of the Church of England,

41. *Ibid.*, 35.

42. For a comprehensive, though superficial, narrative see Robert Hunt Land, "Henrico and Its College," *WMQ*, 2d Ser., XVIII (1938), 453–498.

43. Barbour, *Pocahontas*, 173–174; "Letters Patent to Sir Thomas Gates, Sir George Somers and others . . . , April 10, 1606," Alexander Brown, ed., *The Genesis of the United States* (Boston, 1890), I, 53.

with the proceeds to found and fund a college for the Indians.[44] Grati-fyingly large sums poured into the company's treasury, a thousand acres of land were set aside for the college at Henrico, and a committee of "choice Gentlemen" was set up to supervise the "waighty busines" of the college, it being "so greate, that an Account of their proceedings therein must be given to the State."[45] The crown's earnestness in the project seems beyond question, but the company disposed of what the crown proposed. As the money came in, the company's treasurer "borrowed" from the college fund to pay back debts and finance the company's other business. He proposed in 1619 to put off actual build-ing on the college grounds, suggesting instead that its funds be in-vested and that the college be built out of the annual income rather than out of the capital. His proposal, duly adopted, turned out to be a device to divert the college fund to pay for the company's annual supply ship to Virginia. The excuse given for this diversion was the sending of fifty tenants on that ship to work on the lands set aside for the college. Half the proceeds of their labor theoretically would be put into the college fund.[46] This was the fund's "investment."

After the supply ship brought the tenants to Virginia, they were seized upon by preestablished planters and put to work on private plantations, and the man who had been placed in charge of them (with certain private understandings, as he alleged) was later found guilty by the company in London of reprehensible behavior—which probably means that he had diverted to his own pocket what they had intended for theirs. A dissident faction in the company "confessed that the greatest parte of the stocke belonginge to the Colledge was wasted" in an unsuccessful ironworks.[47]

The college was never built. No indication exists in surviving records that a single Indian was ever proselyted through its agency, with or

44. Peter Walne, "The Collections for Henrico College, 1616–1618," *Virginia Magazine of History and Biography*, LXXX (1972), 259–266; James I to Arch-bishops of Canterbury and York [1617], in Susan Myra Kingsbury, ed., *The Records of the Virginia Company of London* (Washington, D.C., 1906–1935), IV, 1–2; Instructions to George Yeardley, Nov. 18, 1618, *ibid.*, III, 102. Thanks to Philip L. Barbour for showing me the Walne piece.

45. Minutes, June 14, 1619, Kingsbury, ed., *Recs. of Va. Co.*, I, 231; minutes, Nov. 17, 1619, *ibid.*, 268.

46. Minutes, May 26 and June 9, 1619, *ibid.*, 220–221, 226. Treasurer Sir Edwin Sandys had received £1,500 by May 26, 1619. He had already "lent" £700 of it to the company for its commercial purposes. May 12, 1619, *ibid.*, 216. I am indebted to Wilcomb E. Washburn for guidance in this matter. See his "Philanthropy and the American Indian: The Need for a Model," *Ethnohistory*, XV (1968), 53–54.

47. Minutes, Jan. 30, 1622, and Feb. 13, 1622, Kingsbury, ed., *Recs. of Va. Co.*, I, 593–594, 601–604; minutes of the council in Virginia, Nov. 11, 1619, *ibid.*, 226–227; John Rolfe to Sir Edwin Sandys, Jan. 1620, *ibid.*, III, 245–246; John Pory to Sandys, Jan. 16, 1620, *ibid.*, 257–258; "An Answere to a Declaration of the Pres-ent State of Virginia," May 1623, *ibid.*, IV, 141.

without buildings. The famous conversion of Pocahontas occurred before the college's creation. The hard fact is that the Virginia Company never transported a single missionary to America. Some confusion on this point has arisen because of the presence in Virginia of a Mr. George Thorpe, who seems to have talked religion to his Indian neighbors and to have made efforts to ingratiate himself with them, much to the disgruntlement of hard-liners among the English. A minister named Stockam growled that persuasion was useless, that "till their Priests and Ancients have their throats cut, there is no hope to bring them to conversion." In the circumstances, perhaps he was right, for Thorpe was killed in the Indian rising of 1622. Whatever proselyting he had attempted among the Indians had certainly been his personal enterprise. The company had assigned him no such responsibility. His function for the company was to oversee its investment, as the "Deputy of the College Lands."[48]

When a minister named Pemberton offered, July 3, 1622, "to imploye himselfe for the converting of the infidells," the Virginia Company confined its encouragement to giving him the freedom of the colony. On the same day, however, the company appointed the Reverend Patrick Copeland as rector "of the intended Colledge." Copeland had earned high favor by collecting seventy pounds from a warship's crew for a free school in Virginia—an extraordinary feat. But he had paid this donation to the treasurer on November 21, 1621, and the delay of over seven months until his appointment as rector is curious. In any case, his missionary talents were never tested. The Virginia Indian uprising had occurred more than three months before his appointment, and the colonists had become more concerned with exterminating Indians than converting them. Besides this rather decisive circumstance, Copeland's title as rector of the *intended* college only seemed to imply a missionary responsibility, although doubtless that seeming was intentional. The function actually assigned to him was "the Pastorall charge of the Colledge Tenants," who were English workmen.[49]

Fairly plainly, everyone who could get near the college treasure put his fist into it; so far as the company and planters were concerned, the Indians were irrelevant to the whole business except as a pretext to extract money from the gullible English faithful. The Indian rising spoiled everything. Although the company tried hard to keep the college project going,[50] crown officials were so startled by the violence

48. John Smith, *The Generall Historie of Virginia, New England, and the Summer Isles* (1624), in Arber and Bradley, eds., *Travels and Works of Smith,* II, 564, 574–575; Kingsbury, ed., *Recs. of Va. Co.,* I, 594, 603.

49. Kingsbury, ed., *Recs. of Va. Co.,* II, 74, 75–76, 91, III, 531, 537–540.

50. Virginia Company council in London to council in Virginia, Aug. 1, 1622, *ibid.,* III, 671.

that they investigated and found evidence of much mismanagement.

The crown had heard earlier complaints about "abuses" by the Virginia Company. As one of its money-raising devices, the company had conducted lotteries "toward the advancement of that Plantation, and the Relief of the distressed Colonies," but the Privy Council began to wonder who was being advanced and relieved. After complaints by members of the House of Commons, Council suspended the lotteries in March 1621. When the Indian rebellion burst out a year later, it impelled Council to command submission of the company's books for investigation, but the order was resisted and circumvented, whereupon Council confined several company officials to their homes for contempt. Finally the Privy Council seized all the communications on a ship from Virginia. These apparently clinched the case for revocation of the company's charter, and the crown assumed direct government of Virginia.[51]

Until the uprising, however, the Indian college mission device had been most lucrative, and the gentlemen interested in overseas affairs kept it in mind for resuscitation when opportune. Copeland, who claimed that he had been the initiator of the Virginia project, later advised New England's Puritan leaders on missionary methods, and when the Puritans tardily concerned themselves in this field, they immediately solicited a collection in all the churches of England for its financial support. They encountered skepticism and resistance, but they propagandized hard and were rewarded by the formation in 1649 of the President and Society for Propagation of the Gospell in New England.[52]

There was more difference between Protestantism and Catholicism in the seventeenth century than there is today. Both were conquest religions, but with different implications. The Catholic church aspired to convert and include people all over the world. Spain's conquistadors were followed by missionaries who labored mightily in their cause. So also in New France the Jesuits took themselves into Indian villages to endure sacrifice and martyrdom. The Protestants produced no missionary martyrs, though some Protestant clergymen died violently along with laymen during Indian wars. Seventeenth-century Protestant ministers stuck close to their colonial settlements, venturing forth only when a special congregation had been collected to listen to a sermon. This seems odd when one considers the evangelical missionizing fervor

51. Privy Council minutes and orders, Mar. 4, 1621, July 16, 1622, and Dec. 30, 1623, C.O. 5/1354, 206–208, 215, P.R.O.; Captain Butler, "The unmasked face of our Colony in Virginia as it was in the winter of the yeare 1622," C.O. 1/3, 36–37.

52. Copeland to John Winthrop, Sr., Dec. 4, 1639, Massachusetts Historical Society, *Winthrop Papers* (Boston, 1929–1947), IV, 157–159, and see chap. 14 below.

that Protestantism would take on in later centuries, but the data are there.

I do not mean to imply by the contrast in the foregoing paragraph that all Catholic missionaries were possessed of superior virtue or necessarily were sympathetic to Indians or accepted human equality with them.[53] With all homage to Las Casas and others like him, the missionary priest could become the missionary despot easily in any faith. The very condition of being a missionary implied assumptions of superiority in the knowledge of the most important Truth in the world, to which all other knowledge is subsidiary and inferior; and a man with such assumptions is not likely to be modest when he compares himself with his innocent or "evil" charges. One man with God is a majority, it has been remarked, and nobody is more aware of it than the one man. The sincere missionary desired most of all to reduce the heathens to a proper submission to his God, and he would rejoice over their physical calamities when he thought his spiritual goal was furthered by them. This was much in the tradition of the Inquisition's willingness to burn bodies to save souls, and indeed there was burning enough in New Spain.

Nevertheless, the Catholic imperative for converting and including the heathen compelled Catholics to learn something about them in order to do the holy work effectively,[54] while the Protestant principle of elitism worked out in practice to exclusionism and indifference. The difference in attitude is sharply illustrated by contrasting approaches to Indian medicine. New England's Puritan missionaries had so closed their minds that after nearly three decades at their task they knew nothing of Indian medicine. Surviving today is a "Drug List" prepared for the use of Massachusetts troops in "King Philip's War"; it contains not a single medicinal product of American origin. In Canada, however, Jesuit Father Le Mercier carefully distinguished between the Hurons' prayers to the devil and their natural remedies, and he asked for instruction in the remedies.[55] Such contrasts explain why the *Jesuit Relations* are today an invaluable mine of ethnological information in spite of bias and cant. There is nothing comparable in Protestant literature until we reach the reports of Moravian missionaries in the mid-eighteenth century.

53. For a discussion of the way in which French Catholic conceptions of the Indians were influenced by theological disputation, see George R. Healy, "The French Jesuits and the Idea of the Noble Savage," *WMQ*, 3d Ser., XV (1958), 143–167.

54. J. H. Kennedy, *Jesuit and Savage in New France*, Yale Historical Publications, Miscellany, L (New Haven, Conn., 1950), 109.

55. Vogel, *American Indian Medicine*, 10, 42–43.

Chapter 5 ❧ SAVAGE FORM for
PEASANT FUNCTION

In his book on the Canadian fur trade, Harold A. Innis has conceived of the contact between Europe and the Americas, not as a collision of civilization and savagery, but as a meeting of two civilizations, one relatively more complex than the other, but both extremely responsive to each other.[1] Innis's comment referred particularly to economic relations, which will be discussed at length hereafter, but it is also applicable in other contexts. If the two societies were comparable as civilizations, then their member persons were comparable as human beings.

To the persons involved in contact situations there was at first some doubt on this score. For a brief while Columbus's crew were "persons from the sky" to the West Indians, and the Mexicans debated too long for their own good whether Cortés's troops were gods.[2] Indian disillusionment was not long postponed.

Europeans, however, have had a longer struggle with their primitive conceptions. Deluded by successes, they have preserved assumptions that "worked," selecting and perceiving phenomena in accordance with the assumptions. The very name *Indian* bears witness to Columbus's resistance to a novel idea. The modern Mexican scholar Edmundo O'Gorman has argued that America had to be invented because of its explorers' reluctance to discover it.[3]

This chapter is slightly modified from a paper read at the 11th annual meeting of the Northeastern Anthropological Association, Apr. 9, 1971, State University of New York at Albany.

1. Harold A. Innis, *The Fur Trade in Canada: An Introduction to Canadian Economic History*, rev. by S. D. Clark and W. T. Easterbrook (Toronto, 1964), 16.

2. Columbus to sovereigns, Feb. 15, 1493, Morison, trans. and ed., *Journals of Columbus*, 184; Bernardino de Sahagún, *Florentine Codex, Book 12: The Conquest of Mexico*, trans. Arthur J. O. Anderson and Charles E. Dibble, Part XIII (Santa Fe, N.M., 1955), 5–18.

3. Edmundo O'Gorman, *The Invention of America: An Inquiry into the His-*

This study focuses on the conceptions of Englishmen rather than Spaniards, more particularly the varied shapes in which Englishmen conceived the savages of America. A basic rule was that any given Englishman at any given time formed his views in accordance with his purposes. Those who came for quick plunder saw plots and malignancy on every side; in a mirror image of their own intent, their savages were sinister and treacherous—envisioned much as the English saw Turks and Spaniards who were likewise fit objects of prey and likewise intransigent about accepting their role. When Indians were regarded as partners in profitable trade, they appeared less threatening, and their vices were excused. When they resisted eviction from lands wanted by the colonizers, they acquired demonic dimensions. When they were wanted as soldiers for war against the French, the martial abilities of these demons were appreciated rather than decried. In short, like the most modern of architects, the Englishman devised the savage's form to fit his function.[4]

The word *savage* thus underwent considerable alteration of meaning as different colonists pursued their varied ends. One aspect of the term remained constant, however: the savage was always inferior to civilized men. Ethnocentric historians have been quite correct in asserting that English colonizers never adopted the conception of the Noble Savage (although they sometimes looked for noble classes in Indian society). Even William Penn advocated justice for Indians on the grounds that "we make profession of things so far transcending" the conscience of the "poor Indian."[5] The constant of Indian inferiority implied the rejection of his humanity and determined the limits permitted for his participation in the mixing of cultures. The savage was prey, cattle, pet, or vermin—he was never citizen. As the myth of the Ignoble Savage gathered momentum, it came to deny the Indian citizenship even in his own community. Upholders of the myth denied that either savage tyranny or savage anarchy could rightfully be called government, and therefore there could be no justification for Indian resistance to European invasion. Even Helen Hunt Jackson, that staunch champion of "fair" treatment for Indians, rejected "feeble sentimental-

---

torical Nature of the New World and the Meaning of Its History (Bloomington, Ind., 1961).

4. My method of inquiry differs from that of Roy Harvey Pearce, whose excellent studies center on the literature of morals and ideas. I have attempted to see ideas as one factor in a more comprehensive acculturation process. Cf. Pearce, *Savages of America*, and see also his article "The Metaphysics of Indian-Hating," *Ethnohistory*, IV (1957), 27–40.

5. "Penn to Free Society of Traders, 1683," Myers, ed., *Narratives of Early Pennsylvania*, 236.

ism" to declare, "Of the fairness of holding that ultimate sovereignty belonged to the civilized discoverer as against the savage barbarian, there is no manner nor ground of doubt."[6]

This comment hints of one reason for inventing savagery, a reason that was stated more explicitly by Chief Justice John Marshall when he argued with impeccable logic from a false assumption to a conclusion that he admitted would be criminal if not for the assumption. "The tribes of Indians inhabiting this country were fierce savages," wrote Marshall in a landmark decision in 1823, "whose occupation was war, and whose subsistence was drawn chiefly from the forest. . . . That law which regulates, and ought to regulate in general, the relations between the conqueror and conquered was incapable of application to a people under such circumstances."[7]

To invade and dispossess the people of an unoffending civilized country would violate morality and transgress the principles of international law, but savages were exceptional. Being uncivilized by definition, they were outside the sanctions of both morality and law. The condition of savagery therefore involved more than aesthetic sensibilities, and the chief justice of a country espousing separation of church and state could show no official concern about Indians' lack of Christianity as criterion of legal status. For Justice Marshall the fundamental criteria of legal savagery were two: subsistence "from the forest" and the "occupation" of war. Since it could hardly be argued that civilized societies eschewed war or withheld honor from professional soldiers, the critical factor in being savage reduced to a mode of subsistence. In that mode both the kind and place of activity were important. Insofar as the difference between civilized and uncivilized men is concerned, the theorists of international law, whom Marshall followed, have held consistently that civilized people stay in place and thus acquire such right in their inhabited lands as uncivilized wanderers cannot rightfully claim. Emmerich de Vattel, a noted eighteenth-century expounder of international law whose views were influential among American statesmen, used comparison to make the issue precise: "While the conquest of the civilized Empires of Peru and Mexico was a notorious usurpation, the establishment of various colonies upon the continent of North America might, if done within just limits,

---

6. Helen Hunt Jackson, *A Century of Dishonor: A Sketch of the United States Government's Dealings with Some of the Indian Tribes* (New York, 1881), 10.

7. *Johnson and Graham's Lessee* v. *William McIntosh*, 21 U.S. Reports 240, 260–261 (1823). Marshall also wrote that "discovery gave an exclusive right to extinguish the Indian title of occupancy, either by purchase or by conquest." *Ibid.*, 259. His use of "right" here seems like nothing more than a legal-sounding noise, for its objective referent cannot be found in either moral philosophy or law. See also Washburn, *Red Man's Land/White Man's Law*, Pt. III, chap. 2.

have been entirely lawful. The peoples of those vast tracts of land rather roamed over them than inhabited them."[8]

The premises of these legal philosophers corresponded not at all with the actual state of Indian societies at about the time of French and English invasions. The natives of the Atlantic coast and the Saint Lawrence-Great Lakes inland coasts supported themselves by hunting and fishing alone or by hunting, fishing, and agriculture. Since the character of hunter was ascribed to all Indians, it is essential to notice that among the east coast tribes south of present-day Maine hunting was a supplementary activity in a predominately agricultural or, to be precise, horticultural economy.[9]

The quality of both the hunting and the horticulture has been much misunderstood. Even in a land lush with wild life, a hunter has to know the habits of his prey in that locality; he has to know the salt licks and water holes and breeding places, the peculiarities of local climate and weather. Without such specialized information, even the most skillfully trained user of weapons can go hungry in the woods or lose himself and die of exposure.[10] Indian hunters, whether full-time or part-time, worked in well-defined territories in which they claimed varieties of property right.[11] Sometimes they maintained trap lines along fixed routes. Sometimes they preserved particular areas as subsistence hunting territories. Among the agricultural Indians a custom widely prevailed of maintaining large parks for hunting to supplement the produce of tillage. Once or twice each year the men of a village gathered to burn away the brush. Much labor obviously went into these burnings, a

8. Emmerich de Vattel, *Le Droit des Gens; ou, Principes de la Loi Naturelle* (1758), trans. Charles G. Fenwick, Carnegie Institution Classics of International Law (Washington, D.C., 1916), III, 38.

9. Alvin M. Josephy, Jr., *The Indian Heritage of America* (New York, 1968), 82; G. K. Holmes, "Aboriginal Agriculture—The American Indians," in L. H. Bailey, ed., *Cyclopedia of American Agriculture: A Popular Survey of Agricultural Conditions, Practices, and Ideals in the United States and Canada* (New York, 1907–1909), IV, 24–39.

10. A nonhunter, I owe this insight to Dr. Jacques Rousseau, who remarked on the matter at the First Conference on Algonquian Studies, Sept. 13–15, 1968. Cf. Innis, *Fur Trade in Canada*, 13.

11. See John M. Cooper, "Land Tenure among the Indians of Eastern and Northern North America," *Pennsylvania Archaeologist*, VIII (1938), 58–59, and also his "Is the Algonquian Family Hunting Ground System Pre-Columbian?" *Am. Anthro.*, N.S., XLI (1939), 66–90; Frank G. Speck, *Family Hunting Territories and Social Life of Various Algonkian Bands of the Ottawa Valley*, Canada Department of Mines, Geological Survey, Memoir 70 (Ottawa, 1915); Frank G. Speck and Loren C. Eiseley, "Significance of Hunting Territory Systems of the Algonkian in Social Theory," *Am. Anthro.*, N.S., XLI (1939), 269–280; William Christie MacLeod, "The Family Hunting Territory and Lenápe Political Organization," *ibid.*, XXIV (1922), 448–463; and Anthony F. C. Wallace, "Political Organization and Land Tenure among the Northeastern Indians, 1600–1830," *Southwestern Journal of Anthropology*, XIII (1957), 318.

purpose of which was to provide pasture land for deer as well as to ease the passage of the hunters.[12] No distinction is here made between communal property, family property, and personal property. All three kinds seem to have existed and evolved. The point is merely that given localities belonged to particular persons or groups who confined themselves to those territories and excluded outsiders from using them.

Fishing also involved knowledge and craft. Compilers Harold E. Driver and William C. Massey have concluded that "fish were obtained by Indians in every major manner known to modern commercial fishermen." Again knowledge of specific localities was important to the fisherman. Like trap lines, weirs were maintained more or less permanently; one, in Boston, has been dated by carbon 14 analysis as four thousand years old. Shellfish beds were visited regularly by whole villages for harvesting. Need it be argued that oyster beds are not portable?[13]

Indians lacked plows, but their horticulture was both intensive and productive. Their maize complex of crops and cultivation techniques was as productive at their own hands as it is today among the people to whom they taught it, and they grew a great variety of plants besides maize. A student of Indian farming practices makes the interesting suggestion that European "improvements" in cultivation methods "provided the chief requisite for soil erosion by stirring the soil over the entire field. . . . For this reason it appears that the Indians were able to grow corn on the same field longer than the white settlers."[14] A Smithsonian scholar estimated in 1929 that "about four-sevenths of the agri-

12. Morton, *New English Canaan*, 36–37, in Force, comp., *Tracts*, II; Wood, *New Englands Prospect*, 16–17; John Cotton, *A Reply to Mr. Williams his Examination* . . . (1647), ed. J. Lewis Diman, in Narragansett Club, *Pubs.*, II (Providence, R.I., 1867), 46–47; John Smith, *Generall Historie of Virginia*, in Arber and Bradley, eds., *Travels and Works of Smith*, II, 427. The best discussion is Gordon M. Day, "The Indian as an Ecological Factor in the Northeastern Forest," *Ecology*, XXXIV (1953), 334–339. For the effects on the land of certain group hunting methods using fire, see Lindeström, *Geographia Americae*, 161, 213–214, and Lawson, *New Voyage to Carolina*, 79, 206–207.

13. Driver and Massey, *North American Indians*, Am. Phil. Soc., *Trans.*, N.S., XLVII, pt. ii (1957), 201, 203; Frank G. Speck and Ralph W. Dexter, "Utilization of Marine Life by the Wampanoag Indians of Massachusetts," *Journal of the Washington Academy of Sciences*, XXXVIII (1948), 257–265; Charles Rau, "Prehistoric Fishing in Europe and North America," in *Smithsonian Contributions to Knowledge*, XXV (Washington, D.C., 1885), 261–318.

14. G. Melvin Herndon, "Indian Agriculture in the Southern Colonies," *North Carolina Historical Review*, XLIV (1967), 283–297, quote on 287; Guy N. Collins, "Notes on the Agricultural History of Maize," *American Historical Association, Annual Report for 1919* (Washington, D.C., 1923), I, 423; Holmes, "Aboriginal Agriculture," in Bailey, ed., *Cyclopedia of American Agriculture*, IV, 25–26, 31. See also Arthur C. Parker, *Iroquois Uses of Maize and Other Food Plants* (1910), in William N. Fenton, ed., *Parker on the Iroquois* (Syracuse, N.Y., 1968).

cultural production of the United States (farm values) are in economic plants domesticated by the American Indian and taken over by the white man."[15]

Labor was divided on the Indian farm. Men girdled and felled trees to open up crop land and then broke the sod. Women sowed and weeded, "wherein they exceeded our English husband-men," according to William Wood in 1634, "keeping it so cleare with their Clamme shell-hooes, as if it were a garden rather than a corne-field, not suffering a choaking weede to advance his audacious head above their infant corne." Weeding was so constant an activity among Indians that cessation of it drew alarmed attention from the English. In 1644 New Englanders suspected warlike intentions because their Indian neighbors had "left their Corne unweeded." In Virginia shiftless colonists who neglected their weeding were ridiculed by the painstaking Indian women[16] (see figure 1). Before European invasion most eastern Indians subsisted largely on the products of their farms and fishing. A nutritionist has concluded that the Indians of southern New England ate only about half as much meat per capita as Americans do today. A Dutch colonist reported that the Indians "do not eat a satisfactory meal" without cornmeal mush."[17]

The basic difference between Indian and English subsistence economies was not farming but herding. So far as meat products were concerned, this difference was minor, but herding has other implications. Indians had no dairy products in their diet. Although they wove reeds into mats and baskets and practiced finger weaving, they failed to develop looms, and their shortage of textiles was felt so keenly that woolen blankets and garments became the great counter-staple of the "fur" trade.[18]

As regards animal management, the English kept herds of domesticated

15. Spinden, "Population of Ancient America," Smithsonian Institution, *Annual Report* (1929), 465n.

16. Parker, *Iroquois Uses of Maize*, in Fenton, ed., *Parker on the Iroquois*, 21-24; Wood, *New Englands Prospect*, 106; Herndon, "Indian Agriculture," *N.C. Hist. Rev.*, XLIV (1967), 287-290; minutes, Sept. 1644, David Pulsifer, ed., *Acts of the Commissioners of the United Colonies of New England* (Nathaniel E. Shurtleff and David Pulsifer, eds., *Records of the Colony of New Plymouth in New England*, IX-X [Boston, 1859]), I, 26, hereafter cited as Pulsifer, ed., *Acts of United Colonies*. See also Howard S. Russell, "New England Indian Agriculture," *Bulletin of the Massachusetts Archaeological Society*, XXII (Apr.-July 1961), 58-61.

17. M. K. Bennett, "The Food Economy of the New England Indians, 1607-75," *Journal of Political Economy*, LXIII (1955), 394; Van der Donck, *Description of New Netherlands*, N.-Y. Hist. Soc., *Colls.*, 2d Ser., I, 193.

18. Carol King Rachlin, "The Historic Position of the Proto-Cree Textiles in the Eastern Fabric Complex: An Ethnological-Archaeological Correlation," in *Contributions to Anthropology*, 1958, National Museum of Canada, Bulletin 167, Anthropological Series, No. 48 (Ottawa, 1960), 82. Driver and Massey, *North American Indians*, Am. Phil. Soc., *Trans.*, N.S., XLVII, pt. ii (1957), 320; chap. 6 below.

FIGURE 1. *Indians planting a crop. The men break the sod while the women sow.*

Figures 1 through 5 are pictures of Carolina Indians of the sixteenth century made by two artists who accompanied abortive French and English colonizing expeditions. Jacques Le Moyne de Morgues was in the colony sent by Admiral Gaspard de Coligny to Florida in 1564, and John White was sent by Sir Walter Ralegh to Virginia in 1584–1590. Le Moyne and White painted what they saw, although obviously they interpreted some scenes according to the artistic conventions of their time. The artists' paintings were engraved by Flemish goldsmith and publisher Theodore de Bry; the five reproduced here to document points made in the text are from de Bry's first German editions of 1590 and 1591. Figures 1, 2, and 5 are engravings of Le Moyne's paintings in Warhafftige Abconterfaytung der Wilden in America . . . (Frankfurt, 1591), and figures 3 and 4 are from White's pictures in Wunderbarliche doch Warhafftige Erklärung, von der Gelegenheit und Sitten der Wilden in Virginia . . . (Frankfurt, 1590). Figures 2, 3, and 4 follow on pp. 68–70; figure 5 is in chapter 9, p. 167.

(Courtesy of the Lehigh University Library, Bethlehem, Pa.; photographs by Mike Jennings.)

livestock—often letting them run free, however, to forage as they might. (To call swine domesticated, when raised in such circumstances, may be stretching a point.) The Indians' livestock had never been domesticated, except for the dog; but, as has been noticed, Indians created pasture land that attracted grazing animals. After contact with Europeans some Indians came to speak of the deer as their "sheep."[19] In the eighteenth century an Oneida chief rationalized the difference between European and Indian management thus: "The Cattle you raise are your own; but those which are Wild are still ours."[20] Indian pasture was made by communal effort, English by private. Actually the colonists of the early contact period avoided the heavy labor of clearing woods whenever possible, bending their chief efforts instead to acquiring the lands already cleared by Indians.[21]

In respect to herding, Englishmen introduced not only livestock but also the forage crops necessary to the European method of maintaining animals in a narrowly restricted habitat. Forage grasses were unknown in aboriginal America, and the browse that sufficed for deer at scattered intervals was inadequate for the concentrated herding of the colonists. The introduction of "English" grass—blue grasses, rye grasses, bents, and white clover—made large herds of grazing animals possible, manageable, and profitable.[22] The herdsman transformed the browse pasture into the forage pasture, and, in New England particularly, he raised meat for the market as well as for subsistence.[23] Some of our earliest cowboys worked in Harvard Yard.

Contrary to assumptions of inadequate yields from Indian cultivation, there is considerable evidence of production and storage of surpluses.[24]

19. Swanton, *Indians of Southeastern U.S.*, 312.

20. Treaty minutes, Oct. 18, 1758, Samuel Hazard, ed., *Minutes of the Provincial Council of Pennsylvania* ... (Harrisburg, Pa., 1838–1853), VIII, 199, hereafter cited as *Pa. Council Minutes*.

A bibliographical note: When the first three volumes of this set were reprinted, the type was reset with pagination different from that of the original edition. My notes have been taken from various sets, so the page numbers will reflect the discrepancies. Date references provide correction where needed.

21. Edward Waterhouse, "A Declaration of the State of the Colony," in Kingsbury, ed., *Recs. of Va. Co.*, III, 556–557; Amandus Johnson, trans. and ed., *The Instruction for Johan Printz, Governor of New Sweden* (Philadelphia, 1930), 117; *History of the Town of Dorchester, Massachusetts* (Boston, 1859), 23; Herndon, "Indian Agriculture," *N.C. Hist. Rev.*, XLIV (1967), 297; Henry E. Chase, "Notes on the Wampanoag Indians," Smithsonian Institution, *Annual Report* (Washington, D.C., 1883), 879–880; Russell, "New England Indian Agriculture," *Bulletin of Mass. Archaeol. Soc.*, XXII (Apr.–July 1961), 60.

22. Lyman Carrier, *The Beginning of Agriculture in America* (New York, 1923), 239–245.

23. Darrett B. Rutman, *Winthrop's Boston: Portrait of a Puritan Town, 1630–1649* (Chapel Hill, N.C., 1965), 180–185.

24. Regina Flannery, *An Analysis of Coastal Algonquian Culture*, Catholic University of America Anthropological Series, VII (Washington, D.C., 1939), 27–30.

Uniformly the early European colonists depended on such surpluses for survival. On this point Jamestown's John Smith thought that the "worthie discourse" of a stout young Indian deserved to be remembered, and he gave it thus: "We perceive and well know you intend to destroy us, that are here to intreat and desire your friendship and to enjoy our houses and plant our fields, of whose fruits you shall participate, otherwise you will have the worst by our absence, for we can plant any where, though with more labour, and we know you cannot live if you want our harvest, and that reliefe wee bring you; if you promise us peace we will beleeve you, if you proceed in revenge, we will abandon the Countrie." Smith promised peace.[25] At this stage of colonization, notably, the colonists preferred the company of competent farmers to the land that would be free for the taking if the farmers removed themselves. As Arthur C. Parker so eloquently has said, the cultivated maize of the Indians "was the bridge over which English civilization crept, tremblingly and uncertainly, at first, then boldly and surely to a foothold and a permanent occupation of America."[26]

Apart from the desperate situations of the "starving times" of the colonists, Indian surplus crops often became a commodity in trade.[27] In aboriginal times the Hurons of the Great Lakes region had laid the foundations for a "trading empire" by carrying their surplus corn as a commodity to the hunting Indians of northern Canada.[28] In Virginia there were communal storage houses; in New England families kept individual storage bins underground.[29] The Narragansett tribe of New England cleared twice as much ground as was planted each year, in

25. John Smith, Map of Virginia, in Barbour, ed., Jamestown Voyages, II, 443-444.

26. Parker's "bridge" had traffic in both directions. Maize was taken by the Portuguese to Africa, where it was first grown to provision slave ships. With expanded use, it supported a great increase of population simultaneously with the slave trade's depletion of the people. Parker, Iroquois Uses of Maize, in Fenton, ed., Parker on the Iroquois, 15; Reay Tannahill, Food in History (New York, 1973), 244-267, esp. 248.

27. Johnson, ed., Instruction for Johan Printz, 111, 117; Van der Donck, Description of New Netherlands, in N.-Y. Hist. Soc., Colls., 2d Ser., I, 209; Lawson, New Voyage to Carolina, 86; Bradford, Of Plymouth Plantation, ed. Morison, 114-115; Nov. 5, 1634, Winthrop, History, ed. Savage, I, 146.

28. Bruce Graham Trigger, "The Jesuits and the Fur Trade," Ethnohistory, XII (1965), 35, and Trigger, "Destruction of Huronia," Royal Can. Inst., Trans., XXXIII (1960), 42; George T. Hunt, The Wars of the Iroquois (Madison, Wis., 1940), chap. 5.

29. The South: Swanton, Indians of Southeastern U.S., 308-309, and de Bry's engraving in figure 2. New England: Morton, New English Canaan, 30, in Force, comp., Tracts, II; Howard S. Russell, "How Aboriginal Planters Stored Food," Bulletin of Mass. Archaeol. Soc., XXIII (Apr.-July 1962), 47-49.

order to let fields lie alternately fallow.[30] They gave and sold large quantities of corn to the colonists of Massachusetts Bay.[31] In another respect also the English farmer and herdsman depended upon their Indian neighbors; namely, to keep down the numbers of wolves and other predators that otherwise would have "oppressed" the colonists.[32]

Indians were as much tied to particular localities as were Europeans. John Smith carefully itemized the territories of Virginia's natives.[33] Edward Winslow, in 1624, noted that every sachem in New England knew "how far the bounds and limits of his own country extendeth; and that is his own proper inheritance."[34] Whether hunters or farmers, all Indian bands or other organized community groups lived in territories marked by specific natural boundaries such as mountains or streams. Their lives were governed by cycles of movement within their territories. When fish shoaled, plants fruited, and animals seasonally migrated, Indians revisited familiar spots. Both hunters and farmers gathered at certain seasons in tribal centers or villages for the performance of unifying rituals and public business as well as for simple sociability.[35] Agricultural villages had permanent buildings and were occupied during the entire planting season. When the ground became infertile through constant replanting, those Indians who did not fertilize their lands—some of the coastal peoples did—removed their villages to new sites; ordinarily, however, even this movement was cyclical, since the old sites were likely to be reoccupied after a lapse of some years.[36] An Indian who "wandered" into the territory of an alien tribe,

30. John Winthrop, Jr., to Winthrop, Sr., Apr. 7, 1636, *Winthrop Papers*, III, 246.

31. William B. Weeden, *Economic and Social History of New England, 1620–1789* (Boston, 1890), I, 37–38.

32. John Martin, "The manner howe to bringe in the Indians into subjection without making an utter exterpation of them together with the reasons," in Kingsbury, ed., *Recs. of Va. Co.*, III, 705–706.

33. John Smith, *Map of Virginia*, in Barbour, ed., *Jamestown Voyages*, II, 339–344, 371, and map of 1612 facing p. 374.

34. Edward Winslow, *Good Newes from New England* ... (1624), in Alexander Young, ed., *Chronicles of the Pilgrim Fathers of the Colony of Plymouth, from 1602 to 1625* (Boston, 1841), 361.

35. Williams, *Key*, ed. Trumbull, Narragansett Club, *Pubs.*, I, 74–75; Ralph Lane, "Discourse on the First Colony" (ca. 1586), in Quinn, ed., *Roanoke Voyages*, I, 283; Van der Donck, *Description of New Netherlands*, in N.-Y. Hist. Soc., *Colls.*, 2d Ser., I, 197–198; A. F. C. Wallace, "Political Organization and Land Tenure," *Southwest. Jour. Anthro.*, XIII (1957), 304, 311.

36. Day, "Indian as an Ecological Factor," *Ecology*, XXXIV (1953), 340–341; William N. Fenton, "Locality as a Basic Factor in the Development of Iroquois Social Structure," in Fenton, ed., *Symposium on Local Diversity in Iroquois Culture*, Smithsonian Institution, Bureau of American Ethnology, Bulletin 149 (Washington, D.C., 1951), 42.

FIGURE 2. *Jacques Le Moyne's picture of a communal storehouse.*

FIGURE 3. *John White's picture of an open village in Virginia.*

FIGURE 4. *A contrasting picture by John White of a stockaded village (compare fig. 3).*

or who poached on the hunting grounds of a fellow tribesman without permission, committed thereby an offense that might be punished by death.[37] Farmers planted in tracts assigned to them by their chiefs.[38] In the most literal sense every Indian knew his place on the land and was kept in it by enforced custom.[39] The Indian did not wander; he commuted.[40]

In this discussion care has been taken to limit the remarks to subsistence hunting. There was another kind that served as a basis for the far-ranging Indian of the hunter stereotype, but it had not been a feature of aboriginal society. This was the commercial hunting produced by the impact of European colonization, and it was dictated by the combined pressures of the international market in furs and the Indian dependence on European products that occurred after native crafts fell into disuse. An early Dutch observer noted that Indians hunting at a great distance had to take food with them. He clearly distinguished between the subsistence hunting for deer "near the sea-shore and rivers where the Christians mostly reside" and the commercial hunting for beaver that were "mostly taken far inland, there being few of them near the settlements."[41] Whether searching for food or for commodity,

37. A. F. C. Wallace, "Political Organization and Land Tenure," *Southwest. Jour. Anthro.*, XIII (1957), 316–318.

38. Winslow, *Good Newes*, in Young, ed., *Chronicles of Pilgrims*, 361; Wisquannowas's petition, ca. 1675, in Hugh Hastings, ed., *Third Annual Report of the State Historian of the State of New York, 1897* (New York and Albany, 1898), 308–309.

A bibliographic note: Appendix L of Hastings's *Report* (pp. 157–435) prints manuscript volumes XXIII and XXIV of the New York Colonial Manuscripts, N.Y. State Lib., for the years 1673 to 1675 inclusive. This transcript is especially valuable because it was made before the manuscripts were damaged by fire.

39. See Fenton's detailed discussion in "Locality as a Basic Factor," in Fenton, ed., *Symposium on Local Diversity in Iroquois Culture*, 35–53.

40. The practice of cyclical migration was perfectly well understood by the English colonizers in America. As early as 1634 William Wood noted dispersion of Indian villages "sometimes to fishing places, other times to hunting places, after that to a planting place where it abides the longest." When colonists pretended that the Indians were mere nomads, the reason was to invoke international law doctrines applicable to vacant lands; such lands were available for seizure. I have elsewhere documented such a case in 18th-century Pennsylvania. Nicholas Canny observes interestingly that English colonizers in Ireland "took the Irish practice of transhumance as proof that the Irish were nomads, hence barbarians"; I presume that possession of land was also at issue there. Irish transhumance—removing with herds of domesticated animals from one pasture to another—had the same cyclical effect as Amerindian removal from planting sites to hunting and fishing sites. Wood, *New Englands Prospect*, 106; Francis Paul Jennings, "Miquon's Passing: Indian-European Relations in Colonial Pennsylvania, 1674 to 1755" (Ph.D. diss., University of Pennsylvania, 1965), 108–111, 238–239; Canny, "Ideology of English Colonization," *WMQ*, 3d Ser., XXX (1973), 587.

41. Van der Donck, *Description of New Netherlands*, in N.-Y. Hist. Soc., *Colls.*, 2d Ser., I, 209.

the Indian hunter always returned after the chase to his native village.

It is clear enough that there was a difference in quality between the cultures of Indians and those of the colonizing Europeans. What is being argued here is only that the difference was relative rather than absolute. Without the shadow of a doubt it was of a nature that permitted and even encouraged interaction between the cultures and was thus contradictory to John Marshall's edict that Indians were "a people with whom it was impossible to mix, and who could not be governed as a distinct society."[42]

Defined by technological standards, Indian culture has been called neolithic or primitive. By sociopolitical criteria, however, recent theory suggests that Europe's intrusion transformed Indian communities into peasant societies. What has been lacking to make recognition explicit is the realization that invasion-era Indians made up what A. L. Kroeber has called "part-societies." Expounding on Kroeber's concept, Robert Redfield held that "a peasant's community is only a part-community; his society is incomplete without the town or city.... To the extent that the trade of the tribesman with the town becomes necessary to him and requires him to enter into some relationships of personal and moral dependence on the townsman, that tribesman, to that extent and incompletely, is less of a tribesman than he was and more of a peasant."[43]

If such distinctions between primitives and peasants have validity, then the Indians who traded and treated with Europeans in the seventeenth and eighteenth centuries had departed absolutely from their precontact primitive state. It is impossible not to fit the facts of their lives into Redfield's economic criteria for peasantry: "It is the market, in one form or another, that pulls out from the compact social relations of self-contained primitive communities some parts of men's doings and puts people into fields of economic activity that are increasingly independent of the rest of what goes on in the local life. The local traditional and moral world and the wider and more impersonal world of the market are in principle distinct, opposed to each other, as Weber and others have emphasized. In peasant society the two are maintained in some balance; the market is held at arm's length, so to speak."[44]

Eric R. Wolf has substituted political criteria for Redfield's economic

---

42. *Johnson and Graham's Lessee* v. *William McIntosh*, 21 U.S. Reports 260 (1823).

43. Kroeber, *Anthropology*, 284; Robert Redfield, "Tribe, Peasant, and City," in Margaret Park Redfield, ed., *Human Nature and the Study of Society: The Papers of Robert Redfield* (Chicago, 1962–1963), I, 287.

44. Robert Redfield, *Peasant Society and Culture: An Anthropological Approach to Civilization* (Chicago, 1956), 45–46. See also Manning Nash, *Primitive and Peasant Economic Systems* (San Francisco, 1966), 59.

standards, but his model fits Indian contact communities just as closely as Redfield's: "It is the crystallization of executive power which serves to distinguish the primitive from the civilized, rather than whether or not such power controls are located in one kind of place or another. Not the city, but the state is the decisive criterion of civilization and it is the appearance of the state which marks the threshold of transition between food cultivators in general and peasants. Thus, it is only when a cultivator is integrated into a society with a state—that is, when the cultivator becomes subject to the demands and sanctions of power-holders outside his social stratum—that we can appropriately speak of peasantry."[45]

The first thing that European invaders did was to claim the Indians as their subjects and to enforce the claim where feasible. Those Indians who escaped full subjection in fact did so only by becoming clients of one European polity or another, and the acceptance of protection invariably implied acceptance, to greater or lesser degree, of the demands and sanctions of the European power-holders.

By either economic or political criteria, therefore, American Indians departed from the primitive state—the only condition to which the term *savage* has any conceivably objective reference—when European traders and governors appeared on the tribal doorstep.

How, then, did the observed data of the Indian peasant turn into the myth of the roaming savage? Part of the answer is found in the deliberate intent of propagandists to create opinion in England favorable to aggressive policies in America, but another part is contained in the development of connotations that became incorporated in the term and acquired a life of their own. This development was long peculiar to English. In Dutch, Swedish, and German, the Romance word *savage* failed to find a welcome. Colonizers from the Netherlands used *wilden* for the Indians, and German translates "savage people" into *wildes Volk*. In Swedish the Indians were *wildar*.[46] In French *sauvage* was used

45. Eric R. Wolf, *Peasants*, Foundations of Modern Anthropology Series (Englewood Cliffs, N.J., 1966), 11 (quotation by permission of Prentice-Hall, Inc.). Wolf's contradiction of Redfield's emphasis on the city is more apparent than real, for Redfield modified his view to accept a manorial elite in some circumstances to fulfill the city's role. Redfield, *Peasant Society*, 160. See also the definitions of Cyril S. Belshaw, *Traditional Exchange and Modern Markets*, Modernization of Traditional Societies Series (Englewood Cliffs, N.J., 1965), 53-54.

46. Van der Donck, *Description of New Netherlands*, in N.-Y. Hist. Soc., *Colls.*, 2d Ser., I, 190-191; Lindeström, *Geographia Americae*, 191 and n. Lindeström's translator was addicted to "savage," but he gives the original in his note; cf. his rendition of the title page with the photograph of the original following p. xliv. See also Tobias E. Biorck, "The Planting of the Swedish Church in America" (ca. 1725), quoted in C. A. Weslager, "Susquehannock Indian Religion from an Old Document," *Jour. of Washington Academy of Sciences*, XXXVI (1946), 7.

ambiguously with connotations of noble primitivism or of bestiality according to the outlook and mood of the writer. Marc Lescarbot, who used *sauvage* consistently in his own writing, objected to its use in a pejorative sense: "If we commonly call them Savages, the word is abusive and unmerited, for they are anything but that, as will be proved in the course of this history." Throughout the eighteenth century French colonials seem to have used the term as a mere synonym for Indian, and their meanings vacillated with their attitudes. Not until the nineteenth century did French usage harden into the pattern already long established in English.[47]

The Latin root *silva*, meaning woods, took two directions in English to make "sylvan" and "savage." "Sylvan" now portrays woodland serenity and beauty. Through French *sauvage*, however, the idea of ferocious wild beasts came as one of the word's meanings into English. The term did not gain general currency as a substantive denoting a human person of the wilderness until late in the sixteenth century. At that time it was used as an adjective applying indifferently to plant, animal, or person.[48] An early Jamestown narrative refers to "wild and savage people, that live and lie up and downe in troupes like heards of Deare in a Forrest"; these people were "very loving and gentle."[49] The special development of "savage" in English was a stress on beastly ferocity that displaced simple wildness as the dominant meaning of the word. Thus savage persons came to be wild like wolves instead of wild like deer. This development was long and uneven, and only its first phase can be shown here.

As late as 1563 Jean Ribaut's narrative of Florida referred only to "people" and "Indians," who are unfailingly described as gentle; "savage" is not to be seen.[50] In 1566, after the destruction of the Huguenot colony on the Carolina coast, Nicolas Le Challeux survived to take refuge in England. In his account of the colony there were savages, but they were "kind and gentle"; the human beings described as more cruel than wild beasts were the Spanish exterminators of the colony.[51] The simple mean-

47. For the 17th and 18th centuries: Kennedy, *Jesuit and Savage in New France*, chap. 10; Marc Lescarbot, *The History of New France* (1618), trans. W. L. Grant, introduction by H. P. Biggar, Champlain Society Publications, I, VII, XI (Toronto, 1907–1914), I, 33. For the 19th century: Pierre Larousse, *Grand Dictionnaire Universel du XIXe Siecle* (Paris, [1865–1890?]), s.v. "sauvage."

48. *Oxford English Dictionary*, s.v. "savage."

49. [George Johnson], *Nova Britannia: Offering Most Excellent fruites by Planting in Virginia. Exciting all such as be well affected to further the same* (1609), 11, in Force, comp., *Tracts*, I.

50. H. P. Biggar, ed., "Jean Ribaut's Discoverye of Terra Florida," *English Historical Review*, XXXII (1917), 253–270.

51. [Le Challeux], *A true and perfect description, of the last voyage or Navigation, attempted by Capitaine John Rybaut, deputie and generall for the French men, into Terra Florida...* (1566), in Stefan Lorant, ed., *The New World: The*

ing of wild person continued in the extensive use of "savage" by the two Richard Hakluyts, lawyer and geographer, who kept in touch with the explorers and colonizers of their day. In his "Notes on Colonization" (written in 1578, printed in 1582), Hakluyt the lawyer used "savage" more or less synonymously with "inland people."[52]

In 1580 the geographer Hakluyt probably wrote the dedication to the first English translation of Jacques Cartier's travels. It asked pointedly why no effort had been made to send colonies "to reduce this savage nation to some civilitie," and it also described the people, "though simple and rude in manners, and destitute of the knowledge of God or any good lawes, yet of nature gentle and tractable, and most apt to receive the Christian Religion, and to subject themselves to some good government." The translation of Cartier thus introduced was curious in more than one respect. It was a translation of a translation, and it showed a definite feeling by translator John Florio about the use of "savage." Cartier's manuscript had not yet been published in France, so Florio had to work from a version published in Italian by a Venetian geographer. In this the word *salvatichi*—the Italian cognate of "savages"—appeared frequently, but Florio nowhere translated it as "savage persons." In one passage where *detti Salvatichi* appeared three times, Florio Englished it twice as "said wild men" and the third time simply as "said men." On the other hand, Florio translated *le bestie* as "savage beastes." Clearly Florio, who was an Oxford scholar, identified "savage" with wilderness and animals, but distinguished human beings by other words.[53]

In 1583 another member of the Hakluyt circle, Sir George Peckham, emphatically and repeatedly stressed the heathenism of the Indians, arguing "that it is lawfull and necessarie to trade and traffike with the Savages: And to plant in their Countries," his justification being the obligation to save savage souls, and in 1584 the geographer Hakluyt picked up this theme in his highly influential *Discourse of Western Planting*, in which he continued to refer to Indians as "these simple

First Pictures of America (New York, 1965), 88–116; "savage," 92; "kind and gentle," 94; Spaniards, 102 and *passim*.

52. E. G. R. Taylor, ed., *The Original Writings and Correspondence of the Two Richard Hakluyts*, Hakluyt Society Publications, 2d Ser., LXXVI–LXXVII (London, 1935), I, 116–122.

53. Jacques Cartier, *A Shorte and briefe Narration of the two Navigations and Discoveries to the Northweast partes called Newe Fraunce*, trans. John Florio (1580), March of America Facsimile Series, No. 10 (Ann Arbor, Mich., 1966), unpaged preface; Giovanni Battista Ramusio, *Navigationi et Viaggi* (Venice, 1550–1559), III, 435–453. For the strange history of Cartier's meandering narrative see *Dict. of Can. Biog.*, I, s.v. "Cartier, Jacques." I have used the copy of Ramusio's rare work at the Linderman Library of Lehigh University, Bethlehem, Pa., to whose staff I wish to express gratitude for this favor and many others.

people that are in errour into the righte and perfecte waye of their salvacion."[54]

Generally it appears that the Hakluyts and their friends wanted to present Indians in an attractive light because of their desire to interest backers for their colonization schemes. In 1585 the elder Hakluyt (lawyer) set forth his "Inducements to the liking of the voyage intended towards Virginia" in admirably clear and succinct language: "The ends of this voyage are these: 1, to plant Christian religion; 2, To trafficke; 3, To conquer; Or, to doe all three."[55] For such purposes mild and tractable Indians would be best. In the same year colonist Ralph Lane, though apparently brutal in his treatment of the Indians, wrote home from Roanoke to say that "the soil is of an huge and unknowen greatnesse, and very wel peopled and towned, though savagelie." Lane added, "Savages . . . possesse the land."[56]

An interested friend of the Hakluyts was William Shakespeare, whose omnivorous appetite for colorful words did not neglect "savage." Bartlett's *Concordance* quotes forty-two phrases from Shakespeare using "savage," "savagely," "savageness," and "savagery" to express attributes of wildness, rudeness, bestiality, and cruelty; and the words were sometimes applied to persons. But Shakespeare was a wild-eyed poet; the solid, steady scholars who produced the King James Bible in 1611 avoided "savage."[57]

The term gradually gained form and acceptance through its use by the people engaged in colonizing, and they continued to use it uncertainly for a couple of decades. They obviously regarded it as a slur associated with heathenism, nakedness, and general contemptibility, but equally obviously they saw exciting possibilities in the savages for easy exploitation. Although the savages were wild people, and therefore an inferior sort, they were still people.

In 1606 the Virginia Company of London instructed its colonists to buy a stock of corn from the "naturals" before the English intention to settle permanently should become evident. The company's chiefs were sure that "you cannot carry yourselves so towards them but they will grow discontented with your habitation." Nevertheless, the colonists were to offend the natives as little as possible, consistent with their mis-

54. "A true Report of the late discoveries . . . ," in Hakluyt, *Principall Navigations*, II, 705; Taylor, ed., *Writings of the Two Richard Hakluyts*, I, 31, II, 214.

55. In John Brereton, *A Briefe and true Relation of the Discoverie of the North part of Virginia* (1602), March of America Facsimile Series, No. 16 (Ann Arbor, Mich., 1966), 30.

56. Ralph Lane to R. Hakluyt, lawyer, Sept. 3, 1585, Taylor, ed., *Writings of the Two Richard Hakluyts*, 346.

57. John Bartlett, *A Complete Concordance . . . [to the] Dramatic Works of Shakespeare* (New York, 1966), 1321; James Strong, *The Exhaustive Concordance of the Bible* (New York, 1894), 879.

sion of trade and plantation, because the presence of the natives was essential to the mission's fulfilment. So long as trade with the natives remained a dominant purpose, this logic prevailed. "Savages," when so named, were discussed in relatively mild and tolerant terms, and no one tried to exterminate the Indians either factually or metaphorically. The official instructions of the Virginia Company were careful to refer to the Indians as "native people," "naturals," and "country people."[58] In an oddly mixed official publication of a slightly later date, the natives are "Indians" when mentioned in trading contexts, "savages" when the necessity for defense is mentioned. At one point this tract cautions that "there is no trust to the fidelitie of humane beasts, except a man will make league with Lions, Beares, and Crocodiles," but the only specific use of "savages" is distant in the text from this beast imagery.[59] Even tough John Smith, for all his swagger and bluster, was ready to regard Indians as peers when the price was right. Certainly no Christian Englishman should have tolerated the thought of another Englishman in savage servitude, but Smith carried young Henry Spelman off to a nearby chief, and as Spelman later complained, "unknowne to me" Smith "sould me to him for a town caled Powhatan."[60]

Change came with the Indian uprising of 1622.[61] Before that war the Hakluyt tradition had been continued in London by the Reverend Samuel Purchas, who boasted of how carefully the Virginians had conciliated the "salvages" and of how the English paid in valuable commodities for all their newly occupied land—"a thing of no small consequence to the conscience, where the milde Law of Nature, not that violent law of Armes, layes the foundation of their possession."[62] But

---

58. Arber and Bradley, eds., *Travels and Works of Smith*, I, xxxiv–xxxv.

59. *A True Declaration of the estate of the Colonie in Virginia* (1610), 6, 20, in Force, comp., *Tracts*, III.

60. Henry Spelman, "Relation of Virginia," in Arber and Bradley, eds., *Travels and Works of Smith*, I, cii.

61. Wilcomb E. Washburn, "The Moral and Legal Justifications for Dispossessing the Indians," in James Morton Smith, ed., *Seventeenth-Century America: Essays in Colonial History* (Chapel Hill, N.C., 1959), 20–22.

62. Samuel Purchas, *Purchas his Pilgrimage*, 4th ed. (London, 1626), 836. Although I have used the fourth edition, I have inspected it carefully to make sure that it was not revised to take account of events that occurred after the issuance of the last preceding edition of 1615. There is no doubt that the quoted remark was written before the war of 1622.

A bibliographic note: Purchas wrote two books, the first of which was made physically uniform in its last edition with the first edition of the other book. Thus *Purchas his Pilgrimage*, 4th ed., came erroneously to be viewed as Vol. V of *Hakluytus Posthumus or Purchas His Pilgrimes*, 4 vols. (London, 1625). I have used the copies of both works at Linderman Library, Lehigh University. See Sir William Foster, "Samuel Purchas," in Edward Lynam, ed., *Richard Hakluyt and His Successors*, Hakluyt Society Publications, 2d Ser., XCIII (London, 1946), 49–61.

contention over the land was exactly what had precipitated the war. The discovery of tobacco's profitability had altered the Virginians' attitudes toward native neighbors. So long as the colony depended heavily on trade for skins and furs, nearby trading partners were an asset. They changed into a liability when trade became secondary. The colonists could and did raise tobacco by themselves—the Indians had taught them well—and they now coveted their neighbors' cleared lands more than their company. The lucrative weed stimulated a reorganization of Virginian society involving large "grants" of lands, accompanied by rapid growth and scattering of the English population. How Indians were persuaded to part with lands during this period is not clear; despite boasts of purchase, there are no deeds to show for it such as appeared later in New England. Between 1618 and 1622 English numbers appear to have doubled, and Indian hostility grew with them. Finally the alarmed Indians rose in a desperate effort to drive away or exterminate the intruders.

It was then that John Smith and Samuel Purchas gave a sharp twist to the meaning of "savage" that originated its present ugliness. Smith was moved by the Virginia war to dilate upon his habitually uncomplimentary references to Indians. Where formerly he had dwelt on their supposed treachery and other evil qualities in terms that he might have used interchangeably for Turk or Spaniard, he now adopted the beast imagery latent in "savage" and fastened it explicitly upon savage persons. In his *Generall Historie of Virginia, New England, and the Summer Isles*, published in 1624, the "perfidious and inhumane people" became "cruell beasts" with "a more unnaturall brutishness then beasts." Throughout Smith's account of the Indian massacre, "savage" appears prominently. This is the more notable because eight years earlier Smith had railed against a personal enemy for "trecherie among the Salvages" whom he had identified at that time as "poore innocent soules."[63]

Smith's admiring friend Purchas joined him in the turnabout. Purchas contributed complimentary verses to the *Generall Historie*, remarking that "Smiths Forge mends all, makes chaines for Savage Nation / Frees, feeds the rest."[64] A year later Purchas published his own magnum opus, *Hakluytus Posthumus or Purchas His Pilgrimes*, in part of which, contrary to his usual practice of presenting edited versions of others' writings, he spoke at length in his own voice to formulate an elaborate and seminal rationalization for colonization by conquest.[65]

63. Arber and Bradley, eds., *Travels and Works of Smith*, II, 574; *A Description of New England* (1616), *ibid.*, I, 219–220.

64. Arber and Bradley, eds., *Travels and Works of Smith*, I, 283.

65. Purchas, *Hakluytus Posthumus*, IV, Bk. 9, chap. 20: "Virginia's Verger, Or a Discourse shewing the benefits which may grow to this Kingdome from Ameri-

Smith and Purchas presumably were familiar with the circumstances of Virginia related by one Captain Butler "in the winter" of 1622. Butler "unmasked" the colony in a denunciation of its managers for their neglect and exploitation of the settlers. "There haveinge been, as itt is thought, not fewer than Tenn thousand soules transported thether, there are not, through the aforenamed abuses and neglects, above Two thousand of them att the present to be found alive . . . in steed of a Plantacion, itt will shortly gett the name of a slaughter house." Of the 8,000 dead immigrants, 347 had been killed in the Indian massacre. If Indians deserved a bad name because of the 347, what might the Virginia Company's gentlemen deserve to be called for the other 7,600? [66]

But Smith and Purchas were not interested in evenhanded distribution of blame.[67] Both wrote under great pressure to counteract the bad effect on public opinion of the company's bankruptcy and dissolution in 1624.[68] There can be little doubt that the company had been looted by its organizers. If the public were to become generally conscious of its bad management and scandalous peculation, investors would withhold

----

can English Plantations, and specially those of Virginia and Summer Ilands," 1809–1826.

66. Captain Butler, "The unmasked face of our Colony in Virginia as it was in the winter of the yeare 1622," C.O. 1/3, 36–37, P.R.O.; Wesley Frank Craven, *Dissolution of the Virginia Company: The Failure of a Colonial Experiment* (New York, 1932), chap. 6; Alf J. Mapp, Jr., *The Virginia Experiment* (Richmond, Va., 1957), 61.

Butler's manuscript was published in 1906 in Kingsbury, ed., *Recs. of Va. Co.*, II, 374–376, apparently from a different copy than that in P.R.O., but only spelling and punctuation vary; the words are identical. Oddly this extremely important document was merely listed in the *Calendar of State Papers* without being abstracted by editor Sainsbury; it is listed as an enclosure to another document purportedly refuting it. The contents of the "refutation" really add to the power of Butler's indictment. At most the "refutation" insists that "only" 6,000 persons, instead of 10,000, had been transported to Virginia, and it does not dispute Butler's charge that only 2,000 of these remained alive. Blame for the others' deaths was laid upon the previous administration of Sir Thomas Smythe (1607–1619), during which time, as the "refutation" affirmed, there were "wants and miseries of the colony under most cruel laws sent over in print, contrary to the charter. The allowance of food in those times for a man was loathsome and not fit for beasts; many fled for relief to the savages but were taken again, and hung, shot, or broken upon the wheel: one man for stealing meal had a bodkin thrust through his tongue, and was chained to a tree until he starved. Many dug holes in the earth and hid themselves till they famished. So great was the scarcity that they were constrained to eat dogs, cats, rats, snakes, etc. and one man killed his wife and powdered her up to eat, for which he was burned. Many fed on corpses. . . ." Let it be repeated: this is the *defense* against Captain Butler's charge of maladministration. "The Governor, Council, and Assembly of Virginia to the King" [Feb. 1623], W. Noel Sainsbury, ed., *Calendar of State Papers, Colonial Series, 1574–1660* (London, 1860), 38–40.

67. Purchas disingenuously tried to make the Indians responsible for casualties that had occurred before they fought. *Hakluytus Posthumus*, IV, 1816.

68. Arber and Bradley, eds., *Travels and Works of Smith*, I, 274.

funds from the future colonization to which Smith and Purchas were committed. A scapegoat was needed—a manageable scapegoat that could be heaped with blame for past disasters, then safely got out of the way to remove fears of the future. Smith's book provided the goat. Purchas sacrificed it.[69]

Purchas's unique distinction was the invention of the nonperson-nonland qualities of savages and the world they lived in—the depersonalization of persons who were "wild." Turning away from his pre-war boasts of how Englishmen had conciliated the savages, Purchas justified (in 1625) the Virginians' retaliatory massacres of the Indians. He argued that Christian Englishmen might rightfully seize Indian lands because God had intended his land to be cultivated and not to be left in the condition of "that unmanned wild Countrey, which they [the savages] range rather than inhabite."[70]

It is instructive to dwell for a moment on that last phrase. Purchas may have picked it up from the Jesuit missionary Pierre Biard, who had described the Indians living farther north: "Thus four thousand Indians at most roam through, rather than occupy, these vast stretches of inland territory and sea-shore. For they are a nomadic people, living in the forests and scattered over wide spaces as is natural for those who live by hunting and fishing only."[71] But Purchas knew perfectly well that the Virginia Indians were sedentary and agricultural and that the Jamestown colonists had been preserved from total starvation by Indian farm produce.

Before Purchas wrote, a Jamestown colonist had actually gloated over the occurrence of the Indian uprising, for reasons that make stark comment on Purchas's trustworthiness.

We, who hitherto have had possession of no more ground then their waste, and our purchase ... may now by right of Warre, and law of Nations, invade the Country, and destroy them who sought to destroy us: *whereby wee shall enjoy their cultivated places*, turning the laborious Mattocke into the victorious Sword (wherein there is more both ease, benefit, and glory) and possessing the fruits of others labours. *Now their cleared grounds in all their villages (which are situate in the fruitfullest places of the land) shall be inhabited by us*, whereas heretofore the grubbing of woods was the greatest labour."[72]

---

69. The interpretation is mine. Smith's most recent biographer, whose scholarship is exemplary, distinguishes sharply between the two men while describing their cooperation in publishing matters. Philip L. Barbour, *The Three Worlds of Captain John Smith* (London, 1964), 297, 364-367, and *passim*.

70. Purchas, *Hakluytus Posthumus*, IV, 1814.

71. "Roam through, rather than occupy," is a translation of Biard's Latin "*non tenentur, sed percurruntur.*" *Letter from Port Royal in Acadia* ... (1612), in Thwaites, ed., *Jesuit Relations*, II, 72-73.

72. Waterhouse, "State of the Colony," in Kingsbury, ed., *Recs. of Va. Co.*, III, 556-557. Emphasis added.

Although Purchas's "range rather than inhabite" phrase was contrary to known fact, it held the magic of a strong incantation and the utility of a magician's smokescreen. It became an axiom of international law (although it does not appear in the works of Hugo Grotius, the so-called founder of international law),[73] and its capacity to smother fact was still so highly valued as late as 1830 that Secretary of War Lewis Cass synonymized it elegantly ("traversed but not occupied") to justify the expropriation of the sedentary and agricultural Cherokees.[74]

Purchas's chief pronouncement was that the Indians had become "Outlawes of Humanity." He fumed against "the unnaturall Naturalls" who had forfeited by "disloyal treason" their "remainders of right." He verbally abolished their personal existences along with the rights natural to persons. They became "like Cain, both Murtherers and Vagabonds in their whatsoever and howsoever owne," and therefore "I can scarcely call [them] Inhabitants." Having committed their monstrous crime against English humanity, they had "lost their owne Naturall, and given us another Nationall right . . . so that England may both by Law of Nature and Nations challenge Virginia for her owne peculiar propriety."[75]

Having laid claim to Virginia, Purchas prescribed the righteous duty of its colonists "not to make Savages and wild degenerate men of Christians, but Christians of those Savage, wild, degenerate men." Even the land was transformed with wordplay characteristic of the then fashionable literary style: "All the rich endowments of Virginia," he declared, "her Virgin-portion from the creation nothing lessened," were "wages" for converting the "Savage Countries."[76]

It is all true and it is all false—true as metaphor in a system of ideas designed for a conqueror's needs, and false as representation of fact. Certainly Purchas understood what he was doing, and he was never foolish enough to believe that Virginia was really virgin land devoid of natives. Pursuing a constant practical objective, he advocated that the metaphorical noninhabitants "be servilely used; that future dangers

---

73. Grotius's modern translator turned Latin *ferina* into "savages" at one point although the translator of the 17th-century English edition had rendered it "brutish." The versions: original, "*Bella quae utroque causarum genera carent, ferina esse*"; 1682, "The War that hath neither of these, is brutish"; 1925, "Wars which lack causes of either sort are wars of savages." Hugo Grotius, *De Jure Belli Ac Pacis Libri Tres* (1646), Vol. II, trans. Francis W. Kelsey, Carnegie Endowment for International Peace Classics of International Law, III (Oxford, 1925), I, 384, II, 547; Hugo Grotius, *His Three Books Treating of the Rights of War and Peace*, trans. William Evats (London, 1682), 404.

74. Lewis Cass, "Removal of the Indians," *North American Review*, XXX (1830), 77.

75. Purchas, *Hakluytus Posthumus*, IV, 1811, 1813.

76. *Ibid.*, 1811.

be prevented by the extirpation of the more dangerous, and commodities also raised out of the servileness and serviceablenesse of the rest."[77]

Before Purchas, his mentor Richard Hakluyt had also waxed euphuistic about metaphorical virginity and his patroness queen,[78] but Elizabeth had been two decades dead when Purchas wrote. Hakluyt had been very much interested in savages as persons to be traded with and ruled over; rhetorical virginity in the land waited for Purchas to define it as nonhabitation.

The process of reifying metaphor into purported actuality developed further in New England, where Purchas's logic was refined into the practical form of a legal fiction—an abstract idea accepted by courts as though it were a fact—akin in factuality and function to the fiction that General Motors or the Standard Oil companies are persons. This development was contributed by a Puritan lawyer, Governor John Winthrop, Sr., of Massachusetts Bay. Winthrop was not interested in fanciful plays on the idea of virginity in the land, but he seized on the equivalent conception that it had never been used. Responding to scrupulous objections against seizing Indian property, Winthrop declared in 1629 that most land in America fell under the legal rubric of *vacuum domicilium* because the Indians had not "subdued" it and therefore had only a "natural" and not a "civil" right to it.[79] Such natural right need not be respected in the same way as civil right; only the latter imposed the obligations of true legal property. Morally (and pragmatically) Winthrop's Puritans were obliged to leave individual Indians in possession of tracts actually under tillage, because such small plots of cultivated land obviously qualified as "subdued" according to English cultural assumptions, but hunting territories were regarded as "waste" available for seizure, no matter what status they held in native custom. Inherent in this doctrine was the notion that no Indian government could be recognized as sovereign over any domain, and therefore no legal sanction could exist for Indian tenure of real estate.

Seizure of open lands was nothing new to Englishmen. Since the Statute of Merton in 1235 A.D., English manorial lords had been enclosing lands—sometimes "waste," sometimes commons, and sometimes cropland—with little regard for the welfare or customary rights of local peasants.[80] Massachusetts's Puritans carried on this ancient practice with

77. *Ibid.*, 1819.

78. Taylor, ed., *Writings of the Two Richard Hakluyts*, 367.

79. John Winthrop, Sr., "General considerations for the plantation in New England, with an answer to several objections," *Winthrop Papers*, II, 120. Winthrop apparently was indebted to Purchas's "Virginia's Verger" chapter for many specific formulations, but he made a concise selection instead of taking over the entire battery of Purchas's arguments.

80. See W. E. Tate, *The Enclosure Movement* (New York, 1967), chaps. 2, 3, 4, 7.

only a slight change of rationalization. To meet moral criticism on this issue (as on others also) they relied on their status as the Elect of God.

For their ultimate authority the Puritans scorned matters of mundane fact to appeal to Holy Writ in a neat selection of texts. They quoted Psalms 2:8: "Ask of me, and I shall give thee, the heathen for thine inheritance, and the uttermost parts of the earth for thy possession." For enforcement of this large donation they cited Romans 13:2: "Whosoever therefore resisteth the Power, resisteth the Ordinance of God, and they that resist, receive to themselves damnation."[81] References to such biblical texts were incorporated into the laws that ostensibly guaranteed Indians a title to land, so that once the scriptural citations were included, they too became an integral part of the law.[82]

For convenience the Puritans reinforced Scripture with the temporal authority of their patent from the king of England. Difficult subjects though they were, they recognized his sovereignty (as they recognized Indian property) for the single purpose of conveying the recognized right to themselves.[83] An anonymous humorist has summarized all this authority in a syllogism that he attributed—apparently apocryphally —to a Puritan town meeting: "Voted, that the earth is the Lord's and the fulness thereof; voted, that the earth is given to the Saints; voted, that we are the Saints."[84] Whether or not any town was ever indiscreet enough to commit such a resolution to record, that was the Puritans' logic. People possessed of such marvelously self-serving doctrine had no difficulty in classifying land as vacant or virgin when it actually held inhabitants with aboriginal rights of tenure. In the Puritans' rationalization the land had never been made property by English law —or, more properly, by provincial law—and it was therefore vacant in fact.

The deductive imperatives of authority were reinforced in the nineteenth century with developed conceptions of inequality and Social

81. These texts appeared on the title pages of, respectively, Gookin, "Historical Collections," Mass. Hist. Soc., *Colls.*, 1st Ser., I, 141, *The Book of the General Laws and Libertyes Concerning the Inhabitants of the Massachusetts* (1648), reprinted with an introduction by Max Farrand (Cambridge, Mass., 1929).

82. Minutes, Oct. 19, 1652, in Nathaniel B. Shurtleff, ed., *Records of the Governor and Company of the Massachusetts Bay in New England* (Boston, 1853–1854), III, 281–282, hereafter cited as *Recs. of Mass.*

83. See the oath required of all freemen of Massachusetts and the associated declarations of the General Court, May 14, 1634, *Recs. of Mass.*, I, 117; cf. the wrangle in 1664 between the General Court and the royal commissioners, *ibid.*, IV, pt. ii, 157–273. Although the latter is a self-serving and often false document prepared as a brief by the General Court, it is useful for its exposition of the Puritan viewpoint. The student will do best to consult the primary sources in this matter; the secondary studies are often unreliable.

84. George F. Willison, *Saints and Strangers . . .* (New York, 1945), 392; Louis B. Wright, *Religion and Empire: The Alliance between Piety and Commerce in English Expansion, 1558–1625* (Chapel Hill, N.C., 1943), 158.

Darwinism. Francis Parkman pronounced the Indian to be "a true child of the forest and the desert. The wastes and solitudes of nature are his congenial home."[85] George E. Ellis echoed that "the Indians simply wasted everything within their reach. . . . They required enormous spaces of wilderness for their mode of existence."[86] Frederick Jackson Turner conceived this wilderness as "free land," and Walter Prescott Webb brought the whole process back to its beginnings, upside down. He took the myth that had formed from a legal fiction and converted it into the "fact" that made an action legal: this free land, as he saw it, was "land free to be taken."[87]

85. Parkman, *Conspiracy of Pontiac*, I, 3.

86. George Edward Ellis, "The Indians of Eastern Massachusetts," in Justin Winsor, ed., *The Memorial History of Boston, Including Suffolk County, Massachusetts, 1630–1880* (Boston, 1880–1881), I, 248.

87. Turner, *Frontier in American History*, 3; Webb, *Great Frontier*, 3.

Chapter 6 ❧ UNSTABLE SYMBIOSIS

Francis Parkman, who has often been called the greatest of American historians, wrote in the nineteenth century that "the Indians melted away, not because civilization destroyed them, but because their own ferocity and intractable indolence made it impossible that they should exist in its presence."[1] Setting aside ferocity for later treatment, let us now examine a giant social organization that stands in manifest refutation of the other myths in this capsule of ideology. The intersocietal institution of economic exchange, imprecisely called the fur trade, required enormous labor from Indians and depended utterly for its existence upon cooperation between Indians and Europeans.

The trade was possible because of compatible traits in the two cultures. Europeans seeking wealth and dominance in America found peoples there who already understood and practiced division of labor and exchange of commodities. Contact and trade between the two societies caused internal change in both. For the Indians there was paradox. Contact with the more complex culture of Europe did not stimulate the development of greater complexity in Indian culture. On the contrary, Indian industry became less specialized and divided as it entered into closer relations of exchange with European industry. For the Indians *intersocietal* commerce triumphed by subordinating and eliminating all crafts except those directly related to the European-Indian trade, while *intertribal* trading relations survived only insofar as they served the purposes of intersocietal trade.

Precontact trade between Indian tribes had involved a variety of goods. Copper was mined in northern Michigan and traded over great distances; the colonists of Jamestown found it among their neighboring Indians. Catlinite stone used in the manufacture of ceremonial peace pipes (calumets) was quarried in Minnesota. Mica has been found in the great temple mounds of Ohio, although it does not occur naturally in that vicinity. Flint and flintlike stones formed an object of exchange. Obsidian for the making of arrowheads was brought into the east

1. Francis Parkman, *The Jesuits in North America in the Seventeenth Century* (1867), New Library ed. (Boston, 1909), 418.

coast region from distances as great as seventeen hundred crow-flight miles away. In the reverse direction, multicolored stratified slate was traded from the coast to the Mississippi River.[2] One tribe became known as the Tobacco Indians because of its production of that crop in quantity for trade. The agricultural Hurons traded maize for the meat and fish of the Nipissing hunters of the north. Only one tribe in all of North America has ever been discovered that did not possess objects obtained through trade with other tribes; the exception was the Polar Eskimos, who lived so isolated an existence that they believed themselves to be the only people on earth.[3]

The nature of this intertribal trade was transformed by the introduction of European trade goods among the eastern tribes. New commodities displaced old. Iron and steel implements made copper and stone obsolete. Instead of exchanging surpluses of their own products, the tribes abandoned their crafts in order to concentrate on obtaining surpluses of the goods desired by Europeans. Their new objectives created intertribal tensions where former trade had favored the friendship born of mutual advantage. Interior tribes that once had desired trade with eastern peoples came to regard the easterners as obstacles to a more desirable trade with Europeans. The eastern tribes strove to keep the advantage of brokering from the coast to the interior, and previous intertribal cooperation turned into competition and conflict.

While trade with Europeans transformed intertribal relations, it also metamorphosed the tribes' internal economies. All attention was turned to acquiring the goods produced by Europe's more advanced technology, and all energies were bent toward the means required for getting those precious goods. Because Europeans would readily exchange their commodities for furs, Indians turned to hunting with an intensity previously unknown. No longer did they merely "harvest" the game to satisfy needs for meat and garments. Their new circumstances required them to produce great surpluses of peltry for exchange; in short, they added commercial hunting to subsistence hunting.

2. Charles Rau, "Ancient Aboriginal Trade in North America," Smithsonian Institution, *Annual Report, 1872* (Washington, D.C., 1873), 348–394; Smith, *Map of Virginia*, in Barbour, ed., *Jamestown Voyages*, II, 353–355. Rau's evidence is the more significant because it ran counter to his bias. As he conceived Indians, "They shared the fate of every inferior race that takes up the contest with one occupying a higher rank in the family of man." *Ibid.*, 394.

3. Driver and Massey, *North American Indians*, Am. Phil. Soc., *Trans.*, N.S., XLVII, pt. ii (1957), 375, 379n; Trigger, "Jesuits and the Fur Trade," *Ethnohistory*, XII (1965), 35. Frederick Jackson Turner remarked on the "extensive intertribal trade" that laid the foundation for European-Indian trade ("forest commerce"). Turner recognized that the trade with Europeans was more complex than just a trade in furs; he called it the "Indian trade." "The Character and Influence of the Indian Trade in Wisconsin," in Louise Phelps Kellogg, ed., *The Early Writings of Frederick Jackson Turner* (Madison, Wis., 1938), 90–93.

Just as commercial agriculture producing staples for the market differs from subsistence farming, so commercial hunting differs from subsistence hunting. Subsistence hunters restrain themselves to preserve breeding stock; they conserve as well as kill. But to supply European demands for fur the Indians had to hunt with such destructive intensity as to exterminate commercially valuable game. Thus they eventually destroyed the basis for the very economy they were trying to practice and, in the end, rendered themselves superfluous to the European traders on whom they had come to depend.

As Indians devoted increasing amounts of time and energy to activities associated with the fur trade, the resulting processes came to stand in direct contradiction to Frederick Jackson Turner's suggestion of "a return to primitive conditions on a continually advancing frontier line."[4] Primitive conditions do not include a world market. The frontier "line" was dotted with trading posts connected directly to the world market through European merchants. Indians may be said to have entered the market through trading post gateways, and the gates swung only inward. Once inside, the Indians became dependent upon the Europeans who controlled the market's functioning in America. For both Indians and Europeans the trade was a movement forward but not always upward. A return to primitive conditions for Indians would have been a return to increased agricultural production for self-sufficiency in an ecologically balanced habitat.[5] Primitive conditions for Euramericans would have obliged them to hunt their own peltry instead of importing cloth and firearms from Europe to pass on to Indians for furs.

Although the trade was ultimately self-destructive, it served while it lasted as a means to draw Indians and Europeans together. The Swede Peter Lindeström once remarked on the futility of attempts to exterminate Indians, explaining that "the trade, traffic and commerce of the Christians would be of small value" without Indians.[6] In essence the trade was a means of unstable symbiosis for two societies. Europeans benefited from it both in the colonies and on their home continent. Europe's industries were stimulated by what Harold A. Innis has char-

---

4. Turner, *Frontier in American History*, 2.

5. For a different view see E. E. Rich, "Colonial Settlement and Its Labour Problems," in E. E. Rich and C. H. Wilson, eds., *The Cambridge Economic History of Europe*, IV (Cambridge, 1967), 358–359. Rich wrote that Indians did not allow their dependence on European trade goods to affect their lives in essentials. The Indian "remained a wanderer, a hunter, and—at the cost of great precariousness —independent." Therefore he "could not in any sense be called the worker for the white man." Rich's primary focus of study was the Hudson Bay area, where agriculture was not practiced and where European colonization was restricted to thinly manned trading posts. Wholly different conditions prevailed in the vicinity of the the English colonies on the Atlantic coast.

6. Lindeström, *Geographia Americae*, 212.

acterized as the "overwhelming" task of "continuously supplying goods to the Indian tribes of North America, of maintaining the depreciation of those goods, and of replacing the goods destroyed."[7] For the colonists the trade was generally beneficial long after their settlements had become stable and permanent, because the trade yielded a continuing income and especially because that income was derived from an extractive industry that produced goods that Europe wanted and could not produce itself. Thus peltry provided a means of reducing the colonists' perpetual deficit in the balance of payments of their own trade with Europe.[8]

For Indians the advantages of the trade were local and temporary. Over the long term the commercial transformation of their society implied its decay. To the calamities of epidemic disease and alcoholism were added trade wars of the most destructive sort. Firearms acquired in trade enabled particular tribes to gain advantage and supremacy in competition with other tribes, but the general effect of the trade wars was depletion of all the participants, victors and vanquished alike. With these large-scale "beaver wars" Indians truly entered upon an era of self-destructive frenzy.

The trade became omnipresent in Indian society and ramified extensively in Europe. It has become a research specialty for historians, anthropologists, geographers, and economists who follow the French and English traders westward to where they encountered the Russians who had traded eastward through Siberia and Alaska. Only a brief overview can be given here of the trade's effects on the cultures of northeastern Indians and northwestern Europeans. The particulars of market diplomacy, transportation routes, and routines of commerce, fascinating in themselves, have been capably and lucidly reported elsewhere. What follows in this chapter will first attend to the trade as it appeared in Indian society and then as it appeared in Europe and will conclude with a brief comparison of the two cultures.

The trade was a process of exchange between two industries. We are accustomed to the notion that European trade goods were the product of manufacture, but somehow the Indians' furs and hides seem like raw materials or natural resources, that is, objects consonant to a savage society. In fact, the peltry was the product of extensive labor and organization and much skill; it was raw material for further processing only in the sense that a bolt of cloth is raw material for tailoring. Although the Indians' industry involved operations at widely dispersed

7. Innis, *Fur Trade in Canada*, 16.
8. See, e.g., Albright G. Zimmerman, "James Logan, Proprietary Agent," *Pennsylvania Magazine of History and Biography*, LXXVIII (1954), 174.

sites, it may be considered by three criteria as analogous to cottage industry in Europe: (1) the Indian's own home in his own village served as the base of all operations; (2) the hunting Indian was a self-employed craftsman who purchased his own tools and sold semifinished products; and (3) the workman often operated on credit supplied by a merchant entrepreneur.[9]

The factors of an extractive industry, as identified in the terms of abstract economic analysis, existed in real circumstances peculiar to Indian society and culture. The simple barter of the earliest days of the trade provided Indians with steel hatchets and knives and later with firearms—implements by means of which their craft could be conducted more efficiently.[10] After the trade had become well established, Indians regularly obtained goods and implements on credit, to be repaid by their peltry product; that is, they borrowed operating capital from European traders.[11] Other articles of operating capital, such as canoes, were created by the Indians themselves because their product was superior to anything Europe had to offer.[12] Land was the Indians' own contribution until such time as they were dispossessed. Labor was varied in a number of operations and was performed by both men and women. Men in work gangs traveled for months away from home and lived at their site of operations. They located the special kind of raw material incorporating their desired commodity—the beaver and other fur-bearing animals—and extracted the raw material from its site. This extraction involved a number of processes hidden under the rubric "hunting," and it required skilled labor as well as the expenditure of operating capital. Having acquired his raw material, the Indian hunter turned skinner, spending more labor on extracting the commercially valuable part of the material from its associated waste product. He then became porter and freight manager to get his peltry back to his village, and on the way he might be obliged to turn soldier to protect it from hijackers. At the village further work was done, comparable to a tanner's, to dress the skins. Then the Indian transported his product once again—sometimes for distances of hundreds of miles—to the marketplace maintained by a European merchant, and there the Indian turned trader. Sometimes, if

9. Cf. E. Lipson, *The Economic History of England*, rev. ed. (London, 1937–1943), II, 1–6.

10. Innis, *Fur Trade in Canada*, 18–19.

11. In the early days of the trade all transactions seem to have been immediate exchanges, but credit later became important. See, for example, Le Tort's accounts of debts due him, Oct. 1704, Logan Papers, XI, 4, and the accounts—undoubtedly inflated but with basis in fact—of the "Suffering traders," Etting Collection, Ohio Company Manuscripts, I, both in Historical Society of Pennsylvania, Philadelphia. See also Wilbur R. Jacobs, ed., *The Appalachian Indian Frontier: The Edmond Atkin Report and Plan of 1755* (Lincoln, Neb., 1967), 22–23.

12. E. E. Rich, *Montreal and the Fur Trade* (Montreal, 1966), 6–7.

he could not get the terms he wanted, he might pick up his goods and carry them to another market; but if he was in debt he was obliged to deal with his creditor. When the merchant packed peltry for shipment to Europe, it was already a semimanufactured product that had been handled and treated many times. No living, breathing, raw-material beaver got into the cargo.[13]

The sheer hard work, as well as the technical skills, involved in this industry has become hidden behind the myth of the lazy savage, perhaps because hunting is recreation rather than work for so many modern Americans. Europeans of colonial times were content to leave the production of marketable peltry entirely in the hands of Indians until Daniel Boone and other Kentucky hunters revolutionized the trade, late in the eighteenth century, by substituting themselves in the Indians' roles. Massachusetts's William Wood observed in 1634 that the beaver, whose pelts were the most wanted products of Indian industry, were "too cunning for the English, who seldome or never catch any of them, therefore we leave them to those skilfull hunters whose time is not so precious, whose experience bought-skill hath made them practicall and usefull in that particular."[14] A nineteenth-century scholar remarked slurringly that "organized commerce could compel industry, could exact all the spasmodic labor possible to the barbarian."[15] The seventeenth century knew the worth of that "spasmodic" labor: Adriaen Van der Donck wrote that "the Indians, without our labour or trouble, bring to us their fur trade, worth tons of gold, which may be increased, and is like goods found."[16] Van der Donck's final phrase is at the heart of the confusion: the peltry was raw material for *European* commerce and industry. The trading post was the only point of contact between the industries of Europeans and Indians, and no European concerned himself to study the processes of Indian industry as a whole until modern scholars began to reconstruct it from bits and pieces of description.

Some of those processes are worth a moment's attention. Although some Indians hiked to the hunt, others anticipated the burden of a peltry pack by traveling via canoe and portage. First, however, they had to make their canoes. For birchbark canoes the materials had to be col-

---

13. Eccles, *Canadian Frontier*, 110. Roger Williams noted division of labor by crafts among the Narragansetts: "They have some who follow onely making of Bowes, some Arrowes, some Dishes, and (the Women make all their earthen Vessells) some follow fishing, some hunting: most on the Sea-side make Money, and store up shells in Summer against Winter whereof to make their money [wampum]." Williams, *Key*, ed. Trumbull, Narragansett Club, *Pubs.*, I, 179–180.

14. Wool, *New Englands Prospect*, 100.

15. Weeden, *Economic and Social History*, I, 39.

16. Van der Donck, *Description of New Netherlands*, in N.-Y. Hist. Soc., *Colls.*, 2d Ser., I, 236.

lected in the summer while the bark would peel off easily. At the time of construction the stored bark and other materials were assembled by a crew of workers, ideally two men and four women, over a period of ten days to two weeks. With care the canoe might last several years, but birchbark canoes were fragile and easily damaged. Harold E. Driver and William C. Massey have observed that "the making of a good birchbark canoe is a detailed and skilled task which no doubt required some centuries to perfect."[17]

Roger Williams described the construction of the alternate type of canoe, the dugout. The craftsman went alone into the woods with some parched corn for sustenance. There, according to Williams, he "continues burning and hewing until he hath within ten or twelve dayes (lying there at his worke alone) finished."[18] It will be noticed that those were dawn-to-dusk days.

About the journey to distant hunting territories, two facts may be noted: the hunters moved over networks of trails that were soundly enough laid out to serve as the basis for the wagon roads and automobile highways of times to come; and the journey was made in all sorts of weather.[19] Adriaen Van der Donck described how the Iroquois organized a commercial hunt. "For beaver hunting," he wrote, "the Indians go in large parties, and remain out from one to two months, during which time they subsist by hunting and on a little corn meal which they carry out with them, and they frequently return home with from forty to eighty beaver skins, and with some otter, fishers and other skins also."[20] Taking all of Van der Donck's estimates at maximum, eighty beaver skins does not seem like an overwhelming reward for two months of seven-day work weeks of a "large" party. The travel itself could be heavy going, as we are quick to concede when we describe the fatigues and travails of white frontiersmen wading through streams up to their necks and shuddering dry without a fire for fear of betraying their whereabouts, or getting caught in rain or snowstorms far from the comforts of home. Although Indians had conditioned themselves to stoic endurance, such experiences were no more pleasant for flesh in red skins than in white. We need not and should not give way to romantic senti-

17. Driver and Massey, *North American Indians*, Am. Phil. Soc., *Trans.*, N.S., XLVII, pt. ii (1957), 289. See also E. T. Adney and H. I. Chapelle, *The Bark Canoes and Skin Boats of North America*, Smithsonian Institution, Bureau of Ethnology, Bulletin 230 (Washington, D.C., 1964).

18. Williams, *Key*, ed. Trumbull, Narragansett Club, *Pubs.*, I, 131–132.

19. Paul A. W. Wallace, *Indian Paths of Pennsylvania* (Harrisburg, Pa., 1965), 2. Wallace described and mapped 131 routes in this one state. See also Leaman F. Hallett, "Indian Trails and Their Importance to the Early Colonists," *Bulletin of Mass. Archaeol. Soc.*, XVI (Apr. 1956), 41–46.

20. Van der Donck, *Description of New Netherlands*, in N.-Y. Hist. Soc., *Colls.*, 2d Ser., I, 209–210.

mentality in order to recognize the very plain fact that hunters and warriors loafed in the villages—where Europeans saw and described them—in order to rest and recuperate from the exhaustion of the hunt—where the writing kind of European does not seem to have followed.

Sir William Johnson was one of the eighteenth century's most acutely perceptive observers of Indian culture. He understood well the Indian men's "disinclination to remain long in one place without action." It was a "certain Maxim," he wrote, "that altho in their own Villages they spend much of their time in indolence, yet, when abroad they must be employed in War, Hunting, conferences, or Trade." [21]

When the Indian man returned from the hunt, there was work for the Indian women. If he brought back beaver skins she scraped their inner sides and rubbed them with marrow. Then she trimmed each one into rectangular shape and sewed together about half a dozen with moose sinews. The robes thus made were worn by the Indians with the fur next to the body for fifteen to eighteen months, after which the furs commanded top price in the market. [22]

In southern regions deer skins became the staple of the trade. These too required special treatment to enhance their value. In the mid-eighteenth century James Logan of Pennsylvania classified them into three types at corresponding prices: "Ordinary" at one shilling each; "Fall" at one shilling and ninepence each; and "Indian drest" at three shillings and sixpence each. [23] What "Indian drest" meant was described by an English observer of the late eighteenth century, who transmitted to the Royal Society a description of "the Indian way of Dressing Buckskins with Brains in Carolina." This was always done by women, and the job was so complex and tedious that no more than eight or ten skins could be prepared per day by a single worker. It involved soaking and scraping the skins, heating them together with the animal's dried brains in a kettle, scouring them, twisting and untwisting them, and forcing the water out of them by rubbing them with a dull hatchet until they became perfectly dry. Clearly this was an industrial process. [24]

Villages not connected directly with the hunt might yet participate indirectly through the manufacture of wampum out of sea shells. Authorities differ as to whether wampum had been used as native money

21. Sir William Johnson to Gen. Thomas Gage, May 3, 1764, in James Sullivan et al., eds., The Papers of Sir William Johnson (Albany, N.Y., 1921–1965), XI, 174, hereafter cited as Sir William Johnson Papers. See also the comment in Wilbur R. Jacobs, Dispossessing the American Indian: Indians and Whites on the Colonial Frontier (New York, 1972), 141.

22. Innis, Fur Trade in Canada, 14.

23. Treaty minutes, Aug. 2, 1735, Pa. Council Minutes, III, 604.

24. Oct. 7, 1791, Classified Papers, III (2), 1, Royal Society, London (microfilm, American Philosophical Society, Philadelphia, Pa.).

for purely commercial purposes before contact with Europeans. They agree, however, that the painstakingly wrought strings of shell beads were highly valued by all coastal Indians as objects for use in religious and governmental procedures and for personal adornment.[25] Under the stimulation of European trade, the eastern Indians carried wampum to the interior and acquainted landlocked tribes with its many functions. For a while in the seventeenth century, wampum as a medium of exchange was as necessary to European colonists as to Indians. In a period when the hard coins of Europe had to be reserved for purchases in Europe, colonists adopted wampum as legal tender for internal circulation.[26] Indians were the mintmasters of this shell currency because of the specialized skills and painstaking labor required in its production. Counterfeits produced by colonial or European manufacture were readily recognized as an inferior product; although the sheer necessity for a circulating medium often made them pass, they sold at discount. Genuine wampum set the standard.[27]

Wampum production was localized where beaches could be harvested for the right kind of shells. On the north Atlantic coast the periwinkle used for the purpose did not spawn north of Cape Cod. "Mints" were located among the Narragansetts and other coastal Indians of the mainland and among the Indians of Block Island and Long Island, especially around Gardiner's Bay.[28] These tribes were blocked from access to commercial hunting territories, but they participated in a subsidiary branch of the trade through their specialized industry. J. N. B. Hewitt has described the manufacture of wampum as follows:

The process, though simple, required a skill acquired only by long practice. The intense hardness and brittleness of the materials made it impossible to wear, grind, and bore the shell by machinery alone. First the thin portions were removed with a light sharp hammer, and the remainder was clamped in a scissure sawed in a slender stick, and was then ground into an octagonal figure, an inch in length and half an inch in diameter. This piece being ready for boring was inserted into another piece of wood, sawed like the first stick, which was firmly fastened to a bench, a weight being so adjusted that

25. George S. Snyderman, "The Function of Wampum in Iroquois Religion," Am. Phil. Soc., *Procs.*, CV (1961), 571–608, and his "Functions of Wampum," *ibid.*, XCVIII (1954), 469–494; J. S. Slotkin and Karl Schmitt, "Studies of Wampum," *Am. Anthro.*, LI (1949), 223–236; Frank G. Speck, "The Functions of Wampum among the Eastern Algonkian," American Anthropological Association, *Memoirs*, VI (1919), 3–71.

26. Weeden, *Economic and Social History*, I, 40–41.

27. Lawson, *New Voyage to Carolina*, 193; Williams, *Key*, ed. Trumbull, Narragansett Club, *Pubs.*, I, 181; Morton, *New English Canaan*, 29–30, in Force, comp., *Tracts*, II; Hodge, ed., *Handbook of N. Am. Indians*, s.v. "wampum."

28. Williams, *Key*, ed. Trumbull, Narragansett Club, *Pubs.*, I, 173; Gookin, "Historical Collections," Mass. Hist. Soc., *Colls.*, 1st Ser., I, 152; Benjamin F. Thompson, *The History of Long Island*, 2d ed. (New York, 1843), I, 87–88.

it caused the scissure to grip the shell and to hold it securely. The drill was made from an untempered handsaw, ground into proper shape and tempered in the flame of a candle. Braced against a steel plate on the operator's chest and nicely adjusted to the center of the shell, the drill was rotated by means of the common hand-bow. To clean the aperture, the drill was dextrously withdrawn while in motion, and was cleared by the thumb and finger of the particles of shell. From a vessel hanging over the closely clamped shell drops of water fell on the drill to cool it, for particular care was exercised lest the shell break from the heat caused by friction.[29]

And so forth. In New England the beads were usually valued from four to six to the penny, and a "fathom" of 240 to 260 beads was worth five shillings, or sixty pence.[30] It seems plain enough that such prices would not pamper a lazy workman who had to go through what Hewitt described in order to make one bead.

Another specialized occupation connected with the trade showed itself among the Huron Indians, who became brokers between French merchants and the hunting Indians of the distant west and north.[31] Other tribes seem to have practiced similar brokerage at least some of the time. In the eighteenth century the Caughnawaga Indians were hired by provincial merchants to pack furs and trade goods in a heavy illicit traffic between Albany and Montreal.[32] Similarly the Indians who lived near Niagara hired themselves out as laborers for the portage required there.[33]

Finally there were extremely intricate and time-consuming political processes connected with Indian industry and commerce that were prerequisite to their success. Hunters passing into or through other Indians' territories traveled on sufferance of the local people. Permission might be obtained through alliance or by payment of toll. It might be forced by fighting. It could never be taken for granted, and the time and energy devoted to obtaining it were never negligible. For Indians as for Europeans, trade followed the flag.[34]

One student has remarked that "trade and war appear as alternative forms for Huron dealings with contiguous non-Hurons," and his com-

---

29. Hodge, ed., *Handbook of Indians*, s.v. "wampum."

30. Weeden, *Economic and Social History*, I, 37.

31. Trigger, "Jesuits and Fur Trade," *Ethnohistory*, XII (1965), 35; Hunt, *Wars of the Iroquois*, chap. 5, and map between pp. 7 and 8.

32. Cadwallader Colden, "A Memorial concerning the Fur Trade of the Province of New York" (1724), in E. B. O'Callaghan and Berthold Fernow, eds., *Documents Relative to the Colonial History of the State of New York* (Albany, N.Y., 1856–1887), V, 732, hereafter cited as *N.Y. Col. Docs.*

33. Donald H. Kent, *The French Invasion of Western Pennsylvania, 1753* (Harrisburg, Pa., 1954), 46.

34. Trigger, "Destruction of Huronia," Royal Can. Inst., *Trans.*, XXXIII (1960), 23, 28. See also the discussion in Abraham Rotstein, "Fur Trade and Empire: An Institutional Analysis" (Ph.D. diss., University of Toronto, 1967), chap. 3.

ment seems applicable to other tribes as well.[35] The collapse of inter-tribal trade in Indian commodities surely contributed to a general increase in hostilities by establishing competition as a greater source of advantage than cooperation. There can be no doubt at all of the increase in hostilities stimulated by the arrangements of the new trade with Europeans. Although the resulting carnage has been called the "beaver wars," it might be as justifiably called the "firearm wars," "kettle wars," or "blanket wars."

Competition and conflict between Indians arose from two sources. In part it reflected the competition between Europeans of diverse nationalities and interests whose client tribes were drawn into the patrons' struggles, and this source of conflict increased in importance as the Europeans consolidated their positions and increased their dominance. In the sixteenth and early seventeenth centuries, however, the tribes often warred on their own initiative for what they perceived as their own interest. Aimed at control over movement of goods and access to suppliers, these wars for tribal supremacy ranged over the entire space from trapline to trading post. Relations between tribes were strongly influenced by their locations in the configuration and movement of the trade. The tribe neighboring a trading post could gain a broker's profit as long as it could block more distant tribes from direct access to the post. Distant tribes could get better prices by breaking through the obstruction. European attitudes were mixed. Although nearby tribes were more manageable and reliable as allies, the traders' basic policy was to keep the channels of supply free of hindrances. Like the more distant tribesmen, European traders also wanted to eliminate the Indian middleman's profit. The mixture of parties, motives, and goals kept the trade constantly in a state of tension and flux.

Historically the trade began at the coast and remained a fully commercial exchange between societies until Euramericans began hunting for themselves late in the eighteenth century. The basic strategy of the European trader in America was not to get at the animals but rather to get at the Indians, either by going directly to them or by bringing the Indians to himself. In the earliest years, while substantial populations of Indians and game animals still lived in coastal regions, the traders needed only to make their presence known. C. H. McIlwain has remarked that, as far as we can look back, "in the very earliest recorded voyages we find that the Indians had collected stores of skins in anticipation of trade with the Europeans, and that the voyagers in turn had invariably brought with them goods for this traffic."[36] Sometimes, indeed, the voyagers

35. Trigger, "Destruction of Huronia," *Royal Can. Inst., Trans.,* XXXIII (1960), 21.

36. Charles Howard McIlwain, "Introduction," in Peter Wraxall, *An Abridgment*

prepared so carefully as to bring counterfeit wampum, as in the case of John Winthrop's journey of 1629–1630.[37]

Fishermen trading on the beaches where they dried their catch were followed by explorers who engaged in trade in order to pay the costs of "discovery." French trade began at least as early as Cartier's voyages in 1534 and 1535.[38] After the explorers, came the merchant ships that ranged the coasts only for trade (or a little piracy if opportunity offered). From trading on shipboard the merchants moved naturally, as they gained confidence, to setting up stations on shore, manned by a few men who collected and stored skins while awaiting the ship's return journey. These transient settlements were followed by the colonizing ventures of the great companies, which were always placed in locations that promised enough trade to make the colonies profitable.

The early Europeans mostly preferred to stick close to the ports that seemed like the uttermost outreach of their familiar homelands, but they soon learned the lessons of interposition and leapfrogging. Very early in the seventeenth century Quebec and Fort Nassau (near Albany) were founded on navigable streams far inland, and some enterprising Virginians set up a trading post where the Susquehanna River falls into Chesapeake Bay.[39] Montreal took Frenchmen deeper inland to a strategic juncture of waterways in 1642, and Frenchmen soon afterward plunged deep into the woods to get the commercial advantage of dealing directly with the interior tribes. The coureurs de bois of Canada made possible the early exploitation of the tremendous Great Lakes–Saint Lawrence waterway system and the Mississippi River network, and it was renegade coureurs de bois who taught the English of New York and Pennsylvania how to voyage inland.[40] Not a single step of all this inland journeying was taken out of idle curiosity, and none was done alone. Every voyager directed himself toward communities of Indians. Every voyager had business with the Indians as his purpose. As soon as he left the decks of European ships or the close environs of a European settlement, every

of the Indian Affairs, Contained in Four Folio Volumes, Transacted in the Colony of New York, from the Year 1678 to the Year 1751, ed. Charles Howard McIlwain, Harvard Historical Studies, XXI (Cambridge, Mass., 1915), xiii, hereafter cited as Wraxall, Abridgment.

37. William Iredell Roberts, "The Fur Trade of New England" (Ph.D. diss., University of Pennsylvania, 1958), 80.

38. Cartier, Narration, I, 28.

39. Petition of Wm. Clayborne, Feb. 26, 1638, Browne et al., eds., Archives of Md., III, 66.

40. Lanctot, History of Canada, I, 194; Eccles, Canadian Frontier, 7–10; Allen W. Trelease, Indian Affairs in Colonial New York: The Seventeenth Century (Ithaca, N.Y., 1960), 132, 246–247; Evelyn A. Benson, "The Huguenot Le Torts: First Christian Family on the Conestoga," Journal of the Lancaster County Historical Society, LXV (1961), 98–99; Francis Jennings, "The Indian Trade of the Susquehanna Valley," Am. Phil. Soc., Procs., CX (1966), 409–410.

voyager was taken along his route by Indian guides and was fed and sheltered in Indian villages. As the French became more familiar with the trails and tribes, they established lightly manned outposts as far inland as Michilimackinac at the juncture of Lakes Superior, Michigan, and Huron.

The Dutch and English produced few frontiersmen to rival the coureurs de bois. Until the eighteenth century they continued to rely on Indians to do their inland commercial traveling. When the English did move inland, they, like the French, followed the trails of the trade; but, unlike the French, they moved massively and displaced Indian communities in order to occupy new territories with their own people. For Indians, therefore, trade with Frenchmen had different consequences than trade with Englishmen. Dealings with the French brought Indians into economic and political dependency, but dealings with the English brought dispossession also.

The swift penetration of the North American continent profoundly modified the history of Europe and Euramericans as well as that of Indians. Europe sought trade with Indians because Europe needed what the Indians had to offer. Indian commodities became an important factor in the European commercial system, Indian demands stimulated particular European industries, and the meshing of the Indian trade into the world market modified to a degree the functioning of that market and the relationships of its national components.

European trade in furs long antedated 1492. In medieval Europe winters were cold, open hearths gave little warmth into drafty halls, and fur garments proclaimed the wealth and status of their wearers.[41] In the "Dark Ages" of small population and great forests, local hunting in central and eastern Europe provided a sufficiency; but as human populations grew and wild animal populations declined, trading organizations reached farther and farther east for sources of supply. Medieval Kiev had traded extensively in furs with Byzantium, and the Russians had become adept in the dressing of the peltry as well as in its acquisition. In the sixteenth century England and the Netherlands began to develop trade with Muscovy via the Baltic Sea, and during the seventeenth and eighteenth centuries Russian traders and hunters worked their way ever deeper into Siberia. A European market in furs grew up, with its major headquarters in Amsterdam.[42]

41. Elspeth M. Veale, *The English Fur Trade in the Later Middle Ages* (Oxford, 1966), chap. 1.

42. Raymond H. Fisher, *The Russian Fur Trade, 1550–1700*, University of California Publications in History, XXXI (Berkeley and Los Angeles, 1943), 190–193. For a brief historical summary of the Russian expansion into Siberia, see James R. Gibson, *Feeding the Russian Fur Trade: Provisionment of the*

This market was an immense and complicated structure that marched over the land masses of the north as the market in spice and sugar sailed to the islands of the tropics. As in all markets fluctuations in one sector affected all the others. The extent of interdependence is curiously illustrated by one practice of the ubiquitous Dutch merchants. After they had opened trade with American Indians, they often carried furs all the way from America to Russia. It seems like carrying coals to Newcastle, but it worked. Age-old familiarity with furs had taught Russian craftsmen techniques for combing beaver pelts in such a way as to remove the "woollen" hairs that felted best for hat manufacture, while leaving intact the "guard" hairs that were necessary to the fur's quality as a coat. Thus the Russians converted one Indian-caught pelt into two commodities for Dutch merchants. The Dutch returned to pick up the treated furs for transport back to their market at Amsterdam, profiting at every stage in the cycle.[43]

The anticipated and real demands of Indians as consumers shaped imperial policies and influenced the development of England's greatest industry, the wool trade. In 1584 Sir Walter Ralegh commissioned Richard Hakluyt to argue that "after the seekinge the advauncemente of the Kingedome of Christe, the seconde chefe and principall end" of colonization should be "the vent of the masse of our cloths and other commodities of England, and in receaving back of the nedeful commodities that wee nowe receave from all other places of the worlde." Hakluyt noted that the imports would not be finished products like those of France and Flanders, but rather "all substaunces unwroughte, to the ymploymente of a wonderfull multitude of the poor subjects of the realme."[44] These motives continued to carry weight in England. In 1681 William Penn echoed Hakluyt with a suggestion that Englishmen should "consider how many thousand Blacks and Indians are also accommodated with Cloaths and many sorts of Tools and Utensils from England, and that their Labour is mostly brought hither [to England] which adds Wealth and People to the English Dominions."[45]

Such expectations were soundly based. Although decline in Indian population implied correlated decline in consumption of trade goods, Indians manned the markets, so to speak, until English colonial populations acquired significant purchasing power. Contrary to the popular

Okhotsk Seaboard and the Kamchatka Peninsula, 1639–1856 (Madison, Wis., 1969), 3–24.

43. E. E. Rich, The History of the Hudson's Bay Company, 1670–1870 (London, 1958–1959), I, 47.

44. "Discourse of Western Planting," in Taylor, ed., Writings of the Two Richard Hakluyts, II, 274, 238.

45. Penn, "Some Account of the Province of Pennsilvania" (1681), in Myers, ed., Narratives of Early Pennsylvania, 204.

impression that Indians traded mostly for gimcracks and baubles, traders soon discovered that the goods most in demand were those adapted to practical use in the Indian way of living. Firearms and ammunition were extremely important, of course, as necessary implements in the hunting industry and in war. Woolen cloth and cloth garments also made up a major proportion of all goods traded.[46]

The Indian trade affected England's wool production quantitatively and regionally. Although statistics are not at my disposal, the circumstances in America suggest that woolens entering English colonial ports were traded and retraded far inland to be consumed not only by Indians under English protection but also by the "Farr Indian" clients of France.[47] Indian customers were the more appreciated because English woolen exports to the continent of Europe were encountering difficulties in the seventeenth century.[48]

One region, in particular, had reason to be pleased with the Indian trade. The scarlet and blue cloth made in the Stroud or Stroudwater valley of Gloucestershire became an Indian favorite and remained so during the eighteenth century. The valley was distant from the great highways leading to London, and its clothiers turned naturally to nearby Bristol for outlet. Merchants trading with Indians in the colonies kept in touch with Bristol because the cloth they wanted was cheaper there than in London.[49] The clothiers of the Bristol region enjoyed their greatest prosperity between 1690 and 1760, the span of greatest activity in the English-Indian trade.[50]

It was in this West Country wool district that English weavers first sank from the status of self-employment to that of hired hand. To pursue the subject further is impossible here, but we can speculate: Did the profits accumulated from Indians make possible the proletarianization of these English workmen? Credit was the mechanism through which the weavers mortgaged their tools and property and finally lost them to the wealthy entrepreneur who could ride out the bad times while the workmen lost their savings. Stroudwaters were dyed cloths and, as

46. Colden, "Memorial concerning the Fur Trade," *N.Y. Col. Docs.*, V, 728–730.

47. *Ibid.*, 729.

48. Hakluyt, "Discourse of Western Planting," in Taylor, ed., *Writings of the Two Richard Hakluyts*, II, 236; J. H. Parry, "Transport and Trade Routes," in Rich and Wilson, eds., *Cambridge Economic History of Europe*, IV, 175–177.

49. Albright G. Zimmerman, "The Indian Trade of Colonial Pennsylvania" (Ph.D. diss., University of Delaware, 1966), 81, 94, 116–125; Colden, "Memorial concerning the Fur Trade," *N.Y. Col. Docs.*, V, 729.

50. Ruth F. Butler, "Social and Economic History," in William Page, ed., *The Victoria History of the County of Gloucester* (London, 1907), II, 160, 163–164. The dates coincide roughly with the abolition of chartered monopolies at the beginning of the period and the Seven Years' War at the end.

such, were far more profitable than the cheap undyed textiles sold to Flanders and France. Some, at least, of the money lent to the English workmen had been made from the Indians.[51]

First the Netherlands and then England became the most advanced industrial nation of Europe. In the same sequence they built the greatest merchant and naval fleets to command the sea lanes to America. And in the same sequence also, they administered trade at the location called Fort Orange by the Dutch and Albany by the English. The great activity generated at this spot created competition with New France that became an important factor in the diplomacy of the powers in their homelands.

Trade goods at this location were almost always cheaper and more plentiful than in New France. Sometimes Montreal's prices were double Albany's for the same sort of goods. Price-conscious Indians preferred to trade in Albany when the proper arrangements could be made, which meant when the Mahican and Iroquois tribes of that vicinity would permit.[52] French strategy for overcoming this handicap relied on gaining advantage at the other end of the trade. While the Netherlands and then England mastered the westward-moving supply of European manufactures, France concentrated on controlling the eastbound products of Indian industry.[53] The French were helped by an accident of geography: they had been first in the Saint Lawrence–Great Lakes system of waterways, and the cold regions first penetrated by their explorers and colonists supported an animal population with furs thick enough to withstand subarctic winters. Such furs moved at the top of the market. What first fell to the French by chance, they subsequently took pains to maintain. By diplomacy and military action they repelled every effort of Dutch or English agents to reach their controlled tribes.[54]

The historical importance of Albany and its Indian trade can be seen in patterns in the American economy today. If we think only in terms of port cities and their physical hinterlands, the whole Great Lakes area should naturally be the hinterland of Quebec, and the Mississippi Valley

51. Paul Mantoux, *The Industrial Revolution in the Eighteenth Century: An Outline of the Beginnings of the Modern Factory System in England*, trans. Marjorie Vernon, rev. ed. (New York, 1961 [orig. publ. New York, 1928]), 62–66.

52. Colden, "Memorial concerning the Fur Trade," *N.Y. Col. Docs.*, V, 730; Chevalier de Callières's price list, 1689, *ibid.*, IX, 408–409; Louis XIV to Messrs. de Denonville and de Champigny, Mar. 30, 1687, *ibid.*, 323.

53. Bruce G. Trigger, "Champlain Judged by His Indian Policy: A Different View of Early Canadian History," *Anthropologica*, N.S., XIII (1971), 87–88.

54. E. B. O'Callaghan, ed., *The Documentary History of the State of New-York* (Albany, N.Y., 1849–1851), I, secs. iii, vii, xi; Jean Delanglez, *Frontenac and the Jesuits* (Chicago, 1939), 3; Guy Johnson to Charles Inglis, Apr. 26, 1770, *Sir William Johnson Papers*, VII, 596–602, esp. 598; Jacobs, ed., *Appalachian Indian Frontier*, 9–11.

commerce should be at the command of New Orleans. In spite of the compulsions of geography, however, New York City exerts enormous influence in the basins of the Lakes and the Mississippi. The city's success is only partly owing to the Erie Canal and the New York Central Railroad; these constructions merely improved a trade route that had previously been active for nearly two centuries. By means of Albany's market, New York City began to exert its sway over the Lakes' hinterland Indian populations long before the Midwest was resettled by Euramerican immigrants. The immigrants followed the Indian trade routes westward and continued to use them for their own trade.

In the seventeenth century the French contended against Albany and Albany's client tribes by spreading themselves thinly over vast territories. From the base of their communities on the Saint Lawrence, they extended trading posts halfway across the continent. Jesuit missions became resorts for coureurs de bois who were followed by government administrators. Robert Cavelier de La Salle carried goods and the flag down the Mississippi. After some hesitation in Paris a policy of imperial expansion was adopted, and in 1700 a new French colony was founded in Louisiana to complete the military "encirclement" of the English colonies. Vast distances between forts make the idea of effective encirclement seem silly on the map, but the open spaces were inhabited by Indians controlled through the trade conducted at the forts. Each fort functioned like a medieval castle as an administrative center for a native dependency or province. The fort secured the trade, the trade secured the people, and the people under France's direction genuinely did encircle the English colonies, as the Seven Years' War in America would amply prove.[55]

English counterstrategy varied with time. During the seventeenth century, except for a few turncoat coureurs de bois, the English depended on their allied Indians to find the way to the interior peltry and bring it back to market. Far-reaching adjustments in Indian demography and diplomacy were implied by these commercial travels. Some western tribes came east to be within easier reach of English markets. All the tribes trading with the English became pioneers for the English trading system's penetration of the French protectorate, and they were necessarily thrown into attitudes of hostility toward the French and their allies. However, as tribes were dispossessed and forced westward, their functions and relationships changed. English traders followed them over

55. Louis XIV to Messrs. de Callières and de Champigny, May 31, 1701, *N.Y. Col. Docs.*, IX, 721; Gov. Hunter to the Council of Trade and Plantations, July 7, 1718, W. Noel Sainsbury *et al.*, eds., *Calendar of State Papers, Colonial Series, America and West Indies* (London, 1860–), *August 1717–December 1718*, doc. 600; Jacobs, ed., *Appalachian Indian Frontier*, 4–6.

the Appalachian Mountains so that the familiar journey to the market towns became largely a thing of the past. Sharing habitation in territories claimed by France and France's allies required negotiation of political arrangements in which automatic hostility to France also receded into limbo. In brief, no matter how unintendingly, the English forced "their" Indians into the arms of France at precisely the historic moment when the French became most anxious about the survival of their empire. The horror that ensued was called by the English, "The French and Indian War."

Although the trade was as eagerly sought by Indians as by Europeans, its effects upon the two societies were conditioned diversely by preexisting traits of their cultures. In the long run it helped to make Europeans dominant and Indians dependent. It stimulated European industry and enriched European merchants while destroying Indian crafts and impoverishing the tribes. It opened to the Europeans vast new territories and provided the means for their acquisition, but it set the Indians against each other in a deadly competition for subordinate supremacy that ultimately resulted in the dispossession of them all.

Apart from the incessant demographic erosion of disease and war, what traits in Indian culture made the trade itself so deleterious? The myth of shiftlessness has already been disposed of, but we cannot be fully satisfied with European avarice and villainy as explanation. Rampant as these unlovely characteristics were, they were not monopolized by Europeans. Indians also showed themselves capable of cutthroat dealings in trade. Although the Indians never quite acquired the ability to meet Europeans as full peers in that sort of skill, Sir George Clark's comment on seventeenth-century business practices can be applied to both societies: "Armed aggression, when all is said, was the heart of commerce."[56]

Undoubtedly merchant controls over credit played a part in America as in England, but this still falls short of sufficiency to account for the phenomena. Although some English workmen broke out of their class ranks to rise in the world, Indians failed to amass property as defined by Europeans. The tribute paid to chiefs did not become the chiefs' property; rather it was a sort of trust fund out of which the trustee chief cared for visitors and the indigent and provided for hard times generally.[57] Indians who constantly engaged in trade never got rich at

56. G. N. Clark, *The Seventeenth Century*, 2d ed. (New York, 1947), 59.

57. Winslow, *Good Newes*, in Young, ed., *Chronicles of Pilgrims*, 360–363; "Penn to Free Society of Traders, 1683" Myers, ed., *Narratives of Early Pennsylvania*, 233.

it even under the most favorable circumstances. Frequently selling their rights to large territories, they soon dissipated the sometimes considerable payments they received. In this sense, and in terms of European values, the Indians were indeed improvident. They failed to acquire property because they did not accept the European cultural trait of capital accumulation.

In commerce every Indian traded for himself, even the chiefs. Apparently Indian culture provided no means of adapting the shared economy of the kin group to more purely specialized commercial activity. Although the Hurons specialized in trade, they were a tribe of traders rather than a trading tribe.[58] No equivalent to a joint-stock company or a European merchant's rationalized organization came into being anywhere among Indians. Perhaps the Indian's utter individualism in commerce derived from his identification of trade as an extension of the tribal custom of "prestation," or gift-giving between peers.[59] Such a conception would block understanding or acceptance of the hierarchical and bureaucratized structure of European business organization. Certainly lavish distribution of presents militated against capital accumulation by the tribal leaders, who would naturally have become property owners under other sanctions.[60] The Indian's culture permitted and encouraged him to become a trader, but it forbade him to be a merchant.

In a sense one can say that the Indians universally failed to acquire capital because they did not want it. Thereby they sacrificed status as well as opulence and incapacitated themselves for assimilation to the dominant European society except as laborers, fighters, or small peddlers. In this respect the cultural values of Europeans proved as unalterable as the Indians'. Despite the loftiest sentiments of morality and religion, Europeans have never been able or willing to devise a secure place in their midst for persons, other than those in holy orders, who care nothing about wealth. Nor have the Americans of European extraction been willing even to leave Indians alone so long as the latter occupied land that could be turned into wealth. Ironically it has been the Indian's

58. For description of the fairs held when the Huron fleet came to Montreal, see [Louis-Armand de Lom d'Arce], Baron de Lahontan, *New Voyages to North-America* (1703), ed. Reuben Gold Thwaites (Chicago, 1905), I, 92–95; W. J. Eccles, *Frontenac: The Courtier Governor* (Toronto, 1959), 86–87.

59. Cf. Belshaw, *Traditional Exchange and Modern Markets*, 46–49.

60. Nicolas Perrot remarked that only the Indians who lived in close association with the French became "less liberal . . . [and] fully as selfish and avaricious as formerly they were hospitable." Nicolas Perrot, *Memoir on the Manners, customs, and religion of the savages of North America*, in Emma Helen Blair, trans. and ed., *The Indian Tribes of the Upper Mississippi Valley and Region of the Great Lakes* . . . , I (Cleveland, Ohio, 1911), 23–272.

egalitarianism and generosity—traits much admired in European culture—that doomed him to the lowest echelon of the European social structure. This is a far cry from the mythical attributes of laziness and shiftlessness. Perhaps there was a certain nobility about this savage after all.

Chapter 7 ❧ LORDSHIP
and VASSALAGE

Europeans used a great variety of means to attain mastery, of which armed combat was only one. Alternative means were adjusted to definable, attainable, and gainful goals. In sum and in time these goals, along with their unplanned accompaniments, added up to conquest by Europeans generally over Indians generally, but along the way to that epochal climax specific situations required particular Europeans to cooperate with particular Indians. In pursuit of an immediate end the actual historical Europeans of events (as distinct from the abstract Europeans of theory) allied themselves with certain Indians on terms of formal equality. As occasion permitted, the Europeans pressed to turn alliance into clientage and clientage into subjection, with variable success.

The European assumed the sovereignty of his own Christian prince over the American land and its heathen inhabitants claimed by that prince, but this assumption was shared neither by the natives nor by competing Europeans. The natives, of course, held the naive view that they were entitled to rule themselves in their own lands. All Europeans agreed on the error of that belief. Sooner or later the "natural" subordination of the Indians was to be translated into formal subjection. For Europeans the issue was not *whether* they should rule, but *which* of them should do it.

Five principles were available to a European sovereignty for laying claim to legitimate jurisdiction over an American territory and its people: papal donation, first discovery, sustained possession, voluntary self-subjection by the natives, and armed conquest successfully maintained. Protestants and French Catholics could not hope for papal donation, but they used the other four principles in a wide variety of situations. In practice the claim to sovereignty impressed no one until a colony had been planted on the territory at issue. The colony was the means of translating a formal claim into the effective actuality of government, and it was "colonial" in both senses of that ambiguous word. The huddled villages of Europeans were colonies in the sense of being offshoots or reproductions of their parent societies, and these villages exerted power over larger native populations in the sense more clearly implied by the word *colonialism*.[1]

Formally the colonies were created in the same way that the frontiers of feudal England or Charlemagne's empire were conquered and organized, and to some extent settled, by emigrants. This was the process of chartered expansion, the stages of which were as follows: (1) a head of state laid claim to territories previously outside of his government; (2) he authorized a person or an organized group by charter to conquer the claimed territory; and, (3) if the conquest was successful, the conquering lord (whether personal or collective) became the possessor and governor of the territory, subject to the terms of the charter and his acknowledging the sovereignty of the charter's issuer.[2]

Thus, England's expansion in the seventeenth century was not without precedent. The Plantagenet kings had ruled over a feudal empire that comprised vast and varied "dominions" overseas as well as the sceptered realm. By the time Jamestown was planted the English Chancery had been familiar for centuries with the functions of a colonial governor, though, as Julius Goebel points out, the office was known "under such aliases as seneschal, king's lieutenant, warden, or lord deputy." In one royal dominion especially, that of Ireland, striking resemblances have been seen between the general situation respecting law administration in the thirteenth century and the situation that later developed in the American colonies. More than coincidence was involved. Ireland had been the one medieval dominion where an Anglo-Norman colony was sent forth from England, was planted in the midst of a native population that successfully resisted total conquest, and was governed by royal authority with frequent royal intervention.[3]

In America the chartered lords of Virginia and Massachusetts were companies. In Maryland, Lord Baltimore preserved the personal feudal pattern beyond a shadow of doubt. The duke of York's conquest of New Netherland, under sanction of his brother the king, filled in the space between New England and Maryland, and Pennsylvania was carved as a fief out of New York. Connecticut and Rhode Island were invaded by adventurers on their own account, who hastened to legitimize themselves with royal charters. Plymouth failed to obtain a

1. For a new look at the complexity of such relationships, see Ronald J. Horvath, "A Definition of Colonialism," *Current Anthro.*, XIII (1972), 45–51.

2. See Louise Phelps Kellogg, "The American Colonial Charter: A Study of English Administration in Relation Thereto, Chiefly after 1688," American Historical Association, *Annual Report* (Washington, D.C., 1903), 191–201.

3. See Julius Goebel, Jr., "The Matrix of Empire," introductory essay to J. H. Smith, *Appeals to the Privy Council from the American Plantations* (New York, 1950), xiii–lxi, quote at xvii.

charter and was gobbled up by Massachusetts as New Haven had earlier been swallowed by Connecticut. Maine was the chartered fief of Sir Ferdinando Gorges.

The language of these charters, it is nothing new to say, was feudal through and through. Some were modeled on the charters of the march-land palatine counties of Durham and Chester.[4] As has often been re-marked, the crown lawyers knew no other forms in which to phrase their documents, but it would be wrong to infer that any other form would have been appropriate, for the substance of the charters' powers and duties was as feudal as their terminology. The crown lawyers ex-plicitly stated their understanding of the status of colonial govern-ments as that of lordship. In *Calvin's Case* (1608), Sir Edward Coke reached back to medieval precedent to define the colonies as dominions of the king, distinct from the realm. The practical effect of *Calvin's Case* was to assure that these dominions would be supervised by the Privy Council instead of Parliament.[5]

As late as 1702, when the crown moved to revoke colonial charters, it described the grantees as "proprietors of the soil and Lands com-prehended within the said places but also Lords and Governors thereof." Named explicitly as falling within this description were the diverse gov-ernments of Massachusetts Bay, New Hampshire, Rhode Island and Providence Plantations, Connecticut, East and West New Jersey, Pennsylvania, Maryland, Carolina, and the Bahamas (Virginia and New York having previously been transformed by law into royal provinces).[6]

The direct tie of vassalage between the colonial lord and the king was so clearly understood that Parliament refrained from interposing its own authority except during the Commonwealth, when Parliament substituted itself for the king. The colonies were supervised by the king in his council, and when their affairs became complex the king estab-lished a special council to manage the details. In the reign of William III, when Parliament moved to set up a system of select councils for colonial supervision, William forestalled the encroachment on his pre-rogative by setting up his own Board of Trade and Plantations. After the Board of Trade's creation and until the Seven Years' War in America, Parliament confined itself, with insignificant exceptions, to regulating the

4. Kellogg, "American Colonial Charter," Am. Hist. Assn., *Annual Report* (1903), 192. See the interesting discussion of Pennsylvania's charter in Joseph E. Illick, *William Penn the Politician: His Relations with the English Government* (Ithaca, N.Y., 1965), 27–40.

5. J. H. Smith, *Appeals to the Privy Council*, 466–469, and Goebel, "Matrix of Empire," *ibid.*, lx–lxi.

6. Facsimile transcript of "An Act for reuniting to the Crown the Govern-ment of several Colonies and plantations in America," P.R.O. Proprieties, B.T. 6/1, 16, in *Records in the British Public Record Office Relating to South Carolina, 1701–1710* (Columbia, S.C., 1947), 72–74.

colonies in their external relations only; and when Parliament later began to intervene in internal affairs the colonies apprehended the new policy as encroachment on their own rightful domains, and they went to war to stop it. Although their Declaration of Independence loaded blame on the king (and the crown was surely striving to reduce the colonies to a state of meek subjection), the constitutional issue of the Revolution was hammered home by a deluge of pamphlets. It was, in the first place, Parliament's attempt to nationalize the colonies by legislating directly for them that the colonial lordships would not tolerate.[7]

This situation was not new in British history. In 1460 the Anglo-Norman colonists of Ireland had tried something similar when their "Irish" parliament declared the land not subject to the laws of the English Parliament while continuing to acknowledge allegiance to the English king. The precedent aborted, however, when those colonists failed to make their independence good. They knuckled under with "Poynings' Laws" in 1494–1495, by means of which their parliament abjured its attempts to legislate independently of royal approval.[8]

The nature of lordship is to stand intermediate between sovereign and subjects, but to so state the case is to prejudice it toward the legal ideal of a nation-state. Practically speaking, lords assume powers and privileges based on custom or simple gall and become to a degree autonomous. Persons theoretically subject to the king were practically ruled by their lords and were never permitted to forget the fact. This contradiction is familiar enough to medievalists who routinely examine feudal social relationships for the specific "liberties" of each lord and the specific obligations of his dependents.[9] However, some American historians have dwelt on our origins in terms that vaguely imply that the colonies had always been a nation-state in embryo—that the developed nation of England had reduplicated itself in its colonies. Charles and Mary Beard, for example, remarked that "to this continent the English colonial leaders, like the Greeks in expansion, transported their

7. Charles M. Andrews, *The Colonial Period of American History* (New Haven, Conn., 1934–1938), IV, 58–59. In the pamphlets of American Revolutionists the argument for lordship takes the form of a theory of divided sovereignty (and the U.S. Constitution was later founded on such a rationale). Pennsylvania's James Wilson reached back to *Calvin's Case* for legal authority. Bernard Bailyn, *The Ideological Origins of the American Revolution* (Cambridge, Mass., 1967), 198–229, esp. 225. The colonists opposed the substance of sovereignty rather than the form of monarchy until they suddenly attacked the king as a way of unifying their people. Lawrence Henry Gipson, *The British Empire before the American Revolution*, XII (New York, 1965), 366–367.

8. Lydon, *Lordship of Ireland*, 263–265; Goebel, "Matrix of Empire," in J. H. Smith, *Appeals to the Privy Council*, lvi–lvii.

9. Otto Brunner, "Feudalism: The History of a Concept," in Fredric L. Cheyette, ed., *Lordship and Community in Medieval Europe: Selected Readings* (New York, 1968), 37.

own people, their own economy, and the culture of the classes from which they sprang, reproducing in a large measure the civilization of the mother country."[10] Insofar as such general statements suggest that the colonies were miniature Englands, they are erroneous in several respects. Although colonial politicians frequently appealed to parliamentary examples and to the laws of England, colonial governments and laws evolved on paths distinct from the evolution of English government and law. For example, no colony had a house of lords, and in no colonial assembly did there develop a responsible cabinet system of government, such as grew up in eighteenth-century England.

The English crown had neither the technical resources nor the inclination to establish a developed bureaucracy within each colony. Grappling with the semantics of definition, C. M. Andrews concluded that "in reality these settlements were not colonies; they were private estates."[11] His remark appears baffling to the logician. When is a colony not a colony? The answer is, When it is an issue in law. Andrews perceived the distinction between a colony as a social phenomenon (a community) and as a legal construction (a province). Because the early English "settlements" could not conform to the type of the bureaucratically administered province, he resorted to the name "estates" to clarify their legal status, and the "colonies" simply disappeared. Such verbal magic works only on the beholder; the colonies continued to exist both as settlements and as estates, and as estates they included claimed jurisdiction over natives as well as immigrant settlers.

Andrews simply ignored the problem of native jurisdiction, as he generally ignored the Indians' existence. The Beards reduced the problem to a dilemma that enabled them to dismiss it in a sentence: "Instead of natives submissive to servitude, instead of old civilizations ripe for conquest, the English found an immense continent of virgin soil and forest, sparsely settled by primitive peoples who chose death rather than bondage."[12] This is good melodrama and it has stalked many a stage, but we are dealing with real life rather than heroic bombast. Few Indians *chose* either death or bondage, and the colonists were rarely able or eager to enforce such a limited choice. They aimed instead at reducing the Indians to political "subjection" or "dependency," and they were often obliged to reconcile their de jure assumptions in this regard with an acute de facto awareness of deficiency in the power necessary to translate Indian subjection from theory to fact. It was not always a sensible procedure for a handful of Europeans to inform the

10. Charles A. and Mary R. Beard, *The Rise of American Civilization*, rev. ed. (New York, 1934), I, 11.
11. Charles M. Andrews, *The Colonial Background of the American Revolution: Four Essays in American Colonial History*, rev. ed. (New Haven, Conn., 1931), 6.
12. Beard and Beard, *Rise of American Civilization*, I, 11.

chief of thousands of nearby warriors that a piece of paper had reduced the chief and his people to subjection. Even the sometimes stupendous arrogance of seventeenth-century Europeans knew some prudence. Responsible men of affairs temporized onward and upward, grasping power "by little and by little." [13]

Lacking royal armies and royal courts of law, and seeing the royal navy only at such moments as suited the royal convenience, colonial lords reverted to methods tested in the feudal era of their own homelands. They tried to make inferior vassals out of Indian chiefs. [14] Up to a point this effort succeeded, but it encountered difficulties inherent in the differential development of the two societies. After their improvised beginnings colonial governments were under constant pressure from abroad to rationalize their organization and to imitate the forms already developed in the increasingly bureaucratic nation-state in Europe, though colonial conditions did not permit exact miniaturization of England's governmental forms. Indian society, which was structured by kinship and tradition, more strongly resisted the impersonal forms of rationalization becoming dominant in European-style government. The "kinship states" of the Indians could not be integrated with the developing bureaucratic states of the Europeans.

The irreconcilability has served as still another proof to some students that Indians were incapable of civilization; that, in fact, the Indians had no genuine government at all, since true government (like true religion) existed only in the "civil society" patterned on European conceptions of law and the institutions for its enforcement. Indian resistance to a particular alien culture of written laws and stratified hierarchy became an Indian incapacity for civilization per se. Lewis Henry Morgan believed that "the passion of the red man for the hunter life" required that Indian government be "adapted to the hunter state"; thus, "the effect of this powerful principle has been to enchain the tribes of North America to their primitive state." It followed that "the red race has never risen, or can rise above its present level." Using Morgan as a source, historian Francis Parkman described Iroquois government at length and concluded that no Iroquois was "for a moment divorced from his wild spirit of independence," explaining further that, "where there was no property worthy the name, authority had no fulcrum and no hold." A multitude of writers have worked variations on these themes. [15] It was true that unassimilable tribal blocs maintained villages

---

13. The quoted phrase was a favorite of John Winthrop, Sr.'s.
14. See Wesley Frank Craven, "Indian Policy in Early Virginia," *WMQ*, 3d Ser., I (1944), 70; Nash, "Image of the Indian," *ibid.*, XXIX (1972), 214.
15. Morgan, *League of the Iroquois*, 57–58; Parkman, *Jesuits in North America*, 57–58.

and territories separate from the European colonists (sometimes, indeed, by force of colonial segregation laws) and held to their own custom rather than accept European law.[16] The only political point of contact between colony and tribe was the treaty conference where lord and chief negotiated.

The ideology of power produces many contradictions; Europeans' pronouncements that Indians had no government were contradicted by their practice of dealing with Indian chiefs through the protocol of diplomacy with sovereign states. The bulk of evidence about Indian communities implies structures of political association irreconcilable with assumptions of anarchy. From anthropology comes the root conception of the "kinship state," a community of families and clans in which some of the ordering functions of society are performed by the kin groups individually while others are assigned to officers and councillors chosen cooperatively.[17]

In this structure, as European observers were quick to notice, there was no law in the European sense, and no specialized apparatus of law enforcement. Binding decisions were made by legitimate officers, however, and before the intervention of Europeans eroded the chiefs' authority there were forceful sanctions for both occasional decisions and enduring customs. In a community where every man bore arms no need existed for a corps of specialized police; any man could be appointed to act guard or do executioner's duty.[18] Early seventeenth-century observers reported that the paramount chiefs of the tribes sometimes inflicted corporal punishment upon criminals with their own hands.[19] Families also bore responsibility for protecting their kinsfolk, and the accompanying threat of vengeance sanctioned by custom proved an effective deterrent to potential wrongdoers. Such sanctions in their social context were more effectual than European procedures of criminal justice; Adriaen Van der Donck wonderingly noticed "how uncommon" crimes were among the Hudson River Indians. "With us," he continued, "a watchful police is supported, and crimes are more frequent than among them." Not recognizing the sanctioning functions performed by means that he had himself described, he was baffled to understand how there could be so little crime "where there is no regard paid to

16. For segregation laws see General Court minutes, Aug. 26, 1642, Dec. 1, 1642, J. Hammond Trumbull, ed., *The Public Records of the Colony of Connecticut* (Hartford, Conn., 1850–1890), hereafter cited as *Recs. of Conn.*

17. Fenton, "Locality As a Basic Factor," in Fenton, ed., *Symposium on Local Diversity in Iroquois Culture*, 39, 51.

18. John Smith, *Map of Virginia*, in Barbour, ed., *Jamestown Voyages*, II, 371–372.

19. Winslow, *Good Newes*, in Young, ed., *Chronicles of Pilgrims*, 364–365; Williams, *Key*, ed. Trumbull, Narragansett Club, *Pubs.*, I, 166.

the administration of justice."[20] A lawyer himself, Van der Donck could recognize due process only when it appeared in the forms to which he had been trained. That fault was shared by other Europeans contemporary with himself and in following generations.

Indian processes of internal criminal justice might stimulate mild curiosity among Europeans, but other functions of government excited the most intense and sustained interest. These had to do with what would traditionally be called foreign relations. Naturally enough, Europeans best understood those processes and agencies with which they regularly dealt directly. They were concerned with military power and the means of controlling and directing it. They were also much concerned about territorial jurisdictions and the means of withdrawing land from tribal jurisdictions to bring it under their own.

Pursuing such objectives, Europeans learned that Indian communities were not so unqualifiedly egalitarian as myth maintains. Although social status was less stratified than in Europe, the Indians did recognize distinctions of hereditary right as well as individual accomplishment. A great warrior might become a military chief, but he could not succeed to the supreme leadership of his tribe unless he had been born within the appropriate degree of kinship to the incumbent paramount chief. A common rule among the Algonquians, for example, was the election of the new paramount chief from the sons of a sister of the old one—a procedure that guaranteed blood lines more effectively than Europe's patrilinear system.[21]

Chiefs were not always male. "Queens" occurred among some Algonquian tribes. Among the Iroquois certain old clan matrons were the kingmakers.[22] The titles of chiefs were generally rendered into European spelling as *cacique* in Florida, *werowance* in the Chesapeake Bay region, and *sachem* or *sagamore* farther north. In upper New England a *sagamore* might be the principal leader, but in lower New England he was more likely to be a subchief. I use the phrase "paramount chief" as a neutral term of classification rather than as a specific title.[23]

The paramount chief's duties probably varied from tribe to tribe.

20. Van der Donck, *Description of New Netherlands*, in N.-Y. Hist. Soc., *Colls.*, 2d Ser., I, 212.

21. John Smith, *Map of Virginia*, in Barbour, ed., *Jamestown Voyages*, II, 371; "Penn to Free Society of Traders, 1683," Myers, ed., *Narratives of Early Pennsylvania*, 234–235.

22. Cara Elizabeth Richards, "The Role of Iroquois Women: A Study of the Onondaga Reservation" (Ph.D. diss., Cornell University, 1957), 82–83. See accounts of Awashonks, Magnus, and Weetamoo in Samuel G. Drake, *Biography and History of the Indians of North America from its First Discovery . . .*, 11th ed. (Boston, 1856), scattered pages, see index; Hodge, ed., *Handbook of N. Am. Indians*, s.v. "women."

23. A concise description is in Lawson, *New Voyage to Carolina*, 195.

Among the Carolina Algonquians he was responsible for a community storehouse to provide against famine.[24] New England Algonquian chiefs also stored food that had been collected as tribute by subchiefs and distributed it to the needy, besides using some for hospitality to travelers and diplomats.[25] Some examples show Algonquian paramount chiefs leading their men to battle, but the Iroquois tribes divided responsibility among war chiefs and peace chiefs, who alternated in primacy according to circumstances.[26] In some tribes the paramount chief allocated cleared lands to each family for tillage.[27] In all tribes he was the guardian of the tribal territory.[28]

The paramount chief ruled with the advice and consent of a council. As Roger Williams wrote, from his experience with the tribes of lower New England, "The Sachims, although they have an absolute Monarchie over the people; yet they will not conclude of ought that concernes all, either Lawes, or Subsides, or warres, unto which the people are averse, and by gentle perswasion cannot be brought." Williams's comment is typical of those of other observers. Even John Smith, who liked to portray Powhatan as the complete despot, noted that "the lawes whereby he ruleth is custome," and that "his inferiour kings" were "tyed to rule by customes" although they had "power of life and death as their command in that nature."[29]

The qualifications for council membership and the duties attached to it seem to have been insufficiently studied in general, but we know that the political ingenuity of the much-researched Iroquois tribes produced an astonishingly elaborate traditional structure of offices and responsibilities.[30] It seems reasonable to assume that the neighbors of the Iro-

24. See de Bry's engravings in figs. 1 and 2, chap. 5 above.

25. Winslow, *Good Newes*, in Young, ed., *Chronicles of Pilgrims*, 362–363.

26. Algonquians: John Smith, *Map of Virginia*, in Barbour, ed., *Jamestown Voyages*, II, 361–362; de Bry's engravings in fig. 5, chap. 9 below, and in Lorant, ed., *New World*, 63; Aug. 1643, Winthrop, *History*, ed. Savage, II, 130. Iroquois: William N. Fenton, "Iroquoian Culture History: A General Evaluation," in William N. Fenton and John Gulick, eds., *Symposium on Cherokee and Iroquois Culture*, Smithsonian Institution, Bureau of American Ethnology, Bulletin 180 (Washington, D.C., 1961), 269.

27. Winslow, *Good Newes*, in Young, ed., *Chronicles of Pilgrims*, 362; Williams to Mass. General Court, May 12, 1656, John Russell Bartlett, ed., *Letters of Roger Williams, 1632–1682*, Narragansett Club, *Pubs.*, VI (Providence, R.I., 1874), 300–301.

28. See chap. 8, "The Deed Game."

29. Williams, *Key*, ed. Trumbull, Narragansett Club, *Pubs.*, I, 164; John Smith, *Map of Virginia*, in Barbour, ed., *Jamestown Voyages*, II, 371.

30. In 1907 J. N. B. Hewitt found that "for most of the tribes of North America a close study and analysis of the social and political organization are wanting." Hodge, ed., *Handbook of N. Am. Indians*, II, 498. In 1957 Anthony F. C. Wallace wrote that "we are only now beginning to be able to focus attention on the subject of primitive political organization." "Political Organization," *Southwestern Journal of Anthropology*, XIII (1957), 302.

quois, whose cultural development was of the same general level, would have possessed at least a substantial portion of their political sophistication. William Fenton has noted more cultural resemblances between the Iroquois and nearby Delawares than between the Iroquois and their linguistic relatives the Cherokees.[31] The assumption of regional diffusion of political sophistication gains weight from the consideration that Iroquoian dominance over neighboring tribes did not become a fact until after European contact altered all the political rules.[32]

Scholars have condemned the European explorers' habit of referring to Indian chiefs as kings and emperors, and certainly no valid comparison could be made between the state of a Powhatan and that of a Stuart or Bourbon.[33] However, it seems extremely unlikely that such a comparison was ever intended by the ethnocentrically proud Europeans. Their language is explained by their own history. Anglian and Saxon chiefs of the tribes who invaded Britain after Rome's withdrawal were called kings because they headed kins or kindreds.[34] Kings long antedated the nation-state in Europe. Englishmen knew no other title for King Ethelbert of seventh-century Kent, for example, who was overlord of the other tribal chieftains, also called kings, of Essex, Wessex, Sussex, East Anglia, Mercia, and Northumbria, all of whom together ruled a territory roughly equal to that of modern New York State, all of whom ruled over heathen, clan-structured polities and led companionships of warriors, and none of whom controlled an impersonal bureaucracy.[35] Powhatan could well deserve a title to compare with Ethelbert's. Through the fourteenth century the native Irish chiefs of kindreds styled themselves kings of nations and were so described by Anglo-Norman colonists, who simultaneously asserted that these Irish kings were vassals of the king of England.[36]

This seemingly trivial semantic issue holds importance because the identification of Indians as kings has been waved aside as another ex-

---

31. Fenton, "Iroquoian Culture History," in Fenton and Gulick, eds., *Symposium on Cherokee and Iroquois Culture*, 262–263. See also Anthony F. C. Wallace, "Woman, Land, and Society: Three Aspects of Aboriginal Delaware Life," *Pennsylvania Archaeologist*, XVII (1947), 8–9.

32. E. M. Ruttenber, *History of the Indian Tribes of Hudson's River* (1872), Empire State Historical Publications Series No. 95 (Port Washington, N.Y., 1971), 52–53; Trelease, *Indian Affairs in Colonial New York*, 23–24.

33. Cf. Anthony F. C. Wallace, review of Albert Cook Myers, ed., *William Penn's Own Account of the Lenni Lenape or Delaware Indians*, in *Pennsylvania History*, XXXVIII (1971), 325.

34. *Oxford English Dictionary*, s.v. "king."

35. F. M. Stenton, *Anglo-Saxon England*, The Oxford History of England, 2d ed., II (Oxford, 1947), chap. 2.

36. Lydon, *Lordship of Ireland*, 16–17, 71, 257.

ample of how the early explorers did not really understand what they were looking at. While it is true enough that they did not see through our eyes, we should not be so quick to waive the rules of historical evidence, one of which commands us to try to look through theirs. We do not have to agree with their interpretation of what they saw, but we must try to understand it. Whatever the defects in observation of these adventurers and colonizers, they knew how to discover holders of power, and they were adept at dealing with them.

A government constructed on the basis of kinship can be effective only insofar as genetic or fictive kin relationships are conceivable.[37] By its nature such a government depends on clearly understood interpersonal relationships, which must be maintained in a preliterate society through face-to-face contacts. Kinship states are local governments.[38] This fact in no way diminishes their effectiveness within their bounds; but the bounds are small, and the number of independent governments is large. Indian governments, like nation-states, were potentially or actively hostile to all other governments with which they had not concluded agreements of amity or alliance. Many governments produced many wars, but the same logic that multiplied the wars kept them small. They were not anarchic, however, for they conformed to the definition of war as conflict between organized governments, and they were conducted in aboriginal times according to forms prescribed by well-established customs.[39] The complexity of this subject requires separate discussion in chapter 9, below.

An Indian "emperor," or paramount chief, was head of a confederation of local governments and was obliged to exert his authority, whatever it may have been, through their means. Individually the local chiefs were formally subordinate to the paramount chief; collectively, however, because of his dependence upon them, they were his master. In this dependence lay a weakness in Indian confederations that exposed them to European manipulation. Lacking a standing army, a paramount chief had few alternatives when a subordinate chief chose to secede. Indeed secession seems to have been tolerated by custom in much the manner that Europe's Middle Ages permitted free men to transfer their

---

37. Elisabeth Tooker stresses that the conception of kinship was often more important than the actuality: "Clans may be primarily a device for classifying people who are not well known, not a device for retaining knowledge of genealogical relationships." Elisabeth Tooker, "Clans and Moieties in North America," *Current Anthro.*, XII (1971), 359.

38. Fenton, "Locality as a Basic Factor," in Fenton, ed., *Symposium on Local Diversity in Iroquois Culture*, 35–54.

39. George S. Snyderman, *Behind the Tree of Peace: A Sociological Analysis of Iroquois Warfare*, entire issue of *Pa. Archaeol.*, XVIII, Nos. 3–4 (1948), 7.

allegiance from one lord to another.[40] Indian tradition is full of stories about groups breaking away from parent communities to migrate and establish new tribes; at a certain density of population the practice would be simple common sense.[41] While secession cannot be reconciled with the demands of total sovereignty, it once seemed consonant with civilized government to a large body of Americans in the eighteenth century, and again in the nineteenth century, nor is it wholly inconceivable as a future response to gigantism and oppression. Indian toleration of secession, however, provided Europeans with ready-made handles for breaking off bits and pieces of tribes; and when the process incensed a tribe to consider forceful recovery of the seceders, Europeans interposed their own protection.[42] Such seceders, of course, gained merely the illusion of independence; when they changed protectors they changed masters.

Europeans adopted the detaching tactics as a second choice; they would have preferred to keep tribes intact under the management of chiefs unqualifiedly loyal to themselves. Toward this end the Jamestown colonists received orders from London to acquire formal suzerainty over Powhatan's whole "empire" by a vassalizing ceremony in which Powhatan was to be crowned as a subject king of England's James I. John Smith wrote of inviting Powhatan to "come to his Father Newport" to receive presents and be crowned. Powhatan immediately recognized that acceptance of presents from a "father" would imply his acceptance of a filial relationship, "whereunto the subtile Salvage thus replied. 'If your king have sent me presents, I also am a king, and this my land; 8 daies I will stay to receave them. Your father is to come to me, not I to him, nor yet to your fort, neither will I bite at such a baite.' " Shrugging the rebuff aside, Captain Christopher Newport doggedly went on with his intended ritual at Powhatan's capital instead of his own.

In Smith's account the result was farce.

All things being fit for the day of his coronation, the presents were brought, his bason, ewer, bed and furniture set up, his scarlet cloake and apparel (with much adoe) put on him (being perswaded by Namontacke they would doe him no hurt.) But a fowle trouble there was to make him kneele to receave his crowne, he neither knowing the majestie, nor meaning of a Crowne, nor bending of the knee, indured so many perswasions, examples, and instruction, as tired them all. At last by leaning hard on his shoulders, he a little stooped, and Newport put the Crowne on his head.

40. Gookin, "Historical Collections," in Mass. Hist. Soc., *Colls.*, 1st Ser., I, 154; A. F. C. Wallace, "Political Organization," *Southwest. Jour. of Anthro.*, XIII (1957), 309.

41. The Nanticokes, Conoys, Shawnees, and Mahicans claimed a common origin with the Lenni Lenape. Hodge, ed., *Handbook of N. Am. Indians*, s.v. "Delaware."

42. E.g., grand sachem Miantonomo and subsachem Pumham. See chap. 15 below.

In the midst of it all, Powhatan kept his head. With simple symbolism he demonstrated unmistakably the terms on which he had accepted Newport's presents: "he gave his old shoes and his mantle to Captain Newport." A "subtile Salvage" indeed.[43]

In the conditions of the time there was no way to erect a bureaucracy for direct government of the tribe as a whole even if it accepted subjection; the only possible way of regularly controlling its conduct was through the voluntary cooperation of its effective chiefs. It was not the absence of Indian government that baffled the English, but rather the effective resistance to subjection by the stubbornly existing governments. With time, however, the English learned how to combine force and favor to persuade certain chiefs to acknowledge a degree of subordination to the Great King over the Water. The final sticking point came when the local colonial lords demanded the further subordination of the Indian chiefs to themselves. The chiefs would not be vassals of vassals. In one instance the Narragansetts subjected their whole tribe directly to England's crown precisely in order to avoid coming under the rule of Massachusetts Bay,[44] and the Iroquois Five Nations repeatedly stressed that their acknowledgment of subjection to the crown did not imply an obligation to take orders from New York. They were a free people, they insisted, and their cooperation with the colony had to be renegotiated every year. There is an echo here of medieval Irish kings who accepted the distant overlordship of the king of England, but would not tolerate another lord—a "mesne lord"—between them and the sovereign. Iroquois statements on the matter of subjection often seem contradictory, being influenced by expediency and pressures. The actual situation has to be deduced from the Indians' actions rather than their equivocal words. Although New York claimed the Five Nations as a "dependency," and France recognized England's suzerainty over them after 1712, the Iroquois treated with whatever colonies they pleased, including New France. Perhaps the best description of their status is their own characterization made in 1684: a "free people uniting them selves to the English."[45] English officials understood this. In a letter to Sir William Johnson, dated October 7, 1772, General Thomas Gage remarked, "As for the Six Nations [the original Five

---

43. John Smith, *Map of Virginia*, in Barbour, ed., *Jamestown Voyages*, II, 410–414.

44. See chaps. 15 and 16 below.

45. Lydon, *Lordship of Ireland*, 167; "That being a free people uniting them selves to the English, it may be in their power to give their land to what Sachim they please": "Abstract of the Proposalls of the Onoundages and Cayouges Sachims at New Yorke 2. August 1684.," *N.Y. Col. Docs.*, III, 347.

Nations plus the Tuscaroras] having acknowledged themselves sub-jects of the English, that I conclude must be a very gross Mistake ...
I know I would not venture to treat them as Subjects unless there was a Resolution to make War upon them."[46]

The vassalage of Indian chiefs whose tribes held together was not quite the same thing as the vassalage of lesser lords in Europe's fully developed feudal era. The Indian chief made a restricted and temporary contract of allegiance or alliance. In practice the realities of politics and economics usually attached him and his tribe for long periods in a factual dependence upon one colonial lord; in form, however, the dependence manifested itself as an alliance repeatedly renewed rather than a legal bond perpetually continued. And there were tribes who changed al-liances. (The Shawnees, especially, moved restlessly about.)

Allowing for this formal distinction, the effect of which was real and substantial, we must still face the relationship that quickly became normal after the establishment of permanent colonies; namely, an al-liance that was in fact clientage and that was renewed so regularly that its parties functioned in effect as lord and vassal—most of the time. It cannot be pinned down to any formula without qualification because it was an arrangement construed by the different parties according to their different preconceptions and expectations. Accordingly it was like one of those gadgets, beloved of souvenir collectors, that display a certain picture when tilted at one angle and show a wholly different image in the same space when turned to another angle. The image of colonial-Indian relationships was changed by the different angles of view created by the Europeans' acceptance and the Indians' rejection of the conception of European sovereignty. Tilted away from that conception, agreements between Indian and European are alliances. Tilted toward European sovereignty, the agreements display the Indian chief as vassal and his tribesmen as subjects. Events sometimes rocked the images back and forth in considerable confusion.

There seems to be no word in English that properly fits the situation. Our language tidily sorts out dependence, independence, and inter-dependence, of which the last comes closest to defining the whole re-lationship between Indians and Europeans; but if we want to categorize the special status of Indians as both dependent and independent the language fails us. Perhaps we should coin a new term, such as "am-bipendence" or "ambigupendence," that could be useful generally to identify such objective situations as often exist where the subjective at-titudes of people are ambivalent.[47] Indians had to cope with "am-

---

46. *Sir William Johnson Papers*, XII, 995.
47. For example, married persons seem to be "ambipendent" as individuals

bipendence" for centuries. Like other handicapped people they evolved customary routines for living with their problems, and some of these routines became the institution familiar to historians as the Indian treaty.

In its fully developed form the Indian treaty is represented by innumerable examples recorded by colonial scribes, and it has long been regarded as a curious branch of literature.[48] But it was not intended as literature: it was both an agreement and the meeting that produced it. *Treaty* is one of our ambiguous English words that can refer either to a process or a product.

Reserving discussion of the product to a later place, let us examine the procedure here. It was as serious and ritualized an affair as anything that happened over the baize-covered tables in London or Paris, and although what might be called the high-church treaty—the full-protocol solemnity—grew slowly out of Indian rather than European antecedents, the procedure was easy for English colonial lords to adjust to. Fourteenth-century Anglo-Norman lords in Ireland had routinely treated with Gaelic chieftains, even forming alliances with those who were technically "Irish enemies."[49]

It is essential for the student to recognize in all such arrangements, whether in Ireland or America, the distinction between forms and functions. The English had a long tradition of suspending, without entirely abandoning, jurisdictional pretensions that were practically unenforceable, and their justifications for pragmatic procedures sometimes muddled together a mixture of propaganda, wishful thinking, and excuses that reveal more about their prejudices than about the objects of description. An example in point is the splutter of William Samuel Johnson in the eighteenth century when he reconciled his hurt pride to the necessity for negotiating with Indians.

When the English Treated with them it was not with Independent States (for they had no such thing as a Civil Polity, nor hardly any one Circumstance essential to the existence of a state) but as with savages, whom they were to quiet and manage as well as they could, sometimes by flattery, but oftener by force. Who would not Treat if he saw himself surrounded by a Company of Lyons Wolves or Beasts whom the Indians but too nearly resembled, ready to fall upon him and even call them Friends and allies too, if he thought it would for a Moment repress their Rage, and give him time to take measures for his security; but you would not therefore Im-

---

though interdependent as a pair. While married, each depends much on the other, but each also preserves enough independence to survive separately. It hardly needs arguing that ambivalent attitudes occur in marriage.

48. See the introduction in Julian P. Boyd, ed., *Indian Treaties Printed by Benjamin Franklin, 1736–1762* (Philadelphia, 1938).

49. Lydon, *Lordship of Ireland*, 196.

mediately call them an independent State (though Independent enough God knows) because they hunted the same Forest or Drank at the same Brook.... This Notion of their being free States is perfectly ridiculous and absurd. Without Polity, Laws etc. there can be so such thing as a State. The Indians had neither in any proper sense of the words.[50]

Regardless of such outbursts Indians and Englishmen developed customary procedures for negotiations that took the form of agreement between governments. At first the English paid little attention to Indian protocol. Early meetings typically show an Indian chief or his ambassador (with entourage) appearing before a colonial council, and the negotiations appear as an item of business on the council's agenda; or a European presents himself to an Indian council and becomes part of its business. As time went on the Europeans adapted themselves to Indian forms of ritual in order to ingratiate themselves with the chiefs or to create a sense of solemn obligation, and the treaty conference became an affair in its own right in which the councils of both sides met each other on formal terms of parity.[51] Such master diplomats as Canada's Count Frontenac and New York's Sir William Johnson even joined the natives in ceremonial dances. (It makes a vivid scene—the elegant gentleman, in his silks and laces and ribbons and plumes, stomp-dancing with the sweaty warriors in the flickering firelight and no doubt sweating a bit himself.)

From the records familiar to me (a small portion of the available total), I have formed an impression that the treaty protocol of the northeastern region was developed primarily by the Iroquois Five Nations and taught by them to both Indians and Europeans with whom they did business.[52] The beginnings are discernible in the late seventeenth century, and the minutes of mid-eighteenth-century treaties show the full pomp. The fully elaborated treaty form required due notice to be given by one side and accepted by the other. Advance preparations sometimes involved both Indians and Englishmen in exploratory discussions with their tribal or colonial allies. When the treaty conference convened, whether outdoors around a council fire or inside the Albany town hall (for example), the Indians formed themselves in a semicircle on one side, with their great chiefs in front and the younger men well to the rear, and the English lined up facing them. The meeting opened with the formal expression of condolences by one side for the death of leaders of the other side.[53] Presents would be offered as part of the

50. Quoted in J. H. Smith, *Appeals to the Privy Council*, 434–435, n. 109.
51. Johnson to Gage, Feb. 19, 1764, *Sir William Johnson Papers*, IV, 330–331.
52. See Snyderman, "Functions of Wampum," Am. Phil. Soc., *Procs.*, XCVIII (1954), 473. This article has a full description of treaty protocol. See also Speck, "Functions of Wampum," Am. Anthro. Assn., *Memoirs*, VI (1919), 3–71.
53. Fenton has pointed out the transition of the Requickening Address of the

consolation for the afflicted. A calumet pipe of tobacco might be handed about and a puff or two taken by each leader in turn as a means of showing goodwill, invoking divine "medicine," and inducing a meditative frame of mind.

One side's spokesman would step forward and line up a series of strings and belts of wampum before him as tokens of agenda. Taking them up in turn, he recited the "proposition" accompanying each and passed it to the other side. If the wampum was accepted, the recipient was understood to have taken its proposition under consideration, but a reciprocal belt was required to signify agreement; refusal to accept a belt denoted immediate rejection of its proposition. The size of the wampum symbol signified the importance attached to its proposition, ranging from small single strings for relatively trivial business to broad belts "seven hands" long for matters of utmost urgency. White wampum went with peaceful issues, black with propositions or declarations of war. Figures in the belts gave them the individual identities necessary to distinguish propositions of the same importance but different substance. For the Indians these belts served as mnemonic devices and permanent records. They were carefully preserved in council houses and reviewed regularly by the old chiefs, who recited their contents to younger men and required the latter to memorize them as a way of preserving continuity of tribal policy—and as a further means of keeping a check on the written minutes of the English scribes, who were deservingly suspected by the Indians of biasing the records. The student of treaty minutes should always note carefully, in cases of dispute, whether wampum was passed when the disputed proposition was made. Remarks without wampum were just talk—trial balloons, perhaps, or polite diplomatic hypocrisy—that carried no obligation whatever though scribes might try to give them the appearance of pledges.[54]

As in European diplomacy speeches were translated after having been delivered in the speaker's own language. The interpreter often became a very influential person, for his skill and intentions might make or break a treaty. Few Europeans spoke Indian languages, so the colonial governments depended heavily on certain individuals who acquired status as diplomats in their own right instead of being merely translators. Pennsylvania's Conrad Weiser comes to mind.

Indian "speakers" at the treaties often were not the great chiefs of

Condolence Council from the internal affairs of the Iroquois League to the diplomatic meetings of the League with the English colonies. "Iroquoian Culture History," in Fenton and Gulick, eds., *Symposium on Cherokee and Iroquois Culture*, 272.

54. Cadwallader Colden, *The History of the Five Indian Nations Depending on the Province of New-York in America* (Ithaca, N.Y., 1958 [orig. publ. 1727–1747]), Pt. ii, chap. 10, 139.

their tribes. They might be lesser chiefs chosen for oratorical skill,[55] and many an Englishman complained privately of their infernal long-windedness; other English, especially those who knew Indian languages, acquired a taste for Indian rhetoric. Dead silence and absolute decorum prevailed while the speaker had the floor: Robert Beverley tells of a Virginia chief who tomahawked a tribesman for the presumption of interrupting the chief in the midst of a treaty speech.[56] The silent solemnity remained unbroken throughout a treaty conference, except when a chief invited his company to intone a ritual "yo-hah" to show hearty agreement or gratitude.[57]

Indian custom ordinarily dictated that no proposition should get a response on the same day it was offered, and sometimes the chiefs would cause an English aristocrat to fume in wounded pride for days while awaiting an answer to an imperious demand.[58] After both sides had presented their initial propositions the meeting adjourned till the morrow, and the sides withdrew to council separately. During these intervals there might be informal discussions between leaders of both sides, or individuals might conduct an intrigue, commonly involving bribery. This sort of affair could be lucrative to individual chiefs and was often winked at by their fellows, but it could also be unhealthy for the chief who had lost touch with tribal opinion. The famous Iroquois speaker Canasatego may have been executed by his tribesmen for unacceptably wide discrepancy between his cupidity and their policy.[59]

A conference lasted at least two days and might go on for many more. At its end each side gave presents to the other. As a matter of prestige the English customarily calculated the value of the Indian gifts and returned a value noticeably greater.[60] Astute Indians would devote weeks to accumulating as large a stock as possible for their treaty donation, obviously in expectation of making a large profit on the exchange, but the ritual of present giving must not be too simplistically dismissed. It had deep roots in Indian custom, and the mere fact that the English took such pains to give the greater value shows their understanding of the act's importance for establishing respect and preserving loyalty. The present giving, in some instances, came to be the reason for holding

55. A. F. C. Wallace, "Political Organization," *Southwest. Jour. of Anthro.*, XIII (1957), 305.

56. *History of Virginia*, ed. Wright, 225.

57. Paul A. W. Wallace, *Conrad Weiser, 1696–1760: Friend of Colonist and Mohawk* (Philadelphia, 1945), 68–69.

58. Treaty minutes, Sept. 10, 1722, *N.Y. Col. Docs.*, V, 674–675.

59. P. A. W. Wallace, *Conrad Weiser*, 313–314.

60. E.g., Indian delegations in 1712 presented a total of £31 7s. 6d. in furs to the government of Pennsylvania, in return for which the Pennsylvanians presented goods worth £50 6s. 6d. to the Indians. Oct. 14, 16, 1712, *Pa. Council Minutes*, II, 559, 561.

the treaty. Annual or occasional presentation of English gifts became a form of tribute, demanded by the Indians and much grumbled at by some gentlemen who thought the lowly Indians should be paying the tribute to their betters. But policy-makers understood the delicate balance of power between the colonies of France and England and wooed the Indians who could tip the scales. Realistically they were also aware that the money would all come back through profits in the Indian trade.[61]

Depending on the negotiators' credentials and instructions, they might be able to arrive at a binding agreement during the treaty conference, or they might have to take their treaty home for ratification by the tribal or colonial council, or both. This point is especially worth noting because much error has been perpetuated in our histories through the interpretation of unratified treaties as binding contracts, and much invective has been directed at tribes who "broke their promises" or "betrayed their trust" when they were really deciding that the promises in question were such as they did not care to make.[62]

Let it be repeated that the foregoing description in its fullness applies to eighteenth-century treaties. The forms and processes of the seventeenth century were more varied. The later model has been described here because elements of it appear in even the earliest years, which may be best understood in the perspective of their continued evolution. In any case, the treaty institution plainly was not the product of a society that lived in conditions of wild anarchy. Nor was it something invented by the English to shape up the Indians to make them governable. Treaty protocol was of Indian manufacture.[63] Englishmen adapted, not always willingly, to a device that made coexistence possible between two organized societies, interdependent and "ambipendent."

By the end of a successful treaty conference the parties had made a contract that existed in two forms, wampum belts and treaty minutes. Sometimes the English asked the Indian chiefs to subscribe their marks on an especially important contract to validate it indisputably, but the student who considers these documents must preserve some skepticism about that indisputability. The question is always to be asked, Did the

61. Present giving has been treated comprehensively in Wilbur R. Jacobs, *Diplomacy and Indian Gifts: Anglo-French Rivalry along the Ohio and Northwest Frontiers, 1748–1763* (Stanford, Calif., 1950).

62. See, for example, Francis Jennings, "A Vanishing Indian: Francis Parkman Versus His Sources," *Pennsylvania Magazine of History and Biography*, LXXXVII (1963), 306–323.

63. William N. Fenton, "The New York State Wampum Collection: The Case for the Integrity of Cultural Treasures," Am. Phil. Soc., *Procs.*, CXV (1971), 442.

Indians know what they were signing? The answer varies. Procedure usually called for the English to read the document aloud to the Indians before the signing, and they did not always read what was on the paper. The Indians signed for what they had heard. The English held them to what was written.[64]

Treaty contracts could be made for any sort of mutual interest or enterprise, but the bulk of them dealt with military affairs, trade arrangements, and land cessions. In return for untroubled frontiers an English colony would undertake to protect the Indians from disturbance by its own people or other English colonies. It sometimes pledged protection against the French also, but such promises were rarely fulfilled militarily; they usually produced legal maneuver and indignant letters, which the French responded to as they chose. Trade agreements and land cessions were made in complex circumstances that are treated more fully in chapters 6 and 8 of this study.

The net effect of all these agreements was to create a symbiotic political relationship between a colony and the tribes it contracted with regularly—often mentioned as "our" Indians—the colony's government being the stronger, dominant partner. This relationship usually created channels of trade, and it enabled the colony to do things through Indian agency that it otherwise dared not or could not undertake. To see these maneuvers we must look past the issue of Indian versus European to focus upon the ever-present issue of European versus European. European lords aimed at dominion not only over the natives but over each other. At a time when chartered boundaries often overlapped and had rarely been surveyed, lords resorted to the ancient principle that actual possession, if maintained long enough, would sooner or later be recognized as legitimate jurisdiction. Possession might or might not be attained through direct action. If the lord preferred to act indirectly, he might make use of Indians in a variety of ways.

Most obviously, Indians were military manpower. Overtly they might be hired, as individuals or by the tribe, to fight the lord's "lawful" battles; i.e., those taking place when empires were at open war or when colonies declared war on other Indians. Covertly, it seems, Indians were used by one colony to harass another at times when they were formally at peace. So, at least, the colonists believed. Charges abound in the sources, in a round robin of Swede against Dutchman, Dutchman against Englishman, Englishman against Frenchman, and so on. Nor were Englishmen of one colony free of suspicion about other Englishmen in competing colonies.

---

64. Francis Jennings, "The Constitutional Evolution of the Covenant Chain," *ibid.*, 94–95, n. 44; Jennings, "Glory, Death, and Transfiguration," *ibid.*, CXII (1968), 52.

Rarely were Indians instigated to attack Europeans in such covert battles. The basic strategy generally was to hurl the Indians allied with Colony A against other Indians allied to Colony B. Until the conflict, B was understood to have an overlord's claim to the territory of its Indian allies. Upon their defeat, A claimed their territory and persons by right of conquest, thus canceling out B's previous claim and enlarging A's jurisdiction beyond its chartered bounds.

The rights-of-conquest device had numerous variations. A successful one was Connecticut's use of the Mohegan Indians to gain dominion over the territory of the defeated Pequot tribe. Although Massachusetts claimed part of the Pequots' territory and authorized its allied Narragansetts to hunt and fish in the disputed lands, the Mohegans harassed the Narragansetts and occupied the territory. Eventually Connecticut made good its claim.[65] On the other hand, a later attempt by New York to claim Detroit, on the basis of an Iroquois conquest of a bygone time, was ridiculed by the French because the Iroquois had been unable to maintain occupation—had in fact been driven out of their "conquest." Nevertheless, the English crown lawyers argued New York's case in international negotiations, and it has often been repeated in histories.[66]

George Edward Ellis has remarked that "only because Indians were set against Indians, giving opportunity to the whites to find most effective allies in their forest warfare, could the early colonists from Spain, France, or England have been so uniformly the conquerors," adding trenchantly that "if the natives of this continent had been at peace among themselves, and had offered a united resistance to the first feeble bands of European intruders, its occupation would have been long deferred."[67] The truth of his observation is not lessened by his evident desire to make Indians share the moral responsibility for their own conquest. European desire to make use of Indians was matched by the readiness of many Indians to be made use of, and the phenomenon had varied implications.

The reasons for Indians to curry European favor depended on their status. Common to all were the desires to obtain favorable conditions of trade and to ward off European hostility. The very universality of those aspirations led to competition among Indians, not just for favor, but for greater favor than their fellows enjoyed. A most-favored chief might be permitted and aided to make war for his own immediate interests. A subchief or common warrior might be encouraged to break

65. See chaps. 12 and 13, below.
66. Treaty minutes and deed, July 19, 1701, *N.Y. Col. Docs.*, IV, 906, 908–910; Gov. Burnet to Council of Trade and Plantations, Oct. 16, 1721, *ibid.*, V, 633.
67. Ellis, "Indians of Eastern Massachusetts," in Winsor, ed., *Memorial History of Boston*, I, 252.

away from his customary allegiance or to vie for his tribe's paramount chieftainship. The government of his sponsoring European colony could promote his interests by supplying him with goods or weapons, but it had also the often decisive instrument of diplomatic recognition. When a challenging Indian was recognized for treaty purposes as sachem by a colonial government, the challenged leader had to have strong loyalty among his people to keep from being deposed.[68]

Such relationships and processes gave Europeans a measure of control over the internal political institutions of Indian tribes. Since clientage of one sort or another was necessary to the tribe's political survival, its leaders sooner or later became those persons who were most adept at finding effective European patrons. In many situations such Indian leaders seem to have played a role comparable to that of vassalage in feudal Europe. Maintained in power over specified persons and lands by the recognition and patronage of a colonial lordship, their reciprocal obligation was to provide troops and sometimes tribute on demand.

Outright vassalage of this sort did not occur everywhere. Some tribes learned the knack of playing off one colony against another so as to be able to maintain their traditional processes of selecting tribal leadership and keeping it responsible to the tribal membership. Of these the Iroquois Five Nations were the most successful. Paying a hideously costly tuition, the Iroquois learned some of the lessons of realpolitik and managed to make themselves into a sort of intermediate lordship between the English colonies and other Indian tribes.[69] In the end even the Iroquois went down before the relentless drive of Europeans to dispossess and evict. However (to repeat), the cooperation of some Indians was essential to the process of dispossessing all. Indians were the colonists' foremost pioneers politically as well as physically. After a client tribe had subdued the environment or another tribe, colonists would acquire permission to share its territory. More colonists moved in, and at a critical moment the Indians were forced out.

In achieving dominance over Indians, Europeans in North America have had to come to terms with tribal institutions of government from the seventeenth century to the present day. During all this time Euramerican governments have also been evolving, sometimes very rapidly, in structure, function, and rationale. As the military and economic strength of the two societies changed in relation to each other, their devices of accommodation reflected the realities, but Euramerican ra-

68. E.g., see Francis Jennings, "The Delaware Interregnum," *PMHB*, LXXXIX (1965), 174–198.
69. P. A. W. Wallace, *Conrad Weiser*, chap. 6.

tionalizations for exerting power have more and more diverged from the realities.

Colonizing Englishmen maintained themselves as an ethnic caste enforcing colonialism upon the Indians of their vicinity. In this colonial society a fundamental inequality existed between all Indians and even the most lowly Englishman, but so long as the Indians could preserve solidarity within their tribes and a minimum distance from Euramerican communities, they could keep a degree of independence within their caste. The thrust of Euramerican power has been to destroy the tribes and the ever-diminishing degree of personal independence preserved within the tribes, thus converting the Indian person from membership in an unassimilable caste to membership in a social class integrated into Euramerican institutions. In myth, however, the Euramerican pleads "not guilty" to killing tribal government. He could not have committed such a crime, he says, because the victim never lived.

The logic is as simple, faulty, and compelling as that of most other fallacies: Civilization is that quality possessed by people with civil government; civil government is Europe's kind of government; Indians did not have Europe's kind of government; therefore Indians were not civilized. Uncivilized people live in wild anarchy; therefore Indians did not have any government at all. And *therefore* Europeans could not have been doing anything wrong—were in fact performing a noble mission—by bringing government and civilization to the poor savages.

Chapter 8 ✌ THE DEED GAME

During the whole of the "colonial" period
Amerindians and Euramericans lived as neighbors in the long strip of country between the Appalachians and the Atlantic. Necessarily they adjusted to each other's presence by arrangements to share the land, generally in separate communities under separate governments. The ultimate effect of those arrangements was to dispossess the Indians, depriving them simultaneously of government over persons and ownership in land. In legal terms they lost both sovereignty and property.

The distinction must be closely attended to. Conquest by Europeans of other Europeans, though resulting in transfer of sovereignty, did not necessarily imply depriving the vanquished of their property. When, for example, the duke of York conquered New Netherland, he left Dutch landholders in full possession of their own, requiring only that they transfer allegiance from the Netherlands to himself. York's conquest destroyed the political entity of New Netherland, but he recreated former property rights under the laws of New York.[1]

Abstractly property is a legal right derivative from the sovereignty that recognizes and enforces it. When an old sovereign power departs, its laws and institutions go with it. The new sovereignty creates its own laws. Although they may be word for word the same as formerly, their source of authority and enforcement is the new sovereign. So also with property: it does not legally exist until recognized by the new sovereign. Prior possession may be generally accepted as a moral right, but legal sanction is required to create property right.

It follows that the acquisition of landed property by Euramericans from Amerindians was a function of relationships between their respective governments as well as the result of negotiations between buyer and seller. Loose talk of the "conquest" of the Indians has obscured the fact

---

This chapter is adapted from material previously presented as a paper and a journal article. The paper was read at the First Conference on Algonquian Studies, sponsored by the Canadian National Museum of Man, at Saint-Pierre de Wakefield, Quebec, Sept. 13–15, 1968. The article appeared as "Virgin Land and Savage People," *Am. Qtly.*, XXIII (1971), 519–541.
1. John Romeyn Brodhead, *History of the State of New York* (New York, 1859–1871), II, 19, 25, 36.

that Indians relinquished much jurisdictional territory by negotiated voluntary cession appearing in the form of the sale of property.[2]

My phrasing uses terms of European law. Warner F. Gookin has given an Indian formulation: "The 'sale' in the Indian's mind meant the admission of the white man to a Sachem's rights within the area specified."[3] I would add, however, that the European not only was admitted to the rights of the sachem; he was substituted for the sachem in the enjoyment of those rights.

Thus it was not possible for a free Indian, living under his independent tribal government, to sell only his property, unencumbered by jurisdictional ties, to a Euramerican living under a colonial government. Such a transaction was impossible in law. The Euramerican would not accept the sanctions of the tribe; when he bought, he intended to put his land under the jurisdiction of his own colonial government and to secure recognition from *that* government of his property right.[4] Neither was it possible for an Indian to enjoy property under colonial law while he refused to subject his person to colonial jurisdiction. There was a sort of legal valve controlling the conveyance of land so that it always moved from Indian to Englishman and never reversed direction. This situation was peculiar to colonialism; it did not apply between the subjects of different European nations. A Frenchman, for instance, might buy an English estate while still preserving his French nationality and allegiance, and his property right would be recognized and protected by English law.

The Indian tribe gave up jurisdiction simultaneously as the Indian landlord quitted his property (whatever that may have been).[5] From the Indian side the transaction was therefore absolute and final unless an easement had been reserved, as frequently happened, to permit the Indian grantor to hunt and fish and perhaps to maintain a residence and

2. For theory consistent with this thesis, see the superb study of A. Irving Hallowell, "The Nature and Function of Property as a Social Institution," *Culture and Experience* (Philadelphia, 1955), 236–249; and Thomas E. Davitt, *The Basic Values in Law: A Study of the Ethico-legal Implications of Psychology and Anthropology*, Am. Phil. Soc., *Trans.*, N.S., LVIII, pt. v (1968), 86–96.

3. Warner F. Gookin, "Indian Deeds on the Vineyard," *Bulletin of Mass. Archaeol. Soc.*, XIII (Jan. 1952), 7.

4. "The law of the place where real estate is situated (*lex loci rei sitae*) governs its tenure and transfer.... The *lex loci rei sitae* determines what is to be considered real estate." *Encyclopaedia Britannica*, 11th ed., s.v. "real property."

5. Theoretically such a transaction is incompatible with the theses of the frontier historian Frederick Jackson Turner, who did not recognize political boundaries between colonial and tribal jurisdictions. Turner did write of a "frontier of military defense" in the latter part of the 17th century, attributing it to "European backers" of "the Indians," without distinguishing between one tribe and another. Turner, "The First Official Frontier of the Massachusetts Bay," in *Frontier in American History*, 41.

cultivate a garden in one corner of his former estate. But what the English purchaser got depended on his status. It was impossible for a private person to acquire governmental jurisdiction by purchase, and there could be no property where there was no jurisdiction to sanction it. The land covered by a deed to a private person therefore legally became no-man's-land until an English government assumed jurisdiction. The bulk of Indian territory was conveyed in large cessions to purchasing or conquering governments, which then parceled out the land by means of patents of property to private individuals. Strictly speaking, then, an Indian "deed" was not a deed at all as that term is understood in Anglo-American law. When it was written in favor of an English government it was a deed of cession, and when it was written in favor of a private person it was a quitclaim rather than a conveyance.[6]

These complicated readjustments often appear in highly ambiguous forms, and each transaction must be interpreted according to the circumstances then prevailing. Sooner or later, all colonial governments outlawed the purchase of Indian land by private persons, because the practice had led to circumvention of laws regarding the distribution of property.[7] Privately purchased "Indian titles" frequently conflicted with governmental intentions and also led to endless litigation over purchase of fraudulent titles.[8] At certain times and places private purchases of the same land were made by persons subject to different colonial governments, whereupon their property claims became the basis for competition over jurisdiction.[9] As Joseph Henry Smith has remarked, the crown came to recognize "some sort of status in the tribes ... for the safeguard of the crown's own property rights."[10]

6. William Penn referred to Indian rights as the "Indian incumbrance," and he pledged to eliminate it so as to guarantee good title to his patentees. "Some Account of Pennsilvania," in Myers, ed., Narratives of Early Pennsylvania, 208.

7. See Clarence White Rife, "Land Tenure in New Netherland," Essays in Colonial History Presented to Charles McLean Andrews by His Students (New Haven, Conn., 1931), 49–50.

8. The most extensively prolonged wrangle over Indian title was probably the case of the Mohegan Indians v. Connecticut. Its legal implications were so profound that upon its appeal to the Privy Council it was characterized as "the greatest cause that ever was heard at the Council Board." J. H. Smith, Appeals to the Privy Council, 422–442, quote at 418. A substantial body of source manuscripts are in the Beinecke Rare Book and Manuscript Library of Yale University, cataloged as "The Mohegan Indian Case," Z117/0047.

9. See Richard S. Dunn, "John Winthrop, Jr., and the Narragansett Country," WMQ, 3d Ser., XIII (1956), 68–86.

10. J. H. Smith, Appeals to the Privy Council, 417. The issue of crown-recognized native land rights is still alive in the courts of successor states to former British colonies other than in the U.S. Correspondents have called my attention to recent cases in Australia and Canada. See Geoffrey Lester and Graham Parker, "Land Rights: The Australian Aborigines Have Lost a Legal Battle, But...," Alberta Law Review, XI (1973), 189–237; Kenneth M. Narvey, "The Royal Proclamation

It took some while for all these possibilities to appear in practice. Each colony experimented in its own way and at its own rate of progress. In the earliest years of English colonization, purchases from Indians were mere expedients without valid legal significance in English eyes. When John Smith and other Virginians gave goods for land, they were merely pacifying the natives. Thus they did not bother to make records of the transactions, because the records would have served no useful purpose.[11] The Virginians' problem with the natives was only to get them to remove with the least possible trouble. They did not get property from the natives; they got it from the Virginia Company.

When the Pilgrims landed in New Plymouth, their problem appeared in a different form, because they had no charter and therefore no legally sanctioned claim to territory. They made a mutual assistance pact with the Wampanoag Indians, which they chose to regard as a deed of cession legitimizing their seizure of unspecified acreage.[12] The Wampanoags tolerated their intrusion as a matter of political realism. The land in question had no Indian residents, having been depopulated by an exterminating epidemic, and the weakened tribe was not eager to launch itself against English weaponry. Plymouth also offered protection for the Wampanoags against the encroachments of the nearby Narragansett tribe. Although this protection quickly established a patron-client relationship, the Wampanoags retained formal independence until 1671.[13] In the meantime New Plymouth adopted the practice of territorial purchase under circumstances to be discussed below.

Two events transformed Euramerican attitudes and practices in confusingly opposed ways. As already noticed in chapter 5, the Indian rising of 1622 in Virginia helped inspire rationalizations about virgin land, free for the taking. In contrast, the Dutch West India Company entered colonial competition and, for its own reasons, decided to recognize Indian jurisdictions at just the historical moment that the English were determining to ignore them. The Dutch company had been chartered as a commercial monopoly with semisovereign powers but without a grant of territory.[14] It could not appeal to papal donation or

of 7 October 1763, the Common Law, and Native Rights to Land within the Territory Granted to the Hudson's Bay Company," *Saskatchewan Law Review*, XXXVIII (1974), 123–133. My thanks to Geoffrey Lester and Imre Sutton.

11. John Smith left unrecorded the transaction by which he exchanged Henry Spelman for an Indian town called Powhatan. Arber and Bradley, eds., *Travels and Works of Smith*, I, cii.

12. Treaty text: Bradford, *Of Plymouth Plantation*, ed. Morison, 80–81.

13. Minutes, Sept. 13, 1671, and treaty, Sept. 29, 1671, in Nathaniel B. Shurtleff and David Pulsifer, eds., *Records of the Colony of New Plymouth in New England* (Boston, 1855–1861), V, 77, 79, hereafter cited as *Recs. of Plymouth*.

14. Text of charter in A. J. F. van Laer, trans. and ed., *Van Rensselaer Bowier Manuscripts: Being the Letters of Kiliaen Van Rensselaer, 1630–1643, and Other*

first discovery to support its jurisdictional claims, and it proposed to colonize in lands where England had established prior claims. Like New Plymouth, the Dutch were obliged to create a new rationalization to validate their presence.

Out of prior experience in competition with England halfway around the world, the Dutch devised a strategy. In the Spice Islands of the East Indies, they and the English had invoked against each other the vague law-of-nations doctrines that heathens and their territories belonged by right to that Christian prince whose subjects had made first discovery or conquest. In practice these doctrines had proved inconclusive. In 1580 the English government had propounded "possession" instead of just "discovery" as the basis of Christian right, and in 1619 the East Indies companies of England and the Netherlands temporarily abated their conflict in the Moluccas by stipulating that each should keep the areas it already possessed.[15] The Dutch perceived possibilities in this formula: "possession" did not have to coincide fully with habitation. A few Dutchmen living in one town could "possess" the region or country surrounding the town. Legal possession could be created out of material such as natural rights by the simple process of manufacturing legal forms. Therefore the Dutch West India Company instructed its resident director of New Netherland in 1625 that Indian claims to land should be extinguished by persuasion or purchase, "a contract being made thereof and signed by them [the Indians] in their manner, *since such contracts upon other occasions may be very useful to the Company*."[16] The point is unmistakable, because the legitimacy of a contract in Indian eyes did not depend on its being in written form. The "other occasions" foreseen by the Dutch were their approaching clashes in America with other European—especially English—claimants. When the Dutch became embroiled in the Delaware and Connecticut valleys with Swedes and assorted English provincials, they pulled out their deeds.[17]

Documents Relating to the Colony of Rensselaerswyck, New York State Library, *90th Annual Report*, II (Albany, N. Y., 1908), 86–125.

15. A. L. Rowse, *The Elizabethans and America* (New York, 1959), 7, 31–32; Masselman, *Cradle of Colonialism*, 406–407.

16. Instructions for Willem Verhulst, Jan. 1625, in A. J. F. van Laer, trans. and ed., *Documents Relating to New Netherland, 1624–1626, in the Henry E. Huntington Library* (San Marino, Calif., 1924), 51–52 (emphasis added). See also Article 26, Charter of Freedoms and Exemptions of the Netherlands West Indian Company, June 7, 1629, in van Laer, trans. and ed., *Van Rensselaer Bowier Manuscripts*, 151.

17. C. A. Weslager, in collaboration with A. R. Dunlap, *Dutch Explorers, Traders and Settlers in the Delaware Valley, 1609–1664* (Philadelphia, 1961), 135–157. Even while the Dutch exploited the deed device, they held amused contempt for English legalism. In 1663 Peter Stuyvesant advised the West India Company directors to get an "Acte, Commission, Patent or Letter, howsoever

The issue actually arose first in Europe early in 1632 when port officials of Plymouth, England, seized the Dutch ship *Eendracht* while it sheltered in their harbor with a rich cargo of furs from New Netherland. Ambassadors from the Dutch States General immediately protested the seizure on the formal grounds that no potentate could "prevent the subjects of another to trade in countries whereof his people have not taken, nor obtained actual possession from the right owners, either by contract or purchase." This was especially true in the instant case, they said, when Dutch subjects, rather than Englishmen, had "acquired the property, partly by confederation with the owners of the lands, and partly by purchase."[18] To this argument the English crown entered a flat denial that Indians could be considered legal possessors of lands, having a bona fide right "to dispose of them either by sale or donation," and the wrangle went on.[19] But the Dutch had taken the high ground, and subsequent events demonstrated that their technical advantage had impressed their equally legalistic English adversaries. English colonials began to strengthen their territorial claims by acquiring written Indian deeds like the Dutchmen's, and in due course they adapted and adopted the Dutch rationale.

But not everywhere, all at once. New Plymouth, in its charterless state, was quick to seize on the device. Massachusetts Bay, however, had been founded in 1630 with a charter of ample authority for jurisdiction over a bounded grant of territory, and so its leaders made no move to buy from Indians until opportunity tempted them beyond chartered bounds.

Plymouth traders competed with the Dutch at various points, struggling to keep from being overwhelmed by the Dutch commercial colossus. Each party attempted to build permanent trading posts at key points and to establish regular trading relationships with the surrounding Indians. One such key point lay in the upper Connecticut Valley where canoe-borne peltry from the northern interior could be intercepted before it got within the reach of coastwise traders. Dutchmen and Englishmen alike understood the strategic value of controlling the Connecticut trade. On June 8, 1633, the New Netherland Dutch purchased a tract of land for a trading post where Hartford, Connecticut, now stands. They bought from the grand sachem of the

---

called" to establish Dutch jurisdiction over Long Island because, "were this sealed with their High Mightinesses' Great Seal, at which an Englishman commonly gapes as at an idol ... it would, in our opinion, help matters somewhat." *N.Y. Col. Docs.*, II, 488.

18. *N.Y. Col. Docs.*, I, 45–50; quote from West India Company to States General, May 5, 1632, *ibid.*, 52.

19. Answer to the Remonstrance of the Dutch Ambassadors, ca. May 23, 1632, *ibid.*, 58.

Pequot Indians with the consent of the Pequots' tributaries resident at the place. In so doing, the Dutch created the first deed of sale of Indian territory in the region of lower New England. Plymouth's traders, having no other weapons, fought back with the Dutchmen's own.[20]

Breaking with their own nonpurchasing precedents, Plymouth's traders acknowledged Indian tenure rights in principle in order to turn the principle against the Dutch. They neatly accomplished this feat by recognizing and purchasing the right of a different Indian than the one from whom the Dutch had bought—an Indian who had earlier been defeated in battle by the Pequots and had been driven from his former territory. Plymouth's men, although strong advocates of the rights of conquest when it suited their purposes, now contended that their client Indian had not lost his true rights through the Pequot conquest and solemnly set up their own deed against the Dutch deed.[21] Similar transactions later occurred in a wide variety of circumstances, but one general principle underlay them all: Euramericans competing for Indian lands—whether governments, companies, or individuals—legitimized their claims by recognizing or inventing whatever purported rights might be severally available to them.[22]

Massachusetts Bay did not soon follow Plymouth's example in pur-

---

20. Deed, June 8, 1633, *ibid.*, II, 139–140. Addendum: After this book had been set in type, my attention was called by Dr. Alvin H. Morrison (to whom thanks) to an Indian deed of 1625 in Maine. It purports to convey a large territory at Pemaquid from sagamores Samoset and Unongoit to colonist John Brown of New Harbor. Printing schedules prevent my investigating further before publication, but the deed appears spurious on its face because supposedly the Englishman paid in skins to the Indians—a highly unlikely possibility. As Dr. Morrison comments, the deed "is remarkably complex for being the first of its kind." If valid, the deed might be an exception to some of my remarks herein, but it would not disturb the general thesis; the cited evidence for that is highly explicit and positive. See Alvin Hamblen Morrison, "Dawnland Decisions: Seventeenth-Century Wabanaki Leaders and Their Responses to the Differential Contact Stimuli in the Overlap Area of New France and New England" (Ph.D. diss., University of New York at Buffalo, 1974), 105–106, and n. 29, pp. 150–151; Henry S. Burrage, *The Beginnings of Colonial Maine, 1602–1658* (Portland, Me., 1914), 177–178.

21. Edward Winslow to John Winthrop, Sr., Apr. 6, 1644, in *New England Historical and Genealogical Register*, XXIX (1875), 239; minutes, Apr. 1653, Pulsifer, ed., *Acts of United Colonies*, II, 16.

22. See C. A. Weslager, *The English on the Delaware, 1610–1682* (New Brunswick, N.J., 1967); Weslager and Dunlap, *Dutch Explorers in the Delaware Valley*; Gary B. Nash, "The Quest for the Susquehanna Valley: New York, Pennsylvania, and the Seventeenth-Century Fur Trade," *New York History*, XLVIII (1967), 3–27. See also the following articles by Jennings: "Glory, Death, and Transfiguration," Am. Phil. Soc., *Procs.*, CXII (1968), 15–53; "Constitutional Evolution of the Covenant Chain," *ibid.*, CXV (1971), 88–96; "Delaware Interregnum," *PMHB*, LXXXIX (1965), 174–198; "Incident at Tulpehocken," *Pa. Hist.*, XXXV (1968), 335–355; and "The Scandalous Indian Policy of William Penn's Sons: Deeds and Documents of the Walking Purchase," *ibid.*, XXXVII (1970), 19–39.

chasing Indian land.[23] Although Massachusetts's parent company in England had issued instructions in 1629 for the colonists to make "reasonable composition" with the native landowners so as to be free of any "scruple of intrusion," this directive was not carried out. John Endecott, who received the instruction at Salem, showed no interest in Indian purchases. His replacement as governor in 1630 was John Winthrop, a lawyer who held views about Indian property rights that were thoroughly inconsistent with the company's instruction, and Winthrop escaped the authority of the English company's directors by taking the colony's royal patent to America.[24]

Before migrating, Winthrop had adopted Samuel Purchas's dictum about the virginity of American land. Lawyer that he was, Winthrop declared that most land in America was *vacuum domicilium*—i.e., legally "waste"—because the Indians had not "subdued" it by methods recognized in English law and therefore had no "natural" right to it; the alternative of "civil" right was impossible for Indians because they did not have civil government. In operational terms civil government meant European government.[25]

Morally and pragmatically Winthrop's Puritans were obliged to leave individual Indians in possession of tracts actually under tillage, for such small plots of cultivated land obviously qualified as "subdued," but legally they recognized as real property only those lands whose claimants could show deeds from grants made by the Massachusetts Bay Company. Inherent in this doctrine was the notion that no Indian government was sovereign over any domain claimed by the English crown, and therefore no legal sanction could exist for Indian tenure of real estate except as derived, directly or indirectly, from the crown. Since the Puritan magistrates interpreted their royal patent as having delegated

23. July 12, 1633, Winthrop, *History*, ed. Savage, I, 105 and ed. n.; Bradford, *Of Plymouth Plantation*, ed. Morison, 257–259 (Morison's notes here are erroneous). See also Bernard Bailyn, *The New England Merchants in the Seventeenth Century* (Cambridge, Mass., 1955), 23–26; McIlwain, "Introduction," in Wraxall, *Abridgment*, xxxi.

24. Letters dated Apr. 17 and May 28, 1629, *Recs. of Mass.*, 394–400; Frances Rose-Troup, *The Massachusetts Bay Company and Its Predecessors* (New York, 1930), chap. 9.

A bibliographic note: This English historian, who worked directly with the manuscripts of the Massachusetts Bay Company, found in them "inserted passages, usually in different hands," and complained of editor Nathaniel B. Shurtleff's practices in editing them for publication in the *Recs. of Mass*. Her suggestion for "competent" editing of them remains unfinished business. Rose-Troup, *Massachusetts Bay Company*, vii. An even sharper criticism of Shurtleff had been made 40 years earlier by a student who found that Shurtleff had altered texts in publishing them. His comments have also been ignored. William H. Whitmore, ed., *The Colonial Laws of Massachusetts. Reprinted from the Edition of 1660, with the Supplements to 1672* (Boston, 1889), viii–x.

25. See chaps. 5 and 7, below.

the crown's rights and powers to themselves, their doctrine meant in practice that there could be no property in the territorial jurisdiction of Massachusetts except what Massachusetts law created.[26] Regardless of habitation by living persons, Indian lands were *legally* vacant.

Winthrop's logic chopping cut more than one way. In creating a magisterial monopoly on the creation of property in land, he not only denied Indian rights but also forestalled the possibility of private colonists creating property for themselves out of Indian rights. This was a living issue in early Massachusetts, as will be shown in Part II of this study.

Lesser men than Winthrop interpreted Indian sanctions over the land quite differently. Early seventeenth-century English observers had quickly concluded that New England's Indians held land among themselves under customs not very different from the relationships prescribed by English law and custom. Explicit testimony exists for the Wampanoag, Narragansett, and Mohegan "nations," and circumstantial evidence implies like customs among the Massachuset and Pequot "nations," to the following effect. The grand sachem of each Indian nation held a jurisdictional right, like that of eminent domain, over all the territory of the nation. Subordinate sachems held property rights in hunting tracts and fishing stations within the national territory. Early data indicate that cropland was held as commons, the sachem assigning annually the land to be tilled by each family; however, as native institutions adjusted to English practices, croplands seem to have become fixed in the possession of their cultivators.[27]

Epidemics preceding and accompanying English colonization catastrophically reduced Indian populations without effecting concomitant reduction of customary rights and claims. Property rights were bequeathed to surviving heirs, and the jurisdictional rights of the grand sachems remained theoretically intact. The land that was *vacuum domicilium*, or "waste," in English eyes was completely covered by In-

26. May 14, 1634, *Recs. of Mass.*, I, 117.

27. Winslow, *Good Newes*, in Young, ed., *Chronicles of Pilgrims*, 361–363; Williams, *Key*, ed. Trumbull, in Narragansett Club, *Pubs.*, I, 120–180; Cotton, *Reply to Mr. Williams*, ed. Diman, *ibid.*, II, 44–48. For ethnohistorical background to interpret these sources, see the references in n. 11, chap. 5.

To these and the following remarks about Indian property holding, I must add a prompt disclaimer: these comments are not intended to describe the aboriginal societies before European invasion. The evidence cited was written by Europeans as their observations during the macrocontact period. Many profound changes occurred during a historically brief period of time, and the validity of contemporary observations was a function of the situations existing when the observations were made. I thankfully relinquish to experts in ethnology the "upstream" interpretation of such data to draw inferences about the precontact era. For a discussion of "upstreaming," see William N. Fenton, "Collecting Materials for a Political History of the Six Nations," Am. Phil. Soc., *Procs.*, XCIII (1949), 233–238.

dians with property and jurisdictional rights. Generally when English-men were willing to recognize these customary rights, Indians were willing enough to sell functionally surplus lands. Some students have doubted that Indians understood how they were dispossessing themselves by sale of land to Europeans. Perhaps that was so in the earliest transactions, but Indian sophistication grew rapidly. European power soon drove home the lesson that a land sale involved full and final alienation of right.

A conveyance of land to an Englishman necessarily implied its removal from the domain governed by the tribe's paramount sachem. For such a transaction to be legitimate in Indian eyes it had to be approved by the grand sachem, just as European cessions of territory from one sovereignty to another could only be legitimized by the sovereign power itself. The proper procedure, therefore, was for English purchases from free Indians to be made directly from their grand sachem, with compensation being given also to the particular Indian who had held personal tenure.

Evidence for these inferences exists in both personal and official sources. Roger Williams's comment is deservedly well known: "The law and tenor of the natives, (I take it) in all New England and America, viz.: that the inferior Sachems and subjects shall plant and remove at the pleasure of the highest and supreme Sachems." Less famous than Williams, Francis Brinley arrived in America via Newport in 1652 and took up residence in the midst of what he estimated to be thirty thousand Indians. He remarked: "To these [Chief] Sachems belongs the power of disposall of Lands, to which their people Subject themselves, as a power due to them, Some gratuity being usually bestowed upon the possessors by the Purchasers to make them the more free to remove and depart." The formula of the deed to Shawomet, Rhode Island, dated January 12, 1643, is expressed as the chief sachem selling "with the Free and joint consent of the present inhabitants, being natives." The pattern outlined by these remarks is confirmed by two quite diverse official agencies—the Royal Commissioners of Charles II and the General Court of New Plymouth.[28]

Such data seem to lend credence to the often-repeated assertion that all of New England's territory was purchased at one time or another

---

28. Williams to Mass. General Court, May 12, 1656, Bartlett, ed., *Letters of Williams,* Narragansett Club, *Pubs.,* VI, 300—301; Brinley, "Brief Narrative," R.-I. Hist. Soc., *Pubs.,* VIII (1900), 73. Deed: Winthrop, *History,* ed. Savage, II, 121, ed. n.; commissioners: "Cartwright's Answer to the Massachusetts Narrative of Transactions with the Royal Commissioners," Jan. 5, 1666, "The Clarendon Papers," N.-Y. Hist. Soc., *Colls.,* Publication Fund Series, *1869* (New York, 1870), 90–91; minutes, Sept. 20, 1672, *Recs. of Plymouth,* V, 102. Cf. this last ref. to King Philip's treaty stipulation, Sept. 29, 1671, clause 6, *ibid.,* 79.

from Indian landholders. Regardless of the merits of that claim in its fullness, the matter now at issue is exactly when the purported transactions are supposed to have occurred. No deeds exist today for any purchases before the 1633 Plymouth acquisition on the Connecticut, simply because none were written. Numerous extant deeds from post-1633 purport to be "confirmations" of transactions supposed to have occurred at earlier dates, but, closely examined, each of these turns into an effort to meet a later political crisis.[29] Most notably, Sir Edmund Andros's assumption of government over the Dominion of New England in 1686 sent people scurrying for these "confirmations." George Edward Ellis has tartly suggested that the deed to Boston's site "was shrewdly contrived by the astute authorities of the town, as they were trembling over the royal challenging of their Colony Charter, the fall of which might render worthless all grants of parcels of territory that depended upon legislation under it."[30]

John Winthrop's behavior has provided one source of confusion about the interpretation of New England's Indian deeds. Although Winthrop never renounced his doctrine of *vacuum domicilium* or explicated an alternative, in 1642 he bought 1,260 Indian-held acres on the Concord River, being careful to take and register a deed for them. Few acres have ever been bought more cheaply—Winthrop paid only his proportion of a joint purchase price amounting to about one pound in money—but the point is that he acted in direct contradiction to his earlier-stated principle.[31] Winthrop's change of heart is all the more curious because, when in the mid-1630s the principle had been challenged by dissenters, he had reaffirmed it vigorously. To see how and why he later abandoned the principle requires close attention to a series of detailed events.

The Indian-right principle first showed itself in Massachusetts as a threat not only to Winthrop's ideas but to the power of the whole ruling oligarchy among whom Winthrop stood out. The source of this danger lay in the town of Salem, where both leaders and commonalty struggled against the assumption of superior jurisdiction by the magistrates at Boston.[32]

29. See Jennings, "Virgin Land," *Am. Qtly.*, XXIII (1971), 526–528. Reference is to lower New England. See n. 20 above.

30. Ellis, "Indians of Eastern Massachusetts," in Winsor, ed., *Memorial History of Boston*, I, 250; Richard S. Dunn, *Puritans and Yankees: The Winthrop Dynasty of New England, 1630–1717* (Princeton, N.J., 1962), 248. See also Theodore B. Lewis, "Land Speculation and the Dudley Council of 1686," *WMQ*, 3d Ser., XXXI (1974), 255–272.

31. Deed, June 20, 1642, *Suffolk Deeds*, I (Boston, 1880), 34. This is the first Indian deed officially reported in the registry. Earlier transactions, not so recorded, are mentioned in the General Court minutes (*Recs. of Mass.*).

32. The orthodox interpretation of this famous event was sketched by William Hubbard in *A General History of New England* ... (Mass. Hist. Soc., *Colls.*, 2d

The situation is best understood in the perspective of a few years. The community of Salem consisted of a mixed lot of people who had come to America at various times preceding Winthrop's great fleet of 1630 and who were therefore self-consciously "Old Planters." Besides the feeling of privilege and status naturally deriving from such identification, these Old Planters held other peculiar distinctions. Among them were Church of England adherents faithful to the very doctrines regarded as odious by the Puritans. Even the dissenters at Salem differed from the dissenters who had come with Winthrop: the Salem church was established on such purely Separatist principles that Roger Williams could accept the post of minister there after having rejected membership in the Boston church. Williams first went to Salem, however, only as an assistant to the minister, and he was not long permitted to stay there. Pressure from Governor Winthrop and his associates achieved Williams's removal to Plymouth, outside Massachusetts's jurisdiction. Besides its religious distinctiveness, Salem also preserved remembrance of its political independence under Governor John Endecott prior to Winthrop's arrival and his supersession of Endecott. The demoted Endecott held aloof from the newcomers. Salem sought to maintain as much autonomy as possible under the new regime, clinging to the name "General Court" for its own town meeting.[33]

For a time Salem's effort to go its own way was aided by members of other towns, all seeking to wrest some degree of autonomy from the supreme power asserted by the magistrates at Boston. These rebels shared the demand that each town control the allotment of land to its own inhabitants.[34] Implied in this demand, also, was the claim that each should

Ser., V-VI [Boston, 1815]), I, 166, 202-213; hereafter cited as Hubbard, *History of New England*. Hubbard's view has been translated into modern idiom by Edmund S. Morgan in *The Puritan Dilemma: The Story of John Winthrop* (Boston, 1958), chap. 9. In this view Salem's Roger Williams was a fanatic who "bewitched" his followers (Hubbard) or "charmed" them (Morgan, p. 119), but was frustrated by the steady watchfulness of the Massachusetts magistrates. Samuel Hugh Brockunier differed from this view to present Williams as a champion of dissenters' rights and a precursor of democracy; but Brockunier agreed in making Williams the charismatic leader of Salem. *The Irrepressible Democrat: Roger Williams* (New York, 1940), chaps. 4-6. In my own interpretation Williams was the spokesman for, rather than the creator of, the dissent at Salem.

33. Andrews, *Colonial Period*, I, 351-354, 378-381, 434-435; Lawrence Shaw Mayo, *John Endecott* (Cambridge, Mass., 1936), 64-67; Joseph B. Felt, "Who Was the First Governor of Massachusetts?" Essex Institute, *Historical Collections*, 1st Ser., V (1863), 73-84; William P. Upham, ed., "Town Records of Salem, 1634-1659," *ibid.*, 2d Ser., I (1869), 7, 16.

34. Rutman, *Winthrop's Boston*, 44-47, 61-67. That the dispute was about authority in general rather than narrowly limited to land is further shown by the withholding by Salem and Saugus of payment of their levies (imposed by the General Court) for construction of the fort at Boston. Nov. 1633, Winthrop, *History*, ed. Savage, I, 117-118.

have the power to enlarge its bounds of its own volition. The magistrates yielded so far as to permit towns to control distribution of lands within their established limits but held fast to their final authority to set the territorial limits. Their authority, said the magistrates, was vested in their central government by its royal patent, which had granted the soil of Massachusetts Bay. It was this final line of defense of magisterial prerogative that Roger Williams assaulted when he wrote a treatise, while still at Plymouth, affirming that the royal patent could not lawfully convey rights to the soil. Title to the land, said Williams, rested in the aboriginal owners, the Indians, and could be lawfully acquired only by purchase from them.[35] What seemed to turn this essentially legal argument into a theological dispute was Williams's characteristic designation of the magistrates' reliance on their patent as sinful. We do not know what else Williams said in his "large treatise," but his argument plainly implied that any town or any person could go directly to the Indians to buy any quantity of land without prior authority from king or magistrate; in fact, he had done just that, albeit discreetly outside the chartered limits of Massachusetts.[36]

In August 1633 Williams returned to Salem to resume his assistance to the town's minister, much to the disturbance of the magistrates.[37] The action represented defiance on two counts: though Williams's position was not a formal office of government, his acceptance by the church was a reversal of Salem's previous compliance with the magistrates' wishes in regard to Williams's church status, and it also seemed to constitute an endorsement of his views opposing the magistrates' patent-derived authority.[38] If Williams were to be allowed to preach as the Word of God that the very foundation of the magistrates' authority was invalid, how long could it be before Salem seceded entirely to set itself up in competition with the Bay? The General Court responded with a series of new laws, the first of which banned the purchase of Indian lands *except* when such purchase had the Court's prior approval.[39]

The General Court also ordered a survey and registry of all lands and meaningfully stipulated that no agency other than itself might "dispose of land, viz., to give and confirm proprietyes." Joined to the latter order was the enactment of an oath to be required of all free men that

35. Dec. 27, 1633, Winthrop, *History*, ed. Savage, I, 122.
36. "Confirmatory Deed of Roger Williams and his wife . . . ," Dec. 20, 1661, in John Russell Bartlett, ed., *Records of the Colony of Rhode Island and Providence Plantations, in New England* (Providence, R.I., 1856–1865), I, 22–25, hereafter cited as *Recs. of R.I.*
37. Mayo, *John Endecott*, 79–81.
38. For comment on Endecott's support of Williams, see Jennings, "Virgin Land," *Am. Qtly.* XXIII (1971), 534n.
39. Minutes, Mar. 4, 1634 (Old Style 1633), *Recs. of Mass.*, I, 112.

in effect transferred allegiance from the English crown to the government of Massachusetts Bay.[40] What has been less noticed by historians is that the oath also destroyed all possibility of transcendent allegiance to autonomous towns within the territory claimed by Massachusetts.

Sorting out parties and sides in the confusion is not easy, but it seems clear that Salem and Roger Williams were steadily losing ground, both in metaphor and in actuality. Salem had claimed jurisdiction over the tract of territory called Marblehead Neck, which the General Court refused to recognize. In May 1635 the Court ordered a new "Plantation" and required Salem's inhabitants to sell their Marblehead lands to the new planters at cost.[41] Williams then rose in Salem's pulpit to denounce the authorities, "teaching publickly against the king's patent" and against the magistrates' "great sin in claiming right thereby to this country."[42] The General Court responded in September 1635 by appointing a commission "to sett out the bounds of all townes not yet sett out, or in difference betwixte any towne, provided that the committees of those townes where the difference is shall have noe vote in that particular," and Salem's claim to Marblehead was overborne.[43] It is also noteworthy that Salem's "General Court" was here casually reduced to the rank of a "committee."

Tension mounted as Williams and many of his supporters refused the Bay government's oath of allegiance and pitted Salem church against the doctrine that magistrates should have power to punish heresy. In the midst of the quarrels Salem church formally elevated Williams from his assistantship to the post of minister. Magistrates and orthodox clerics alike were outraged by the town that wanted autonomy and the minister who wanted liberty. Clergy thundered their wrath and called it God's, thus defining Williams as the sort of heretic that magistrates had power to punish. Salem's deputies were expelled from the General Court, and Williams was brought to trial and sentenced to banishment explicitly because he had "broached and dyvulged dyvers newe and dangerous opinions, against the aucthoritie of magistrates, as also writt lettres of defamation, both of the magistrates and church *here* . . . and yet maineteineth the same without retraction."[44] As the Reverend William Hubbard would later remark, "Mr. Williams did lay his axe at the very

40. Minutes, Apr. 1 and May 14, 1634, *ibid.*, 116–117.

41. Joseph B. Felt, *Annals of Salem*, 2d ed. (Salem, Mass., 1845–1849), I, 206; William Bentley, "A Description and History of Salem," Mass. Hist. Soc., *Colls.*, 1st Ser., VI (Boston, 1800), 248. See also the controversy over Bentley's article, *ibid.*, VII (1801), iii–v, VIII (1802), 1–4.

42. Nov. 27, 1634, Winthrop, *History*, ed. Savage, I, 151.

43. Minutes, Sept. 3, 1634, *Recs. of Mass.*, I, 125.

44. Brockunier, *Irrepressible Democrat*, chaps. 5, 6; minutes, Sept. 3, 1635, *Recs. of Mass.*, I, 160–161. I have italicized one word to show the error of the view that Williams was banished for opposing the authority of the king.

root of the magistratical power in matters of the first table [i.e., the first four of the Ten Commandments]."[45]

In the historical controversy that has been waged over precisely which issue dominated the magistrates' minds, S. H. Brockunier's judgment seems best: "Heresy and sedition in Massachusetts were inextricably joined."[46] For present purposes it may be observed that, despite the gravity of other charges, much of the trial court's time was spent on Williams's ideas about Indian rights. Williams reaffirmed his belief that it was "a National sinne" to claim right to Indian lands by virtue of the royal patent "and a Nationall duty to renounce the Patent," which, the magistrates thought, "to have done, had subverted the fundamentall State and Government of the Countrey."[47] They were correct, of course. Only a quite different sort of government could have functioned on Williams's principles.

In the management of power these magistrates were wholly rational. Having expelled Williams and having briefly punished John Endecott for abetting him, they accepted Salem's and Endecott's submissions. Salem's deputies were restored to the General Court, and in March 1636, Salem, meek and penitent, even received the Marblehead lands that had been denied to Salem, proud and challenging—though perhaps not as much land as had been claimed.[48] There was no longer any question about who held final authority; Salem had obtained that land only on the terms of the General Court. A few years later, when tension again mounted, the Court again asserted its ascendancy. In March 1640 Salem appointed a "Mr. Sharpe" to keep the records of town lands, but in October the General Court overrode the town by installing Winthrop's brother-in-law Emanuel Downing in that office. The nature of the controversy is suggested by the fact that the last entries of Elder Sharpe, who had been one of Roger Williams's strongest supporters, are missing from the record. Downing's substitutions for them provided that Marblehead's inhabitants could have only such lands "as have not been formerly granted to other men," leaving no doubt of the Court's revocation of at least some of the claims of the Salem-Marblehead people.[49]

No Indian purchase sullied the Court's supreme prerogative at the

---

45. Hubbard, *History of New England*, I, 166.

46. Brockunier, *Irrepressible Democrat*, 71.

47. Roger Williams, *Mr. Cottons Letter Lately Printed, Examined, and Answered* (1644), ed. Reuben Aldridge Guild, in Narragansett Club, *Pubs.*, I (Providence, R.I., 1866), 324–325; Cotton, *Reply to Williams*, ed. Diman, *ibid.*, II, 46–47.

48. Brockunier, *Irrepressible Democrat*, 82; *Recs. of Mass.*, I, 165.

49. Upham, ed., "Town Records of Salem," Essex Inst., *Hist. Colls.*, 2d Ser., I, 5, 101, 111. Salem's leaders continued afterwards in an "Essex County clique" antagonistic to the Bostonians. See Ronald D. Cohen, "New England and New France, 1632–1651: External Relations and Internal Disagreements among the Puritans," Essex Inst., *Hist. Colls.*, CVIII (1972), 252–271.

time, and none was made until half a century later when Massachusetts Bay was incorporated into the Dominion of New England. The extinction then of the old government raised a specter of possible invalidation of land titles acquired irregularly, and Salem men hastened to buttress their possessions with an Indian quitclaim. Dated October 11, 1686, this stipulates on the part of its Indian sellers that *"untill the ensealing and delivery of these presents,* they [the Indians] and their ancestors were the true, sole and lawfull owners of all the afore bargained premises, and were lawfully seized of and in the same, and every part thereof in their own proper right."[50] Thus Salem fended off a review of its land titles by the new royal governor, Sir Edmund Andros, whose known rule was that title could not be fully valid while Indian claims existed.

But this all happened long after Roger Williams's tilt with the Massachusetts General Court. In the 1630s the magistrates alternated between assertions of principle and acts of expedience. By overriding Salem they temporarily silenced arguments that Indian purchases were legally prerequisite to good land titles, but they acted to forestall future difficulties of a like nature by ordering a series of purchases to be made from Indian landowners along the coast between Boston and Ipswich. This was done for convenience, without rationalization or concession of right, and no special fuss was made about it.[51]

When a new situation arose that gave an appearance of advantage for Massachusetts in Williams's rejected principle of Indian right, the magistrates suddenly abandoned their old hostility and laid a loving clutch upon the former anathema. John Winthrop's startling change of heart (and the other magistrates' also) occurred in 1641 when an opportunity arose for Massachusetts to gain an opening onto Narragansett Bay. Pursuing the chance, Winthrop mounted an invasion of a small non-chartered colony already existing at Narragansett, doing so with an elaborately concocted formal justification in terms of Indian rights. Besides, "the place was likely to be of use to us," he noted succinctly.[52] The story of that adventure will be narrated below in chapter 15. The point here is simply that Winthrop and the other Massachusetts magistrates were very ready to abandon their early theses about Indian land

50. Felt, *Annals of Salem*, I, 28–33, quote on p. 30 (emphasis added).

51. As of Mar. 13 and Sept. 6, 1639, the Massachusetts General Court ordered compensation to "the Indians" for their rights at Lynn, Watertown, Cambridge, and Boston; and John Winthrop, Jr., paid £20 for an Indian right to Ipswich. But young Winthrop had founded Ipswich in 1633. The six-year interval between demographic settlement and financial settlement robs the payment of the character of a negotiated purchase price in which the seller would be free to refuse an unacceptable offer. *Recs. of Mass.*, I, 243, 252, 254; Robert C. Black III, *The Younger John Winthrop* (New York, 1966), 67–68.

52. Sept. 8, 1642, Winthrop, *History*, ed. Savage, II, 84–85; minutes, Sept. 8, 1642, *Recs. of Mass.*, II, 26–27.

being free for the taking when the takers were people other than themselves.

Further study of deed games will shed light on the complex maneuvers of interprovincial aggression through which the early colonists established their boundary lines. Generalizations will not suffice. Each situation requires attention to its own circumstances, because official acceptance of Indian property right did not guarantee ethical practices in Englishmen's acquisition of those rights.

Within the limits of a jurisdiction, as well as across boundary lines, colonials everywhere used numerous identifiable devices (and doubtless others) to seize Indian property with some show of legality. One method was to allow livestock to roam into an Indian's crops until he despaired and removed. Even when the Indian uncharacteristically fenced his cropland, he found that there was something nocturnally mysterious that did not love an Indian's wall. The Indian who dared to kill an Englishman's marauding animals was promptly hauled into a hostile court.[53] A second method was for Englishmen to get the Indian drunk and have him sign a deed that he could not read. A third method was to recognize a claim by a corrupt Indian who was not the legitimate landlord and then to "buy" the land from him.[54] A fourth method, highly reminiscent of feudal Europe, was a simple threat of violence. A timorous Indian—there were many—would turn over his property for no other reason than the "love and goodwill" he bore the man behind the gun; he was then permitted to remain as a tenant on a corner of the land he formerly had owned.[55] A fifth method, which seems to have been a favorite in

53. The law stated that the Indian had to "make proof" of whose livestock had transgressed before he could get redress. Entirely different treatment was accorded to Englishmen whose fields were invaded by livestock of other Englishmen. If "Indians" harmed English cattle, "the Governour or Deputie Governour with two of the Assistants or any three Magistrates or any County Court" could "order satisfaction according to law and justice." Since no particular law was specified, this meant that justice was what the judge decided. *The Laws and Liberties of Massachusetts. Reprinted from the Copy of the 1648 Edition in the Henry E. Huntington Library*, with an Introduction by Max Farrand (Cambridge, Mass., 1929), 28–29; *Recs. of Mass.*, I, 150.

54. Sometimes the drunk technique was combined with the fraudulent claimant approach. "Cartwright's Answer . . . ," Jan. 5, 1666, "Clarendon Papers," N.-Y. Hist. Soc., *Colls., 1869*, 90–91.

55. See John W. De Forest, *History of the Indians of Connecticut from the Earliest Known Period to 1850* (Hartford, Conn., 1851), 83; deeds to New Haven, Nov. 24 and Dec. 11, 1638, in Charles J. Hoadly, ed., *Records of the Colony and Plantation of New Haven, from 1638 to 1649* (Hartford, Conn., 1857), I, 1–7. The New Haven "gift" came shortly after a massacre by the English at the same spot: Richard Davenport to Hugh Peter, ca. July 17, 1637, *Winthrop Papers*, III, 452–454. I like particularly the understatement of Cassawashat's deed to Thomas Stanton, Jan. 14, 1660, which conveys land without compensation "for good Reasons leading me heereunto." *Suffolk Deeds*, III, 482.

New England, was the imposition of fines for a wide variety of offenses, the Indian's lands becoming forfeit if the fines were not paid by their due date. The offenses ranged from unauthorized riding of an Englishman's horses to conspiracy against English rule.[56] Small or great, the offense was likely to incur a fine larger than the offender could probably pay. An Englishman would "rescue" him from his straits, paying his fine for a short-term mortgage on his land and later foreclosing.[57]

These were devices to put a fair face on fraud. When taken at face value, they present a rosy picture of upright, fair-minded Euramericans giving value for value in honest business transactions. Only when surrounding circumstances are taken into account is the fraud revealed.[58]

Fraud was widespread though not universal, but even when the Indian was dealt with fairly, as also happened, the cession of his land was traumatic for himself and his society. Whether negotiated by diplomatic treaty or commercial contract, the effect of systematic dispossession cannot be overestimated. The selling Indians had only two choices: to retreat into the interior with the hope of being accepted as guests in other tribes' jurisdictions or to accept subjection and exploitation in the lands of their former freedom.

Peaceful purchase of Indian territory was more drastic in its consequences than many armed conquests of one European power by another. It was a *double* conquest in which Indians lost not only sovereignty but also commons and severalty, and it established the harshest possible terms for the Indians who might hope to assimilate into "civilization." Property and liberty were synonyms in the seventeenth and eighteenth centuries. When the Indian was dispossessed of his land, he lost all hope of finding any niche in the society called civilized, except that of servant or slave.

56. Minutes, Sept. 12, 1662, Pulsifer, ed., *Acts of United Colonies*, II, 281–282, and Sept. 6, 1660, *ibid.*, 247–248; mortgage, Sept. 29, 1660, *ibid.*, II, 449.

57. Dunn, "Winthrop, Jr., and the Narragansett Country," *WMQ*, 3d Ser., XIII (1956), 73.

58. For a thesis that the Puritans were fair and pure in their land dealings with the Indians, see Vaughan, *New England Frontier*, 104–114. A ruthlessly candid, but often mistaken, counter thesis was advanced by George E. Ellis, "Indians of Eastern Massachusetts," in Winsor, ed., *Memorial History of Boston*, I, 247–250. An interesting survey of issues and a sampling of cases are in Cyrus Thomas's introduction to *Indian Land Cessions in the United States*, Smithsonian Institution, Bureau of American Ethnology, *Annual Report*, XVIII, pt. ii. (Washington, D.C., 1896–1897), 527–647.

Chapter 9 ❧ SAVAGE WAR

Myth contrasts civilized war with savage war by accepting the former as a rational, honorable, and often progressive activity while attributing to the latter the qualities of irrationality, ferocity, and unredeemed retrogression. Savagery implies unchecked and perpetual violence. Because war is defined as organized violence between politically distinct communities, some writers have questioned whether savage conflicts really qualify for the dignity of the name of war. By whatever name, savage conflicts are conceived to be irrational because they supposedly lack point or objective beyond the satisfaction of sadistic appetites that civilization inhibits, and savages are ferocious through the force of these appetites.

These images are by-products of the master myth of civilization locked in battle with savagery. Civilized war is the kind *we* fight against *them* (in this case, Indians), whereas savage war is the atrocious kind that they fight against us. The contrast has been sustained by means of biased definition on the one hand and tendentious description on the other. Savage war has been dismissed as mere "vengeance" or "feud," and writers have made it seem incomparably more horrible than civilized war by dwelling upon the gory details of personal combat, massacre, and torture on the Indian side while focusing attention diversely on the goals and strategy of wars on the European side.

Still another circumstance has contributed to the myth. Indian governments held jurisdiction over relatively small territories, and there were a great many of them. No supreme power existed to suppress conflicts; the tribes settled their differences themselves by negotiation or struggle. With so many possible combinations of interest groups, statistical odds dictated frequent intertribal conflicts. European governments, in comparison, extended over larger territories, and thus the possible number of international wars was statistically a good deal less. Furthermore, European society may have deferred some "organized" warfare, not by abolishing violence, but by internalizing much of it.

This chapter is based on a paper read at the Fourth Conference on Algonquian Studies, Sept. 26, 1971, at Big Moose, N.Y.; in revised form it was read again at the Seventh Annual Bloomsburg State College History Conference, "War and Peace," May 2, 1974, Bloomsburg, Pa.

Nearly all the violence of Indian society expressed itself intertribally in the form of war, but internal violence in the European states required a vast apparatus for its suppression, the means of which were also violent: Londoners could always find sadistic entertainment at Tyburn or the Tower, and the gaolers buried more prisoners than they discharged. There were also means of violent struggle between nation-states other than declared war; Sir Francis Drake sacked Spanish towns in time of peace, and pirates were ever present on all the seas. We tend to glorify these "sea dogs" instead of putting them on the same low level as Indian raiders, but the victims in both cases went through much the same experiences. If we focus entirely on internal order, the Indian village was a peaceful place compared to the European town. If we focus instead on relations between polities, the nation-states were under tighter controls than the tribes.[1] It seems to me that a proper comparison should include both internal and external relations and should examine the total level of violence in each society, its forms and motives, and the methods used to control and direct it. From this perspective aboriginal Indian society appears to have been far less violent than seventeenth-century European society. The wasting wars so prominent among Indians in historic times were a factor of adaptation to European civilization.

Indian tribes were internally more peaceful than European nations partly because of the kin-oriented sanctions pervading Indian villages, as distinct from the greater impersonality of European social relationships, and partly because Indian custom defined and punished fewer crimes than European law. If there is merit in the argument that psychological aggressions are the cause of social violence (and, like most psychological explanations, this one permits large flights of fancy), then the aggressive feelings of Indians were vented mostly upon persons outside the protection of kin obligation—that is to say, outside the clan and tribe. The same customary sanctions were notably tolerant of many sorts of behavior that Europeans classed as crime, especially regarding deviant sexual and religious conduct. There was no crime of fornication or "unnatural vice" among Indians, nor was there any heresy as that was defined by European law.[2] All sex relations except rare cases of rape were personal matters outside the jurisdiction of sachem and council, and religious *belief* was totally personal. Although participation in rituals was expected, the punishment for withdrawal was limited to public obloquy; in extreme cases the offender might be be-

1. Kennedy, *Jesuit and Savage in New France*, 114-115, 130.

2. Fornication and adultery comprised most of colonial New England's court load. Edmund Morgan, "The Puritans and Sex," *New England Quarterly*, XV (1942), 596.

witched or poisoned by the tribal powwow, but such acts were clandestine. Indians knew nothing of the whole class of offenses called by European lawyers "crimes without victims." When one considers the floggings, jailings, hangings, torture, and burnings inflicted by European states for the multitude of crimes that did not even exist in Indian society, one becomes painfully aware that an incalculably great proportion of European violence against persons was inflicted by the very agencies whose ostensible function was to reduce violence. In due course "civil society" would seek to tranquilize its communities by emulating savage toleration of human variety, but even today this has still only begun.

Of crimes common to both societies, murder requires special notice. It was conceived of differently by Indian and European and was therefore punished by different processes. In Europe murder was an offense against the state; among Indians it was an offense against the family of the victim. European law demanded the murderer's life as atonement to the state; Indian custom made his life forfeit to his victim's family. In Europe the state apprehended the murderer; among Indians it was the family's obligation to do so. European observers tagged the Indian custom "revenge" and blathered much about the savagery revealed by it. Yet, as compared to the state's relentlessness, the tribe provided an institution carefully and precisely designed to stanch the flow of blood. The obligation of blood for blood could be commuted into a payment of valuable goods by the murderer's own kinsfolk to the relatives of his victim.[3] This custom (which had been known centuries earlier in Anglo-Saxon England as *wergild*) was a widespread stabilizer of Indian societies, forestalling the development of obligatory revenge into exterminating feuds. Although the term *feud* has been used freely by the condemners of savage society, Marian W. Smith has been unable to find the phenomena properly denoted by it. "True feud," she remarks, "in its threat of continued violence between particular groups, is surprisingly rare in the New World."[4]

Europeans understood the *wergild* custom and used it themselves in their dealings with Indians, but only unilaterally. Europeans would pay blood money to avert Indian revenge for the killing of an Indian, but Indians were not permitted to buy absolution for the killing of a Euro-

3. Gookin, "Historical Collections," Mass. Hist. Soc., *Colls.*, 1st Ser., I, 149; Elisabeth Tooker, *An Ethnography of the Huron Indians, 1615–1649*, Smithsonian Institution, Bureau of American Ethnology, Bulletin 190 (Washington, D.C., 1964), 28; "Penn to Free Society of Traders, 1683," Myers, ed., *Narratives of Early Pennsylvania*, 236; Snyderman, *Behind the Tree of Peace*, in *Pa. Archaeol.*, XVIII (1948), 31; David H. Corkran, *The Creek Frontier, 1540–1783*, Civilization of the American Indian Series (Norman, Okla., 1967), 26.

4. Marian W. Smith, "American Indian Warfare," New York Academy of Sciences, *Transactions*, 2d Ser., XIII (June 1951), 352.

pean. In the latter case the Europeans demanded the person of the accused Indian for trial in a European court.[5] In the event of nonapprehension of the suspected culprit, mass retribution might be visited upon his village or tribe.[6] The savagery of revenge, therefore, was simply a semantic function of its identification with an Indian; European revenge was civilized justice.

When Indians stirred abroad they were safe in their own territory and in those of tribes with whom they were at peace. The hospitality trait so prominent in all the tribes guaranteed to the traveler not only security but also shelter, sustenance, and sometimes sexual entertainment, all free of charge. Europeans traveling through Indian territory received the same treatment.[7] But travelers in seventeenth-century Europe risked life and property on every highway and in many inns, and they paid for all they got.

The violence and horrors of civil war were rare among Indians, probably because they tolerated secession, while England underwent the Puritan Revolution and France the Catholic-Huguenot agonies, to say nothing of dynastic upheavals by the score. Nor were there class wars or riots in Indian society. Nor did aboriginal Indians experience drunken orgies with their attendant tumults until rum and brandy were poured into the villages from Europe. Thereafter, however, drunken rage became a recurring menace everywhere.

When all this has been said, there still remains the problem of conflict between the tribes. The traditional conception of savage war depicts it as so unrelenting and frightful as to be incapable of proper comparison with the purposeful and disciplined processes of civilized war. No less an authority than A. L. Kroeber has attributed to the east coast Indians of North America a kind of "warfare that was insane, unending, continuously attritional, from our point of view." It was nightmarish— "so integrated into the whole fabric of Eastern culture, so dominantly emphasized within it, that escape from it was well-nigh impossible. Continuance in the system became self-preservatory. The group that tried

5. Trigger, "Champlain Judged by His Indian Policy," *Anthropologica*, N.S., XIII (1971), 96–97; *A Relation of Maryland* (1635), in Clayton Colman Hall, ed., *Narratives of Early Maryland, 1633–1684*, Original Narratives of Early American History (New York, 1910), 88–90; minutes, Jan. 27, 1672, and Lovelace to Salisbury, Jan. 27, 1672, in Victor Hugo Paltsits, ed., *Minutes of the Executive Council of the Province of New York: Administration of Francis Lovelace, 1668–1673* (Albany, N.Y., 1910), I, 156–157, II, 756–757.

6. John Smith, *Generall Historie of Virginia*, in Arber and Bradley, eds., *Travels and Works of Smith*, II, 538–539.

7. Beverley, *History of Virginia*, ed., Wright, 186–189; Corkran, *Creek Frontier*, 23–25; Morgan, *League of the Iroquois*, 327–329; Williams, *Key*, ed. Trumbull, Narragansett Club, *Pubs.*, I, chap. 11; Heckewelder, *Account of the Indian Nations*, ed. Reichel, Hist. Soc. Pa., *Memoirs*, XII (1876), 148–149.

to shift its values from war to peace was almost certainly doomed to early extinction."[8] This harsh indictment would carry more weight if its rhetoric were supported by either example or reference. The only example that comes to mind in support of Kroeber is the Lenape mission of the Moravian church in the mid-eighteenth century. The Indians of that mission took their Christianity seriously, became absolute pacifists, and were unresistingly massacred. But their experience does not quite illustrate Kroeber's point, for their killers were not other Indians but backcountry Euramerican thugs, also Christian after a fashion, who were rather less ready to attack the old-fashioned pagan sort of Indian that fought back.[9]

Kroeber's implication of heavy casualties in aboriginal warfare is contradicted by seventeenth-century reports of Europeans with attitudes as diverse as those of Roger Williams and Captain John Underhill. From his observation post among the warring Narragansett and Pequot Indians, Williams saw that their fighting was "farre lesse bloudy and devouring than the cruell Warres of Europe."[10] Underhill was contemptuous of what Williams approved. He sneered at the Indian warriors who called off a battle after inflicting only a few deaths, and he reported complacently the Narragansetts' protest against his English-style war that "slays too many men."[11]

Imagined dogmas about warriors' lethal accomplishments have led sober scholars into impossible contradictions. For instance, Harold E. Driver has remarked, on the one hand, that "the greed, cupidity, deceit, and utter disregard of Indian life on the part of most of the European conquerors surpassed anything of the kind that the Indian cultures had been able to produce on their own in their thousands of years of virtual independence from the Old World." But Driver has also written, in conformity to savagery mythology, that "no young man ever thought of getting married or of being accepted as an adult citizen until he had slain an enemy and brought back a scalp to prove it."[12] The mathematical implications of the latter statement are wondrous. To demonstrate what it would mean in practice, let us imagine a situation in which two villages are perpetually raiding each other as they would be obliged to do in order to qualify their males for manhood and matrimony. Assuming that the age of eighteen is the threshold of manhood, we find that all of the eighteen-year-old men of one village achieve the right to

8. Kroeber, *Native North America*, 148.

9. Edmund De Schweinitz, *The Life and Times of David Zeisberger* (Philadelphia, 1870), chap. 35.

10. Williams, *Key*, ed. Trumbull, Narragansett Club, *Pubs.*, I, 204.

11. John Underhill, *Newes from America; or, A New and Experimentall Discoverie of New England*... (London, 1638), 26, 42–43.

12. Harold E. Driver, *Indians of North America* (Chicago, 1961), 384, 370.

marry by killing off an equal number of males in the other village. The total population of both villages would thus be reduced annually by the total number of eighteen-year-old men (at least this is so if the eighteen-year-olds from the two villages avoided killing each other). This is the minimum implication of one coup per warrrior. If some braves showed more than minimum enthusiasm and skill, the whole process would be speeded up accordingly. Such a process would lead inexorably, year by year, not just to a low level of population, but to total extinction. The thing is impossible, of course, and so is the dogma on which it is predicated. Clearly there were young men in Indian society who got married before they ever killed anyone, and the mathematics imply that a lot of old Indian men also died without having killed. What really made an Indian youth a citizen of his community was an initiation ritual, and the process has been observed and reported thousands of times. William Penn reported that young Delawares were permitted to marry "after having given some Proofs of their Manhood by a good return of Skins" and that almost all of them were wed before they reached nineteen years of age.[13] Among the Delawares, therefore, a man could marry when he could demonstrate the ability to support a family. How many Euramerican parents have drilled that notion into their offspring? That the young Indian could gain prestige and status by killing and scalping is undeniable, and that many youngsters itched for such fame is as plain as the enlistment of European mercenaries for pay and plunder. But universal generalizations should be grounded in some minimum quantity of evidence and common sense.

Suppose it be argued that the disastrous demographic implications just presented are fallacious because warriors might diffuse the population loss by taking scalps from women and children. Deductively such an objection might have merit if not for the inductive evidence available. Contact-era Europeans agreed that, with few exceptions that occurred in the confusion of battle, Indians killed only men.[14] The cultural imperative may have been a survival trait rather than pure sentiment, because one reason for sparing these noncombatants was to assimilate them into the victorious tribe, thus to enlarge and strengthen it.[15] Some tribes

13. "Penn to Free Society of Traders, 1638," Myers, ed., *Narratives of Early Pennsylvania*, 231.

14. Sagard, *Long Journey to Hurons*, ed. Wrong, trans. Langton, 140; Van der Donck, *Description of New Netherlands*, in N.-Y. Hist. Soc., *Colls.*, 2d Ser., I, 211; John Smith, *Map of Virginia*, in Barbour, ed., *Jamestown Voyages*, II, 372; Heckewelder, *Account of the Indian Nations*, ed. Reichel, in Hist. Soc. Pa., *Memoirs*, XII, 337–339; David Pietersz. de Vries, *Short Historical and Journal notes Of several Voyages made in the four parts of the World, namely, Europe, Africa, Asia, and America* (1655), trans. Henry C. Murphy, in N.-Y. Hist. Soc., *Colls.*, 2d Ser., III (New York, 1857), 116.

15. Snyderman, *Behind the Tree of Peace*, in Pa. *Archaeol.*, XVIII (1948), 13–15.

were observed to begin war for the specific purpose of augmenting their female population.[16] Whatever the motive, the merciful custom was universal in regard to women and children.

Treatment of captured men was more varied. Early southern accounts indicate that all male prisoners were put to death except the chiefs.[17] By the seventeenth century torture of men was practiced fairly extensively, although some doubt exists about how widespread this trait had been at an earlier time. An ameliorating custom decreed the sparing of a large proportion of male captives, however. Again, the custom may have arisen out of the dire pressures of population decline, in this case pinpointed on particular families. Women among the victors, who had lost a husband or kinsman, held unchallengeable individual right to "adopt" a prisoner in his place, and the man so chosen became immediately assimilated into the tribe as well as the family. (In our terminology he was naturalized as well as adopted.[18]) Perhaps the most famous example of the custom is Pocahontas's rescue of John Smith, although Smith rejected assimilation at the first opportunity to escape. Not every European captive followed Smith's example. It was a constant crying scandal that Europeans who were adopted by Indians frequently preferred to remain with their Indian "families" when offered an opportunity to return to their genetic kinsmen.[19]

The adoption custom grew in importance with the intensification of war during the macrocontact era. Of all the Indians, the Iroquois, who are generally agreed to have been the most militaristic and to have suffered the most debilitating casualties, seem to have practiced adoption more than any other tribe. At one time adoptees constituted two-thirds of the Iroquois Oneidas.[20] The Senecas adopted whole villages of Hurons after the breakup of the Huron "nation" under Iroquois attack,[21] and various Iroquois tribes struggled for possession of Susquehannocks after the latter's dispersal under attack from Maryland and Virginia.[22]

Still another Indian custom served (aboriginally) to reduce the

16. John Smith, *Map of Virginia*, in Barbour, ed., *Jamestown Voyages*, II, 360.
17. *Ibid.*, II, 361; Lescarbot, *History of New France*, trans. Grant, I, 88.
18. Morgan, *League of the Iroquois*, 341–344; Snyderman, *Behind the Tree of Peace*, in *Pa. Archaeol.*, XVIII (1948), 18; Heckewelder, *Account of the Indian Nations*, ed. Reichel, in Hist. Soc. Pa., *Memoirs*, XII, 217–218; Colden, *History of Five Nations*, Pt. I, chap. 1, 8; Lowery, *Spanish Settlements*, I, 37.
19. Barbour, *Pocahontas*, 23–25. I thank James Axtell for providing an advance copy of his article "The White Indians of Colonial America," *WMQ*, 3d Ser., XXXII (1975), 55–88. This is the first objective treatment, to my knowledge, of the European prisoners who refused repatriation.
20. Letter of Jacques Bruyas, Jan. 21, 1668, Thwaites, ed., *Jesuit Relations*, LI, 123.
21. Letter of Jacques Fremin, n.d. ("Relation of 1669–1670"), *ibid.*, LIV, 81–83.
22. Jennings, "Glory, Death, and Transfiguration," Am. Phil. Soc., *Procs.*, CXII (1968), 40.

deadliness of war. Indians refrained from the total war that involved systematic destruction of food and property—until its use by Europeans roused the Indians to reprisal.[23] In this respect, as in so many others, the English continued a tradition of long standing from their devastations in Ireland.[24] Burning villages and crops to reduce Irish tribesmen to subjection under Elizabeth I led naturally enough to using the same tactics against the tribesmen of Virginia.[25] A "relation" of 1629 tells how the Virginia colonists compelled a hostile Indian chief to seek peace, "being forc't to seek it by our continuall incursions upon him and them, by yearly cutting downe, and spoiling their corne."[26] The same practice was used everywhere in North America when Indian guerrilla tactics prevented Europeans from gaining victory by decisive battle.[27] According to Indian logic, such destruction doomed noncombatants as well as warriors to die of famine during a winter without provisions.

These remarks are not intended to suggest that Indians of precontact days were gentle pacifists whom the Europeans seduced to evil warlike ways. On the contrary, all evidence points to a genuinely endemic state of sporadic intertribal violence. Had this base not been present, Europeans could not so readily have achieved hegemony by playing off one tribe against another. But the dispersion of violence tells nothing of its intensity. What is especially at issue here is the significance of the data in comparison with the phenomena of war in European society. As the history of feudal Europe well exemplifies, endemic war does not necessarily imply, although it may be associated with, population decline. The fact is unlovely, but growth in human societies is demonstrably compatible with bellicosity, up to a critical level of mortality. We have no difficulty in perceiving this rule at work in, say, ancient Greece; yet we deny that the rule also applied to Amerindians when we attribute to them a savage kind of war that supposedly was incomparably more continuous, more widespread, more integral to cultural values, and more senseless in the long view than the dedicated vocation of backward but civilized Sparta—or of Athens, for that matter. To show the falsity of these absolute antitheses is a primary objective here. Indians could be and often were as stupid and vicious as Europeans, which is to say that they belonged to the same human species. They were never so much more devoted than Europeans to killing each other that their uniquely

23. Minutes, Aug. 26, 1645, Pulsifer, ed., *Acts of United Colonies*, I, 44.
24. For the practice of Richard II in the late 14th century, see Lydon, *Lordship of Ireland*, 234.
25. *Encyclopaedia Britannica*, 11th ed., s.v. "Ireland (History from the Anglo-Norman Invasion)."
26. Capt. William Perse, "Relation," Aug. 1629, C.O. 1/5, Pt. 1, fol. 69, P.R.O.
27. E.g., the French foray against the Mohawks in 1666. O'Callaghan, ed. *Doc. Hist. of N.-Y.*, I, 70.

violent natures or cultures doomed their societies to perpetual stagnation.

To discover the nature of aboriginal Indian war requires a skeptical and analytical approach not only to European sources but to Indian sources as well. Like old tales in other cultures, Indian "traditions" were of several sorts: some preserved the memory of historical events, and others were invented to amuse or edify. Wendell S. Hadlock has shown how legends diffused rapidly, being adapted to the local settings of different tribes so that "a single occurrence in history has been told in varying ways so as to appear like many incidents."[28] Sometimes one may doubt whether the "single occurrence" ever did happen anywhere.

One genre of such legends, dealing with the "grasshopper war," has been interpreted by chroniclers in its multiple manifestations as literal fact demonstrating the terrible carnage that Indians would wreak over such trivial causes as a children's quarrel about possession of a grasshopper. That grasshopper hopped over a lot of territory. He spilled the same mythical blood by gallons from the Micmacs of Newfoundland to the Shawnees, Lenape, and Tuscaroras of western Pennsylvania. The story seems to have been in the same class as Aesop's fables. Whatever may have been its remote origins, it diffused so widely because of its didactic utility rather than its historical reality. Hadlock associated it with a table of similar stories that "are not so much an explanation of a war incident as philosophical explanations of tribal fission."[29]

To Frank G. Speck it was fiction, and Speck's interpretation implies bittersweet irony as to how the Indian myth was absorbed and transformed in the European myth of savagery: "In the 'grasshopper war' legend we have an example of the type of Algonkian moral teaching with which the ethnologist has long been familiar. Need the moralist point out that its clarified motive is to portray the consequences of grown-ups taking over the disputes of children, the curse of partisanship in disputes of a trivial nature, the abomination of giving way to emotional impulses? The myth is a great composition for the lesson it carries extolling self-restraint and the virtues of deliberation before taking action that may lead to disastrous outcome."[30]

By the transforming power of the savagery myth, a fable denouncing

28. Wendell S. Hadlock, "War among the Northeastern Woodland Indians," *Am. Anthro.*, N.S., XLIX (1947), 217–218.

29. Wendell S. Hadlock, "The Concept of Tribal Separation as Rationalized in Indian Folklore," *Pa. Archaeol.*, XVI (1946), 84–88.

30. Frank G. Speck, "The Grasshopper War in Pennsylvania: An Indian Myth That Became History," *Pa. Archaeol.*, XII (1942), 34. See also C. E. Schaeffer, "The Grasshopper or Children's War—A Circumboreal Legend?" *ibid.*, XII (1942), 60–61; John Witthoft, "The Grasshopper War in Lenape Land," *ibid.*, XVI (1946), 91–94.

war's irrationality was converted into evidence of the real existence of widespread irrational bellicosity. The Indian could not even preach against war without convicting himself of obsessive love for it. By the same logic Quakers would be the most militaristic of Euramericans.

Historical sources strongly suggest that aboriginal war among the hunting Indians of the cold north differed markedly from the wars carried on by the agricultural tribes farther south. During most of the year the hunters lived dispersed in family bands that were occupied full-time in making a living. Opportunity to organize concerted tribal wars existed briefly during the summer months when the bands congregated at tribal centers and had some leisure. Wars could then be organized, but they were sporadic, individualistic affairs.[31] A Jesuit observer condemned both the Indians' motives and scale of operations with a succinct phrase—"their war is nothing but a manhunt"—and narrated how a war party of thirty men dwindled to fifteen who returned home satisfied after they had taken the scalps of three unoffending members of a friendly tribe.[32] In Europe such waylaying would have been called brigandage rather than war.

Farming Indians operated on a larger scale and under the direction of tribal purposes and policies. Their more complex culture provided a variety of motives. Sometimes they fought to gain territory, although apparently not in the fashion of European empire building; when Indians fought for territory as such, they wanted to displace its occupants rather than to subject them. Lands thus made available might be occupied by the victors, left empty for use as hunting grounds, or kept as a protective buffer against distant enemies.[33]

Sometimes, it seems, agricultural Indians fought to achieve dominance —to make the defeated tribe confess the victor's preeminence. The symbol of such acknowledgment was the payment of tribute. Because the tributary role has been much confused, it needs a moment of special attention. First, tribute should be distinguished from plunder. When the Niantics raided Long Island's Montauks for wampum in 1638, they were after loot.[34] When the Iroquois Five Nations—the Mohawks among them—required wampum from the Lenape of the Delaware Val-

31. Hadlock, "War among Northeastern Indians," *Am. Anthro.*, N.S., XLIX (1947), 211–214.

32. Andre Richard, "Relation of 1661–1662," Thwaites, ed., *Jesuit Relations*, XLVII, 221–239.

33. Occupation: Pequot displacement of Niantics. Hodge, ed., *Handbook of N. Am. Indians*, s.v. "Pequot." Hunting grounds: Five Nations displacement of tribes around Lake Erie. Five Nations deed, July 19, 1701, *N.Y. Col. Docs.*, IV, 908. Buffer lands: Hadlock, "War among Northeastern Indians," *Am. Anthro.*, N.S., XLIX (1947), 217.

34. Thompson, *History of Long Island*, I, 89–90.

ley in the eighteenth century, they wanted ceremonial recognition of a confederate relationship in which the Iroquois were superior.[35] Several contrasts mark the difference. Loot was seized by a raiding party; tribute was presented by a diplomatic mission. Loot's value increased precisely in accordance with quantity; tribute's value was primarily symbolic, secondarily quantitative. The taking of loot was a one-sided transaction; the presentation of tribute was reciprocated by a counter presentation of wampum to confirm the tributary agreement.

The last difference was especially important, because tribute symbolized subordinate alliance rather than subjection and thus entailed obligation on the part of the superior tribe as well as the tributary. In essence the alliance entitled the tributary to freedom from molestation by its patron and to protection by the patron against attack by a third party. In return the tributary was expected to give ceremonial deference on all occasions, to allow free passage through its territory by members of the patron tribe, and to permit or encourage the recruitment of its own young men to join the patron's war parties. This sort of mutual obligation can be identified in the historic period, but it does not appear that all tributary relationships were the same; there seem to have been grades and degrees of obligation,[36] and the word *tribute* was also applied to payments of wampum or other valuable goods in the nature of a toll. For instance, English officials agreed to pay tribute to the Illinois tribes in 1764 for the privilege of unobstructed passage through the tribes' territory, and the Indians knew perfectly well that the English were not submitting or subjecting themselves by the payment.[37]

It may be said quite positively that a tributary tribe did not necessarily give up title to its lands when it presented tribute. After the defeat of the upper Hudson Mahicans by the Mohawks in 1628, the Mahicans offered tribute as a means of purchasing peace, but they also sold land to the Dutch without Mohawk objection, and after two years of tribute payment they "got drunk and lost the pouch [of wampum]." Mohawk sachem Joseph Brant, who told the story, commented that the Mohawks

---

35. Minutes, May 19, 1712, *Pa. Council Minutes*, II, 546; draft minutes of treaty, Sept. 15, 1718, Logan Papers, XI, 7, and Sassoonan's speech, Aug. 7, 1741, Records of the Provincial Council and Other Papers, boxed manuscripts, fol. 1740–1749, both in Hist. Soc. Pa., Philadelphia.

36. Snyderman, *Behind the Tree of Peace*, in Pa. *Archaeol.*, XVIII (1948), 33; Anthony F. C. Wallace, *King of the Delawares: Teedyuscung, 1700–1763* (Philadelphia, 1949), 195–196, and his "Political Organization," *Southwest. Jour. of Anthro.*, XIII (1957), 308–309; Beverley, *History of Virginia*, ed. Wright, 174; Flannery, *Analysis of Coastal Algonquian Culture*, 117–118; Jennings, "Evolution of Covenant Chain," Am. Phil. Soc., *Procs.*, CXV (1971), 90–94.

37. Gen. Thomas Gage to Johnson, May 28, 1764, *Sir William Johnson Papers*, IV, 433–434; Johnson to Gage, June 9, 1764, *ibid.*, XI, 223.

did not "take it hard" when payment ceased.[38] Four decades later, when the Executive Council of New York considered purchase of land from the "Wickerscreek" (Wecquaesgeek) tribe, the council had to consider whether the Wickerscreeks could deliver good title, "now they are beaten off" by the Mohawks. The Indians replied that the Mohawks would not "have any pretence to their Land, though being at Warre they would destroy their Persons, and take away their Beavers and Goods."[39]

The "sales" by dominant tribes like the Pequots and Iroquois of their rights in tributaries' territory were in the nature of quitclaims, without prejudice to the tributaries' retained rights of habitation and enjoyment. The Pequots quit their own claims to the Connecticut Valley and permitted Englishmen to settle there, but after the English evicted a tributary chief, the Pequots attacked in reprisal.[40] When the Iroquois were bribed by Pennsylvanians in the eighteenth century to "quit" a claim they had never made to the Delaware Valley, the swindle ruptured their confederacy.[41]

The customary situation was summarized by General Thomas Gage in the course of his systematic correspondence on Indian affairs with Sir William Johnson. Gage's confidential letter also clarifies the English motives that often led to the muddying of the formal records. "It is asserted as a general Principle that the Six Nations having conquered such and such Nations, their Territorys belong to them, and the Six Nations being the Kings Subjects which by treaty they have acknowledged themselves to be, those Lands belong to the King. I believe it is for our Interest to lay down such principles especially when we were squabbling with the French about Territory, and they played us off in the same stile of their Indian Subjects, and the right of those Indians." Gage went on to define the Indian customs as he privately understood them. "I never heard that Indians made War for the sake of Territory like Europeans, but that Revenge, and an eager pursuit of Martial reputation were the Motives which prompted one Nation to make War upon another. If we are to search for truth and examine her to the Bottom, I dont imagine we shall find that any conquered Nation ever formaly ceded their Country to their Conquerors, or that the latter ever required

38. Douglas W. Boyce, ed., "A Glimpse of Iroquois Culture History through the Eyes of Joseph Brant and John Norton," Am. Phil. Soc., *Procs.*, CXVII (1973), 290; Bruce G. Trigger, "The Mohawk-Mahican War (1624–28): The Establishment of a Pattern," *Canadian Historical Review*, LII (1971), 281.

39. Minutes, Oct. 30, 1671, Paltsits, ed., *Minutes of Council of N.Y.*, I, 105.

40. See chaps. 12 and 13, below.

41. Jennings, "Delaware Interregnum," *PMHB*, LXXXIX (1965), 174–198; A. F. C. Wallace, *Death and Rebirth of the Seneca*, 154.

it. I never could learn more, than that Nations have yielded, and acknowledged themselves subjected to others, and some ever have wore Badges of Subjection."[42]

Gage's remark refers to the most frequently mentioned motive for Indian war—behavior that is almost invariably termed *revenge*. Like most effective propaganda language, the term has a referent in reality, and also like most propaganda, it distorts that referent in the mere naming of it. Our English word implies an act of retaliation intended to inflict suffering upon an enemy and performed in part for the emotional satisfaction that the avenger will achieve from contemplation of that suffering. (Who has not hated the villainous Iago?) Revenge connotes ferocity—personal, unrestrained by charity or mercy or any of the nobler impulses of humanity—in short, savagery. The actual phenomenon in Indian society to which this name has been given did not conform to these connotations. As it manifested itself intratribally, we have already noticed revenge as an obligatory retaliation for murder, together with the commutation custom by which the obligation might be discharged in lieu of blood for blood.[43] *Intertribal* retaliation for wrongs done or fancied (a real and omnipresent occurrence) was also bound up in motives and restraints imposed by custom and social purpose, including commutation by payment between tribes as well as between families. As Marian W. Smith has noted, such retaliations bear "a legalistic tinge. They serve as mechanisms for righting the balance of sanctions in the society, and the reprisal is seen as justified, in view of the fact that it reestablishes the validity of customs which had been violated."[44]

Smith wrote in the formal language of the twentieth-century scholar. A seventeenth-century Lenape Indian phrased the "justified reprisal" idea—which in Europe might readily have been classed as "just war"—in simpler language when he told a Pennsylvanian, "We are minded to live at Peace: If we intend at any time to make War upon you, we will let you know of it, and the Reasons why we make War with you; and if

42. Gage to Johnson, Oct. 7, 1772, *Sir William Johnson Papers*, XII, 994–995.

43. See the description by missionary Francesco Bressani (1653) who remarked, "it is the public that gives satisfaction for the crimes of the individual, whether the culprit be known or not. In fine, the crime alone is punished, and not the criminal; and this, which elsewhere would appear an injustice, is among them a most efficacious means for preventing the spread of similar disorders." *Thwaites*, ed., *Jesuit Relations*, XXXVIII, 273–287, quote at p. 277.

44. M. W. Smith, "American Indian Warfare," N.Y. Acad. Sciences, *Trans.*, 2d Ser., XIII (1951), 352. See also the discussion of revenge in Snyderman, *Behind the Tree of Peace*, in Pa. *Archaeol.*, XVIII (1948); A. F. C. Wallace, *Death and Rebirth of the Seneca*, 44–48; Heckewelder, *Account of the Indian Nations*, ed. Reichel, in Hist. Soc. Pa., *Memoirs*, XII, 175–176; Tooker, *Ethnography of the Huron Indians*, 28; Lawson, *New Voyage to Carolina*, 199; Driver, *Indians of North America*, 354.

you make us satisfaction for the Injury done us, for which the War is intended, then we will not make War on you. And if you intend at any time to make War on us, we would have you let us know of it, and the Reasons for which you make War on us, and then if we do not make satisfaction for the Injury done unto you, then you may make War on us, otherwise you ought not to do it." To one looking back from the twentieth century this sounds quaintly moralistic. In the era of total "preventive" war, what is one to make of "otherwise you ought not to do it"?[45]

Marian W. Smith identifies a "mourning-war" complex of traits correlating to the northern distribution of maize agriculture. By implication she makes it a development of the revenge trait, but her definition is brief and unenlightening: it is "an elaborate socio-religious complex relating individual 'emotion' to social reintegration through group activity and sanctioned homicide."[46] This seems more to describe what happens psychologically to a tribe after it has gone to war than to explain the reasons for its choosing to fight a particular foe at a certain time and place; further, it could as well apply to the nations of World War II as to aboriginal Indians.[47] Pursued to their logical assumptions, such psychological explanations of war, primitive or modern, take one ultimately to a neo-Calvinist faith in the innate depravity/bellicosity of man, a position both unwarranted by science and vicious in effect and, ultimately, a self-fulfilling prophecy that stultifies investigation of the empirical sources of war and thus guarantees war's perpetuation. We shall do better to stick with Smith's genuine insight into Indian war as a means of reestablishing the validity of violated customs; it raises questions that can be answered historically.

In sum, the motives for aboriginal war appear to have been few, and the casualties slight. Contact with Europeans added new motives and weapons and multiplied casualties. The trade and dominance wars of the macrocontact era were indeed beyond the sole control of aboriginal cultural and political institutions, because they were bicultural wars, the motives and promptings for which originated in colony and empire as well as in tribe. These wars were truly attritional for Indians—appallingly so—but they were the result of civilization's disruption of aborigi-

45. Thomas Budd, *Good Order Established in Pennsilvania & New-Jersey in America* (1685), March of America Facsimile Series, No. 32 (Ann Arbor, Mich., 1966), 33.

46. M. W. Smith, "American Indian Warfare," N.Y. Acad. Sciences, *Trans.*, 2d Ser., XIII (1951), 359.

47. See W. W. Newcomb, Jr., "Toward an Understanding of War," in Gertrude E. Dole and Robert L. Carneiro, eds., *Essays in the Science of Culture in Honor of Leslie A. White* (New York, 1960), 322–324, and Newcomb, "A Reexamination of the Causes of Plains Warfare," *Am. Anthro.*, LII (1950), 328–329.

nal society rather than the mere outgrowth of precontact Indian culture.

Most discussions of Indian war have probably concerned themselves less with the Indians' motives than with their manner of fighting. Every "frontier" history abounds with tales of grim figures skulking through the woods, striking from ambush, spreading havoc and desolation, and culminating their horrors with scalping, torture, and cannibalism. In many instances the tales are verifiable, and no attempt will be made here to palliate their horrors. But when atrocity is singled out as a quality exclusive to tribesmen (Indians or others), myth is being invoked against evidence—indeed against the sorrowful experience of our own twentieth century and our own "highest" civilization of all time. The Indians of the macrocontact era, and presumably their aboriginal ancestors also, undoubtedly showed plenty of ferocity when aroused; what will be argued here is that the records of European war of the same era display the same quality in ample measure also. There were no Indians in Ireland when Cromwell's armies made it a wilderness, nor were there Indians with Wallenstein and Tilly during the Thirty Years' War in central Europe. If savagery was ferocity, Europeans were at least as savage as Indians.

Many of the aspects of so-called savage war were taught to Indians by European example. As to torture, for example, a systematic examination of the documents of the early contact era, published by Nathaniel Knowles in 1940, found no references to torturing by Indians of the southeast coast region "until almost 200 years after white contact." Knowles added, "It seems even more significant that there are no expressions by the early explorers and colonizers indicating any fear of such treatment. The Europeans were only too willing in most cases to call attention to the barbarity of the Indians and thus justify their need for either salvation or extermination."[48] Among the northeastern Indians, Knowles found that deliberate torture, as distinct from simple brutality (i.e., unplanned and unorganized cruelty), had not been practiced in

---

48. Nathaniel Knowles, "The Torture of Captives by the Indians of Eastern North America," Am. Phil. Soc., *Procs.*, LXXXII (1940), 202. This is a systematic study fundamental to any study of torture in North America. Knowles remarked that Ponce de Leon in 1613 had met a Florida Indian who understood the Spanish language, "thus making it apparent that the atrocious cruelty of the Spanish for some twenty years in the West Indies had become known to the inhabitants of the mainland prior to the discovery of the continent by the whites" (p. 156). Knowles cites the speculation of Lowery that the Floridians' resistance to the Spaniards indicated "they had learned somewhat of the treatment they were to expect at the hands of such conquerors." Lowery, *Spanish Settlements*, I, 144-145. In 1642 the Canadian Jesuit martyr Father Isaac Jogues wrote, "*Never till now* had the Indian [torture] scaffold beheld French or other Christian captives." *N.Y. Col. Docs.*, XIII, 581 (emphasis added).

aboriginal times except by the Iroquois, who associated it with the practice of ritual cannibalism. These usages seem to have been derived from an ancient complex of customs connected with human sacrifice and perhaps tracing back to similar practices in Mexico. Iroquois torture secondarily served as a terrorist device to keep surrounding tribes in fear, but its usefulness for this purpose declined as some neighbors adopted the same trait in reprisal, much as the southern Indians had retaliated against such European tortures as burning at the stake.[49] After describing the torture of an Iroquois prisoner by Samuel de Champlain's allies, Marc Lescarbot remarked, "I have not read or heard tell that any other savage tribe behaves thus to its enemies. But someone will reply that these did but repay the Iroquois who by similar deeds have given cause for this tragedy."[50] Lescarbot stated positively that "our sea-coast Indians" did not practice torture, and his modern translator added a note of confirmation.[51] Although some Indians practiced the ritual cannibalism that Europeans had sublimated many centuries earlier into symbolic acts of "communion," other Indians abominated man-eating as much as the Europeans themselves. Algonquian speakers used a contemptuous epithet meaning "man-eaters" to refer to their Iroquois neighbors: it took the forms of Mengwe, Mingo, Maqua, and finally, in English, Mohawk.[52]

Europeans and Indians differed in the publicity given to torture. Europeans burnt heretics and executed criminals in ingeniously agonizing ways, but much European torture was inflicted secretly for the utilitarian purpose of extracting confessions from suspects. Public or private, European torture was performed by specialists appointed by governmental authority, whereas torture among Indians was a spectacle for popular participation as well as observation. It seems reasonable to infer that comparably painful practices in the two societies were sharply distinguished in European minds by what was conceived as their relative lawfulness. Torture by commission of civil authority was merely execution of the law, often highly approved as a means of preserving order, but torture by a self-governing rabble was savagery. The *Encyclopaedia*

49. Knowles, "Torture," Am. Phil. Soc., *Procs.*, LXXXII (1940), 190–191, 213, 215; Heckewelder, *Account of the Indian Nations*, ed. Reichel, in Hist. Soc. Pa., *Memoirs*, XII, 343.

50. Lescarbot, *History of New France*, trans. Grant, III, 13–15.

51. *Ibid.*, III, 20–21.

52. Trelease, *Indian Affairs in New York*, 41. But see a dissenting meaning for "Mohawk" given by Mohawk sachem Joseph Brant who held that it came from the Mahican word *munkwas*, meaning "fish dryed." Brant may have been a little sensitive on the subject. Boyce, ed., "Glimpse of Iroquois Culture History," Am. Phil. Soc., *Procs.*, CXVII (1973), 291.

Britannica has noted that the name of torture has been historically used "especially" for those modes of inflicting pain "employed in a legal aspect by the civilized nations of antiquity and of modern Europe."[53] In such a context the remark of seventeenth-century friar Louis Hennepin becomes ironic: "We are surprised at the cruelty of tyrants and hold them in horror: but that of the Iroquois is not less horrible."[54]

Plenty of sadism was evident in both cultures. Indians vented it directly upon the person of their victim, hacking and slashing at his body democratically with their own hands. Even old women would satisfy some horrid lust by thrusting firebrands at his genitals or chewing off the joints of his fingers. Their culture sanctioned what they did in the same way that local and regional cultures in nineteenth- and twentieth-century America sanctioned somewhat similar practices by white supremacists at lynching parties. In the more authoritarian seventeenth century the European populace in general was not allowed to participate except as spectators in the tortures prescribed for condemned persons. When we consider that crowds brought their lunch along to be enjoyed during such entertainments as disemboweling and slow immolation, we may wonder about the significance of the cultural difference. We have no way of knowing how many Europeans were prevented from soaking their own hands in blood only by the state's armed guards. Equally we have no way of knowing how many of the persons in an Indian village were active participants in the grim sport of torture, or how many just looked on. The diverse qualities of character that we recognize as distinguishing one European or Euramerican from another are ignored or denied among Indians. Savages are homogeneously cruel.

In America, Europeans sometimes turned captives over to allied Indians for torture in order to make hostility between two tribes irrevocable. Their own complicity was not felt keenly enough to shame the Europeans into silence; after having thus condemned a victim they would sometimes fastidiously deplore the sadistic appetites of the Indian torturers who were carrying out the Europeans' own desires.[55] One French officer, after "prudently" consigning an old Onondaga to the torture in 1696, considered that the *victim's* taunting defiance "will be

53. *Encyclopaedia Britannica*, 11th ed., s.v. "torture."

54. Louis Hennepin, *A Description of Louisiana* (1683), trans. John Gilmary Shea, March of America Facsimile Series, No. 30 (Ann Arbor, Mich., 1966), 311–312.

55. Heckewelder, *Account of the Indian Nations*, ed Reichel, in Hist. Soc. Pa., *Memoirs*, XII, 343–344; *Dict. Can. Biog.*, I (1966), s.v. "Buade de Frontenac et de Palluau, Louis de." Sir William Johnson followed the same practice but masked it under euphemisms. For example, he told Cadwallader Colden, Mar. 16, 1764, "I was obliged to *give* them People 5 Prisoners for their good behaviour." To General Gage, on the same day, Johnson wrote that the Indians had "kept" the five prisoners. *Sir William Johnson Papers*, IV, 365, 368–369 (emphasis added).

found perhaps to flow rather from ferociousness, than true valour."[56]

One thing is not in doubt: as befitted its greater progress in technology, Europe had designed a variety of implements for the specific purpose of creating agony, not merely death, in human bodies. Their function was to make pain excruciating—a word that itself commemorates one of the pioneering inventions in that field and recalls its connection with European worship. Indians never achieved the advanced stage of civilization represented by the rack or the Iron Maiden. They simply adapted instruments of everyday utility to the purposes of pain. It may be worth a moment to reflect on the cultural traits imaged in the specialized torture technology of Europe. Something more than sudden emotional impulse will have to be taken into account.

I have an impression that about midway through the seventeenth century the outlook toward torture began to change in opposite directions among the two peoples. It seems to me from general reading that European attitudes toward mutilation of the human body began to turn negative. The old delight in hacking enemies' corpses in the public square and exposing their heads on palings went out of fashion—gradually and with conspicuous exceptions such as the displays made of sachem Philip and "squaw sachem" Weetamoo in "King Philip's War."[57] Slowly the use of torture for extracting information from political prisoners came under disapproval and ultimately under official ban. At the same time, torture was increasing among Indians as trade wars multiplied and European conflicts dragged Indian allies along. It is easy to understand why the Europeans, who were apparently trying to overcome their own worst traits, should have found relief and a sense of superior righteousness by rejecting torture and cruelty as things foreign to their own best impulses and therefore to civilization per se. No one dreamed at the time that the increase of torture by Indians could have come as the result of exposure to the uplifting influence of Europe, but the idea seems more credible nowadays after the revelations of German and Russian secret police practices, French policy in Algiers, Mississippi justice, and the ministrations of nice young American boys in Vietnam.

Every day brings revelations of secret tortures committed as deliberate instrumentation of governmental policy. Today's newspaper leads off an article with this paragraph: "Amnesty International, the organization dedicated to assisting political prisoners, has charged that torture as a systematic weapon of control is being used by almost half the world's governments and is spreading rapidly." The civilized world's response to this information is symbolized by the United Nations Educational, Scientific, and Cultural Organization. UNESCO withdrew

56. O'Callaghan, ed., *Doc. Hist. of N.-Y.*, I, 334.
57. Drake, *Biography and History of the Indians*, 189–190, 227.

from Amnesty International the offer of its facilities because the torture report implicated more than 60 of UNESCO's 125 member countries.[58] Clearly civilization is not a homogeneous whole, whatever it may otherwise be. Nor was it in the seventeenth century.

Apart from torture, some Europeans have domineered over Indians, when they could, with a reign of terror functioning through indiscriminate cruelty. In early Virginia the curtain was opened briefly on the reality behind self-serving and self-glorifying reports when Englishmen slew twelve Chickahominy Indians without cause and by treachery. Relatives of the victims retaliated against ten colonists and then fled into the woods. The rest of the villagers, abused by both sides, "much feared the English would be revenged on them"—a fear they had unquestionably been taught by the swaggering Virginians. Grand sachem Opechancanough "saved" the village from causeless slaughter, and incidentally revealed the motive behind the English menaces, by ceding the village to the colonists.[59] On a larger scale, after the much-provoked Virginia Indians rebelled in 1622, English writers fumed against the Indian massacre even as English soldiers multiplied their vengeance massacres beyond counting. Virginian Dr. John Pott became "the Poysner of the Savages thear" in some sort of episode so shocking that the earl of Warwick insisted it was "very unfitt" that Pott "should be imployed by the State in any business." But Pott became governor.[60]

Virginia was not exceptional. Puritan New England initiated its own reign of terror with the massacres of the Pequot conquest. David Pieterszoon de Vries has left us an unforgettable picture of how Dutch mercenaries acted, under orders of New Netherland's Governor Willem Kieft, to terrorize Indians into paying tribute.

About midnight, I heard a great shrieking, and I ran to the ramparts of the fort, and looked over to Pavonia. Saw nothing but firing, and heard the shrieks of the Indians murdered in their sleep.... When it was day the soldiers returned to the fort, having massacred or murdered eighty Indians, and considering they had done a deed of Roman valour, in murdering so many in their sleep; where infants were torn from their mother's breasts, and hacked to pieces in the presence of the parents, and the pieces thrown into the fire and in the water, and other sucklings being bound to small boards, and then cut, stuck, and pierced, and miserably massacred in a manner to move a heart of stone. Some were thrown into the river, and when the fathers and mothers endeavoured to save them, the soldiers would

58. *New York Times*, Dec. 16, 1973: "64 Nations Charged in Report as Users of Torture."

59. John Smith, *Generall Historie of Virginia*, in Arber and Bradley, eds., *Travels and Works of Smith*, II, 528, 538–539.

60. See Craven, "Indian Policy in Early Virginia," *WMQ*, 3d Ser., I (1944), 73; Warwick to Sec. Conway, Aug. 9, 1624, C.O. 1/3, 94; C.O. 1/5, Pt. 2, fol. 206, Public Record Office.

not let them come on land, but made both parents and children drown—children from five to six years of age, and also some old and decrepit persons. Many fled from this scene, and concealed themselves in the neighbouring sedge, and when it was morning, came out to beg a piece of bread, and to be permitted to warm themselves; but they were murdered in cold blood and tossed into the water. Some came by our lands in the country with their hands, some with their legs cut off, and some holding their entrails in their arms, and others had such horrible cuts, and gashes, that worse than they were could never happen.

And the sequel: "As soon as the Indians understood that the Swannekens [Dutch] had so treated them, all the men whom they could surprise on the farm-lands, they killed; but we have never heard that they have ever permitted women or children to be killed." [61]

Indians have often been charged with senseless bloodlust in their fighting, even to the point of treacherously murdering people who had befriended them. The variety of friendship claimed for the victims of such murders should always be investigated in particular detail. The purported friend often turns out to be no more than someone who lived close to the Indians in order to exploit them more efficiently than he could from a distance—his "friendship" is proved by nothing more than his toleration of their persons—or one who warded off other exploiters in order to preserve his own monopoly. For reasons of space and proportion, the subject cannot be fully discussed here, but examples can be cited of real discrimination by Indians in favor of persons that they recognized as friends. David de Vries, himself one such person, was able, after Kieft's massacre, to walk alone, unmenaced and unscathed, in the midst of the very Indians whose kinsfolk had been treated so cruelly.[62] The most startling example is to be found in eighteenth-century Pennsylvania, where the entire Religious Society of Friends, whose members were settled the length and breadth of the colony, was excepted from the raids of the Seven Years' War. In 1758 the Yearly Meeting held at Burlington for New Jersey and Pennsylvania recorded its "Thankfulness for the peculiar favour extended and continued to our Friends and Brethren in profession, none of whom have as we have yet heard been Slain nor carried into Captivity." In consideration of Indian willingness to reciprocate benevolence, the Yearly Meeting displayed an unusual form of racist thinking: it urged all Friends to show their gratitude practically by freeing their slaves.[63]

Indian war, like European war, changed with time and circumstance.

61. De Vries, *Voyages*, in N.-Y. Hist. Soc., *Colls.*, 2d Ser., III, 115–116.
62. *Ibid.*, 116–120.
63. Minutes, 1758, Minutes of the Yearly Meeting Held at Burlington for New Jersey and Pennsylvania, Manuscripts, Bk. A3, 121, Department of Records, Philadelphia Yearly Meeting, Society of Friends, 302 Arch St., Philadelphia.

The guerrilla raids of small war parties became more common after the introduction of firearms made massed attack suicidal. Firearms also reduced the value of stockades around villages even as they had destroyed the invulnerability of walled castles in Europe. The most militaristic of Indians, the Iroquois, adapted to fighting with guns by casting aside their encumbering wooden and leather body armor to gain greater mobility. The naked warrior of the savage stereotype became real enough, but among the Iroquois, at least, he was the product of acculturation rather than an aboriginal prototype.[64]

The influence of European contact on Indian warfare is quite plain. In New England, for instance, until the Pequot conquest, the tribes marched to war en masse, but the Pequots recognized that such tactics would be futile against English firepower (see figure 5, following). They therefore approached the Narragansetts to propose joint harassment of the English rather than confrontation. They would kill livestock, waylay travelers, and ambush isolated farmers. The Narragansetts rejected this proposal in favor of an English alliance and later fought a battle against the Mohegans with the traditional tactics of a large army; but when they were finally forced into open violence against the English in "King Philip's War," they adopted the Pequots' proposed guerrilla tactics, to New England's great distress. Cultural change in response to the contact situation was not one-sided, however. While Pequots and Narragansetts changed traditional tactics to cope with English colonials, the Englishmen were also modifying ancient military wisdom to meet the needs created by Indian guerrilla war. In James Axtell's words, "From these opponents the English gradually learned to fight 'Indian-style,' an ability that once again spelled the difference between their destruction and survival in the New World."[65]

Customs and practices changed from decade to decade, even in regard to the trait of scalping, which, while apparently Indian in origin, did not exist among many Indian tribes in the early seventeenth century. It seems to have been adopted in New England, for example, as a convenient way to collect provincial bounties for heads without having to lug about the awkward impedimenta attached to the scalps.[66]

Both Indians and Englishmen took heads as trophies and put them on show, and the practice of paying bounties for heads was well established among Englishmen. It had been conspicuous in the wars in Ireland in

64. Keith F. Otterbein, "Why the Iroquois Won: An Analysis of Iroquois Military Tactics," *Ethnohistory*, XI (1964), 57–59; Snyderman, *Behind the Tree of Peace*, in *Pa. Archaeol.*, XVIII (1948), 75–77.

65. Bradford, *Of Plymouth Plantation*, ed. Morison, 294–295, 330–331; James Axtell, "The Scholastic Philosophy of the Wilderness," *WMQ*, 3d Ser., XXIX (1972), 340.

66. Hodge, ed., *Handbook of N. Am. Indians*, s.v. "scalping."

FIGURE 5. *Jacques Le Moyne's picture of combat between two tribes,
one of which is assisted by French soldiers. Masses of warriors are
shown marching against each other in a style of warfare that European weapons made obsolete. (See the legend to fig. 1, chap. 5.)*

the thirteenth and fourteenth centuries.[67] In the sixteenth century Sir Humphrey Gilbert had terrorized the Irish by ordering that "the heddes of all those (of what sort soever thei were) which were killed in the daie, should be cutte off from their bodies and brought to the place where he incamped at night, and should there bee laied on the ground by eche side of the waie ledyng into his owne tente so that none could come into his tente for any cause but commonly he muste passe through a lane of heddes which he used *ad terrorem*. . . . [It brought] greate terrour to the people when thei sawe the heddes of their dedde fathers, brothers, children, kinsfolke, and freinds. . . ."[68]

As Europeans taught Indians many of the traits of "savage" war, so also their intrusion into Indian society created new situations to which the Indians responded by cultural change on their own initiative. The attritional warfare of the macrocontact era did indeed justify A. L. Kroeber's indictment of having become so integrated in the culture that escape from it had become impossible, but it was not the aboriginal culture that took such a grim toll. It was instead a culture in which European motives and objectives of war multiplied war's occasions and casualties. Four different kinds of war took place in the macrocontact era: European versus European, Indian versus Indian, intermixed allies versus other allies, and, rarely, European versus Indian. In all of them the influence of European political or economic institutions is apparent. Many of the Indian versus Indian combats were really European wars in which the Indians unconsciously played the role of expendable surrogates. The curbs and restraints of aboriginal custom held no power over Europeans, and particular tribes were in various states of dependency or "ambipendency" with regard to particular colonies. Continual European initiatives and pressures for war created a *macrocontact* system in which tribal bellicosity was indeed self-preservatory for particular groups in particular circumstances, even though it worked general calamity upon the whole of Indian society.

There were no innate differences between Indians and Europeans in their capacity for war or their mode of conducting it. Their differences were matters of technology and politics.[69] Only a few generations before the invasion of America, Europeans had conducted war according

67. Lydon, *Lordship of Ireland*, 195.

68. Canny, "Ideology of English Colonization," *WMQ*, 3d Ser., XXX (1973), 582.

69. The only extended discussion seems to be one without visible virtues: Henry Holbert Turney-High, *Primitive War: Its Practice and Concepts* (Columbia, S.C., 1949). This is an unreliable, superficial, Colonel Blimp sort of repetitive dogma and slippery semantics. The author repeatedly expresses his contempt of the social sciences and declares that any noncommissioned officer knows more than all the social scientists. He hastens to add that he was himself a commissioned officer.

to feudal rules very different from those of the nation-state but start-lingly similar in many respects to the practices of Indian war. Admit-tedly Indian society was not class-stratified like feudal society, and the Indian warrior differed from the feudal knight by being an all-purpose man who turned his hand to peasant occupations between battles. Clearly, also, Indians did not build or besiege castles, or fight with metal weapons and armor. But let not reality disappear behind the knight's armor plate; there was a naked warrior within. From childhood he had received special training in the use of arms, and he spent much time in strenuous sports that would strengthen and condition his body for war. So did the Indian. Both were hunters, and in the hunt both maintained their skill in the use of weapons. Like the Indian the medieval knight hunted for food as well as for sport and training; and, as with the Indian's hunting territories, unauthorized persons were forbidden to hunt in the knight's domain.[70]

A special purification ritual admitted the European esquire into the status of warrior; so also for the Indian, although in his case the ritual was also an ordeal. Knight and warrior mobilized for war in similar ways: the knight responded, if he felt like it, to the call of a lord to whom he had commended himself as vassal; the warrior responded, if he felt like it, to the invitation of an admired chief. No warrior was con-scripted against his will. In neither case was there a bureaucracy to re-cruit and organize a fighting force; such loyalty as existed was that of man to man and family to family. Naturally enough, such soldiers knew nothing of Prussian discipline. Knights and warriors were free men fighting in wars and battles of their own choosing, unlike the hireling standing armies of the nation-state, who accepted orders with their wages.

One of the most striking parallels between the customs of feudal knights and those of Indian warriors was a code of behavior that in Europe is called chivalry. The sparing of women and children in In-dian warfare fits snugly into the doctrines of chivalry avowed by feudal knights (and even practiced by them when the women and children were of their own religion). The practice was abandoned by the more rational or efficient killing machines organized by the nation-states; chivalry belonged to the knights, and the knights belonged to the Mid-dle Ages. Chivalry, in short, was barbarous.

70. A. F. C. Wallace has erroneously extrapolated the American custom of freedom to hunt on unposted lands back into European times, and the error is repeated by Vaughan; but hunting in Europe was stringently limited to the no-bility and to "stinted" limits of rights in commons for the lower orders. Wallace, "Political Organization," *Southwest. Jour. of Anthro.*, XIII (1957), 312, n. 7; Vaughan, *New England Frontier*, 108; E. C. K. Gonner, *Common Land and In-closure* (London, 1912), 14–16.

Perhaps an opportunity exists here to use the parallel between America and Europe to learn more about Europe. A customary explanation of chivalry's rise has been that the sweet moan of minnesingers and troubadours softened the hearts and manners of the great hulks on horseback. This lacks persuasion. Indians had a different sort of explanation for their own variety of chivalry: they needed to rebuild their declining populations. Feudal Europe was a time of population uncertainty, and the damsels spared by gallant knights were prime breeding stock—a fact sometimes put to test by the knights. In this respect the Indians seem to have been the more chivalrous, for they were observed everywhere to refrain from sexual molestation of female prisoners; they took the women and girls, untouched, back to the captors' villages for assignment to families as wives and daughters.[71] The knight, however, though he served the public interest by preserving his prisoners' lives, served himself also by demanding ransom.

Knight and warrior both gave first allegiance to their kin. This reservation of loyalty from the monopoly demanded by the nation-state was the unforgivable sin that has roused nationalists to denounce the special barbarity of feudal Europe and the special savagery of Indian America. That all war is cruel, horrible, and socially insane is easy to demonstrate, but the nationalist dwells upon destiny, glory, crusades, and other such claptrap to pretend that his own kind of war is different from and better than the horrors perpetrated by savages. This is plainly false. The qualities of ferocity and atrocity are massively visible in the practices of European and American powers all over the world, quite recently in the assaults of the most advanced civilized states upon one another.

71. Hodge, ed., *Handbook of N. Am. Indians*, s.v., "captives"; Heckewelder, *Account of the Indian Nations*, ed. Reichel, in Hist. Soc. Pa., *Memoirs*, XII, 339–340.

Chapter 10 ᔰ PIONEERS

In one way or another the question frequently arises, How substantially have Indians contributed to the society and culture of modern America? The most common answer to this question is, Very little. It seems to me that there are different ways of defining the issue and that valid answers will vary according to the way the question is put. The processes of trait diffusion and cultural cumulation have not ceased to work upon either Amerindian or Euramerican since 1492. Seventeenth-century European culture is as much dead and gone (thank goodness) as is seventeenth-century Indian culture.

Nevertheless, modern American society owes more of its apparent features to European antecedents than to Indian, and its component traits have been contributed overwhelmingly from non-Indian sources that include Asian and African traits picked up both directly and through European carriers (for example, jazz music, Korean-Chinese printing, and Hindu-Arabic numerals). Attention has been given in foregoing chapters to varied Amerindian contributions to Europe and, by way of Europe, to the world, but it may be argued that these became mere accretions to European culture without substantially transforming it in any fundamental way. (Much depends, of course, on how culture is defined and identified.) Indian agriculture contributed new crops, but it did not cause Europe to forsake the plow. Indian herbs were added to the European pharmacopoeia without changing the physician into a powwow. Indian warriors fought with and against European soldiers and taught the value of guerrilla tactics in certain circumstances; but drill, discipline, and a hierarchical command structure remain basic to modern military forces. Indian voluntarism and equalitarianism struck the European political imagination, but the nation-state grew ever more centralized and bureaucratic and acquired new techniques for compelling its subjects to obedience and conformity. Even if it is assumed that the Indians addicted Europe to nicotine, the change can be seen as just one more relatively minor vice added to an already imposing pile. If the Indians had gotten Europeans to *substitute* smoking for drinking, the change would have been undeniably basic; but puffing while we pour has mostly added to our bills.

It is valid to say that very little of Indian culture survives to modern times in its original forms except in the enclaves of tribal reservations. The identifiably Indian cultural traits still with us have been assimilated into Euramerican culture and adapted and conformed to structures of European institutions and ideas. Our culture has consumed Indian traits the way our language has gobbled up words: as Danish and French words have come into the English language without bringing along Danish or French grammar, so canoes have been adopted without displacing sails or oceanic navigation. Like other peoples, Indians have also contributed heavily to the vocabulary of English without affecting its mode of movement, particularly in the realm of geographical names.

Another way of asking what modern society owes to the Indians produces an equally valid answer with a different significance. Regardless of vestiges and residues of aboriginal cultures still recognizable, suppose it be asked what modern America would be like if Indians had not been here to receive Europe's vanguard. Could Europeans have established their beachheads and penetrated so swiftly to the heart of the continent without the stimulus of Indian exploitation and the help of Indian persons and technology? What would Boston, New York, and Philadelphia be if Shawmut, Manhattan, and Passayonk had not preceded them? How many times would Jamestown have followed Roanoke into oblivion if Powhatan's maize had been unavailable? How long would it have taken Champlain to get past the Saint Lawrence rapids without Indian canoes, and why would he have bothered if the interior had been uninhabited wilderness? Is there any good reason to think that the Mississippi Valley would be more highly developed today than the Australian outback if the Indians of North America had not existed? Although second-guessing history is a risky business, it may be said fairly confidently that both American and European society would be vastly different today if not for the interaction of Europeans with Indians.

So much is fairly generally accepted by historians nowadays. Samuel Eliot Morison, for example, has written in a widely circulated text of the profoundly enriching and transforming effect the Indians had upon European immigrants. But Admiral-Professor Morison continued his remark with a description of historical process squarely in the tradition of the civilization-savagery myth. What we more especially owe to the Indians, in his view, is that they forced our ancestors to fight for what they got. "As the Algonquian warrior of old drank the blood of his fallen enemy in order to absorb his courage, so the people of America may thank the brave redskins who made their ancestors pay dear for the mastery of a continent."[1] Ignoring the blood and thunder, we may

1. Samuel Eliot Morison, *The Oxford History of the American People* (New

say that Morison's analysis is a little deficient. As we have seen, Europeans went through a far more complex historical process than just fighting their way into the New World. What they did was to enter into symbiotic relations of interdependence with Indians (and Africans), involving both conflict and cooperation, that formed the matrix of modern American society.

Another kind of fallacy is propounded by the "transit of civilization" historians who trace modern American society directly back to Europe. It is as though European culture were to be derived directly from Rome without notice of the matrix of medieval times. Superficially a case could be made for such a derivation by someone willing to ignore the data of a millennium. For example, the governments of modern Europe and ancient Rome have been characterized by bureaucratic states administering written codes of law; how easily one might skip over the long era in between when lordship, custom, and contract prevailed. Ancient and modern times alike have been dominated by large cities bustling with industry and commerce, but the historical link between them was rural and its commerce largely local. Historians know well that a host of "barbarian" peoples intervened between ancient and modern cultures and entered fully into the creation of modern Europe. The Lombards have disappeared into Italy, the Angles into England, the Gauls into France. Except for the archaeologist and the etymologist, theirs are vanished cultures, but no one will dispute that all those peoples and cultures have gone into the modern mix.

Modern America is descended from formative "colonial" America—not merely from transplanted Europeans—with all the cultural and ethnic complexity that characterized that effervescent era. The colonial mold has vanished, as the Middle Ages are gone from Europe, but the final product could not have achieved its form if the mold had been other than it was. In the last analysis, what American society owes uniquely to the Indian component of our matrix is its exploration, development, settlement, and cultivation of the continent. Every European "discoverer" had Indian guides. Every European colonizer had Indian instruction and assistance. Ethnocentric semantics have hidden the chief role of Indians in the creation of American society by reserving exclusively for Europeans the honorable title of "pioneer" and contrasting it to the lowly status of "native," but the European vanguard were pupils in the Indian school. Indians brought to their symbiotic partner-

---

York, 1965), 15–16. The remark represents considerable advance in Morison's thinking. Less than a decade earlier he had written of "backward peoples getting enlarged notions of nationalism and turning ferociously on Europeans who have attempted to civilize them." Morison's introduction to Leach, *Flintlock and Tomahawk*, ix.

ship with Europeans the experience and knowledge of millennia of genuine pioneering. What American society owes to Indian society, as much as to any other source, is the mere fact of its existence.

Part Two ❧ *THE HEATHEN*
FOR INHERITANCE,
AND THE EARTH
FOR POSSESSION

> *It is painful to advert to these things. But our forefathers, though wise, pious, and sincere, were nevertheless, in respect to Christian charity, under a cloud; and, in history, truth should be held sacred, at whatever cost. We, who are stationed, as it were, at the portals of history, are peculiarly bound ... to enter the lists against that blind zeal, which is all the blinder and more pernicious because it will not see; and especially against the narrow and futile patriotism, which, instead of pressing forward in pursuit of truth, takes pride in walking backwards to cover the slightest nakedness of our forefathers.*
>
> COLONEL THOMAS ASPINWALL

Chapter 11 ❧ THE DREAD LORD
and LORDS of
NEW ENGLAND

We turn now to examine how the abstractions and theoretical propositions of the foregoing pages hold up when applied to a substantial unit of historical experience: seventeenth-century New England—a busy place, copiously documented, in which contact phenomena moved swiftly to a climax.

New England in the early seventeenth century was both a rather vague geographical expression and a name for a particular group of English settlements within the region. After the founding of Massachusetts Bay in 1630 and its swift growth through mass migration, New England came to apply in practice to the colonies of that particular vicinity. Puritans used the name with even more restriction, for only the colonies controlled by brethren of their own faith or such close cousins as the New Plymouth independents.

The territorial New England to which this book attends is effectively what we now call southern New England, including the modern states of Massachusetts, Connecticut, and Rhode Island (see map 1, p. 200). These polities represent a coalescence of colonies that started out as New Plymouth, Salem, Massachusetts Bay, Martha's Vineyard and Nantucket, Providence Plantations, Shawomet-Warwick, Aquidneck-Rhode Island, Connecticut, New Haven, and some smaller ephemera. Most of them shook down into their present containers during the period prior to 1677, and Plymouth was merged with Massachusetts soon afterward.

The people who lived in this territory had not yet come to be called New Englanders, and there is difficulty even now in comprehending them under a single rubric. General practice gives the name *Puritan* to the culture and people of the region overall, reserving special identification for other persons and communities. In this book, however, that name is reserved for the members and supporters of a specific church and the governments with which it was affiliated. It seems important to stress that Puritans were a minority of the whole population during a not precisely determined period of time, because the history to be narrated is largely an account of how that minority labored incessantly to impose its power on the rest. For reasons set forth in chapter 2 above, it is accepted herein that an overwhelming majority of New England's population in the early seventeenth century were Indians. Besides Indians there were an unknown number of dissenters from Puritanism, the most significant concentration of whom were settled on the islands and shores of Narragansett Bay. For convenience they will be called (anachronistically) Rhode Islanders. Although the Puritan colonies excluded the dissenters of Rhode Island from the dissenter establishment of the United Colonies of New England, there is every reason for a historian to include them in the population of New England. They were there.

The period of this study embraces the two great wars of Puritan conquest and their interval—roughly from 1634 to 1677. Among its subjects are the processes by which the English colonies acquired their present shapes. These processes were intimately involved with the colonists' policies toward, and relations with, the Indian tribes whose territories they had invaded. New England displays, in a relatively small extent of space and time, patterns that spread more diffusely in other colonies. The "good" land of New England—soil rich enough and deep enough for easy tillage—is and was comparatively small in area because of ancient glacial scouring, and the colonists hoping to acquire that land immigrated in unmatched numbers in the seventeenth century's second quarter. Newcomers' pressures for ownership were briefly alleviated by the availability of land that had been voided of Indian inhabitants in the epidemic of 1616, but as immigrants arrived en masse they turned their desires to the lands still held and used by surviving Indians. Until these pressures reached the bursting point, colonists in New England pursued trade and alliance with Indian tribes much after the pattern of colonists elsewhere.

The moment of traumatic change came with the colonization of Connecticut. That event stirred up latent antagonisms not only between Indians and colonists but between the two Puritan colonies of Massachusetts and Connecticut. Indeed the Puritans' quarrel was decisive for initiating the first Puritan war, the conquest of the Pequots. Between the first and second Puritan wars was a span of nearly forty years during which colonist and Indian lived in uneasy accommodation. The bulk of the fur trade moved westward to the line of the Connecticut River, where it was conducted with interior tribes. The eastern Indians did not follow after it. None of the Wampanoags, Massachusets, Nipmucks,

Pequots, or Narragansetts went west (or east or north or south) until their tribes had been smashed by armed conquest or subjection under menace. Until the second Puritan war many Indians assisted in the economic growth of the colonies by working for wages, making wampum currency and paying wampum tribute, and selling meat and fish as retail provisioners.[1] Many others participated in colonial progress through the new institution of the missionary reservation by means of which "praying Indians" were simultaneously converted into church congregations and formidable auxiliaries of Massachusetts Bay's armed forces.[2]

The founding of Connecticut, instead of assuaging Puritan appetites for land, stimulated Connecticut and Massachusetts to accelerated acquisition, and the rise of heterodox Providence Plantations heightened the stimulation with yet another competitor. All the colonists knew that the availability of landed property to an individual depended upon the extent of territory under his government's jurisdiction. All the colonies struggled anxiously to gain preemptive dominion over Indian territories while the Indians were yet in occupation. By averages there was still plenty of land for everyone, and Indian populations opened still more room by continuing to decline, but statistics were not at issue. What concerned each magistrate and colonist was how much land there was *for him.*

Until the second Puritan war the colonies constantly struggled to maintain and expand their jurisdictions against the Indians and against one another. The territory of the Narragansett tribe, the largest and most powerful of the region, became a special object of desire and contention. In an oversimple way, one might say that all intercolonial relations were motivated or shadowed by efforts to acquire Narragansett land. After the Narragansetts were smashed in what is misleadingly called "King Philip's War," colonial boundary disputes of southern New England were settled in court. "Free" tribal government disappeared from southern New England except for the dependably subservient Mohegans in Connecticut and the Eastern Niantics in Rhode Island.[3] The interior frontiers of the Puritan colonies were ringed by tribes having the strong support of other European colonies: those on the north and

---

1. Weeden, *Economic and Social History*, I, 37–39, and his *Indian Money as a Factor in New England Civilization*, Johns Hopkins University Studies in Historical and Political Science, 2d Ser., VIII–IX (Baltimore, 1884), 407.

2. See chap. 14, below.

3. For the Mohegans, see Carroll Alton Means, "Mohegan-Pequot Relationships as Indicated by the Events Leading to the Pequot Massacre of 1637 and Subsequent Claims in the Mohegan Land Controversy," *Bulletin of the Archaeological Society of Connecticut*, XXI (1947), 26; Drake, *Biography and History of the Indians*, 149–165.

east were backed by the French, those on the west and south by New York. With the elimination of Indian enclaves, New England acquired a continuous frontier line prophetic of the line that would be established for all the colonies by royal proclamation in 1763. In neither case was it a line between civilization and savagery; it was the line between effective colonial jurisdictions and effective tribal jurisdictions.

Traditional histories tell a different tale that need not be repeated here. The novelty of my findings derives, I believe, from unorthodox assumptions about persons and a critical attitude toward the evidence of familiar sources. In contrast with traditional assumptions that Puritans possessed the humanity implied by civilization while Indians lacked it, I have assumed that both Indians and Puritans were neither more nor less than human. My argument for the Indians' humanity has already been presented in Part I of this study. As for Puritans, I have found no substantiation for the filiopietist portrayal of them in a semidivine state superior even to the humanity of the garden variety of civilized people. In this exalted state the Puritan is actuated only by noble motives and can tell no fibs—anyway, not about Indians. In the words of Alden T. Vaughan, the Puritans "had no reason to conceal their attitudes or actions toward the Indians."[4] I have found plenty of reason.

The Puritan mind was intensely interested in much more than the content of sermons. No more than other people did Puritans refrain from behavior they defined as sin; and, also like those other people, they found rationalizations for forbidden conduct.[5] Although power, wealth, and land were immediate objects of temptation for even the most self-righteous of the Puritan gentry, the sins of pride and covetousness that they prompted were the sort that a wrathful God could forgive in his favorite children. Was it not true that as the Lord's Chosen acquired greater power they could better do His will? And would not their acquisition of land enable them better to bring the land's inhabitants under His government? Massachusetts's Governor John Winthrop, Sr., meditated on his responsibilities and opportunities while en route from England to his new home. His Puritans would build a "Citty upon a Hill" for the admiration and emulation of mankind. Thus far that thought has been respectfully quoted many, many times. But Winthrop also referred, in less quoted phrases, to the sanction for his enterprise: "Thus stands the case between God and us. Wee are entered into Covenant with him for this worke. Wee have taken out a Commission. The Lord hath given us leave to drawe our owne articles...." To finance the con-

4. Vaughan, *New England Frontier*, vi–vii.

5. A psychoanalytical thesis is advanced in Neal Emerson Salisbury, "Conquest of the 'Savage': Puritans, Puritan Missionaries, and Indians, 1620–1680" (Ph.D. diss., University of California, Los Angeles, 1972), 13–20, and throughout.

struction of that city on the hill, God had signed a divine blank check.[6]

Roger Williams thought otherwise. In his usual zealous manner he denounced the Bay Puritans' "depraved appetite after the great vanities, dreams and shadows of this vanishing life, great portions of land, land in this wilderness, as if men were in as great necessity and danger for want of great portions of land, as poor, hungry, thirsty seamen have, after a sick and stormy, a long and starving passage. This is one of the gods of New England, which the living and most high Eternal will destroy and famish."[7]

New England's historians habitually have adopted more of Winthrop's view than of Williams's, and their attitudes have made a strong impression on the historiography of the United States. During the nineteenth century and much of the twentieth, the whole historical profession was dominated by historians who not only were trained in New England but at the same time were steeped in the accepted traditions of that region. Our histories generally show their imprint. Critics of the Puritans have been attacked as merely venting hostility (remarkably in the pattern of Freudian responses to criticism), and the substantial evidence presented by the critics has been passed over with silence or authoritative epithet.

This won't do. Contemporary opponents of the Puritan gentry, who included a remarkable number of less powerful Puritans, were as much witnesses to their time, and certainly as honest, as the oligarchs, and their voices must be heard with at least equal respect. Quite simply, they told the truth more frequently and more reliably than the servants of New England's Leviathan. I have arrived at this finding through subjecting the source documents to standard procedures of textual comparison and analysis similar to the tests commonly applied by historians to documents of other countries and other times. With respect to methodology, my attitude contrasts as strongly with that of the traditionalists as do our assumptions about the comparative humanity of Puritan and Indian. They accept the Puritans' documents as gospel. I have regarded the sources as the writings of persons with interests to serve and have interpreted them accordingly.

I propose to show in the following narrative why and how the interests of the various parties in New England conditioned their reporting. In this chapter it may suffice to show that the Puritans themselves readily acknowledged that they summoned "history" to their support. The highest status in the Puritan oligarchy was held by the

6. John Winthrop, "A Modell of Christian Charity," in *Winthrop Papers*, II, 294.

7. Williams to Major Mason, June 22, 1670, Bartlett, ed., *Letters of Williams*, Narragansett Club, *Pubs.*, VI, 342.

Commissioners of the United Colonies of New England, and these gentlemen concisely expressed their own notion of how history should be oriented. In 1646, after having menaced the Narragansett Indians into a treaty of territorial dispossession, the Commissioners thought to take account of public opinion. They "desired" that "all the Colonies (as they may) would collect and gather up the many speciall providences of God towards them, ... how his hand hath bene with them in laying their foundations in church and comon wealth, how he hath cast the dread of his people (weake in themselves) upon the Indians ... that history may be compiled according to truth with due weight by some able and fitt man appointed thereunto."[8]

Among the commissioners subscribing to this resolution was John Winthrop, Sr., whose *History of New England* has had the same sort of importance in its field as John Smith's histories have had for Virginia.[9] Winthrop's *History* is compiled in journal form, and there is no way of knowing when it was undertaken or whether the dated entries were composed ex post facto from notes, but its compilation form met the Commissioners' prescription; and, more important, Winthrop's "truth with due weight" does indeed show, at large and in detail, how God's hand had been with the Puritans. An unbeliever could say that it presented history with a slant. An investigator may add that it is curiously selective and that the documents interpreted by Winthrop have had a high mortality rate. Especially as regards Indian affairs, his interpretations have had to be accepted in lieu of the prime sources because of the latter's disappearance. In the tons of paper squirreled away by Winthrop and his descendants, the only text of an Indian treaty surviving from his lifetime is the one written in 1645, one year before the Commissioners formally decided to give truth its due weight. As will be shown, the prime texts did exist once upon a time. The process of natural selection by which they became unfit to survive must be matter of speculation, but one can say with confidence that the interpretations provided in Winthrop's *History* are unlikely to be accurate representations of the vanished texts. All this sounds like innuendo so let it be said forthrightly: Winthrop probably rewrote the substance of the Indian treaties to meet the Puritans' political and ideological needs, and then he or a devoted descendant destroyed the originals. The case cannot be proved because the essential evidence is gone. The common sense of the case, with the remaining circumstantial evidence, is presented in the following chapters.

During their second great war of conquest, the Puritans again took note of history. The Reverend William Hubbard seems to have begun

8. Minutes, Sept. 1646, Pulsifer, ed., *Acts of United Colonies*, I, 83.
9. See the bibliographic note in chap. 2, n. 45, above.

his *Narrative of the Indian Wars in New England* in November 1675. Hubbard worked at his manuscript more than a year and then submitted it for approval (and doubtless revisions also) by a committee appointed for the purpose by Massachusetts's governor and council.[10] While Hubbard toiled, another cleric, the Reverend Increase Mather, hurried together a *Brief History of the War*, which was published in both Boston and London in 1676. Mather's prose is often more revealing than informative. Certainly it discloses, in purest form, the traditional Puritan outlook.[11]

Mather plunged into his text by affirming that the "Lord God of our Fathers hath given us for a rightful Possession" the land of "the Heathen People amongst whom we live" and that said heathens had unaccountably acquired—but without having been injured—some "jealousies." That they had remained quiet so long "must be ascribed to the wonderful Providence of God, who did (as with Jacob of old, and after that with the Children of Israel) lay the fear of the English and the dread of them upon all the Indians. The terror of God was upon them round about."[12] There could be no clearer equation: the dread of the English was the terror of God.

Mather's depiction of terror is confirmed by Roger Williams, but Williams noted that God had had some assistance in being frightful:

Are not all the English of this land, generally, a persecuted people from their native soil? and hath not the God of peace and Father of mercies made these

10. Samuel G. Drake, ed., *The History of the Indian Wars in New England from the First Settlement to the Termination of the War with King Philip, in 1677, from the Original Work by the Rev. William Hubbard* (Roxbury, Mass., 1865), I, xxi, 3.

A bibliographic note: Hubbard's work has confusingly appeared under three distinct titles. The original Boston edition of 1677 is called *A Narrative of the Troubles with the Indians In New-England, from the first planting thereof in the year 1607. to this present year 1677. But chiefly of the late Troubles in the two last years, 1675. and 1676. To which is added a Discourse about the Warre with the Pequods In the year 1637.* The book was reprinted in the same year of 1677 under Hubbard's supervision in London. The London edition is considered better than the first because Hubbard corrected some slight errors. It varies little except in paging and title, which is *The Present State of New-England, Being a Narrative Of the Troubles* . . . , after which it continues with the language of the first title. Samuel G. Drake, as noted above, called his edition *The History of the Indian Wars in New England*. For further discussion, see Drake's introduction and Randolph G. Adams, "William Hubbard's Narrative, 1677: A Bibliographical Study," *Papers of the Bibliographical Society of America*, XXXIII (1939), 25–39.

My citations are to the London edition, using the short form: Hubbard, *Narrative*. References to Drake's editorial comment give his edition under his name.

11. Increase Mather, *Diary, March, 1675–December, 1676. Together with Extracts from Another Diary by Him, 1674–1687*, ed. Samuel A. Green (Cambridge, Mass., 1900), 29.

12. Mather, *Brief History of the War*, 1.

natives more friendly in this, than our native countrymen in our own land to us? Have they not entered leagues of love, and to this day continued peaceable commerce with us? Are not our families grown up in peace amongst them? Upon which I humbly ask, how it can suit with Christian ingenuity to take hold of some seeming occasions for their destructions, which, though the heads be only aimed at, yet, all experience tells us, falls on the body and the innocent.[13]

The governor and council of Massachusetts Bay apparently disliked Mather's boasting about terror at a time when they were trying to convince the English of England that New England was the aggrieved and defensive party in "King Philip's War." They passed over Mather's explanation of the war to put their seal of approval on William Hubbard's. Their action does not signify that they had rejected Mather's ideas; the same assumptions inform Hubbard's work, but his prose is less nakedly passionate. As New England Puritans went, Hubbard was a sophisticate. His book and his person were the chosen instruments for official propaganda in London, where important people doubted New England's property in Jehovah's thunder. The official approval of Hubbard's book is dated March 1677—apparently after it was already in print—and his voyage to London followed so swiftly afterwards that the English edition was licensed in June.[14]

It is worth consideration that there was bad blood between Hubbard and Mather. Unlike Mather's earlier book, Hubbard's work looked backward to the Pequot conquest to fill in background for the contemporary war against Wampanoags, Narragansetts, etc. When Mather learned that the governor and council of New Plymouth privately judged Hubbard's "mistakes" to be "many more than the truths," he leaked this choice bit of gossip.[15] In the ensuing hubbub, Mather felt moved to write another book of his own on the background he had previously neglected. His new Relation of the Troubles referred to Hubbard's book with a polite sneer, acknowledging Hubbard's "Pains and Industry" but insisting that "neverthelesse it hath been thought needful to publish this; considering that most of the Things here insisted on, are not so much as once taken Notice of in that Narrative."[16]

13. Williams to Massachusetts General Court, Oct. 5, 1654, Bartlett, ed., Letters of Williams, Narragansett Club, Pubs., VI, 271.
14. Drake, ed., History of the Indian Wars by Hubbard, I, 3, xxii and n.
15. John Cotton to Increase Mather, Mar. 19 and Apr. 14, 1677, Mass. Hist. Soc., Colls., 4th Ser., VIII (Boston, 1868), 232–235.
16. A Relation of the Troubles which have hapned in New-England, By reason of the Indians there. From the Year 1614. to the Year 1675. (Boston, 1677). This was reprinted as Early History of New England; Being a Relation of Hostile Passages between the Indians and European Voyagers and First Settlers . . . , ed. Samuel G. Drake (Albany, N.Y., 1864). Because of difficulty of access to the first edition, all references are to Drake's. The quotation is on p. 48.

The recitation of such squabbles among the Puritans themselves should be sufficient warning as to the validity of Hubbard's official account, and a little research in the sources confirms the warning. Hubbard's text was put together with the same sort of skilled attention to details of phrase and twist of meaning that medieval monks used when they adjusted scripture to doctrine. Hubbard was fighting for the survival of his church's power, and he used methods that have come naturally to sophisticated theologians in that situation for thousands of years.

For whatever reasons, his account has remained the substantial foundation on which subsequent histories of the Puritan conquests have been erected. Manifestly it and they are incompatible with the analysis of Euramerican-Amerindian acculturation given in Part I of this study. What follows may therefore be considered, in one aspect, as a detailed refutation of Hubbard's book and tradition. However, that feature was a product rather than the purpose of the study. The purpose was to find out, as best the sources would disclose, what did happen in New England, and the narrative aims at outlining the development of events, though the evaluation of evidence intrudes as a necessary task.

In performing that necessary task, it seems fair to say, I have recognized in myself a strong aversion toward the Puritan gentry and have tried to compensate for it by documenting heavily from their own writings whenever possible. It may be well to notice that I have tried to practice restraint but not concealment of my distaste, and to say further that it was acquired in the course of the research. I started the study with pervasive skepticism and busy curiosity, and my present biases are largely the result of wrestling with the Puritan gentry's own writings to extract bits of reliable data from excruciating cant and masterful guile. Those who can swallow the cant, of course, will find it neither painful nor guileful, but they have an obligation to take into account the bits of data.

Chapter 12 ❧ *TWO WAYS*
to CONNECTICUT

An early incident in New England is worth recalling for its demonstration in microcosm of much that was to follow. It concerns the Plymouth colony, whose settlers engaged in the fur trade in the hope of liquidating the colony's debts. Three years after their arrival in America the Saints of Plymouth showed how to wipe out a competitor forcefully without exposing themselves to the crown's justice. The trick was to manipulate the Indians so as to achieve Plymouth's aims while diverting blame to the "savages."

A colony of adventurers sent out by Thomas Weston in 1622 had settled at Wessagusset, on the south side of Massachusetts Bay. The irritated Saints saw only trouble in Wessagusset. It was a possible (Anglican) source of religious "infection," a certain rival in fur trading, and an undisciplined hazard in Indian relations. Suddenly discovering an Indian "conspiracy," Captain Miles Standish and his small troop of Plymouth soldiery marched to "save" the Wessagusset colonists, who, however, showed a singular disinclination to be saved. One of the Wessagusset men vexed Standish by remarking, "We fear not the Indians, but live with them and suffer them to lodge with us, not having sword or gun, or needing the same." Standish promptly created a need for the same. Pretending to the Indians that he had come to Wessagusset to trade, he enticed a few of them into his hands and then massacred them without warning. After this no Englishman could be safe at Wessagusset. Indian avengers, not grasping the difference between the Englishmen of the two colonies, took a toll of three Wessagusset men, and the rest of that unhappy community chose to abandon the site. They showed their confidence in Plymouth by refusing Standish's invitation to return there with him, and they set sail eastward in a small boat to make contact with the Maine fishing fleet. Back in England they proved most vociferously ungrateful for the benefits conferred upon them by Plymouth.

Plymouth, however, had gained its end. Strong enough to defy the particular Indians offended by the massacre, Plymouth resumed its local trade monopoly until new competitors appeared. To counter the "vile and clamorous" comments of the Wessagusset men, Plymouth's leaders edited their records a bit and sent an ingenious young man named Edward Winslow to propagandize for them in England. Winslow, who was to become a specialist in the art, covered Wessagusset's former colonists with sanctimonious abuse and falsified events sufficiently to implicate the Indians as conspirators against Plymouth and to conceal the premeditation of the massacre. He succeeded so brilliantly that the facts of the affair remained buried for more than three centuries.[1]

Plymouth's men were not quite Puritans, to be sure, but in Indian policy they saw eye to eye with the Puritans in most respects, with one conspicuous exception—namely, the identity of the particular beneficiaries of domination over the Indians. The Pilgrims of New Plymouth were to be sadly disappointed as they watched their stronger neighbor on the Bay encroach upon their trading posts and territorial claims.[2] Indeed Plymouth soon became a relatively inconsequential factor in Indian affairs. Soon after the Puritans had established themselves at Massachusetts Bay, their greater numbers and wealth, and their vastly greater influence in England, won them the power of decision. As Plymouth receded in importance, a secessionist offshoot of Massachusetts came rapidly forward to challenge the Bay. While Plymouth dragged its heels and made excuses to avoid involvement, Connecticut and Massachusetts struggled for domination over the Pequot Indians. What then started as a dispute over legal formalities rapidly advanced to a contest over which colony should be first to conquer the Pequots and ultimately petered out in a long squabble over which should enjoy the spoils.

Although minor clashes with the Indians marked the arrival of the Massachusetts Bay settlers in 1630, no major conflict occurred until the outbreak of war with the Pequot tribe. As the first in the long series of

---

1. Willison, *Saints and Strangers*, chap. 15, quote on 226; Winslow, *Good Newes*, in Young, ed., *Chronicles of Pilgrims*, 269–375; Bradford, *Of Plymouth Plantation*, ed. Morison, 116–118.

Winslow's falsified version remained unchallenged until Willison published. Subsequent comment has varied. David Bushnell called Standish's attack "a preventive massacre," adding that "the Pilgrims bore the Indians no ill will." Alden T. Vaughan recited the old Winslow tale with no recognition of its exposure as a fabrication, though Willison's book is in Vaughan's bibliography. George D. Langdon, Jr., omitted the Wessagusset incident entirely. Bushnell, "The Treatment of the Indians in Plymouth Colony," *New England Quarterly*, XXVI (1953), 194; Vaughan, *New England Frontier*, 82–88; Langdon, *Pilgrim Colony: A History of New Plymouth, 1620–1691*, Yale Publications in American Studies, XII (New Haven, Conn., 1966).

2. Bailyn, *New England Merchants*, 23–26.

New England's Indian wars, the "Pequot War" has been much written about by contemporaries as well as historians. Yet, more than three centuries after its occurrence, explanations of it are full of lacunae and contradictions.

Hostilities in the Pequot conquest began in October 1636 with a punitive expedition from Massachusetts Bay, directed first against the subtribe of Narragansett Indians on Block Island and then against the Pequots in their home territory on the coast eastward of the Niantic River (see maps 1 and 2, pp. 200, 219). Ostensibly this expedition sailed to avenge the murders of two traders: Captain John Oldham, who had been killed on Block Island, and Captain John Stone, who had been killed two years earlier on the Connecticut River. Actually, as in many another war, the real causes had been generating for several years before the outbreak of armed conflict, and they must be sought in disputes over sovereignty and tribute.

These disputes had originated in two sets of rivalries for preeminence in the Connecticut Valley. On the one hand, England and the Netherlands both claimed the valley by right of discovery; on the other hand, the Pequot Indians, who had discovered the place rather earlier than the Europeans, claimed supremacy by right of conquest over the indigenous tribes whose priority of discovery was best of all. The Pequots also feuded intermittently with the powerful Narragansett Indians. Although neither the Pequots nor the Narragansetts lived in the Connecticut Valley, each of these two great Indian powers was far too strong for the fragmented Connecticut tribes to resist; the outcome of their contest would determine the ultimate destination of Connecticut Indian tribute. Dutch and English rivals took advantage of these Indian contests in order to convert "rights of discovery" into "rights of possession." The Dutch, who had invented this legal maneuver for precisely such circumstances, made the first move.[3]

In 1632 the Dutch West India Company acted to strengthen its claim to the Connecticut River by purchasing from the grand sachem of the Pequots a small tract at the site of present-day Hartford. At the site the Dutch planned to build a trading post called the House of Hope. Jacob van Curler, who negotiated the land purchase, noted carefully that it had been made with consent of the local sachem, tributary to the Pequots, and also "with the knowledge" of the Narragansetts.[4]

News of this event quickly reached the settlements of New England. Plymouth's Edward Winslow proposed to the Massachusetts Bay magistrates that the two colonies should forestall the Dutch by jointly estab-

---

3. The event has been noticed in another connection in chap. 8 above.
4. Deed, June 8, 1633, *N.Y. Col. Docs.*, II, 139–140.

lishing an English trading presence on the Connecticut. The Bay leaders rejected Winslow's overtures on grounds of excessive risk. Hindsight reveals a second motive; that is, they declined to share Connecticut with Plymouth because they hoped to make it Massachusetts's exclusive possession. For the time being, however, the Bay made no objection when Plymouth decided to establish on its own a post several miles upriver from the Dutch House of Hope, to thus intercept the furs coming from the interior. To Dutch protests about prior rights acquired through land purchase, Plymouth's men retorted with a deed of their own, obtained from a local sachem formerly chased out of Connecticut by the Pequots. The deed game had begun.[5]

The Dutch tried to gain control of the river through another purchase of the lands at its mouth, but before they could erect a fort to control traffic, the Pequots attempted to do some controlling of their own. Violating their pledge to permit unobstructed access to the Dutch House of Hope, the Pequots killed some Indians attempting to trade there—probably Narragansetts or Narragansett tributaries. Both the Narragansetts and the Dutch reacted violently. The Dutch killed the Pequots' grand sachem and closed the House of Hope to Pequot trade, while the Narragansetts mobilized for war.[6]

At this juncture Captain John Stone appeared on the scene. With our knowledge that Massachusetts would later wage war avowedly on account of Stone's murder, we might expect to see in him a respected figure; in reality, however, Stone was a West Indian trader-cum-pirate who had tried to hijack a Plymouth vessel before coming to Massachusetts Bay. Plymouth demanded his blood for that—a rightful remedy in the law of the time—but the Bay magistrates unaccountably smoothed things over until Stone was caught in Boston rolling in bed with another man's wife. Apparently unaccustomed to the sort of official response that Boston made in such matters and far from being contrite or guilt-smitten, Stone "used braving and threatening speeches" to one of the magistrates. For this compounding of crime he was banished from the colony on pain of death if he should ever reappear. On his way to Virginia he detoured up the Connecticut River, where he kidnapped some Indians for ransom. Stone miscalculated badly in his final episode. An earlier ransom kidnapping by a Dutchman on the Connecticut had made the natives knowledgeable about such affairs, and when Stone neglected

5. Bradford, *Of Plymouth Plantation*, ed. Morison, 257–260, 281; Apr. 4, 1631, and July 12, 1633, Winthrop, *History*, ed. Savage, I, 52, 105; De Forest, *Indians of Connecticut*, 76.

6. "Remonstrance of New Netherland," July 28, 1649, *N.Y. Col. Docs.*, I, 287; Nov. 6, 1634, Winthrop, *History*, ed. Savage, I, 148; De Forest, *Indians of Connecticut*, 73.

to keep a careful guard, the Indians seized the chance to kill him and his crew.[7]

Two years later the Bay magistrates chose to ascribe Stone's death as a major cause of their war against the Pequots, and historians have followed their lead ever since. But this strains credulity. On the face of it, Stone's death was a far from likely casus belli. A known freebooter, he was a subject of neither Massachusetts nor Plymouth; moreover, the authorities of both colonies hated him, those of Plymouth having themselves demanded his death. The Indians had ample provocation for revenging themselves upon him, and they did so outside the legal jurisdiction of any New England colony. Even the anathema of an Englishman's death at Indian hands failed to arouse Boston to intervention at the time of the killing; the magistrates only suggested that the governor of Virginia should be informed of the matter.[8] Soon, however, some twists of politics presented Stone to the Bay magistrates in a new light. Stone, dead, became more cherished and more useful than Stone, alive, had ever been. When substantial considerations of plunder and dominion induced the Bay magistrates to conquer the Pequots, they felt obliged to mask their true motives with a semblance of righteous retribution. The time-honored tradition in such circumstances is to wave a bloody shirt. For the Bay's purposes Stone's shirt would serve nicely.

To get at the real motives for the Pequot conquest, we must attend to two major, inextricably interconnected events: the Pequots' negotiation of a peace and friendship treaty with Massachusetts Bay in 1634 and the early colonization of the Connecticut Valley by Englishmen. Because the sources concerning these events are anything but straightforward, it is necessary to examine the texts in minute detail.

Massachusetts's special interest in the Pequots began in November 1634 when a deputation of Pequot chiefs came to the Bay to negotiate for a trade with the English to substitute for the commerce that had been cut off at the Dutch House of Hope. The Pequots also wanted Massachusetts to mediate peace for them with the Narragansetts. It was an occasion for discreet rejoicing in Boston. Only a short time earlier the Puritans had explored Long Island and discovered what may be called the "mint" of the Montauk Indians, the center of manufacture of the best wampum on the northeastern coast of North America. They had also learned that the Montauks regularly delivered large quantities

7. John Romeyn Brodhead, "Memoir on the Early Colonization of New Netherland," in N.-Y. Hist. Soc., Colls., 2d Ser., II (New York, 1849), 365; Hubbard, Narrative, 118; Bradford, Of Plymouth Plantation, ed. Morison, 268–270; entries for June 2, 1633, Sept. 12, 1633, Jan. 21, 1634, and Nov. 6, 1634, Winthrop, History, ed. Savage, I, 104, 111, 123, 148.

8. Jan. 21, 1634, Winthrop, History, ed. Savage, I, 123. The Boston magistrates erroneously supposed that Stone, a West Indian, was a Virginian.

of that wampum in tribute to the Pequots. Now the affluent Pequots needed Boston's help.[9]

The Massachusetts Bay–Pequot treaty negotiated in 1634 is known only in the glosses provided by John Winthrop, Sr.[10] His description obviously emphasizes Indian obligations while minimizing those of the English, and textual analysis suggests that there were oral understandings inconsistent with what Winthrop recorded. By the evidence of his own words he transformed English demands into "agreements" that could not possibly have been made, because the Pequot ambassadors had no power to commit their tribal council beyond the proposals of their instructions. Actually the Pequot council discriminated in its treatment of the Bay's demands upon its ambassadors, accepting some terms, refusing others, and continuing negotiations. Winthrop retrospectively interpreted such discrimination as the breaking of a fair and equitable covenant, which merited terrible retribution.

Besides the internal peculiarities of Winthrop's explanations of the treaty terms, there are discrepancies between them and the events that followed the treaty. When closely examined, these discrepancies suggest that the Pequot treaty was a covenant finally broken by the Puritans rather than the Indians. This is not to say that either party failed to fulfill the terms of what they really agreed on. Rather, Massachusetts retroactively added new demands to the agreement. When the Pequots rejected these, Massachusetts unilaterally denounced the treaty, in form according with diplomatic protocol, after having lived with it for two years.

For its part in the treaty, the Bay government agreed to arrange two urgent necessities for the Pequots: trade with the English and peace with the Narragansetts. In the matter of trade, John Winthrop's own writings evidence his good faith and desire for commercial gain. He told Plymouth's Governor Bradford that the trade was "the chief thing we aimed at."[11] Confirmation may be inferred from the contrast between two letters to his son in London. The first letter, written shortly before the Pequot treaty, does not mention the Pequots but includes a list of articles desired by the colony, all of them obviously for use by the colonists themselves. The second letter, dated December 12, 1634, describes the Pequot treaty and expands the list of desired articles to

9. Oct. 2, 1633, *ibid.*, 112; Thompson, *History of Long Island*, I, 89; Gookin, "Historical Collections," Mass. Hist. Soc., *Colls.*, 1st Ser., I, 152.

10. Nov. 6, 1634, Winthrop, *History*, ed. Savage, I, 148–149. Bradford copied a contemporary letter from Winthrop differing significantly in its description of the treaty's contents. *Of Plymouth Plantation*, ed. Morison, 291. Originally there was a formal treaty document, according to Winthrop, on which the Pequot ambassadors put their marks.

11. Bradford, *Of Plymouth Plantation*, ed. Morison, 291.

include "trading cloth, good store, if money may be had." [12] The point is that trading cloth had been the commodity specifically requested by the Pequots in their treaty conference. [13] Perhaps, however, there was no money to be had, for the records of goods shipped by order of John Winthrop, Jr., do not include trading cloth. [14]

We may feel confident, however, that the Pequots got as much trade as they wanted. Both Winthrops engaged in the Indian trade, through associates and directly, and numbers of Englishmen traded when they could and where they could with Indians of all tribes. [15] Early in 1635 the elder Winthrop mentioned a pinnace that had gone to trade with the Pequots; he expressed distrust of the Indians and disappointment because of the small volume of business. [16] Probably the trader was offering commodities other than the desired but unavailable trading cloth. Whatever the difficulties may have been, it seems likely that Massachusetts Bay attempted to fulfill its treaty promise to open trade with the Pequots. The Bay also promptly discharged its other recorded obligation to negotiate peace between the Pequots and the Narragansetts; the peace was arranged before the Pequot ambassadors left Boston.

On the other side, the Pequots were ready to pay well for their trade and peace, but the magistrates' demands enlarged the price enormously. Here Winthrop's text turns particularly difficult. He relates how the first Pequot messenger "brought two bundles of sticks, whereby he signified how many beaver and otter skins he would give us . . . and great store of wampompeage, (about two bushels, by his description). He brought a small present with him. . . ." This messenger was followed by two ambassadors who brought "another present of wampompeage"—possibly the two bushels mentioned by the messenger. The major offering of the Pequots was something else, as will be noted in a moment. However, the magistrates were very much interested in wampum. Instead of two bushels they demanded four hundred fathoms, besides forty beaver skins and thirty otter skins. [17]

---

12. *Winthrop Papers*, III, 175, 177–178.

13. Nov. 6, 1634, Winthrop, *History*, ed. Savage, I, 148.

14. *Winthrop Papers*, III, 201–210.

15. *Ibid.*, 81–83, 116–118, 120–121, 150–151, 162–163, 234–235, 238. Some writers have mistakenly thought that Winthrop was above mixing in business matters, basing this notion on his pretentious statement to sachem Chickatabot that "English sagamores did not use to truck," but he built the bark *Blessing of the Bay* and sent it to trade along the coast. If he did not "truck" himself, he hired people to do it for him. Entries for Apr. 13, 1631, July 4, 1631, Oct. 2, 1633, Winthrop. *History*, ed. Savage, I, 53–54, 57, 112.

16. Winthrop to William Bradford, Mar. 12, 1635, in Bradford, *Of Plymouth Plantation*, ed. Morison, 291–292.

17. Nov. 6, 1634, Winthrop, *History*, ed. Savage, I, 147–148. As applied to wampum, a fathom was a measure of value. Until 1635 it was worth 9s. to 10s. A fall in value afterwards brought it down to 5s. or 6od. It varied from 240 to 260

The great value of these commodities has to be translated into monetary terms for modern comprehension. The wampum alone was worth from £180 to £200 sterling; beaver skins sold in London for anywhere from 12s. to double that amount per pound of pelt; and good otter skins sold for 10s. each.[18] All in all, the amount demanded by the Bay could be reasonably computed at approximately £250 sterling, which was a very large sum. In the equivalents calculated by one modern student, it would come to $50,000 in terms of currency as of 1965.[19] Another measure is a comparison of the treaty demand with the real and personal property taxes levied upon the colony of Massachusetts Bay in the year of the Pequot treaty, 1634. These taxes totaled £600.[20] A treaty demand that amounted to nearly half of the colony's levies was more than a token.

In fact the demand was for much more than the Pequot ambassadors had been authorized to offer, and it failed of ratification in their council at home. The council's rejection poses a problem of interpretation that cannot be confidently decided in the absence of records of the Pequots' own statements, but the Indians' discriminating reaction to the rest of the treaty terms suggests that the Bay's requirement would have been costly in a second way. Although Winthrop described it consistently as a present, the Bay's hard bargaining divested it of the quality of a free-will offering. Its conversion into a demand transformed the character of the "present" into that of tribute, and tribute implied subordination.[21] It must be remembered that the Pequots had not been at war with Massachusetts and that their treaty was a voluntary act by which they contracted for certain services on terms of certain compensation. In their comprehension the treaty was an engagement between peers; all evidence agrees that they were a proudly independent people who would have drawn the line at any hint of submission.

The Pequot ambassadors had come to Boston prepared with a munificent present of a different sort. "They offered us also," wrote Win-

---

beads according to the exchange rate. Weeden, *Economic and Social History*, I, 37, 40.

18. Weeden, *Economic and Social History*, I, 37, 40; Francis Kirby to J. Winthrop, Jr., June 22, 1632, *Winthrop Papers*, III, 82.

19. He equated the labor costs of the two periods and found that one pound sterling in 17th-century Massachusetts would buy as much labor time as $200 in 1965. Charles T. Burke, *Puritans at Bay* (New York, 1967), 244.

20. Table, "Commonwealth Levies: 1633–42," Rutman, *Winthrop's Boston*, 209.

21. The wampum demand has been fairly consistently suppressed by historians (following Hubbard's example) since Winthrop himself omitted it entirely from the terms described in his letter to Bradford. In recent times Vaughan reports it, calling it an "indemnity," but that term does not appear in the source. The magistrates were not asking wergild for Stone. Bradford, *Of Plymouth Plantation*, ed. Morison, 291; Hubbard, *Narrative*, 117–118; Vaughan, *New England Frontier*, 125.

throp, "all their right at Connecticut, and to further us what they could, if we would settle a plantation there." This was a princely prize, and it was genuine. Until the Pequots were attacked by the English, they offered no interference to the settlement of Connecticut, and they demanded no compensation for their former interest in that place.

Besides the matter of wampum tribute, the issue of Pequot submission to Massachusetts arose when the magistrates discovered at last what Captain Stone was good for. In Winthrop's text, they demanded that the Pequots should "deliver up those who were guilty" of Stone's death, "etc." As the Pequot ambassadors pointed out, "The sachem, who then lived, was slain by the Dutch, and all the men, who were guilty, etc., were dead of the pox, except two." The reported deaths might seem like sufficient retribution for the value of a scoundrel like Stone, and in fact Massachusetts showed some tardiness in pressing enforcement of its demand. While the possibility of profitable trade was being investigated, the Bay let the issue of Stone's death lie dormant—a period of two years. The significance of this retribution demand must be noticed, however. The requirement for revenge on the men who had killed Stone went beyond a mere lust of blood for blood precisely because those men were *not* Pequots. A Connecticut officer, unimpeachably hostile to the Pequots, has revealed that the killers belonged to the Western Niantics, a lower Connecticut River tribe tributary to the Pequots.[22]

22. Nov. 6, 1634, Winthrop, *History*, ed. Savage, I, 148. Winthrop's first notice of Stone's death remarked that Stone had put in "at the mouth of Connecticut ... where the Pequins inhabit," and "was there cut off by them." The Pequots did not "inhabit" the valley of the Connecticut. Their territory lay between Pawcatuck River on the east and the Niantic River on the west. Winthrop never corrected the statement of the Pequots' habitation although there can be no doubt that he learned of its falsity from his son, who lived, traded, and negotiated with Indians at the mouth of the Connecticut. Jan. 21, 1634, *ibid.*, I, 123; Hodge, ed., *Handbook of N. Am. Indians*, s.v. "Pequot."

Connecticut's Captain John Mason wrote unequivocally that Stone's killers "were not native Pequots." However, he attempted to implicate the Pequots ex post facto by adding that the killers "had frequent recourse to them, to whom they tendered some of those goods" that had been plundered from Stone. The remark confirms the Western Niantics' tributary status. John W. De Forest, who had access to the writings of both Winthrop and Mason, recognized the discrepancy between their identifications and attempted to reconcile them by main force: "The perpetrators in the tragedy were undoubtedly Pequots, although among them there may have been some of their tributaries, the Western Niantics." His only citation was Winthrop, who nowhere admitted participation by tributaries. More recently, Vaughan has also tried to have it both ways: he states that Stone's "assassins" could have been either Pequots or tributaries, but he semantically converts the tributaries into a "subservient" tribe, thus implying Pequot responsibility for their deeds. As will appear in the next chapter, neither the Pequots nor the Western Niantics regarded the latter's tributary status as one of subservience. John Mason, *A Brief History of the Pequot War* (1736), March of America Facsimile Series, No. 23 (Ann Arbor, Mich., 1966), ix, 13; De Forest, *Indians of Connecticut*, 77–78; Vaughan, *New England Frontier*, 123.

This single fact opens a new vista upon Massachusetts's concern for Captain Stone. When the Bay demanded that the Pequots deliver up Stone's killers, they asked for much more than satisfaction of Mosaic code justice;[23] they demanded that the Pequots subject themselves to Massachusetts so far as to act as the Bay's police against Pequot tributaries.[24] Specifically, for the Pequots to seize the persons of Niantic tributaries and deliver them to Massachusetts would have violated all Indian conceptions of custom and honor. The Pequots were no exception to the rule that superior tribes were expected to furnish protection in exchange for tribute. Massachusetts's demand could not have been satisfied without setting the Niantics at feud with the Pequots and unsettling the whole tributary system of the latter.

On this point, as on the issue of wampum tribute, Winthrop's version of the treaty is anything but reliable. He tells us in seemingly explicit words that when the Pequot ambassadors "came to the governour, they agreed, *according to the former treaty* [i.e., their meeting with the magistrates one day earlier], viz. to deliver us the two men, who were guilty of Capt. Stone's death, when we would send for them; to yield up Connecticut; to give us four hundred fathom of wampompeage," and so on. But the Pequots had made no agreements at all in the preliminary session that Winthrop semantically inflated to a "former treaty." Winthrop himself reported that in the preliminary session the Pequot ambassadors had only agreed to make recommendations under certain important conditions. About Stone's killers, he noted that, "if they were worthy of death, they [the Pequot ambassadors] would move their sachem to have them delivered (for they had no commission to do it)." Still with reference to the preliminary session: "The governour not being present, we concluded nothing."[25]

In brief, after translating Winthrop's language into plainer English, we find the chronology of treaty making was as follows: some days after a Pequot messenger initiated negotiations, the Pequot ambassadors met with the magistrates, who imposed a series of demands. In response

23. Winthrop's account to Bradford is a model of double-talk. Although it says that the peace was "concluded" on "condition" that the Pequots "deliver up" Stone's killers, it acknowledges that the Pequot ambassadors insisted Stone had been killed "in a just quarrel." Bradford, *Of Plymouth Plantation*, ed. Morison, 291. The "just quarrel" remark is omitted from Winthrop's *History*, ed. Savage, I, 148.

24. This interpretation runs counter to both of Vaughan's theses, which seem inconsistent also with each other; viz., (1) "At bottom it was the English assumption of the right to discipline neighboring Indians that led to war in 1637"; (2) "Most of the blame for the war must fall on the Pequots, who, according to the testimony of all the whites and most of the Indians, were guilty of blatant and persistent aggression." Alden T. Vaughan, "Pequots and Puritans: The Causes of the War of 1637," *WMQ*, 3d Ser., XXI (1964), 268, and *New England Frontier*, 135–136.

25. Nov. 6, 1634, Winthrop, *History*, ed. Savage, I, 148 (emphasis added).

the Pequots stated what they were empowered to offer—which included an open door to Connecticut—and what they were not empowered to do, but they promised to report the Bay's demands back to their council. On that basis, the governor and magistrates concluded a treaty with them.

A further clarification may still be in order about one more enigmatic remark in Winthrop's reporting. He wrote, "And so [we] should be at peace with them, and *as friends* to trade with them, *but not to defend them*, etc."[26] Thus the treaty had no provision for military alliance. Emphatically, the Pequots had not permitted Massachusetts to assume a protectorate over them.

All in all, the peculiarities of Winthrop's description of the treaty proclaim that its actual text—the vanished text—may have differed somewhat from Winthrop's ex post facto version. Suspicion is not abated by the thought that the Bay did not cherish with greatest care this document that was a deed to the Connecticut Valley.

The Pequot council refused to ratify what its ambassadors had not been empowered to accept, and the limits of its rejection should be noted carefully.[27] The Pequots did not threaten to stand in the way if Massachusetts should send its own men to do Puritan justice on the Western Niantics. On the positive side, the Pequots did relinquish their conquest rights over the Connecticut Valley.

Apparently this satisfied the Bay magistrates at the time. For over a year the treaty was in effect according to the Indians' understanding of it. They sent a present to the Bay, and English settlers began to establish towns on the Connecticut. Trade was carried on peacefully. Winthrop found nothing about the Pequots important enough to note in his history all through 1635. The subsequent troubles were initiated by contentions that started within Massachusetts rather than by newly emerging disputes between the Pequots and Massachusetts.

At the center of the strife was the Bay magistrates' desire to control all colonizing in New England. In 1634 many groups disputed the pretensions of the magistrates even within their own colony. We have previously noticed Salem's restlessness (chapter 8). Now we must attend to a substantial group of orthodox Puritans led by the Reverend Thomas Hooker. Puritan historian William Hubbard has remarked that "after Mr. Hooker's coming over, it was observed that many of the freemen grew to be very jealous of their liberties. Some of them were ready to question the authority of the magistrates."[28] It is evi-

---

26. *Ibid.* (emphasis added).

27. Cf. the instructions to John Winthrop, Jr., for treating with the Pequots, July 4, 1636, *Winthrop Papers*, III, 285.

28. Hubbard, *History of New England*, I, 165–166.

dent that Hooker's newcomers of 1634, as well as some of the earlier settlers, demanded more power than the magistrates would concede, and the alienated dissidents then looked for a place where they could get out from under the domination of the Bay. As Winthrop would later report, "The differences between us and those of Connecticut were divers; but the ground of all was their shyness of coming under our government."[29] Connecticut was undeniably outside the limits set by Massachusetts's patent. That fact both attracted the dissenters and stimulated the magistrates to obstruct Hooker's plans to colonize Connecticut. The migration was delayed, but with much bad feeling. In 1635 the people of Dorchester started the trek westward.

The sheer numbers of people involved precluded any thought of forcible prevention, but the magistrates had not given up. Although Hooker had determination, orthodoxy, and people, his new colony lacked legal sanction, and he was proposing to settle it in territory already claimed by two other parties—New Netherland and a group of English gentlemen known as the Saybrook Company. In sum, Hooker's people intended to squat in territory that was already occupied by numerous Indians; that was claimed by Massachusetts, which had just acquired the preeminent Indian right to it; and that was further claimed by duly constituted agencies of both the Dutch and English nations. If Hooker were to have any shadow of legal sanction for his colony, he would have to obtain acquiescence from both the Saybrook Company and Massachusetts.

This was possible, but only if Hooker came to terms with the Winthrops. The Pequot treaty of 1634 had provided means for these astute gentlemen to extend their cooperating powers into the Connecticut Valley before Hooker even got there. The treaty had occurred during the period when the elder Winthrop and his supporters were attempting to dissuade Hooker's people from removing to Connecticut. While that argument was still in progress, Winthrop, Sr., sent news of the treaty to his son in England, being careful to mention the Pequot quitclaim to Connecticut.[30] The younger John Winthrop was in touch with the leading Puritans constituting the Saybrook Company. Although these Saybrook gentlemen had a charter of the utmost vagueness and vastness, and had been doing nothing much about it for several years, they suddenly decided in July 1635 to colonize the Connecticut Valley in a narrowly delimited portion of their claims, a portion that coincided exactly with what the Pequots had renounced and what Hooker's followers were preparing to move into. Considering the circumstances,

29. Dec. 13, 1638, Winthrop, *History*, ed. Savage, I, 284. See also Andrews, *Colonial Period*, II, 83–84.

30. Winthrop, Sr., to Winthrop, Jr., Dec. 12, 1634, *Winthrop Papers*, III, 177.

we cannot find it strange that the governor commissioned by the Saybrook Company for this colony that existed only on paper was John Winthrop, Jr. He hastily embarked with his new commission, to arrive in Boston in the midst of Hooker's migration.[31]

There was an argument. Hooker did not intend to escape the senior Winthrop only to find himself saddled with the junior. By an uneasy compromise, more of form than substance, the Connecticut settlers gained a tenuous claim on legality by accepting formal subordination to both Massachusetts and the Saybrook Company. The Massachusetts General Court commissioned them to set up a limited government in Connecticut, this in behalf of the Court's own members and also of "John Winthrop, Junior, Esq., Governor, appoynted by certain noble personages and men of quallitie interesed in the said ryver, which are yet in England." Significantly for later events, the subordinate authority thus extended to Connecticut's settlers restricted their belligerence explicitly to "defensive" war.[32]

The Winthrops had made the most of their claims and legalities, but Hooker had the people. Even in the act of consenting to the new colony, the Winthrops had confessed their real impotence, for the Hooker settlement was made at a different location from where its supposed governor wanted it. The Saybrook Company had instructed Winthrop, Jr., to establish a plantation at the mouth of the Connecticut River and to fortify there against Dutch intrusion. He dutifully followed the company's orders, but he failed to convince the settlers that they should too. The English migration to Connecticut therefore presented the curious spectacle of a substantial colony upriver, pretending to have a governor, and a fortified governor downstream, pretending to have a colony.[33]

Winthrop, Jr., did build and garrison his fort, as instructed, but his efforts to govern were humiliatingly flouted. As his biographer has remarked, it became "painfully evident that Winthrop's writ ran no further than a cannon shot from Saybrook fort."[34] Angry but helpless, he spent his time trading with the Indians in order to finance his garrison. Among those Indians were the very same Western Niantics whose community included the killers of Captain Stone.[35]

Before proceeding, we should survey the whole territory to mark

31. Commission, July 7, 1635, *ibid.*, 198–199.

32. Andrews, *Colonial Period*, II, 76–79; minutes, Mar. 3, 1636, *Recs. of Mass.*, I, 170–171.

33. Sir Richard Saltonstall to Winthrop, Jr., Feb. 27, 1636, *Winthrop Papers*, III, 229–230; Black, *Younger John Winthrop*, 97.

34. Black, *Younger John Winthrop*, 97.

35. Lion Gardiner, "Leift. Lion Gardener his relation of the Pequot Warres," in Mass. Hist. Soc., *Colls.*, 3d Ser., III (Cambridge, Mass., 1833), 145.

the locations of the interested parties (see map 1, following, and map 2, p. 219). High up on the Connecticut River, the trading posts of the Dutch and of Plymouth continued to do business under hectic pressures from the new settlements of Wethersfield, Windsor, and Hartford. The newcomers were resented by all their predecessors, Indians and Europeans alike, because of their attempts to dispossess and supplant the people already there.[36]

At the mouth of the Connecticut, Winthrop's Fort Saybrook on the west bank looked across the river to the territory of the Western Niantics under their sachem, Sassious.

Eastward, the Pequot country lay on both sides of what was then called the Pequot River, now the Thames. The Pequot chief sachem, Sassacus, lived on the east bank of the river near its mouth (Groton). About twelve miles upriver on the west bank (Norwich) lived a splinter group called Mohegans, led by sachem Uncas. Although Pequots and Mohegans were related by kinship, Uncas had precipitated strife between them by striving to wrest the grand sachemship of the Pequots from Sassacus.[37]

East of the Pequots, at the Pawcatuck River, were the Eastern Niantics, who must be distinguished sharply from Sassious's Western Niantics. In spite of the confusing names and the probability of kinship, the two tribes went separate ways in their politics. The Western Niantics were allied to the Pequots, but these Eastern Niantics were allied to the Narragansetts.

Along the west shore of Narragansett Bay and its adjacent Atlantic coast were the communities of the Narragansetts proper. Their paramount sachems were Canonicus and Miantonomo, and they had acquired new neighbors early in 1636 when Roger Williams and a small band of refugees from Massachusetts Bay founded Providence Plantations at the head of Narragansett Bay.

The whole region was in a most volatile condition. To preexisting Indian feuds the intruding English added their own quarrels and striving. The treaty between Massachusetts and the Pequots, which became also a peace between Pequots and Narragansetts, had brought a lull in violence and had opened the opportunity for orderly English expansion and orderly Pequot withdrawal. The treaty was a master stroke

36. Edward Winslow to Winthrop, Jr., Mar. 21, 1644, in *N.E. Hist. Gen. Reg.,* XXIX (1875), 238; Bradford, *Of Plymouth Plantation,* ed. Morison, 280–283; "Remonstrance of New Netherland," July 28, 1649, *N.Y. Col. Docs.,* I, 286–287; Mar. 30, 1638, Winthrop, *History,* ed. Savage, I, 260.

37. Frances Manwaring Caulkins, *History of New London, Connecticut. From the First Survey of the Coast in 1612, to 1852* (New London, Conn., 1852), 20; Means, "Mohegan-Pequot Relationships," *Bulletin of Archaeol. Soc. of Conn.,* XXI (1947), 26–34; De Forest, *Indians of Connecticut,* 84–86.

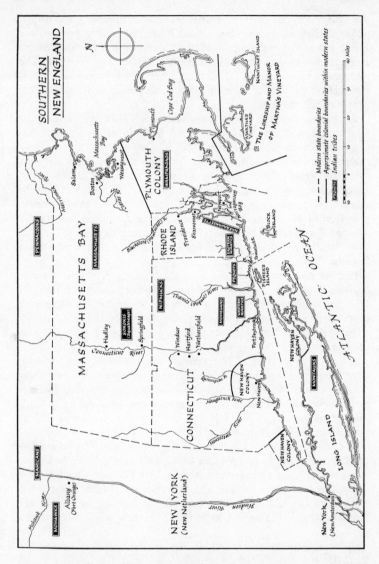

MAP I. *Southern New England, showing locations of Indian tribes mentioned in the text, ca. 1636, and colonial boundaries, ca. 1660. (Drawn by Richard J. Stinely, Williamsburg, Va., from a sketch by the author; base maps from the United States Geological Survey, Department of the Interior, Washington, D.C.)*

of Pequot diplomacy, recognizing the realities of power, retreating from untenable positions, and removing foreseeable causes of war. Ironically, however, its very existence stimulated and accelerated a competition between Massachusetts and Connecticut in which neither colony could succeed without first reducing the Pequots to overt subjection.

Chapter 13 ᔌ "WE MUST
BURN THEM"

In March 1636 the upriver Connecticut mi-
grants had accepted the joint sanction of Massachusetts and John Winthrop, Jr., for their settlement. Their restriction by that sanction to defensive war seems to have been imposed because of overtly evident
bellicosity among the migrants. In spite of restraints the new settlers
immediately began to bully all the persons previously resident in their
vicinity, that is, the traders of New Netherland and New Plymouth
as well as the neighboring Indians.[1]

On June 18, 1636, Plymouth's trader Jonathan Brewster sent a complaint and warning down the river to Fort Saybrook. His message
was based on information obtained from sachem Uncas, the factionalist
chief who had broken away from the Pequots to form his own small
Mohegan tribe. Brewster reported that, according to Uncas, "the Pe-
quents have some mistrust, that the English will shortly come against
them, (which I take is by indiscreet speaches of some of your people
here [in Connecticut] to the Natives) and therefore out of desperate
madnesse doe threaten shortly to sett both upon Indians, and English,
joyntly."[2]

How much of this report was based on fact and how much originated
in Uncas's malicious imagination must be a matter of conjecture. Apparently it sounded credible in Boston, where the younger Winthrop
had immediately forwarded it. The trouble taken by the Bay magistrates
to forbid Connecticut to undertake aggressive war suggests that the
new colonists had been airing notions of conquest even before they
departed from the Bay. Special significance therefore attaches to
Uncas's information that the "indiscreet" speeches threatening war had
been made by Connecticut colonists. I have not found evidence of war
plans in Massachusetts at that time. That the chain of reporting did not

1. Dutch: "Remonstrance of New Netherland," July 28, 1649, in *N.Y. Col.
Docs.*, I, 286–287; Plymouth: Bradford, *Of Plymouth Plantation*, ed. Morison, 280–
284; Indians: minutes, Apr. 5, 1638, *Recs. of Conn.*, I, 19–20.
2. Brewster to Winthrop, Jr., June 18, 1636, *Winthrop Papers*, III, 270–271
(emphasis added).

include any of the Connecticut settlers seems also significant. But we must take into account that the origin of the purported information was Uncas, an ambitious and turbulent chief whose subsequent history strongly suggests that he hoped in 1636 to embroil all the English in war with the Pequots so that he could gain his great end of ruling over the whole Pequot nation after its anticipated defeat.

In Boston the Uncas-Brewster message was considered by the newly created Standing Council composed of Governor Henry Vane, Deputy Governor John Winthrop, Sr., and former Governor Thomas Dudley. The council, which had power over "all military affaires,"[3] could now see the issue in this wise: Connecticut had been chafing at its restraints even in its infancy, and it was growing fast. (Hooker and his congregation had left Massachusetts for Connecticut at the end of May,[4] and Uncas's message was before the Standing Council before the end of June.) If the Bay were to preserve any shadow of authority over the migrants, it would have to act decisively soon. Legalities aside, Massachusetts was powerless to prevent Connecticut from making war on some excuse or other if the Connecticut people were really determined to do so. The Pequots were in the middle between the disputing English colonists, geographically and figuratively. Tales such as Uncas's, of supposed Indian threats to attack the English, never failed to arouse Puritan suspicion; regardless of provocation, the Pequots would have to be called to account and disciplined. But it would never do to let the Connecticut settlers assume that responsibility, for they might then make the Pequots tributaries to themselves or perhaps launch a war to create rights of conquest for themselves. In either event, Connecticut would be building up a legal case for an existence entirely independent from Massachusetts, and it might be able to develop that case into a separate charter from the crown.[5]

The Standing Council moved to forestall such unpleasant possibilities. Its strategy was to strengthen its nebulous controls over the Connecticut colonists by establishing firm controls over the Pequots. To that end it revived the demands that had been set aside after their rejection by the Pequots in the treaty of 1634. Under date of July 4, 1636, the Standing Council sent instructions and a commission to John Winthrop, Jr., at Fort Saybrook to meet with the Pequots and give them an ultimatum.

3. Minutes, Mar. 3 and May 25, 1636, *Recs. of Mass.*, I, 167, 174–175. The settlement of military powers on the Standing Council culminated a long political battle. See also Sept. 3, 1634; Mar. 4, May 6, and Sept. 3, 1635, *ibid.*, I, 125, 138, 146–147, 161, 168.

4. May 31, 1636, Winthrop, *History*, ed. Savage, I, 187.

5. All this motivational description has had to be inferred from the situation. The Standing Council kept no minutes, and it was acting between sessions of the General Court. Winthrop's *History* is silent about the occasion.

Strictly speaking, only two members of the Standing Council signed these documents. This procedure was allowable under the council's rules, but it may be significant that the signers were the men most heavily implicated in the Saybrook Company's affairs: Henry Vane and John Winthrop, Sr. The instructions to the younger Winthrop stated that the Pequots were either to comply with all the terms of the treaty of 1634 (as those terms were *now* interpreted by Massachusetts) or they were to be told that Massachusetts would no longer consider the treaty in force. In the light of Massachusetts's construction of the treaty terms, this new message was a choice of surrender or war.[6]

A conference was held at Fort Saybrook in July 1636. As usual the Winthrops preserved a record of charges and complaints to put the Pequots in the wrong but did not keep the minutes of the conference. In this instance nothing survives of even fragments of Pequot utterance. However, available indirect sources combine to show the substance of the conference's business, and from these sources a roster of participants can be reconstructed, which itself testifies to the importance of the affair. Representing the Saybrook Company were its present and future governors on the Connecticut, John Winthrop, Jr., and George Fenwick, and Winthrop's relative by marriage Hugh Peter. (Fenwick and Peter would later hold high offices in England, where they became prominent in the civil wars.) Fort Saybrook's commander, Lieutenant Lion Gardiner, was also present, along with interpreter Thomas Stanton and possibly the trader John Oldham, who had become a Winthrop confidant. On the Indian side were Sassious, sachem of the Pequots' tributary Western Niantics, and unidentified representatives of the Pequots themselves.[7]

Supposedly the conference had been called because of Pequot menaces to the colonists, but this issue does not appear in the surviving sources as decisive. If the Pequots would "cleare themselves of these Matters," the English would "not refuse to hearken to any reasonable proposition from them for confirmation of the peace." The sticky issue was the peace itself. The English commissioners revived the rejected demands of 1634 as "the very condition of the Peace betwixt us."[8] Unless the full quantity of tribute "presents" was handed over, along with the killers of Captain Stone, the English would regard their peace treaty as

6. Vane to Winthrop, Jr., July 1, 1636, and commission, July 4, 1636, *Winthrop Papers*, III, 282–285.

7. Gardiner, "Relation," Mass. Hist. Soc., *Colls.*, 3d Ser., III, 137–139; affidavit of T. Stanton, 1647, Pulsifer, ed., *Acts of United Colonies*, I, 103. Vaughan states that the Fort Saybrook meeting did not occur. *New England Frontier*, 126.

8. *Winthrop Papers*, III, 285. It will be remembered that when the treaty was made John Winthrop, Sr., had said that trade was "the chief thing we aimed at." Bradford, *Of Plymouth Plantation*, ed. Morison, 291.

null and void and would "revenge the blood of our Countrimen as occasion shall serve." As the Pequots had already given what they considered to be a reasonable quantity of presents in satisfaction for Stone's death, the commissioners were to symbolize their firmness by returning this free-will offering. Nothing but total fulfillment of their demands would be accepted. The Pequots evidently protested, but the English were adamant. As Lieutenant Gardiner remarked, the English delegates "said they would have their lives and not their presents," and he was obliged to witness the return of the voluntary present "full sore against my will."[9]

The Pequots had gone as far as their conceptions of honor and obligation permitted. The next move in this affair was up to their tributary Sassious, sachem of the Western Niantics. Under the pressure of Massachusetts's ultimatum, Sassious improvised a diplomatic maneuver worthy of a Talleyrand. He "gave" his whole country to John Winthrop, Jr., personally; which is to say that, regardless of what he intended that act to mean in terms of ownership of real estate, it definitely transferred the Western Niantics' allegiance from the Pequots. Sassious did not by this act put his people into Massachusetts's hands—neither his entire tribe nor the particular individuals who had killed Captain Stone. It was as a person rather than as Massachusetts's agent or as the Saybrook Company's governor that John Winthrop, Jr., accepted Sassious's grant and took the Western Niantics under his protection. One may doubt how serious either party was in this maneuver because Sassious later fought side-by-side with the Pequots against the English, and Winthrop does not seem to have acted the part of protector in any manner except to lay claim to Sassious's territory. As to the claim, however, the evidence is full and clear.[10]

Winthrop's acceptance of Sassious's fealty exposes the sham of the demand made upon the Pequots for the delivery of Captain Stone's killers. It was entirely within Winthrop's power to withhold his protection until Sassious himself delivered the wanted men; however, the

9. Gardiner, "Relation," Mass. Hist. Soc., Colls., 3d Ser., III, 137, 139.

10. Minutes, July 1647, Pulsifer, ed., Acts of United Colonies, I, 103–104. This transaction has been noticed in Caulkins, History of New London (1852), 27, and again in Black, Younger John Winthrop, 98–99, 375–376, n. 17.

The Western Niantics' disaffiliation from the Pequots is confirmed by a Pequot question to Lt. Gardiner after hostilities had begun. Gardiner reported that the Pequots "asked us if we would fight with Niantecut Indians for they were our friends and came to trade with us." Gardiner replied, however, in a manner showing fear of a trap. "We said we knew not the Indians one from another, and therefore would trade with none." After that the Western Niantics rejoined the Pequots and fought as their allies; but John Winthrop, Jr., continued his claim on their territory as though they had remained his clients. Gardiner, "Relation," Mass. Hist. Soc., Colls., 3d Ser., III, 145 (my emphasis).

real purpose of pressing the Pequots on the issue was not to get the Western Niantic killers but to get the Pequots. That stubborn tribe, however, continued to refuse to be had. The available data show that they made no effort to coerce Sassious into remaining as their tributary. It is reasonable to assume, therefore, that the Pequots thought themselves to have been relieved of the demand to police Sassious's people for Massachusetts. If young Winthrop was to be the Western Niantics' protector, it was up to him to respond to Massachusetts's demand. As in their previous grant of the Connecticut Valley (which remained in force), the Pequots removed cause for contention by relinquishing responsibility—or so they thought. The apparent removal of the problem of the Western Niantic killers left only the rock-bottom question whether the Pequots would pay wampum tribute at the times and in the quantities prescribed by Massachusetts.

The Pequots might readily have failed to interpret the tribute demand as a declaration of hostilities. If the English commissioners followed Massachusetts's instructions to them, they stipulated only that the Bay would take revenge for murdered Englishmen "as occasion shall serve," which would seem to make hostilities dependent on whether the Pequots should commit violence. Perhaps John Winthrop, Jr., had been ambiguous in utterance, as he often was, and had held out hope for reconciliation. Although he would not accept a wampum present smaller than the demanded amount, he did accept personal jurisdiction over the Western Niantics. They would be paying tribute, and they were the responsible parties. Certainly the Pequots did not leave the Fort Saybrook conference with the feeling that they were committed to war. They kept the peace until attacked.

Within a few days after the Winthrop-Pequot-Niantic conference, and apparently unrelated to it, another death transformed the situation. In the same month of July, Captain John Oldham was killed by some Narragansett Indians on Block Island. Oldham's status was very different from that of the Captain Stone, whose murder could be played with in diplomacy as a talking point. Oldham had been trusted with important responsibilities by the Massachusetts government, had been rewarded with a land grant of exceptional size, and had been involved in some special sort of business relationship with the Winthrops. He had been one of the messengers chosen to deliver Massachusetts's ultimatum instructions into the hands of the junior Winthrop at Fort Saybrook, and he may have been present during the conference that followed.[11]

11. Oldham's high status is sometimes overlooked by writers who notice only how he had been discredited by the Puritans a few years earlier when he was associated with their enemy Sir Ferdinando Gorges. His rehabilitation is evidenced

What is especially startling about Oldham's death is that it occurred at the hands of Narragansetts rather than Pequots. As recently as November 1634 the Narragansetts had valued Oldham so highly that they had given him five hundred bushels of corn and had offered him an island in Narragansett Bay if he would come to live among them.[12] Standing against these facts, besides more to be related, the oft-repeated assertion that Oldham was killed for loot by those generous Narragansetts loses plausibility.

Nor is the explanation given by John Winthrop, Sr., any more credible. He quoted Narragansett prisoners as saying that the murder had been arranged because Oldham had gone "to make peace, and trade with the Pekods last year, as is before related."[13] This is far from candid. Winthrop had "before related" that Oldham traded with the Pequots, but it was Winthrop himself who had made the peace. And he neglected to mention Oldham's journey to Fort Saybrook with the commissioners to renounce the peace—information that comes from the independent account by Lieutenant Gardiner.[14] The real sequence of dates makes it appear that Oldham went almost immediately afterward into the Narragansett country. Besides all that, the Narragansetts were allied to Massachusetts and were at peace with the Pequots by mediation of that colony.

The history officially endorsed by the Massachusetts General Court merely adds to the confusion. Author William Hubbard states flatly on one page that the Pequots "treacherously and cruelly murthered Captain Stone . . . and in like treacherous manner slew one Mr. Oldham." On the next page Hubbard concedes that inhabitants of Block Island had killed Oldham, but he then asserts that they "fled presently to the Pequods, by whom they were sheltered, and so became also guilty themselves of his blood."[15] This latter statement is as untrue as the former, as will be shown, and Hubbard probably knew it. Plainly there is something very odd about the Oldham affair. Since the killing became the pretext for beginning war against the Pequots, we must inquire into the confusion surrounding it.

In the absence of reliable information, circumstance must be relied on for clues to motivation. A reasonable guess is that the Narragansetts had come to hold Oldham responsible for an epidemic of smallpox

---

in the following references: *Recs. of Mass.*, I, 119, 125, 145; *Winthrop Papers*, III, 235; *Records of the Court of Assistants of the Colony of the Massachusetts Bay, 1630–1692* (Boston, 1901–1908), II, 43, hereafter cited as *Recs. of Assistants*.

12. Nov. 5, 1634, Winthrop, *History*, ed. Savage, I, 146; Williams to Winthrop, Sr., Oct. 28, 1637, *Winthrop Papers*, III, 502.

13. July 26, 1636, Winthrop, *History*, ed. Savage, I, 191.

14. Gardiner, "Relation," Mass. Hist. Soc., *Colls.*, 3d Ser., III, 137.

15. Hubbard, *Narrative*, 117, 118–119.

among them. In the fall of 1633 he had made the first recorded over-land journey by an Englishman to the upper Connecticut, lodging at Indian villages all the way. Disease broke out soon afterward and ran rapidly through the tribes. The Narragansetts lost seven hundred of their people in the epidemic, which was believed by their sachem Canonicus to have been "sent" deliberately by someone among the English.[16] There are difficulties, however, with the speculation that Oldham personally received blame, for he was in great favor with the Narragansetts shortly after the epidemic's spread. The theory is tenable only on the assumption that belated information reached the Narragansetts. Perhaps a drunken Englishman blurted out a brag or threat? The case is unproven.

Nevertheless something done by Oldham roused the highest possible pitch of indignation among the Narragansetts. Oldham was not murdered by a few local Block Islanders; rather, he seems to have suffered a state execution by the verdict of a number of Narragansett sachems. Just how many were involved is not clear. John Winthrop at first denounced all of the sachems except the two topmost, Canonicus and Miantonomo. Winthrop tacitly modified his view at a later date, but at least four sachems can be counted in the sources.[17] It is not likely that these chiefs had convened in remote Block Island to rob a trader whom they had formerly honored with gifts. Nor is it likely that they murdered Oldham, as the elder Winthrop claimed, because they held him responsible for the period of peace and trade with the Pequots that had been negotiated by the Massachusetts magistrates and ratified by themselves.

The circumstances of the murder have been reported as enigmatically as its motivation, although they certainly were not so mysterious at the time, because John Winthrop, Sr., was in touch with both Indian and English witnesses to the event.[18] Two somewhat discrepant versions

16. Williams to Vane and Winthrop, Sr., [May 15, 1637], *Winthrop Papers*, III, 412–413.

17. July 26 and 30, 1636, Winthrop, *History*, ed. Savage, I, 191. Add to the three anonymous sachems mentioned there the name of Audsah. Williams to Winthrop, Sr., [Sept. 9, 1637], *Winthrop Papers*, III, 494.

18. July 26 and 30, 1636, Winthrop, *History*, ed. Savage, I, 191. Five witnesses to Oldham's killing talked to Winthrop: one Indian prisoner from Block Island, two English servant boys of Oldham's, and two Indians also employed by him. None of their testimony has been preserved except for Winthrop's statement that the Indian prisoner attributed Oldham's peace and trade with the Pequots as the killers' motive. That this prisoner (or Winthrop) was unreliable is indicated by the prisoner's purported further confession that *all* the Narragansett sachems except Canonicus and Miantonomo had been involved. The accusation was implicitly refuted by Winthrop's later concession of Canonicus's "clearing himself *and his neighbors* of the murder." Aug. 8, 1636, *History*, ed. Savage, I, 192 (emphasis added). After that the Bay's demand for delivery of six Narragansett

exist of the discovery of Oldham's body, but neither tells a word about the scene when he was killed. One version is by Winthrop; the other, at second hand, is by the son of the man who discovered Oldham's corpse.[19] Details aside, they agree that Captain John Gallop, Sr., while sailing near Block Island with his sons and a servant, observed Oldham's pinnace being badly handled by an Indian crew. Investigating by violent means, Gallop discovered Oldham's body. How many Indians were killed in the course of this inquiry depends on which version of the story is believed, but both versions present Gallop as taking heavy vengeance —surprisingly without resistance—for Oldham's life. Yet, as it turned out, the man who had actually killed Oldham was not aboard that blood-drenched pinnace. According to Roger Williams, he was sachem Audsah—a man nowhere mentioned in Winthrop's account—and he had fled to the Niantics (probably the Narragansetts' tributary Eastern Niantics), who gave him sanctuary. Miantonomo eventually purchased Audsah's execution at much expense in wampum.[20]

Immediately following Gallop's discovery of Oldham's body, Miantonomo took two hundred warriors in seventeen canoes to Block Island to deal out revenge in Massachusetts's behalf for Oldham's death. Even the stern delegation from Massachusetts conceded "good success" in their subsequent treaty with the Narragansett sachems.[21] But the Boston government saw an opportunity to turn Oldham's death to advantage. The governor and his Standing Council assembled all the magistrates and ministers "to advise with them about doing justice upon the Indians." In their deliberations the Pequots and the Narragansetts were lumped together. In spite of the Narragansetts' full cooperation, the toll of lives already taken, and the Pequot innocence of both Oldham's death and Stone's, the council decided to wreak a lucrative additional vengeance on the Block Island Narragansetts and all the Pequots. On August 25, 1636, a punitive expedition set sail from Boston under the command of John Endecott. "They had commission," wrote Winthrop,

undersachems seems to have been quietly dropped. One has to ask why Oldham's four employees were allowed by his killers to live to bear witness, and even more wonderingly why not one word of what any of the four said has been preserved by the English. Considering New England's fascination with tales of Indian captivities, the most reasonable explanation is that the servants' testimony would have impeded the Bay government's purposes. But what explains the incuriosity of historians?

19. July 20, 1636, Winthrop, *History*, ed. Savage, I, 189–190; Thomas Cobbet, "A Narrative of New England's Deliverances," *N.E. Hist. Gen. Reg.*, VII (1853), 211–212.

20. Miantonomo paid six fathoms of wampum for Audsah, for which he requested reimbursement from Boston. I have found no sign that reimbursement was made. Williams to governor of Massachusetts, [May 13, 1637], *Winthrop Papers*, III, 412.

21. July 26 and Aug. 8, 1636, Winthrop, *History*, ed. Savage, I, 191–192.

"to put to death the men of Block Island, but to spare the women and children, and to bring them away, and to take possession of the island; and from thence to go to the Pequods to demand the murderers of Capt. Stone and other English, and one thousand fathom of wampom for damages, etc., and some of their children as hostages, which if they should refuse, they were to obtain it by force."[22]

The expedition was intended to be highly profitable. Its unpaid volunteer troops were to nourish themselves on plunder. The captured women and children of Block Island would fetch a tidy sum in the West Indies slave markets, and the Pequot wampum would be worth £450 to £500 in itself. Besides all that, the Pequots would have been reduced definitely to the status of tributaries and thus brought safely under the wing of Massachusetts to forestall the expansion by conquest of the upper Connecticut colony.

The expedition turned into an expensive fiasco, however. On Block Island, English guns and armor easily overcame the Indians' brief resistance, but no amount of trudging about that isolated tiny tract of land would disclose the Indians after they had hidden themselves in its then dense forests. The conquerors looted empty villages, destroyed crops, and killed one or a few warriors who had been rash enough to chance arrows against bullets, but instead of a great haul of wampum and slaves they took away only a few utensils and woven mats.[23]

On the mainland they fared no better. When General Endecott arrived at Fort Saybrook at the Connecticut's mouth, he showed his commission to Lieutenant Lion Gardiner, who had been put in charge by the discreetly departed younger Winthrop. Gardiner had been present at the earlier Pequot negotiations at Fort Saybrook and knew of the arrangements that had then been made. Endecott's expedition roused his indignation; he wrote later, "when I had seen their commission I wondered, and made many allegations against the manner of it." He protested also against being left behind in undermanned Fort Saybrook to deal with the aroused Pequots after Endecott's men had struck their intended blow.[24] Brushing Gardiner's objections aside, Endecott went on to make a greater botch in Pequot territory than on Block Island.

One of Endecott's officers, Captain John Underhill, is useful nowadays for his garrulity. Unaware of what the statesmen had been doing behind the scenes, he penned a description of the Pequots widely at variance from the sinister consciousness of guilt officially attributed

22. Aug. 25, 1636, *ibid.*, 192–193.
23. De Forest, *Indians of Connecticut*, 91–92.
24. Gardiner, "Relation," Mass. Hist. Soc., *Colls.*, 3d Ser., III, 140.

to them. In Underhill's story of the punitive expedition's passage along the coast, the Pequots were transparently oblivious of having given any cause for hostilities.

The Indians spying of us came running in multitudes along the water side, crying, What cheer, Englishmen, what cheer, what do you come for? They not thinking we intended war, went on cheerfully until they come to Pequeat river. We thinking it the best way, did forbear to answer them; first, that we might the better be able to run through the work; secondly, that by delaying of them, we might drive them in security, to the end we might have the more advantage of them. But they seeing we would make no answer, kept on their course, and cried, What, Englishmen, what cheer, what cheer, are you hoggery, will you cram us? That is, are you angry, will you kill us, and do you come to fight? [25]

When the English intentions became unmistakably evident, a Pequot sachem engaged the officers in time-consuming discussion until the exasperated Englishmen challenged the Indians to come out and fight European-style in the open fields. Frightened though they were, the Pequots found humor in the sight of the armored Englishmen sweating all in a row in the hot sun while the Indians quietly slipped off into the woods; and the frustrated English, for all their braggadocio, had more sense than to attempt to fight Indian-style by following. They had to content themselves once again with destroying crops and village property. In itself the destruction was no small blow to the people who depended on those crops for their winter provision, but it fell far short of the expedition's goals of subjecting the Pequots and collecting their tribute.[26]

The troops returned to Boston full of self-pity and complaint about the financial losses all had incurred. Far from reaping a profit on the expedition, the General Court was compelled to set up a committee to receive applications for compensation.[27]

As Lieutenant Gardiner had foreseen, the Pequots regarded themselves as wronged, as they had every reason to do. Directing their anger against the nearest Englishmen, who had provided the expedition's last base before its attack, they raided unwary stragglers from Fort Saybrook and besieged the fort itself. Gardiner was competent and kept good watch, so the Pequots got little satisfaction from their effort. The siege is worth a moment's attention, however, for a conversation during its course, reported by Gardiner. As often happened in Indian warfare, there came an interlude for parleying between the attackers and the besieged. "Have you fought enough?" the Pequots asked, still hoping,

25. Underhill, *Newes from America*, 7.
26. De Forest, *Indians of Connecticut*, 94–99.
27. Minutes, Mar. 9, 1637, *Recs. of Mass.*, I, 188.

apparently, to keep the conflict from expanding to full-scale war. If Gardiner had agreed, the Pequots could have returned home satisfied that they had achieved a proper revenge for Endecott's expedition by humbling the English; but Gardiner's carefully nonspecific reply indicated no humility whatever (and Gardiner was not the decision-making authority). The Pequots' next query, shouted over the field to Gardiner, should be hearkened to carefully today. Gardiner noted, "They asked if we did use to kill women and children?"

The importance of this question derives from the fact that New England Indians at that time did not kill women and children in their warfare. The custom was so universal that the Pequots must have been given some reason to ask whether the English would act otherwise. Probably the Dutch had killed indiscriminately in their earlier (undescribed) war against the Pequots; Dutch massacres of other tribes are well documented. The question put to Gardiner, therefore, amounted to negotiation of the rules of combat, and the answer prescribed that the war would be fought with European ruthlessness. "They asked if we did use to kill women and children? We said they should see that hereafter." The Pequots understood him perfectly. "So they were silent a small space, and then they said, We are Pequits, and have killed Englishmen, and can kill them as mosquetoes, and we will go to Conectecott and kill men, women, and children, and we will take away the horses, cows, and hogs." [28]

So many myths have circulated about savage warfare that the civilized European origin of war against noncombatants needs to be explicitly recognized. [29] Armed conquest in New England was a special, though not unique, variant of seventeenth-century war, closely resembling the procedures followed by the English in Ireland in the sixteenth and seventeenth centuries. In these lands the English—Puritan and royalist alike—held the simple view that the natives were outside the law of moral obligation. [30] On this assumption they fought by means that would have been thought dishonorable, even in that day, in war between civilized peoples. Four of their usages, transferred from Scotland and Ireland to America, profoundly affected the whole process of European-Indian acculturation: (1) a deliberate policy of inciting competition between natives in order, by division, to maintain control; (2) a disregard for pledges and promises to natives, no matter how solemnly

28. Gardiner, "Relation," Mass. Hist. Soc., *Colls.*, 3d Ser., III, 145–146.

29. Malone, "Changing Military Technology," *American Quarterly*, XXV (1973), 60–61, and see chap. 9, above.

30. See Canny, "Ideology of English Colonization," *WMQ*, 3d Ser., XXX (1973), 575–598; Samuel R. Gardiner, *History of England from the Accession of James I to the Outbreak of the Civil War, 1603–1642* (London, 1904), I, chaps. 9, 10: "The Pacification of Ireland," and "The Plantation of Ulster."

made; (3) the introduction of total exterminatory war against some communities of natives in order to terrorize others; and (4) a highly developed propaganda of falsification to justify all acts and policies of the conquerors whatsoever. The net effect of all these policies in America has been the myth of the Indian Menace—the depiction of the Indian as a ferocious wild creature, possessed of an alternately demonic and bestial nature, that had to be exterminated to make humanity safe. No Indian people has suffered more from this myth, either in its own time or in the historical records, than the Pequots.

The Pequots were rational strategists within their range of resources and options. Rebuffed by Gardiner, they first tried to gain as many Indian allies as possible. They approached their old enemies the Narragansetts with a realistic proposal to forget old disputes and unite in a guerrilla struggle against the common threat of English encroachment. Had these proposals been accepted by the Narragansetts, there would have without a doubt arisen a genuine Indian menace. Englishmen had not yet learned to fight in the bush, and the united Indians would have outnumbered them many times. All overland communication would have had to cease, and all crops would have had to be raised within fortified walls. Whether the colonies could long have maintained themselves under such conditions is open to serious question.

The foresight of John Winthrop, Sr., saved them. Having surreptitiously aided Roger Williams to become established on Narragansett Bay, Winthrop now disclosed one of the "high and heavenly and public ends" that he had had in mind.[31] He commissioned the exile to break up the Pequot-Narragansett reconciliation, and Williams succeeded just in time. The Narragansetts were giving serious attention to Pequot ambassadors when he thrust himself into the midst of their councils with an offer of alliance with Massachusetts Bay against the Pequots, as an alternative to a Narragansett-Pequot alliance against the English. Williams won and in so doing guaranteed the isolation and ultimate destruction of the Pequots far more effectively than any troops fielded by General Endecott, for example.[32] For his diplomatic triumph Williams was requited meanly by the Puritans; his banishment under pain

31. Williams to Massachusetts General Court, Oct. 1651, Bartlett, ed., *Letters of Williams*, Narragansett Club, *Pubs.*, VI, 231–232. Winthrop also found Williams useful in a business way. See *Winthrop Papers*, III, 502–503, 508, 511. The relationship between them until 1645 was that of patron and client. When Winthrop cut off communication after Williams obtained a charter for Providence Plantations, Williams hastened to cultivate John Winthrop, Jr., to whom he wrote frequently thereafter in much the same obsequious and supplicant tone he had previously used with the father.

32. Williams to Massachusetts General Court, Oct. 1651, and Williams to Major Mason, June 22, 1670, Bartlett, ed., *Letters of Williams*, Narragansett Club, *Pubs.*, VI, 231–232, 338–339.

of death remained in effect during his entire life, and Puritan historian William Hubbard twisted the events to imply that the Narragansetts begged Massachusetts for alliance, thus achieving by one falsification both the demeaning of the Indians and the elimination of Williams's personal role as benefactor of the Bay.[33]

After Williams's success Narragansett sachem Miantonomo accepted a summons to Boston and agreed there to a formal treaty. As happened with tiresome regularity to the records of Indian affairs in early Massachusetts, the text of this treaty has not survived, though it was formally drawn up as a state document subscribed by Governor Vane and several Indian sachems. In making this alliance the Narragansetts still had some freedom of decision because Massachusetts needed them very badly, and undoubtedly they won certain concessions, but the gloss of the treaty provided by John Winthrop is silent about them. In Winthrop's version the Narragansetts unaccountably accept a heavy load of obligations in return for nothing but what they already enjoyed —peace and trade.[34] Stresses between the parties during and after the Pequot conquest hint that Miantonomo had additionally bargained for rights in the persons and lands of the Pequots. What else might have appeared in the treaty is pure guess, but strong evidence exists that the Narragansetts' motivation for making it was something other than vengeful lust for Pequot blood. Deferentially, but unmistakably, Miantonomo asked Roger Williams to notify Boston, "that it would be pleasing to all natives, that women and children be spared, etc."[35]

Months elapsed while these negotiations and other matters distracted Massachusetts from mobilizing. A theological dispute wracked the colony over "antinomianism" and "familism." Like all issues of theology in the Bay, this was also a political struggle, and it ended as usual with the magistrates triumphantly exiling their challengers. Meantime the Pequots, at their pleasure, harried Fort Saybrook and travelers on the Connecticut River.

The garrison at Fort Saybrook had the worst of it. For some reason— perhaps a hope that the treaty of 1634 could still be revived—the Pequots refrained from disturbing the upriver settlements. These were com-

33. To give Hubbard his due, he was only following Winthrop's lead in eliminating Williams's role, but Hubbard distorted even Winthrop's text to make the Narragansetts plead for the English alliance. They had been seriously considering the Pequot proposals until Williams intervened. Hubbard, *Narrative*, 118–122; Aug. 24, 1636, Winthrop, *History*, ed. Savage, I, 196.

34. Oct. 21, 1636, Winthrop, *History*, ed. Savage, I, 199. De Forest thought that "it was evident that the sachems did not understand" the text they had put their signs on. *Indians of Connecticut*, 104. What has disappeared, of course, is what the Indians actually signed.

35. Williams to Vane and Winthrop, Sr., [May 15, 1637], *Winthrop Papers*, III, 414.

placent enough in November 1636, so that they "did jeare or mocke" Lieutenant Gardiner when he requested help.[36] As harassment on the river continued, however, they became less comfortable and began to press Massachusetts to get on with the war. The Bay magistrates in turn pressed the Connecticut settlers to acknowledge Massachusetts's jurisdiction. The settlers evaded that issue by pleading an obligation to wait for word from "the gentlemen of Saybrook"—they were apparently disinclined to pay any attention to the governor appointed by those gentlemen—but they offered to contribute men to Massachusetts's army.[37]

All this was happening while Connecticut remained bound by its agreement to make only defensive war. At some time during the winter or early spring, Captain John Mason took seven men from the settlements down to Fort Saybrook, but as the official records do not mention the matter, he may have been acting privately.[38] Otherwise Gardiner's tiny garrison fought alone until, on April 10, 1637, persons in Massachusetts stirred themselves to help by "lending" twenty men under Captain John Underhill "at the charge of the gentlemen of Saybrook." So far as campaigning on its own was concerned, the Bay government would wait for pleasant weather. The distinction must be well noted, for it means that Captain Underhill was not Massachusetts's representative, but was acting instead in behalf of the Saybrook Company. Massachusetts therefore had neither responsibility for what Underhill did nor claim upon anything he might accomplish. As for what Massachusetts would do on its own account, the magistrates intended to wait until June 1637 and then take charge of the whole situation. Boston proposed then to command an army of 200 men, allocating 120 of its own forces and requisitioning 40 from Plymouth, 10 from Fort Saybrook, and 30 from Connecticut. Assuming a position of preeminence, the Bay made all the decisions and gave orders without so much as consulting the other colonies. Resentment took two forms: Plymouth refused to take part at all, while Connecticut refused to wait until June.[39]

In the meantime three distinct groups had formed in Fort Saybrook who had little to do but maneuver for position in relation to each other.

36. Gardiner to Winthrop, Jr., Nov. 6, 1636, *ibid.*, 320.

37. Apr. 1, 1637, Winthrop, *History*, ed. Savage, I, 217.

38. This would have been in early Apr. 1637. Gardiner put it two days after the arrival of Thomas Stanton, which was dated "some time in April" by De Forest. Gardiner, "Relation," Mass. Hist. Soc., *Colls.*, 3d ser., III, 146; De Forest, *Indians of Connecticut*, 111.

39. Apr. 10, 1637, Winthrop, *History*, ed. Savage, I, 217; Roger Ludlowe to William Pincheon, [May] 17, 1637, "Pincheon Papers," Mass. Hist. Soc., *Colls.*, 2d Ser., VIII (1819), 235–236. For Plymouth's foot-dragging there is an "improved" account by Bradford that is contradicted by Winthrop's letter to him of May 20, 1637. Bradford, *Of Plymouth Plantation*, ed. Morison, 295, 394–396.

Throughout the winter Gardiner had been alone with his original garrison. (His "governor," John Winthrop, Jr., had departed discreetly for the balmier clime of Boston after triggering the hostilities.[40]) As of April 1, 1637, the senior John Winthrop noted that Connecticut was "unsatisfied," and circumstances imply that Captain Mason then took his men to Saybrook to improve Connecticut's condition. Lieutenant Gardiner's welcome was not as ecstatic as one might expect from a lonesome soldier surrounded by enemies. He immediately wrote to Governor Vane in Massachusetts, purportedly asking for more aid, but with Mason's men there the fort was stronger than it had been all winter. Promptly, as of April 10, the associates of the Saybrook Company dispatched Captain Underhill's company to the fort "for fear any advantage should be taken by the adverse party through the weakness of the place."[41] John Winthrop, Sr., who wrote that explanation, was never so roundabout in referring to Pequots; by "the adverse party" he meant the upriver Connecticut settlers, represented by Mason. Underhill's arrival at the fort, with nearly three times as many men as Mason had, caused Mason to abandon whatever enterprise he had had in mind, and he returned upriver with his men. Underhill claimed, possibly correctly, to have been sent "to take the government of that place for the space of three months."[42] Mason later contradicted this statement by explicitly referring to Gardiner as "Chief Commander at Saybrook Fort,"[43] but Gardiner's account is vague about the relative statuses of Underhill and himself.[44] Neither the Connecticut settlers nor the Saybrook Company acted from humanitarian motives by putting men into Gardiner's fort. Both parties had left him alone all winter while he

40. Black, *Younger John Winthrop*, 99.
41. Apr. 10, 1637, Winthrop, *History*, ed. Savage, I, 217.
42. Underhill, *Newes from America*, 16–17.
43. Mason, *Pequot War*, 2.
44. Gardiner, "Relation," Mass. Hist. Soc., *Colls.*, 3d Ser., III, 147–149. Gardiner's version is wholly erroneous about the time of Underhill's arrival in the fort; he placed it "two days after" the killing of one John Tille, which occurred, according to Winthrop, about the middle of Oct. 1636. Oct. 21, 1636, Winthrop, *History*, ed. Savage, I, 200.

A bibliographic note: Some of the confusions and contradictions in the texts pertaining to the Fort Saybrook incidents probably derive from the prolonged litigation between Massachusetts and Connecticut over rights of jurisdiction and property in the Pequot territory. Mason and Gardiner wrote their manuscript accounts several decades after the events, at times when both were under Connecticut's jurisdiction and in the midst of contention over rights of conquest. Thus the accounts became something more than the reminiscences of old soldiers; they were important evidence in the legal and diplomatic proceedings. Gardiner was solicited to write by Mason, and Mason by the Connecticut General Court. Both accounts seem to have been trimmed to the dimensions of Connecticut's case.

was under constant siege. The ostensible reinforcements of both parties were intended to control the fort rather than the Indians.

After Mason returned upriver, Connecticut suddenly acquired a motive for accelerating the tempo of action against the Pequots. The settlers at Wethersfield had dispossessed sachem Sowheag (or Sequin) contrary to their agreement to let him live and make a living in his own lands, and Sowheag had gone to the Pequots for retribution. They accepted his cause and attacked Wethersfield. On April 23, 1637, they raided workers in the fields, killing six men and three women, destroying much property, and taking two girls prisoner. It is worth noting that the settlers had previously been so undisturbed and confident that they did not believe the first alarm given by a rider who had seen the Pequots approaching.[45]

However the rank and file may have reacted, their leaders did not panic. A week went by before the General Court met at Hartford to act in a manner bearing the stamp of cool deliberation. There was no frenzied running about simply to ward off danger. Instead the General Court converted the situation to its own advantage by declaring "offensive warr" on the Pequots.[46] Its undeclared reasons were sound and unemotional. Connecticut could gain nothing but security by staying within its prescribed limits of defense, but it could gain rights of conquest over the Pequot territory by beating the Indians in their homeland.

That the defiance of Massachusetts's sanction against offensive war was consciously done with foreknowledge of the Bay's displeasure is evidenced by a letter that Thomas Hooker felt constrained to write to John Winthrop, Sr. Without the background of interprovincial competition, the spectacle would be curious indeed. Here was Hooker excusing his people for attacking the enemies of Massachusetts, in spite of what seems like ample provocation. And the excuse was lame: Connecti-

---

45. See Sherman W. Adams and Henry R. Stiles, *The History of Ancient Wethersfield, Connecticut* ... (New York, 1904), I, 61; Mar. 30, 1638, Winthrop, *History*, ed. Savage, I, 260; minutes, Apr. 5, 1638, *Recs. of Conn.*, I, 19–20. Winthrop discoursed at length about how the Wethersfield incident eliminated Connecticut's right to call its war against the Indians "just," apparently in order to whittle down Connecticut's claims to rights of conquest that could only be legitimate as the result of a just war. Connecticut confessed that injuries had been committed by settlers against Indians as well as Indians against settlers and that "the first breach was on the said English parte." Connecticut then decided to "compose matters" with the wronged sachem Sowheag. I suppose this was their way of injecting justness into their war ex post facto. Cf. Vaughan's finding that the Sowheag incident was an "example of justice to a minor Indian." Alden T. Vaughan, "A Test of Puritan Justice," *NEQ*, XXXVIII (1965), 339. See also William DeLoss Love, *The Colonial History of Hartford, Gathered from the Original Records* (Hartford, Conn., 1914), 116–117.

46. Minutes, May 1, 1637, *Recs. of Conn.*, I, 9. Mason's retrospective account converts this into "an offensive and defensive War." *Pequot War*, x.

cut's Indian allies, said Hooker, had forced the action: "The Indians here our frends were so importunate with us to make warr presently that unlesse we had attempted some thing we had delivered our persons unto contempt of base feare and cowardise, and caused them to turne enemyes agaynst us: Agaynst our mynds, being constrayned by necessity, we have sent out a company. . . ."[47] Winthrop, of course, knew how to interpret that, but he had to face the fact that Massachusetts's own blundering and delay had provided Connecticut's opportunity. The contest between the two colonies now turned into a race to see who could get at the Pequots first.

Connecticut mobilized a troop of ninety Englishmen under Captain Mason and about seventy Mohegans and "River Indians" under Uncas. These were instructed to attack sachem Sassacus at his main fortified village on the Pequot (Thames) River (see map 2, following). They departed expeditiously, but encountered obstructions at Fort Saybrook, where neither Lieutenant Gardiner nor Captain Underhill showed any great enthusiasm for their mission. "They were not fitted for such a design," said Gardiner, and he raised questions about the competence of Mason's English soldiery as well as the trustworthiness of the Indian allies. Uncas satisfied him as to the latter by killing four Pequots of a company that had just passed by the fort. In the matter of English competence, the officer professionals made two decisions after "five or six days" of argument. They replaced twenty "insufficient" members of Mason's troop with twenty "of the lustiest" of the Saybrook garrison and assigned Underhill to command the replacements. The second decision was to avoid a direct attack on Sassacus's strongly defended main village in order to attack instead from the rear with a large contingent of Narragansett auxiliaries. Following their new strategy, the troops embarked for Narragansett Bay.[48]

Meantime John Winthrop, Sr., in Massachusetts had become disturbed by the news reaching him, but had been immobilized in his current position of deputy governor by the newly developed hostility of Governor Vane. This difficulty disappeared after the May 17 elections, in which Winthrop's faction elected him governor and routed Vane and the antinomians. Winthrop promptly sent forty soldiers by land to Narragansett Bay.[49]

47. *Winthrop Papers*, III, 407–408.

48. Gardiner, "Relation," Mass. Hist. Soc., *Colls.*, 3d Ser., III, 148–149; Mason, *Pequot War*, 2–3; Underhill, *Newes from America*, 23–25, 36. Uncas's Indians brought in a captive Pequot about whom the usual comment is that he was tortured by the Indians and finally put out of his misery by a shot by Underhill. Winthrop wrote, however, that a prisoner was taken "whom the English put to torture." Perhaps Winthrop's access of candor was owing to his antagonism to Underhill. May 24, 1637, *History*, ed. Savage, I, 223.

49. [May] 17, 1637, Winthrop, *History*, ed. Savage, I, 223–224.

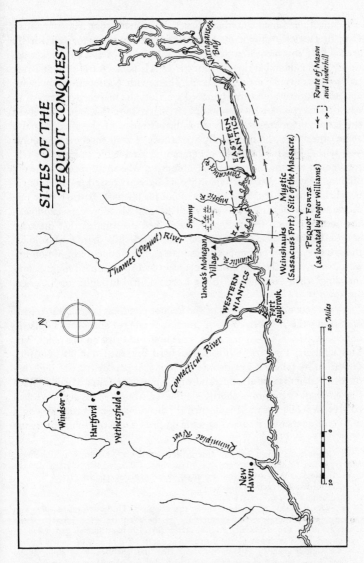

MAP 2. *Sites of the Pequot conquest, 1636–1637. To the west of Mystic, the route shows Mason's retreat from the attacking Pequots to meet his boats. (Drawn by Richard J. Stinely, Williamsburg, Va., from a sketch by the author; base maps from the United States Geological Survey, Department of the Interior, Washington, D.C.)*

Connecticut's men got there first.[50] A runner from Massachusetts's Captain Patrick brought his urgent request for them to wait for his arrival.[51] If anything, it stimulated Connecticut's Mason to quicker action.[52] After disembarking he sent his vessels back to the Pequot River to await his army's arrival by land. Then, with Narragansett guidance and an escort of about five hundred warriors, he marched westward to Mystic River, where the Pequot lesser village stood.[53] Mason had chosen this strategy for reasons set forth in his narrative of the affair, "as also some other" that, he cryptically remarked, "I shall forebear to trouble you with." His forebearance becomes understandable as his other reasons emerge from their intended obscurity. Mason proposed to avoid attacking Pequot warriors, which would have overtaxed his unseasoned, unreliable troops. Battle, as such, was not his purpose. Battle is only one of the ways to destroy an enemy's will to fight. Massacre can accomplish the same end with less risk, and Mason had determined that massacre would be his objective. Gardiner and Underhill, hardened soldiers though they were, had opposed his plan and had concurred, Mason implied, only after the expedition's chaplain had spent a hard night "commending" their "condition" to the Lord and had brought forth clerical approval.[54]

All the secondary accounts of the Pequot conquest squeamishly evade confessing the deliberateness of Mason's strategy, and some falsify to conceal it. Mason's own narrative is the best authority on this point. The Massachusetts Puritans' William Hubbard brazened out his own misquotation by telling his readers to "take it as it was delivered in writing by that valiant, faithful, and prudent Commander Capt. Mason." With this emphatic claim to authority he quoted Mason as saying, "We had resolved a while not to have burned it [the village], but being we could not come at them, I resolved to set it on fire." Despite Hubbard's assur-

50. Connecticut's men headed downriver on May 11. Ludlowe to Pincheon, May 17, 1637, "Pincheon Papers," Mass. Hist. Soc., *Colls.*, 2d Ser., VIII, 235.
51. Patrick to Winthrop, May 23, 1637, *Winthrop Papers*, III, 421.
52. Hubbard, *Narrative*, 124–125.
53. Mason, *Pequot War*, 5.
54. *Ibid.*, 3. Gardiner is silent about the chaplain. Underhill gushes religious rhetoric, but mentions the chaplain only as the recipient of a message about Uncas's killing Pequots. Only Mason states that Chaplain Stone was asked to "commend our Condition to the Lord, that night, to direct how in what manner we should demean our selves," and that the chaplain "had done as he [Mason] had desired, and was fully satisfied to sail for Narragansett." In the context of the other evidence, this seems to mean that Mason had proposed something that the other officers were reluctant to go along with and that the chaplain's approval decided the issue. It strains credulity that three proud and experienced military officers, even among Puritans, would ask a minister to decide the technical question whether to attack a fortified village from front or rear. Clerics are consulted on moral issues.

ance, these were not Mason's words. His manuscript said bluntly, "We had formerly concluded to destroy them by the Sword and save the Plunder."[55]

Not only Mason's prior intent to massacre and plunder was suppressed by Hubbard. The rest of Mason's manuscript revealed what sort of inhabitants had been occupying the Mystic River village and proved conclusively that mere victory over them was not enough to satisfy Mason's purpose. After telling how the attack was launched at dawn of May 26, and how entrance to the village was forced, the account continued thus:

At length William Heydon espying the Breach in the Wigwam, supposing some English might be there, entred; but in his Entrance fell over a dead Indian; but speedily recovering himself, the Indians some fled, others crept under their Beds: The Captain [Mason] going out of the Wigwam saw many Indians in the Lane or Street; he making towards them, they fled, were pursued to the End of the Lane, where they were met by Edward Pattison, Thomas Barber, with some others; where seven of them were Slain, as they said. The Captain facing about, Marched a slow Pace up the Lane he came down, perceiving himself very much out of Breath; and coming to the other End near the Place where he first entred, saw two Soldiers standing close to the Pallizado with their Swords pointed to the Ground: The Captain told them that We should never kill them after that manner: The Captain also said, WE MUST BURN THEM: and immediately stepping into the Wigwam where he had been before, brought out a Fire Brand, and putting it into the Matts with which they were covered, set the Wigwams on Fire.[56]

55. Hubbard, Narrative, 122, 126; Mason, Pequot War, 7-8. Hubbard gratuitously implicated Mason's Indian allies in the massacre, but Mason wrote that he told them to stand aside and watch the English fight. Bradford confirms Mason, but with a slap against the Indians, who, he says, "stood aloof from all danger and left the whole execution to the English." Bradford, Of Plymouth Plantation, ed. Morison, 296.

A bibliographic note: There is a sad story here of editorial shortcoming, not only of Hubbard but also of his 19th-century admirer, the prolific and respected historian Samuel G. Drake. Drake edited reprints of Hubbard's Narrative and Increase Mather's Relation of the Troubles, both under altered titles. The same misquotation of Mason's plunder remark appeared in both, but Drake's editorial treatment of it in Hubbard's book differed sharply from what he had earlier done to the same thing in Mather's. In the Mather book Drake commented that the "Liberty with this important Part of the Narrative is intolerable," and he gave Mason's original text in a note, for comparison. But Drake was silent about the same passage in his edition of Hubbard's book, published later. He omitted to make the comparison with Mason's text, and he praised Hubbard's literary qualities and truthfulness without qualification.

Increase Mather, Relation Of the Troubles which have hapned in New-England ... (1677), ed. Samuel G. Drake as Early History of New England; Being a Relation of Hostile Passages between the Indians and European Voyagers and First Settlers ... (Albany, N.Y., 1864), 133-134, n. 159; William Hubbard, A Narrative of the Troubles with the Indians In New-England ... (1677), ed. Samuel G. Drake as The History of the Indian Wars in New England ... (Roxbury, Mass., 1865), I, xxvii-xxxi, II, 26. See also n. 10 in chap. 11, above.

56. Mason, Pequot War, 8, 10n. Cf. Vaughan: "Fearing that the Pequot's

It is terribly clear from this description that the village, stockaded though it was, had few warriors at home when the attack took place. Mason claimed that 150 Pequots had "reinforced" the village only the day before his attack. Both the number and the suggestion that it supplemented a previous garrison find no confirmation in Mason's own account of the proceedings. There is enough testimony, even in Puritan accounts, of Pequot warriors' willingness to fight to the death, so that one may feel confident that the villagers overwhelmed by Mason were not warriors suddenly and uncharacteristically turned craven.[57] Moreover, Increase Mather's version has revealed that the Pequot warriors had guns, a fact that is substantiated by Lieutenant Gardiner's earlier writing, and nowhere in Mason's account of the Mystic massacre is there mention of Indians with firearms.[58] And if the supposed reinforcements had marched from the major fort at Pequot River to the lesser one at Mystic River, they would have been heading in exactly the opposite direction from the English settlements that Mason said they intended to attack. Such a march would have taken them eastward. Fort Saybrook was to the west, and the upper Connecticut settlements were to the northwest (see map 2, p. 219). There were no "reinforcements," and it was precisely for that reason that Mason struck where he did. Mason and Underhill had had advance intelligence from their Narragansett allies of the Pequots' dispositions, and Mason knew very well that the people at Mystic were the sort who could be destroyed easily "by the sword." The wretches crawling under beds and fleeing from Mason's dripping sword were women, children, and feeble old men.

The Narragansett allies had dissented sharply from Mason's procedures. After his intention became plain to attack Mystic instead of Sassacus's fort at the Pequot River, hundreds of the Indian allies withdrew. (Mason dissembled their motive by accusing them of cowardice.[59]) Not

---

numerical superiority would prove insurmountable, Captain Mason seized a firebrand from a wigwam and thrust it into its straw roof." *New England Frontier*, 144. And Langdon: "In the course of that attack the fort caught fire." *Pilgrim Colony*, 166–167.

57. Mason, *Pequot War*, 10; Gardiner to Winthrop, Jr., Mar. 23, 1637, *Winthrop Papers*, III, 381–383. Underhill and Hubbard omitted the reinforcements assertion. Winthrop assigned as Pequot casualties "two chief sachems, and one hundred and fifty fighting men, and about one hundred and fifty old men, women, and children." May 25, 1637, *History*, ed. Savage, I, 225. Mason's and Winthrop's "reinforcements" thus became Winthrop's total of warrior casualties. Even if this is true, it means that Mason *planned* the attack before those warriors arrived, but the likelihood of its truth is remote. No matter how these wriggly texts are viewed, they testify to Mason's deliberate purpose of massacring noncombatants. He had advance information of the Pequot dispositions. See n. 59, below.

58. Increase Mather, *Early History of New England*, ed. Drake, 123–124.

59. Miantonomo had proposed to Roger Williams that an ambush be laid *between* the warriors and the noncombatants so that warriors attempting to retreat

trusting the remainder to be sufficiently ruthless, Mason and Underhill surrounded Mystic with two concentric rings, relegating the remaining Indian allies to the outer one (see figure 6, following). After firing the village the English closed up their interior ring, and as desperate Pequots tried to break through, the English intercepted and slew them before they could gain sanctuary among their formerly worst enemies. This episode was reported with some finesse by Captain Underhill in language equivocal enough to mislead the uninitiated but to be understood, with a wink, by his fellow participants. In the following passage from Underhill I have italicized key words: "Many were burnt in the fort, both men, women, and children. Others forced out, and came in troops *to the Indians*, twenty and thirty at a time, which *our soldiers* received and entertained with the point of the sword. Down fell men, women, and children; those that scaped *us*, fell into the hands of the Indians that were in the rear of us. It is reported by themselves, that there were about four hundred souls in this fort, and not above five of them escaped out of *our* hands."[60]

Here were the Pequots coming in "troops" to the Narragansetts, but in order to "fall into the hands" of the Narragansetts they had to escape the English. The twists of phrase by which Underhill tried to implicate the Narragansetts in the killing were crude enough to reveal the real situation. In a following passage he was candid enough, or boastful enough, to tell of Indian protest against the killing in words that have been robbed of their full power, unfortunately, by semantic change over the centuries. He wrote that, after the slaughter, "Our Indians came to us, and much rejoiced at our victories, and greatly admired the manner of Englishmen's fight, but cried Mach it, mach it; that is, It is naught, it is naught, because it is too furious, and slays too many men."[61]

In Underhill's day the word *admire* was used to express astonishment or wonder rather than respect, as in Milton's lines, "Let none admire / That riches grow in hell"; and the word *naught* meant bad or wicked.[62] What Underhill smugly passed on as the Indians' comment was their incredulity at the ruthlessness of the English.

---

to the noncombatants could be intercepted. As for the cowardice imputed to the Narragansetts, Miantonomo had earlier offered to attack the Pequots without any English troops to help, if *Massachusetts* would authorize him, but that would have deprived Mason of rights of conquest for Connecticut. The Indians' withdrawal: Mason, *Pequot War*, 5–7; Miantonomo: Williams to governor of Massachusetts, [May 13, 1637], *Winthrop Papers*, III, 411; Williams to Vane and Winthrop, Jr., [May 15, 1637], *ibid.*, 413–414.

60. Underhill, *Newes from America*, 39. Cf. Bradford, *Of Plymouth Plantation*, ed. Morison, 296.

61. Underhill, *Newes from America*, 42–43.

62. *Oxford English Dictionary*.

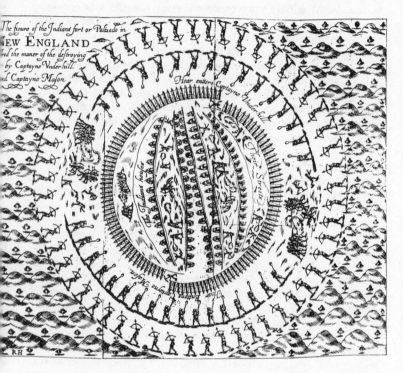

FIGURE 6. Captain John Underhill's portrayal of the attack on the Pequot fort at Mystic, 1637. The picture confirms textual analysis in the following particulars: (1) No Pequot or other Indian is shown with firearms; (2) Englishmen are shown shooting down unarmed Indians as well as those armed with bows and arrows; and (3), on the right, Pequots are shown trying to escape through the English line to the Narragansetts in the outer circle.

(From John Underhill, Newes from America [London, 1638]; courtesy of The Library Company of Philadelphia.)

The toll of Pequot casualties ranges in estimate from three hundred to seven hundred. Of the English, two were killed and twenty were wounded, and some twenty of the allied Indians were also wounded. The allies complained that they had been shot by Englishmen, and one Englishman even seems to have been killed by his own cohorts in the hail of fire they let loose after igniting the village. They must have shot at everything that moved or seemed to move. Mason's men ran low on ammunition, and he had to beat a retreat to his ships to avoid a real battle with Sassacus's warriors, belatedly on their way to help their Mystic kinsfolk. The English retreated by themselves, abandoned by their shocked and guilt-smitten allies.

Now came great irony. Finding out somehow about the English attack, the warriors in Sassacus's fort about five miles away had rushed to Mystic. They arrived too late. At the sight of the smoldering ruins and corpses they gave way momentarily to disabling grief; then rage revived them, and they plunged after the perpetrators for revenge. They encountered the Narragansetts, who had just then drawn away from the English allies of whom they were so ashamed, and the Pequots' furious attack upon those wavering Narragansetts drove the latter back to the covering fire of the English.[63] The allies were helped by the timely arrival of the English pinnaces with reserve ammunition and Massachusetts's company of forty men under Captain Patrick. Thereafter no alternatives but flight, death, or surrender could exist for the demoralized and despairing Pequots.[64]

New expeditions were sent out from Massachusetts and Connecticut to harry and destroy the miserable refugees fleeing into the wilderness. A band of two hundred Pequots surrendered to the Narragansetts without fight. Only two were killed. The rest might have expected humane treatment in accordance with custom. In Roger Williams's words, "I

63. Underhill reported that the retreating English "requested our Indians for to entertain fight" with the "prime men" of the attacking Pequots, because "we saw we could have no advantage against them in the open field." Mason admitted such difficulties that he had to hire Indians to carry his wounded. Roger Williams reported that the Narragansetts fought "thrice that day." Underhill, *Newes from America*, 40–41; Mason, *Pequot War*, 11; Williams to Winthrop, Sr., [ca. June 2, 1637], *Winthrop Papers*, III, 427.

64. Underhill, *Newes from America*, 41–42; Mason, *Pequot War*, 11–13. Underhill and Mason immediately quarreled with Patrick, about whom Mason was careful to write falsely that he was "upon some Service against the Block Islanders." Mason added in undoubted candor, "We did not desire or delight in his Company, and so we plainly told him." *Ibid.*, 12, 13. Winthrop conceded that "Our English *from Connecticut*" had conquered Mystic. May 25, 1637, *History*, ed. Savage, I, 225 (my italics). When Underhill returned to Massachusetts he was immediately attacked by the magistrates in power, partly because of his association with the defeated party of former Governor Vane, but partly also, I infer, for having sided with Connecticut's Mason against Massachusetts's Patrick.

understand it would be very gratefull to our neighbours [the Narragansetts] that such Pequts as fall to them be not enslaved, like those which are taken in warr: but (as they say is their generall Custome) be used kindly, have howses and goods and fields given them: because they voluntarily choose to come in to them and if not receaved will to the Enemie or turne wild Irish themselves." [65] Such prospects faded when a company of Massachusetts's troops seized the captives from the Narragansetts. According to William Hubbard, "The Men among them to the Number of thirty were turned presently into Charons Ferry-boat, under the Command of Skipper Gallop, who dispatched them a little without the Harbour; the Females and Children were disposed of according to the will of the Conquerors [i.e., the English], *some being given* to the Narhagansets and other Indians that *assisted* in the service." [66]

The peculiar virtues of Hubbard's style show vividly in this passage. Not many writers could have so concisely insinuated that the English were really the conquerors of a group taken by the Narragansetts, at the same time suggesting that the Narragansetts bore some responsibility for an atrocity against which they protested. And his sprightly reference to "Charons Ferry-boat" speaks volumes about Puritan wit.

For present purposes we need not pursue every last band of Pequots to its capture and final disposition. There were more atrocities; the whole story of the Pequot "war" is one long atrocity. It is enough here to say that the Pequots scattered far and wide. Some found their way to Long Island. Others, including chief sachem Sassacus, took the tribal wampum treasury to the Mohawks and tried to purchase sanctuary, but the Mohawks killed Sassacus—perhaps because of their alliance with the Narragansetts, or because of fear of the English, or for other reasons. Most of the surviving Pequots hid themselves among Uncas's Mohegans and the Eastern Niantics. Uncas, who had been unable before the war to count more than fifty warriors in his following, suddenly emerged as the ruler of hundreds. Englishmen could not distinguish between a Pequot and a Mohegan—the difference indeed had been political rather than cultural—but the Narragansetts knew the names and pedigrees of individual persons, and they frequently complained to Roger Williams that Uncas had reaped the harvest of their own sweat and sacrifice. The old Narragansett-Pequot feud had not been ended, after all; it had simply become a Narragansett-Mohegan feud, and its rumblings momentarily threatened war once more.

65. Williams to Winthrop, Sr., [ca. June 21, 1637], *Winthrop Papers*, III, 434. Cf. with Williams's wistful remark that Connecticut magistrates Haynes and Ludlow had become "almost averse" to killing women and children. *Ibid.*, 437.

66. Hubbard, *Narrative*, 127 (emphasis added). Gallop was the man who had discovered John Oldham's corpse.

However, it wore an important new aspect. Whereas formerly the Pequots had made a treaty with Massachusetts, now the Mohegans were clients of Connecticut. The Narragansetts continued to hold to their wartime treaty with Massachusetts. Uncas of the Mohegans and Miantonomo of the Narragansetts quarreled for reasons of their own, and their animosity was heightened by the continuing quarrel of Connecticut and Massachusetts. While the Indians struggled for larger shares of the Pequots' persons and former tributaries, the Englishmen strove for wampum and the Pequots' former lands.[67]

The purported cause of the Pequot conquest was quite forgotten. In the wrangling over real issues nobody bothered to pursue "justice" for the killer of Captain Stone, who walked abroad flaunting his identity. In June 1639 the Dutchman David de Vries met him near the mouth of the Connecticut River and was struck by his scarlet mantle. "I inquired," wrote de Vries, "how he came by the mantle. He had some time ago killed one Captain Stone, with his people, in a bark, from whom he had obtained these clothes."[68] That was as much attention as he got. He had served the Puritans' purpose, and they were now giving their energies to interests that had all along lain behind their voluble concern over Captain Stone.

The Pequot conquest did not bring interracial peace to New England. Rather it brought a new set of conflicting alliances in which Indians, as junior partners, fought each other in ways that were permitted and encouraged for particular purposes of particular Puritan colonies. Pequots reconstituted as Mohegans fought Connecticut's covert war against the Narragansetts, which was, at second hand, a struggle with Massachusetts. Uncas understood his dependence and willingly played his role, but though he pulled the trigger, Connecticut provided the gun and prescribed its target.

To the English the experience seemed to prove that they could conquer Indians at will. They gloried in the terror that their conquests had inspired, and they labored as needed to keep it alive. The terror was very real among the Indians, but in time they came to meditate upon its foundations. They drew three lessons from the Pequot War: (1) that the Englishmen's most solemn pledge would be broken whenever obligation conflicted with advantage; (2) that the English way of war had no limit of scruple or mercy; and (3) that weapons of Indian making were almost useless against weapons of European manufacture. These lessons the Indians took to heart.

67. Bradford, *Of Plymouth Plantation*, ed. Morison, 296–297; *Winthrop Papers*, III, 431, 435, 437, 440–448, 450.
68. De Vries, *Voyages*, trans. Murphy, in N.-Y. Hist. Soc., *Colls.*, 2d Ser., III, 86.

Chapter 14 ✌ APOSTLES
to the INDIANS

After the Pequots it was the Narragansetts'
turn to be marked down for conquest. This populous tribe occupied one
of the most attractive situations in New England, and its territory
had never been "granted" to any colony by royal charter (see map 1,
chapter 12, and map 3, chapter 15). For this very reason hundreds of
adventurers and religious dissidents settled along the west shore of
Narragansett Bay and on the bay's islands, well beyond the rule of
Puritan magistrates. Some, like Roger Williams, obtained permission
from native chiefs; others simply elbowed their way in and dared the
Indians to move against them. At another time they might have been
made to regret their intrusion, but the revelations of the Pequot conquest left the Narragansetts shy of challenging Englishmen.

The intruders were almost as averse as the natives to a Puritan conquest. Having created simple institutions of self-government, and seeing
almost limitless opportunities to make themselves rich under their own
rule, they had no wish to see their prospects blighted by the Puritan
oligarchy. Their independence would vanish on the instant that Massachusetts or Connecticut acquired rights of conquest over the Narragansetts. Unlike the Pequots, therefore, the Narragansetts acquired English
allies—weak ones, true enough, but as vociferous and legalistic as the
Puritans themselves, and with attentive correspondents in London. Accordingly the Narragansett conquest became a much more complex and
prolonged affair than the Pequot conquest.

Until 1675 Massachusetts and Connecticut, singly or together, mounted successive diplomatic and military offensives against the Narragansetts, and each time the Indians were assisted by Rhode Islanders of one
stripe or another to wiggle free of subjection. The luck of the Narragansetts finally ran out, and their tribe was destroyed in the climactic
violence of the Second Puritan Conquest. In order to understand that

This chapter has been modified from a paper read at the 17th annual meeting
of the American Society for Ethnohistory, Oct. 25, 1969, and subsequently published as "Goals and Functions of Puritan Missions to the Indians," *Ethnohistory*,
XVIII (1971), 197–212.

FIGURE 7. *Seal of the Governor and Company of Massachusetts Bay, 1629. The Indian is represented as saying, "Come over and help us."*

(*Courtesy of the Archives Division, Office of the Secretary, Commonwealth of Massachusetts, Boston.*)

"hot" war we must first examine two major Puritan institutions of "cold" war: the missionary reservations and the federation of Puritan governments called the United Colonies of New England. Reserving a separate chapter for the United Colonies, let us here attend to the missions.

According to the royal patent of Massachusetts, "the principall Ende of this Plantacion" was to "wynn and incite the Natives of [the] Country, to the Knowledg and Obedience of the onlie true God and Savior of Mankinde, and the Christian Fayth."[1] The great seal adopted by Massachusetts Bay's General Court continued the ostensible motive of religious altruism with its design showing an Indian pleading, "Come over and help us" (figure 7). From the records of the Puritans' activity, however, it would be easy to conclude that "the principall Ende" was not an end at all. In 1642 Thomas Lechford stated unequivocally that "there hath not been sent forth by any Church to learn the Natives language, or to instruct them in the Religion."[2] Although Boston had been founded in 1630, Puritan missionary work did not exist until 1643, and what began then was outside the patronage and control of Massachusetts Bay. It started with the labors of Thomas Mayhew, Jr., in the little island of Martha's Vineyard, where in 1642 a handful of Puritans had established an independent colony, the proprietary fief of Thomas Mayhew, Sr.[3]

The circumstances of settlement conduced to moderate conduct. Perhaps twenty able-bodied Englishmen, with their families, had moved into an island distant from other English colonies and already occupied by three thousand Wampanoag Indians. In the memory of the Indians was the Pequot conquest, and in the minds of the colonists was an acute awareness of the distance between themselves and succor in case of sudden need. Both sides were disposed to accommodation. Besides this favorable circumstance, the ruling Mayhews, father and son, apparently felt quite a serious obligation to win their Indians to the hope of salvation. Both devoted themselves to missionizing, with unmistakable sincerity.

In 1643 an Indian called Hiacoomes approached Thomas Mayhew, Jr., to request Christian instruction. The young colonist took pains with Hiacoomes, who apparently underwent a genuine religious experience and impressed other Indians with his sanctity. Hiacoomes and the Mayhews set going a movement that eventually resulted in the conversion of

1. *Recs. of Mass.*, I, 17.

2. Charles Edward Banks, *The History of Martha's Vineyard, Dukes County, Massachusetts* (Edgartown, Mass., 1966 [orig. publ. 1911–1925]), I, 87.

3. *Ibid.*, I, 213–257; Lloyd C. M. Hare, *Thomas Mayhew, Patriarch to the Indians (1593–1682)* ... (New York, 1932), chap. 9.

the greater number, perhaps all, of the Indians of both the Vineyard and Nantucket. The Christian tradition begun then survives still among the Gay Head Indians of the Vineyard, who, ironically, now send their own Jehovah's Witnesses missionaries to the island's summer visitors.

The Mayhew-Hiacoomes mission was characterized by voluntarism on both sides. Indians came to the missionary, and he went to them without either coercion or material reward.[4] No outside aid of any sort was given to the work until eight years had passed, and the younger Mayhew seems to have continued three years more without regular salary.[5] These facts contrasted absolutely with the later beginnings of Massachusetts's missions. Community and property policies stood in equally strong contrast. On the Vineyard, Indian rights in property were fully respected. When Vineyard converts requested a tract of land to be set aside for a Christian village, they obtained it from the pagan sachems Josias and Wannamanhutt on promise of payment of an annual rent. The government of their town was committed to Governor Mayhew because it was Christian, but outside the town the non-Christian sachems kept their customary prerogatives to govern and to sanction property transfers. Indeed Josias soon complained that the Christian Indians had not paid their rent in accordance with their deed obligation, and he reclaimed and resold part of their town land.[6]

A detailed description of the Mayhew approach to Indian politics has been left for us by one of the family who worked in the mission after coming of age. Matthew Mayhew's report deserves extensive quotation. It tells us that Thomas Mayhew, Sr., informed the Indians "that by order from his Master the King of England, he was to Govern the English which should inhabit these Islands [Martha's Vineyard and Nantucket]; that his Master was in Power far above any of the Indian Monarches; but that as he was powerfull, so was he a great lover of Justice; that therefore he would in no measure invade their Jurisdictions; but on the contrary Assist them as need required; *that Religion and Government were distinct things.* Thus in no long time they conceived no ill Opinion of the Christian Religion."[7]

As the number of Christian Indians increased, Mayhew gradually persuaded the pagan Indians to admit converts to their councils. In "cases of more than ordinary consequence" he offered his "assistance and di-

4. Gookin, "Historical Collections," Mass. Hist. Soc., *Colls.,* 1st Ser., I, 204–205; Banks, *Vineyard,* I, 220–222.

5. Banks, *Vineyard,* 225–226, 231–232.

6. Eleanor Ransom Mayhew, "The Christiantown Story, 1659–1959," *Dukes County Intelligencer,* I (1959), unpaged. See also "Petition of Wisquannowas alias Adam, of Marthas Vineyard, for land," (1675), in Hastings, ed., *Third Report of N.Y. State Historian,* 308–309.

7. M. Mayhew, *Brief Narrative of Martha's Vineyard,* 33 (emphasis added).

rection" to the chief sachem regardless of whether the latter was pagan or Christian, but he maintained that the sachem's assent "was to be obtained." Perhaps the sachem had no real power to refuse assent. Our source document, after all, was written by Mayhew's genetic descendant and vocational successor, who was not likely to explore the informal ways that pressure could be exerted to "obtain" a sachem's assent, and a modern student has characterized the Mayhew policies as "Machiavellian."[8] Whatever the realities of power, Mayhew did preserve the form of Indian independence and the substance of peaceful coexistence. He formally recognized the sachems as his peers in lordship, and they reciprocated by accepting his kind of vassalage to the English crown. As Matthew Mayhew summed up, "Thus within a few years there was a happy Government settled among them [the Vineyard Indians], and Records kept of all Actions and Acts passed in their several Courts, by such who having learned to Write fairly were appointed thereto. The Princes with their Sachims (or Nobles) made Publick acknowledgment of their Subjection to the King of England, being notwithstanding mindful to be understood as Subordinate Princes, to Govern according to the Laws of God and the King."[9]

Even under the conditions of the greatest freedom of action, the mission created tensions and factions among the Indians. Sachems and powwows struggled to keep their followers away from the Christians. Apart from theological issues, the Indian who forsook his powwow was abandoning his physician. He wondered, "When we are sick and wounded, who shall heal our maladies?"[10] Religion and government were so closely allied in Wampanoag society that when the Christian convert rejected powwows he simultaneously rejected the sachem's authority that derived from the ritual and doctrine in the powwows' custody. Considering the tensions thus created, it is remarkable that the Vineyard remained peaceful even throughout the Indian uprising of 1675–1677 that desolated the rest of New England.

In Massachusetts the missions differed from the Mayhew pattern in chronology, policy, and method. The Mayhews started their mission one year after colonizing Martha's Vineyard. Massachusetts waited sixteen years after its founding, and three years after the Vineyard was settled, before sending forth a missionary. The actual creation of Massachusetts's missions, as distinct from proposals and projections for them, emerged as the by-product of an attempt to seize the territory on the west shore of Narragansett Bay. That episode will be fully discussed below, in chapter 15, in its integral relationship to the history of the

---

8. Salisbury, "Conquest of the 'Savage,'" 173.

9. M. Mayhew, *Brief Narrative of Martha's Vineyard*, 34.

10. Gookin, "Historical Collections," Mass. Hist. Soc., *Colls.*, 1st Ser., I, 154.

United Colonies. First we shall step aside for a moment to get an overview.

As on Martha's Vineyard, the year 1643 marked the beginning of serious interest in missions in Massachusetts, but the interest in the Bay colony translated into an approach to Puritans in England rather than an approach to the Indians. Following the precedent set in Virginia from 1618 to 1622, projected Indian missions were used in 1643 to justify an appeal for English donations to Harvard College (among other causes), the grounds being that "some of our godly active young schollars" would "make it there worke to studie [the Indians'] language, converse with them, and carry light amongst them."[11] Massachusetts's agent Thomas Weld remitted £355 from contributors to the appeal. Embarrassingly the money vanished. George Parker Winship has remarked, "There can be no doubt that the proceeds were put to much needed uses in a time of great stringency. What the uses were, however, nobody in England knew at the time, and apparently no one since has found out satisfactorily."[12] At least one fact is certain: as in Virginia the money was not used for any work among Indians at that time. A particular donation may be especially noted. In 1644 the Lady Mary Armine gave an annuity of £20 to support "the Preacher to the poor Indians in New England." This money was assigned to John Eliot in 1647, but its disposition until then is unknown.[13]

Eliot, who was to become known as "the Apostle to the Indians," began to learn an Indian language in 1643. It seems likely, though unprovable, that the prospect of Lady Armine's annuity was his incentive. Nothing in his previous history shows any interest in Indians, any attitude toward them except hostility. In 1634 he had overtly opposed Massachusetts Bay's friendship treaty with the Pequots and had been reproved by the magistrates on that account.[14] When he began his

11. [Thomas Weld and Hugh Peter], *New England's First Fruits, in respect to the progress of learning, in the Colledge at Cambridge in Massachusetts-bay . . .* (1643), *ibid.*, I (Boston, 1792), 249.

12. George Parker Winship's introduction to *The New England Company of 1649 and John Eliot*, Prince Society Publications, XXXVI (Boston, 1920), xii. Weld claimed that most of the money had been paid to four Puritans to cover the expenses of "transportation" of poor children to New England; i.e., the delivery of orphans into indentured servitude. The largest amount, according to his accounting, seems to have been paid to John Winthrop's brother-in-law Emanuel Downing. If Downing ever drew up an account, I do not know of it. Thomas Weld, "Innocency Cleared," (ca. 1649), in *N.E. Hist. Gen. Reg.*, XXXVI (1882), 66.

13. Weld, "Innocency Cleared," *N.E. Hist. Gen. Reg.*, XXXVI (1882), 68; *Recs. of Mass.*, II, 189; Winship, in *New England Company*, xxxiii.

14. Nov. 27, 1634, Winthrop, *History*, ed. Hosmer, I, 142. Hosmer's edition is here cited, instead of Savage's as elsewhere herein, in order to quote the editorial note. Hosmer incorrectly claimed that Eliot remonstrated against the Pequot

Indian language studies he evidently intended his missionary work to be conducted among Indian captives,[15] for the Massachuset language was not the mother tongue of his teacher.[16] That person was conveniently near because he had been "taken in the Pequot Warres, though belonging to Long Island," which is to say that he had been seized as plunder regardless of the fact that his tribe had done no harm to his captors. This less than cheery situation was at first euphemized in Eliot's correspondence to England. He mentioned the captivity of his teacher in the past tense, adding that at the time of the language lessons the Indian was "living with" a Dorchester Englishman. Many years later Eliot edged a little closer to candor with the admission that the Indian "had been a servant" in a colonist's house.[17] A "servant" at that time in New England was sometimes a wage worker, sometimes bound to servitude for a term of years, sometimes a slave. In England, Eliot's remark was ambiguous. New Englanders understood more precisely that an Indian servant captured in war was a slave.

Eliot leisurely pursued his studies in seclusion for the next three years. Meanwhile Roger Williams sailed to England to obtain a charter for his associated towns along Narragansett Bay and on the bay's islands, and Thomas Weld tried to get a "Narragansett Patent" for Massachusetts instead. Weld dutifully played on the mission theme. His proposed patent set forth that Massachusetts should expand over Narragansett Bay not only because of rapidly increasing population but also so "that the Gospell may be speedier conveyed and preached to the Natives, that now sit there in darkness, which by Planting further into the heathens Countrey they [Massachusetts's colonists] may have better opportunity to doe."[18] Weld failed. Important Englishmen were already upset by Thomas Lechford's strictures against New England, which had been

---

treaty "as a friend of the Massachuset Indians with whom his relations were becoming close." No evidence is cited for the remark, and none could be, because the claim was a figment of Hosmer's imagination.

15. John Cotton suggested that Massachusetts's religious instruction of the Indians had begun with those "that live amongst us, and daily resort to us; and some of them learn our language; and some of us learn theirs ... though we never thought it fit to send any of our English to live amongst them, to learn their language: for who should teach them?" *The Way of Congregational Churches Cleared* (1648), in Larzer Ziff, ed., *John Cotton on the Churches of New England* (Cambridge, Mass., 1968), 274–275.

16. Eliot's first preaching to the Massachuset Indians was done through an interpreter. *Ibid.,* 273.

17. Edward Winslow, *The Glorious Progress of the Gospel, Amongst the Indians in New England* ... (1649), in Mass. Hist. Soc., *Colls.,* 3d Ser., IV (Cambridge, Mass., 1834), 90; James Constantine Pilling, ed., *Bibliography of the Algonquian Languages*, Smithsonian Institution, Bureau of American Ethnology, Bulletin 13 (Washington, D.C., 1891), s.v. "John Eliot."

18. Text of the spurious charter, Dec. 10, 1643, C.O. 1/10, 257–258, P.R.O.

published only a year earlier: "They have nothing to excuse themselves in this point of not labouring with the Indians to instruct them, but their want of a staple trade, and other businesses taking them up." [19] Roger Williams added to the disturbance with a treatise in which he remarked that conversion of the Indians would be no great problem at all if anyone should make an effort in that direction. "I can speak it confidently," wrote Williams, ". . . I could have brought the whole Countrey to have observed one day in seven: I adde, to have received Baptisme, to have come to a stated Church meeting, to have maintained Priests, and Forms of Prayer." [20] In people who believed that such observances were quintessential to religion, Williams's remarks stirred up great distress. Lechford had told England that New England had never even tried to proselytize, and Williams had added that even one man could have produced spectacular results. What was wrong with the Puritans of Massachusetts? Why had they been so remiss?

"By these censures," a scholar has written, "the Court of Massachusetts may have been prompted to its action in March, 1644. Some of the sachems, with their subjects were [then] induced to come under a covenant of voluntary subjection." The type of inducement remains murky. No quid pro quo was spelled out in the act of submission; and, considering what the Indians gave up, we may harbor a small doubt about how voluntarily they laid out their sacrifice. On March 8, 1644, five of the sachems living within Massachusetts's chartered limits rendered themselves, their subjects, their lands, and their estates to be governed and protected according to Massachusetts's "just lawes and orders, so farr as wee shalbee made capable of understanding them." As the magistrates would interpret this instrument (until compelled to change), the sachems relinquished their property rights in land as well as their jurisdiction over it. With the priorities of surrender established, the Indians capitulated in second place to the demands of the spirit; they promised in their materially bereft state "to bee willing from time to time to bee instructed in the knowledg and worship of God." [21]

The criticism in England continued. In 1645 an English Presbyterian minister attacked the Congregationalist New Englanders. In a period of intense competition between English Presbyterians and Puritan Congregationalists, the Reverend Robert Baylie made a propaganda point with his condemnation of the Puritans' New England brethren, who, "of

19. Thomas Lechford, *Plain Dealing; or, News from New-England* (1642), ed. J. Hammond Trumbull (1867), new introduction by Darrett B. Rutman (New York, 1969), 56 (p. 21 of orig. ed.).

20. Quoted in editorial note in Williams, *Key*, ed. Trumbull, Narragansett Club, *Pubs.*, I (1866), 160.

21. Ellis, "Indians of Eastern Massachusetts," in Winsor, *Memorial History of Boston*, 259; submission of sachems, Mar. 8, 1644, *Recs. of Mass.*, II, 55.

all that ever crossed the American Seas, . . . are noted as most neglectful of the work of Conversion."[22] Boston took it drowsily. John Eliot remained in his study. The godly young scholars at Harvard stayed at Harvard. The General Court stirred itself in October 1645 only to ask the reverend elders to "returne their thoughts" on the subject of missions. Whatever those thoughts may have been, they did not ripple the even surface of the Court's records.[23]

Events were brewing, however, that would startle Boston into wakefulness. In 1646 two more heretics from Narragansett Bay made their way to London with loud complaint against Massachusetts. Samuel Gorton and Randall Holden told of the magistrates' attacks upon themselves and the Narragansett Indians. Gorton published a book, the very title of which was a manifesto, and members of Parliament read it:

SIMPLICITIES DEFENCE

against

SEVEN-HEADED POLICY.

Or Innocency Vindicated, being unjustly Accused, and sorely Censured, by that Seven-headed Church-Government United in NEW-ENGLAND:

Or That Servant so Imperious in his Masters Absence Revived, and now thus re-acting in New-England.

Or The Combate of the United Colonies, not onely against some of the Natives and Subjects, but against the Authority also of the Kingdome of England, with their execution of Laws, in the name and Authority of the servant, (or of themselves) and not in the Name and Authority of the Lord, or fountain of the Government.

Wherein is declared an Act of a great people and Country of the Indians in those parts, both Princes and People (unanimously) in their voluntary Submission and Subjection unto the Protection and Government of Old England

22. Quoted in editorial note, Lechford, *Plain Dealing*, ed. Trumbull, 54. The remark was also noted and quoted by Cotton. Ziff, ed., *John Cotton*, 268.
23. *Recs. of Mass.*, II, 134.

(from the Fame, they hear thereof) together with the true manner and forme of it, as it appears under their own hands and seals, being stirred up, and provoked thereto, by the Combate and courses above-said.

Throughout which Treatise is secretly intermingled, that great Opposition, which is in the goings forth of those two grand Spirits, that are, and ever have been, extant in the World (through the sons of men) from the beginning and foundation thereof.[24]

Parliament could overlook Gorton's theological haranguing, which was common enough in that day of kaleidoscopic fanaticisms, but statesmen reacted quickly to charges that a colony was acting against the authority of the kingdom of England. Though the kingdom was in the process of shedding its king, the king's authority remained, and the new hands that had grasped it were not ready to let it trickle away. The Narragansett Bay heretics offered their own subjection to the laws of England without reservation or quibble and added to their own the voluntary submission of the Narragansett Indians; in contrast, according to their report, Massachusetts had denied the sovereign power of English law and had overreached the bounds prescribed by England's patent. Parliament was disturbed. Very quickly, Massachusetts Bay became disturbed in turn.

Correspondents in England reported the ominous proceedings to New England. Plymouth's Edward Winslow cautioned Massachusetts's Governor Winthrop about the effects on Parliament of Gorton's representations and also warned of the additional difficulties likely to arise when England should hear of still another heretico-political repression then in process in Massachusetts.[25] Winthrop and the magistrates cautiously awaited developments until a shocking event jolted them into action. Samuel Gorton's associate Randall Holden sailed into Boston harbor on or shortly before September 13, 1646. (The date is crucial.) Holden's arrival was extraordinarily newsworthy as a flamboyant defiance of the magistrates' power, for Holden had been banished from Massachusetts under penalty of death if he ever again set foot in the colony, yet he made no attempt at disguise or concealment. Triumphantly he exhibited Parliament's letter of protection, not only covering his own

24. *Simplicities Defence against Seven-Headed Policy* ... (London, 1646), in Force, comp., *Tracts*, IV.

25. Winslow to Winthrop, Sr., June 30, 1646, "Winthrop Papers," Mass. Hist. Soc., *Colls.*, 4th Ser., VI (Boston, 1863), 181–182.

person but also instructing Massachusetts to cease molesting all of his and Gorton's associates at Narragansett Bay.[26]

The alarmed magistrates took counsel. Holden was grudgingly permitted to pass unharmed through the colony, and decisions were made to restore the Bay's influence in London. The magistrates finally realized the seriousness of the growing rift between themselves and their fellow religionists in England. Their response to political differences was to stress religious likeness and religious duty. The long-gestating mission to the Indians was suddenly perceived as a benefit instead of a nuisance, and it came to birth. John Eliot emerged from his study.

To provide a basis for propaganda in England, Eliot's mission had to appear as an altruistic outpouring of religious benevolence. If seen as a mere maneuver to recover lost influence, it would not make headway against critics. The Puritans, therefore, reported the mission's origins with adjustments of certain data to give the desired image.

Eliot first preached to the Indians under sachem Cutshamoquin at a place called Dorchester Mill. The sources provide us with a choice of two dates. John Winthrop entered the event in his *History* under the date of July 5, 1646, leaving a blank for its description. The anonymous author of a missionary tract (thought to have been John Wilson, the minister of Boston's church) dated the Dorchester Mill preaching at approximately September 15, 1646, which would be about two days after Randall Holden's arrival in Boston harbor. In my interpretation, John Winthrop pushed the mission date back in time to break the connection with Holden. But suppose that Winthrop's date of July 5 be accepted as the time of first preaching at Dorchester Mill. We would then have to take into account the warning that Edward Winslow had written to Winthrop five days earlier; it is clearly dated "June ult. 1646." Winslow had warned of "the evill that I long feared concerning Gorton," and the rest of his letter locates that evil in Parliament. The fact is indisputable that Massachusetts's mission did not begin until after Massachusetts's magistrates began to fear Parliament's reactions to the Gorton-Holden revelations. Compared to that fact, whether the mission originated on July 5 or September 15 is a minor question that may be answered according to one's taste in interpretation without affecting the issue of substance.[27]

There is another curiosity about that first meeting at Dorchester Mill; namely, that Eliot treated it as a nonevent. His terse reference to

26. Sept. 13, 1646, Winthrop, *History*, ed. Savage, II, 273.
27. [John Wilson], *The Day-Breaking, If Not The Sun-Rising of the Gospell With the Indians in New-England* (1647), in Mass. Hist. Soc., *Colls.*, 3d Ser., IV (Cambridge, Mass., 1834), 3–4; Winslow to Winthrop, Sr., "Winthrop Papers," *ibid.*, 4th Ser., VI, 181–182.

it indicates that he was badly heckled: "They gave no heed unto it, but were weary, and rather despised what I said." He refused to consider this failure as part of his missionary career, his logic apparently being that because the meeting was not successful the career had not yet begun: "I first began with the Indians of Noonanetum [Nonantum], as you know; those of Dorchester mill not regarding any such thing." His language is not conclusive in itself, and other narrators have chosen to follow his lead by thrusting the Dorchester Mill meeting out of memory, but Daniel Gookin confirmed the meeting explicitly. Cutshamoquin, he wrote, "was the first sachem and his people to whom Mr. Eliot preached." Equally explicitly the author of the missionary tract of 1647 remarked on the distinction between Eliot's first and second preachings. He dated the Nonantum meeting at October 28, 1646, and remarked happily that the Indians had then behaved "far different from what some other Indians under Kitshomakin in the like meeting about six weekes before had done."[28]

Serious consequences flowed from Dorchester Mill. The magistrates acted swiftly and emphatically to guarantee that that sort of reception would never again be given to one of their missionaries. They took three steps: an immediate executive reorganization of government over the Indians, an enactment at the next session of the General Court for the suppression of native religion, and another legislative enactment for a missionary reservation where praying Indians could be segregated from the recidivist influence of their non-Christian kinsmen.

The first of these decisions is nowhere candidly set down on paper, but it is delineated by the implications of the following circumstances. When Eliot ventured on his second approach to the Indians—the one at Nonantum—he avoided Cutshamoquin as well as the other four legitimate sachems who had formally submitted their people to Massachusetts's government two years earlier. Instead of approaching any of these sachems who governed by native right through native custom, Eliot and three companions took themselves on October 28, 1646, to the village of a man who had no native right whatever. His name was Waban, and his status was described in revealingly variant terms by Eliot and Governor John Winthrop. Well inside his narrative, Eliot characterized Waban as "a man of gravitie and chiefe prudence and counsell among them, *although no Sachem.*" This interesting distinction, casually placed

28. "The Letter of Mr. Eliot to T. S. concerning the late work of God among the Indians," Sept. 24, 1647, in Thomas Shepard, *The Clear Sun-Shine of the Gospel Breaking Forth upon the Indians in New-England* ... (1648), *ibid.*, 3d Ser., IV (Cambridge, Mass., 1834), 50; Gookin, "Historical Collections," *ibid.*, 1st Ser., I; [Wilson], *Day-Breaking, ibid.*, 3d Ser., IV, 3–4. Vaughan cites less evidence than given here and converts the one failure at Dorchester Mill into "intermittent visits" by Eliot "to the neighboring tribes." *New England Frontier*, 247.

in parentheses, was overshadowed by Eliot's other characterization of Waban, in his very first paragraph, as "the chief minister of Justice" among the Indians of Waban's village. The question presents itself: how could an Indian who was not a sachem be a chief minister of Justice? The answer is that the justice was English though the minister was Indian.[29]

John Winthrop seemingly added confusion to the contradiction by terming Waban "a *new* sachem," but Winthrop's remark gives the clue to the misleading partial truths in Eliot's remark as well as his own.[30] The key word is "new." Waban's name does not appear in the records until Eliot's visit. His acquisition of authority preceded the missionary's arrival by a short time, and there is no indication anywhere of the demise or departure of any previous sachem at that time, nor is there any hint by either Winthrop or Eliot that Waban had replaced any other sachem. He was an addition of some sort rather than a successor or substitute. Eliot's precise terms must be observed closely because he carefully distinguished between "sachems of the blood" and "civil rulers," and he repeatedly mentioned Waban in correspondence as a "civil" ruler. It was a standing assumption with English colonials that Indian government could not be civil because the Indians were un-civilized. Clearly, therefore, Waban had not achieved governmental authority by Indian procedures, nor did he rule by Indian custom. Un-derstanding this, we can interpret the cryptic remarks and seeming inconsistency of Eliot and Winthrop. It appears that Waban had indeed not been a sachem before Eliot's first, unsuccessful, attempt at mis-sionizing in sachem Cutshamoquin's village, nor did Waban ever be-come a sachem. In the reaction to Eliot's failure at Dorchester Mill, Waban was made "chief minister of Justice" by English appointment under Massachusetts law, and Winthrop misleadingly equated the new post with the traditional sachemship legitimized by Indian custom. Waban was a good choice from the Puritans' point of view; he used his newly endowed powers to muster a congregation for Eliot and to discipline it to listen respectfully.[31]

Several specimens of Waban's style of exhortation have survived.

---

29. [Wilson], *Day-Breaking*, in Mass. Hist. Soc., *Colls.*, 3d Ser., IV, 3–4 (em-phasis added).

30. Winthrop, *History*, ed. Savage, II, 303–304.

31. Minutes, May 26, 1647, *Recs. of Mass.*, II, 188–189; Eliot to Jonathan Hanmer, July 19, 1652, Wilberforce Eames, ed., *John Eliot and the Indians, 1652–1657* (New York, 1915), 7. It is clear from this letter to Hanmer that Eliot had instituted his civil government system long before the publication of his book describing it; viz., *The Christian Commonwealth: or, The Civil Policy of the Rising Kingdom of Jesus Christ* (1660), in Mass. Hist. Soc., *Colls.*, 3d Ser., IX (Boston, 1846), 127–164. It cannot be reasonably doubted that the mission Indians were kept under tight controls from the very beginning.

One has been preserved by Eliot in a tract extolling his mission's success. Although Eliot admitted to having "cloathed it with our English Idiom," he insisted that the thought was Waban's. Thus spoke Waban the model convert: "These words are a similitude, that as some be sick, and some well; and we see in experience that when we be sick, we need a Phisitian and goe to him, and make use of his Phisick; but they that be well doe not so, they need it not and care not for it: So it is with soul-sicknesse; and we are all sick of that sicknesse in our souls, but we know it not...." Tradition has preserved a rather different sort of rhetoric from the lips of Waban the civil ruler. According to Samuel G. Drake, "The following is said to be a copy of a warrant which he issued against some of the transgressors. 'You, you big constable, quick you catch um Jeremiah Offscow, strong you hold um, safe you bring um, afore me, Waban, justice peace.'" Drake continued, "A young justice asked Wauban what he would do when Indians got drunk and quarrelled; he replied, 'Tie um all up, and whip um plaintiff, and whip um fendant, and whip um witness.'" There are, to be sure, many kinds of English idiom in which thought can be made clear.[32]

Although Waban's power was entirely derivative and subsidiary, the Massachusetts General Court soon gave it impressive magnitude by enactments for the regulation of religion among Indians as well as Englishmen. In its session of November 4, 1646—one week following Eliot's first preaching in Waban's village—the Court enacted "for the honor of the eternall God, whom only we worship and serve, that no person within the jurisdiction, whether Christian or pagan, shall wittingly and willingly presume to blaspheme his holy name, either by wilfull or obstinate deniing the true God, or his creation or government of the world, or shall curse God or reproach the holy religion of God ... if any person or persons whatsoever, within our jurisdiction, shall break this lawe they shalbe put to death." An Indian would think twice about heckling Eliot after learning about that law. To make sure that he should, the Court enacted further that "the necessary and holesome lawes which may be made to reduce them [the Indians] to civility of life shalbe once in the year (if the times be safe) made knowne to them by such fit persons as the Courte shall nominate." In still another enactment the Court outlawed all the ritual of Indian worship by decreeing "that no Indian shall at any time pawwaw, or performe outward worship to their false gods, or to the devill," under "penalty of heavy fines."[33]

The Court conceded, in another connection, that "no human power"

32. [John Eliot], *A further Accompt of the Progresse of the Gospel amongst the Indians in New-England* (London, 1659), 8-9; Drake, *Biography and History of the Indians*, 179-180.

33. *Recs. of Mass.*, II, 176-177, 178.

could constrain men "to beleeve or profess against their conscience," but it simultaneously affirmed a duty to suppress impiety—which meant, of course, the professions of heretical consciences.[34] It is not strange that this terse expression of well-known Puritan principle should have been extended to the Indians as soon as Indian religion became a matter of sufficient concern to stir any activity at all.

Eliot construed freedom of conscience for Indians in a rather constricted sense. When he asked his Indian listeners to submit themselves voluntarily to the worship of the particular entity that he identified absolutely and unqualifiedly as God, he construed voluntarism in a manner peculiar to his coreligionists. That sort of freedom of conscience did not imply freedom to choose any religion other than Eliot's own. He allowed only a choice of degree of commitment to the Puritan religion. The permitted range of choice for mission Indians lay between perfunctory observation of accepted ritual, at minimum, and unqualified profession of faith, at optimum.[35] To go outside that range was to commit the blasphemy for which death was mandatory.

Besides its measures of repression, the General Court took positive action to encourage Eliot's mission in a supporting, though notably thrifty, decree. This provided that two ministers would be chosen by the church elders at each annual Court of Election, to "make knowne the heavenly counsell of God among the Indians in most familiar manner," and that "some thing" should be allowed by the General Court for free distribution "unto those Indians whom they shall perceive most willing and ready to be instructed." The Court also provided for purchase of land for a missionary reservation—the first—but the legislators were not entirely carried away by religious enthusiasm. They added that "the charge this purchase shall amount unto shalbe deducted out of the first gift that shalbe brought over [from England] as given for the good of the Indians."[36]

Decades later Daniel Gookin was to write a defense of this law, rebutting critics who objected that there was no need to provide land for the Indians "forasmuch as it was all their native country and propriety, before the English came into America." Nettled, Gookin claimed English right to the land under Massachusetts's royal patent; besides (he wrote) "the English had the grant of most of the land within this jurisdiction, either by purchase or donation from the Indian sachems."[37] Since very little of Massachusetts's land had been bought as of the time the reservation was enacted, Gookin could only have had reference

---

34. *Ibid.*, 177.
35. Gookin, "Historical Collections," Mass. Hist. Soc., *Colls.*, 1st Ser., I, 182.
36. *Recs. of Mass.*, II, 178–179, 166.
37. Gookin, "Historical Collections," Mass. Hist. Soc., *Colls.*, 1st Ser., I, 179.

to the great donation made by the sachems in 1644, in which they submitted themselves and their lands to Massachusetts's government. It was a grant obviously made under duress and without compensation. In 1646, however, the General Court would not disgorge even enough to provide for Eliot's mission until money was provided from England to pay for it. The incident foreshadowed the history of the missions during the period of this study: the colonials distributed gifts to the missions but did not themselves contribute. All of the missionary financing came from England.[38]

In the matter of Indian land tenure, Massachusetts would be obliged by future events to recede from the position that the Indians had lost all proprietary right by the grant of 1644, but that extreme position was being upheld when the missions were founded. In legal theory at that time, no Indian in the colony's jurisdiction had clear title to as much as an acre until the General Court made its minuscule restitution of reservation land. Indians were not slow to grasp the association: to accept the missionaries was to obtain a secure habitation. The price for them, unfortunately, included more than listening to the ministers.

The first native to show favorable interest in salvation came to minister of justice Waban's village shortly after the November enactments of the General Court. Described as "an inferiour Prince," this visitor had decided to become "more like to the English, and to cast off those Indian wild and sinfull courses they formerly lived in." When opposed by "divers of his men," he argued that "the higher Indian sachems" had only used their tribesmen for personal aggrandizement. It is clear, therefore, that this subordinate chief was attempting to draw his people out of the authority of their old sachem, who would have been Cutshamoquin the heckler. By no great coincidence the seceding subordinate

38. Gookin, who was in a position to know, affirmed only that all expenses of the meetings of the Commissioners of the United Colonies—the disbursing agency—were defrayed by the host colonies "so that *in that respect* New England people are not behind hand in charge towards that work" (emphasis added). To my knowledge, no one has yet produced any other contribution from New Englanders in the 17th century except for the free labor of the Mayhews and possibly a similar contribution from Richard Bourne in Plymouth. Since the United Colonies was founded for political purposes and its Commissioners took advantage of their agency to divert mission funds to ends of their own, the expenses of their meetings do not seem like a very substantial financial contribution by the colonies to the missions. Gookin, "Historical Collections," Mass. Hist. Soc., *Colls.*, 1st Ser., I, 213. See also William Kellaway, *The New England Company, 1649–1776: Missionary Society to the American Indians* (London, 1961), 62–72.

On the other hand, when the Indians' lands were taken from them without compensation through the so-called grant of 1644, distributed to towns or individual persons, and then bought back with company money in order to set up reservation towns, some persons in the colonies were making a nice profit out of the mission funds; and it does not seem strange that the financial records of these transactions have become difficult to follow.

immediately applied for land within the bounds of Concord town. Nevertheless he was unable to persuade all his people to come along. Whoever this inferior prince was, he and some friends paid the price for missionary favor. In January 1647 they agreed to a set of "Conclusions and Orders" that included, among many similar things, fines of twenty shillings for not observing the English sabbath and five shillings for not getting haircuts "comely, as the English do." The source and sanction for such rules hardly needs to be argued.[39]

We have been attending to Eliot's mission as it appeared in Massachusetts, but we must now recall that the primary function of the mission was to make an impression in England. To offset the negative effect on Parliament that had been created by the complaining heretics from Narragansett Bay, the magistrates decided to send an agent to London, as had been earlier advised by Edward Winslow, and Eliot's mission was to be one of the agent's talking points. Winslow himself was chosen for the mission. A week after Eliot's meeting in Waban's village, and in the same session that enacted the legislation mentioned above, the General Court instructed Winslow to tell Parliament's High Commission that Massachusetts had been terribly slandered by its enemies. In this presentation Samuel Gorton and his associates at Narragansett Bay had threatened "the poor Indians . . . who (to avoid their tyranny) had submitted themselves and their lands under our protection and government." For Parliament to countenance Gorton would be to destroy a high and holy work, for the Reverend Mr. Eliot had preached to some Indians in their own language, "all which hopeful beginnings are like to be dashed if Gorton, etc., shall be countenanced and upheld against them and us, which will also endanger our peace here at home." That the Indians of Gorton's acquaintance were rather different people from the Indians of Eliot's mission did not appear in Winslow's documents; all distinctions of persons and places were carefully and expertly obfuscated.[40]

Winslow knew his business. In London he immediately committed himself to polemic war with Massachusetts's critics, exploiting the new mission to maximum effect. Suppressing the fact that the wampum tribute extorted by Massachusetts from various Indian tribes would have financed a considerable missionary effort,[41] Winslow represented

---

39. Shepard, *Sun-Shine*, in Mass. Hist. Soc., *Colls.*, 3d Ser., IV, 38–41.

40. Winthrop, *History*, ed. Savage, II, 359–365; *Recs. of Mass.*, II, 165, 171, 175.

41. Tribute and fines were levied every year by the United Colonies. In 1655 the tribute amounted to £301 1s. 6d. Pulsifer, ed., *Acts of the United Colonies*, II, 141. In 1637 Roger Williams mentioned 100 fathoms of wampum to be paid annually "to Mr. Governour" Winthrop by the Block Island Indians. Williams's phrasing is curious: he said that the Narragansetts acknowledged the Block Islanders to be "wholy Mr. Governours Subjects." It sounds as though the elder

the colony as too poor and struggling to be able to support Eliot's work without English help. On the basis of this asserted poverty, Winslow lobbied with Parliament for a license to solicit funds in all the churches of England.[42] He seems to have been believed in his accounts of pious progress. However, Parliament hesitated to authorize the collection. Perhaps some of its members recalled the fiasco of the Virginia Company's Indian college; whether or not such memories had an effect, there were complaints about New England's unsatisfactory accounting for the moneys collected in 1643.[43] Winslow's job was to arouse enough religious enthusiasm to overcome political and financial skepticism. Apart from his political objectives, he had to get the money out of England for a mission in Massachusetts that the Massachusetts General Court had refused to finance out of its own funds. This was a task of some delicacy, even in an era of fanaticism.

The facts about the Eliot mission were as yet wholly inadequate for Winslow's purpose. Under the most favorable interpretation, Eliot's work was still merely a beginning without any visible accomplishments. Winslow, however, was not a man to be restrained by mere facts or the lack thereof. He seized upon the labors of Thomas Mayhew, Jr., the man who had worked in lonely isolation with never a penny of encouragement from Massachusetts, and gratuitously attributed those labors to Eliot. Editing a book of letters from Eliot, Winslow made Eliot say—or Eliot had himself said prior to the editing—that "our Cutshamoquin [the Massachuset sachem so averse to Christianity that he had rejected Eliot's mission] hath some subjects in Marthas Vineyard, and they hearing of his praying to God, some of them doe the like there, with other ingenious Indians, and I [Eliot] have intreated Mr. Mahew (the young Scholler, son to old Mr. Mahew) who preacheth to the English to teach them; and he doth take pains in their language, and teacheth them not without successe, blessed be the Lord."[44]

Eliot's letter fabricated a role for himself where he had in fact played none. Its assertion about Cutshamoquin was an outright lie: Cutshamoquin had nothing to do with the Vineyard Indians, who were Wampanoags under the general sachemship of Ousamequin, or Massasoit,

---

Winthrop had acquired the Block Islanders personally as his son briefly picked up the Western Niantics. Williams to Winthrop, Sr., ca. Oct. 26, 1637, *Winthrop Papers*, III, 500.

A New England historian has noted that "the United Colonies had devised a scheme by which the native, while being improved off the face of the land, should pay in money for the protection of the paternal government." Weeden, *Indian Money in New England Civilization*, 407.

42. Winship, in *New England Company*, xiv–xix.

43. *Ibid.*, xii–xiii; Weld, "Innocency Cleared," *N.E. Hist. Gen. Register*, XXXVI (1882), 65.

44. Winslow, *Glorious Progress*, Mass. Hist. Soc., *Colls.*, 3d Ser., IV, 81.

who in turn had nothing to do with Massachusetts because he was under the jealous protection of Plymouth Colony.[45] Besides this, when the Vineyard mission began in 1643 Cutshamoquin had not yet subjected himself to Massachusetts and was surely not "praying to God." He was named with the clearly deceitful intention of establishing a semantic connection by which Eliot could be presented as having initiated Mayhew's Vineyard mission.[46]

What made the Vineyard fabrication especially credible in Winslow's publication was its accompaniment in the same book by a seemingly substantiating letter from Thomas Mayhew, Jr.[47] In time, however, the facts of Mayhew's mission were exposed by an accident of the winds. A Connecticut minister named Henry Whitfield was blown out of his course on a voyage and forced to take shelter at Martha's Vineyard. Harboring there for ten days, Whitfield talked with Mayhew and observed the island mission in operation. He went on to Boston and then to England with knowledge gained from direct observation that directly contradicted Eliot's claim to have instigated the mission.[48] It would seem that he had also discussed the matter with Eliot. But Whitfield had no desire to scandalize another minister of his own church or to spoil the pious endeavors then in progress. When he published he permitted Eliot a face-saving "explanation," though he vexed Eliot by keeping silent instead of adding his own word in support of Eliot's strained tale.[49]

The explanation simply disregarded Eliot's former statement about sachem Cutshamoquin. Who in England would know anything about the intricacies of Indian jurisdictions thousands of miles away? The problem that could not be disregarded was Eliot's statement that "I have intreated Mr. Mahew" to preach to Indians that Mayhew had been converting three years before Eliot came out of his study. To explain away this too-obvious fabrication, Eliot wrote that his former letter had had "a great (I) redundant which maketh the sence untrue," brightly adding that everything would read quite accurately if only

45. Gookin, "Historical Collections," *ibid.*, 1st Ser., I, 148; Bradford, *Of Plymouth Plantation*, ed. Morison, 80–81.

46. In 1671 Eliot repeated the trick of fraudulently taking credit for another man's work, in this instance Plymouth's Richard Bourne. Like Mayhew, Bourne had begun to proselytize before Eliot's first effort; and, also like Mayhew, Bourne had worked without compensation. Cf. John Eliot, *A Brief Narrative of the Progress of the Gospel amongst the Indians in New-England, in the Year 1670* (London, 1671), 3; Bushnell, "Indians in Plymouth Colony," *NEQ*, XXVI (1953), 207.

47. Winslow, *Glorious Progress*, in Mass. Hist. Soc., *Colls.*, 3d Ser., IV, 77–79.

48. Henry Whitfield, *The Light appearing more and more towards the perfect Day. Or, a farther Discovery of the present state of the Indians in New-England* ... (1651), *ibid.*, 107–118.

49. Eliot to Winslow, Oct. 20, 1651, *N.E. Hist. Gen. Reg.*, XXXVI (1882), 292.

"that (great I)" were left out.[50] Suppose we do what Eliot suggested, and take that great I out of the passage quoted above. The grammatical subject of his sentence would then change from himself in the singular to a plural number of Indians thus: "Our Cutshamoquin hath some subjects in Marthas Vineyard, and they ... have intreated Mr. Mahew ... to teach them." If Eliot had really not meant to grab credit for himself, he would not have interjected Cutshamoquin and he would not have made Hiacoomes into a multitude. The falseness of his "correction" must have been understood by clergy and magistrates alike in both Massachusetts and Plymouth, and certainly on the Vineyard. Like Whitfield, however, all these pious folk were willing to maintain silence for the benefit of the propagation of the faith—or unwilling to risk the wrath of Eliot's powerful sponsors.

In England the whole performance was a great success. Winslow used Eliot's letters, including the I/Indians/Hiacoomes one, to win Parliament's authorization for a nationwide collection of missionary funds, and an organization with a long name was established to transmit the funds to Eliot's mission. The New England Company, as it is usually called more shortly, became a permanent center of activity for well-wishers of Massachusetts, enlisting the aid of wealthy and important people who thus became committed to active advocacy of the colony's interests. It stood as a perpetual testimonial to the colony's presumed benevolence toward the Indians, and it regularly published tracts extolling Eliot and his associates. Modern propagandists might well admire the ingenuity that created it, for none of this activity or publicity cost Massachusetts a penny.[51] Indeed the company transmitted much more money than was ever accounted for in mission records or activity, and it drastically revised its financing procedures after its agents in America failed to give satisfactory accounting. Among other uses, the colonies spent mission funds on arms and ammunition (to the great distress of the company's officers) and on the construction of the grandest edifice of Massachusetts's newly founded Harvard College—a two-story brick building blandly and uncandidly described to the company as "one entire room."[52] As many as two Indians are known to have

50. Whitfield, *Light appearing*, Mass. Hist. Soc., *Colls.*, 3d Ser., IV, 122–123, 108–109, 118.

51. In the 18th century, when Eleazar Wheelock, an Anglican, got a "bushel of money" out of England for an Indian charity school and diverted it to the founding of Dartmouth College, his maneuver was recognized and opposed in Congregationalist Boston. To Dartmouth's great credit, it has published the whole story. Leon Burr Richardson, ed., *An Indian Preacher in England*, Dartmouth College Manuscript Series, II (Hanover, N.H., 1933), 75, 81, 137; Harold Blodgett, *Samson Occom*, Dartmouth College Manuscript Series, III (Hanover, N.H., 1935), 85–86.

52. For the expenditures for arms, see Neal Salisbury, "Red Puritans: The

been in residence at one time, but not a second time; other uses were found for the excess space.[53]

Meanwhile, John Eliot became an important figure in New England diplomacy, important to both Englishmen and Indians because of the effects of proselytizing on political institutions. Indian communities were cemented by traditional rituals under the direction of priests closely allied to the sachems. Both the rituals and the priests were known as powwows. Both kinds of powwow were intensely attacked by the missionaries and their converts. As Neal Salisbury has written, "In requiring the potential convert to reside in a praying town, Puritan missionaries demanded nothing less than a complete repudiation of not only his culture but his community."[54] In 1650 Eliot had a showdown with sachem Cutshamoquin, in Eliot's words, "because the Indians that pray to God, since they have so done, do not pay him tribute as formerly they have done.... And further [Cutshamoquin] said, this thing are all the Sachems sensible of, and therefore set themselves against praying to God."[55]

Nor was Eliot content to dissolve and reorganize the institutions of Indians who offered formal submission to his government. He and his associates regarded the mission reservations as bases from which praying Indians could be sent to subvert the independent tribes. As one missionary put it, "Religion would not consist with a mere receiving of the word.... Practical religion will throw down their heathenish idols and the sachem's tyrannical monarchy."[56] An English royal commissioner commented that Massachusetts's missionaries proselyted In-

'Praying Indians' of Massachusetts Bay and John Eliot," *WMQ*, 3d Ser., XXXI (1974), 41.

53. Morison writes that the English society "instructed" the United Colonies to erect the building, but Kellaway describes a procedure in which the New Englanders first proposed use of mission funds for Harvard, which proposal was rejected in England because "the Society could not fall in with such a facile diversion of the funds from their proper purpose"; after that the New Englanders twisted an English suggestion for educating the Indians into authorization to spend a large amount of money on Harvard. The cost of the "Indian College" building came to about £350. (Missionaries were paid on the order of £10 and £20 annually.) Morison's misleading phrasing in this instance shakes confidence, but his account of Harvard's venture into Indian education seems to be otherwise a fair description. Samuel Eliot Morison, *Harvard in the Seventeenth Century* (Cambridge, Mass., 1936), I, chap. 17, "instructed," p. 342; Kellaway, *New England Company*, 110; Margery Somers Foster, *"Out of Smalle Beginings...": An Economic History of Harvard College in the Puritan Period (1636 to 1712)* (Cambridge, Mass., 1962), 144. See also the introduction to *Harvard College Records*, I (Colonial Society of Massachusetts, *Publications*, XV [Boston, 1925]), lxxii–lxxxv; Winship, in *New England Company*, xix–xxi.

54. Salisbury, "Conquest of the 'Savage,'" 201.

55. Whitfield, *Light appearing*, in Mass. Hist. Soc., *Colls.*, 3d Ser., IV, 139–140.

56. Gookin, "Historical Collections," *ibid.*, 1st Ser., I, 208–209.

dians "by hyring them to hear sermons, by teaching them not to obey their heathen princes, and by appoynting rulers amongst them over tenns, fifties, etc."[57] Wampanoag sachem Philip told some Rhode Islanders that the Indians "had a great Fear to have any of their Indians should be called or forced to be Christian Indians. They said that such were in everything more mischievous, only Dissemblers, and then the English made them not subject to their Kings, and by their lying to wrong their Kings." The Quaker reporter remarked, "We knew it to be true."[58]

Confirmation of such comment can be gleaned from guarded statements in Eliot's own correspondence. "Messengers and instruments" are mentioned repeatedly. These were his active leading converts. "Messengers and instruments look for their pay," he wrote in December 1671 to the New England Company's treasurer, "and if that fail, the whole moves very heavily and will quickly stand still."[59] Shortly earlier he had been more explicit with the company's bursars in New England, knowing that these local dignitaries shared his own view of the utility of Indian converts as an instrument of expansion. To these gentlemen he confided that "God put it into the heart of the church to send some of their brethren to sundry parts of the country, to call in their countrymen to pray unto God. I forsaw this would be chargeable." Since Eliot himself was the voice of God to his converts, his foresight on the occasion is not strange. He knew exactly why the enterprise would be "chargeable," and he explained it. "Captain Gookings will inform you of some charges in powder and shot for their necessary defence in these times of danger." Such "defence," of course, would be conducted in those "sundry parts of the country" where Eliot's messengers and instruments were wrestling for the souls of the benighted. These zealots carried more than one kind of persuasion when they called on other Indians to pray. On this occasion Eliot armed them to go among the Nipmuck Indians to "teach them the fear of the Lord."[60] When "King Philip's War" broke out four years later, these Nipmuck ingrates repaid the missionary's solicitude by becoming Philip's first allies against the English.[61]

The Nipmucks were not the only ostensible converts to turn hostile. Every missionary town contributed warriors to the rebel bands. Even James the Printer, the Indian who had helped print Eliot's translation

57. George Cartwright, "Account of Massachusetts" (1665), in "Clarendon Papers," N.-Y. Hist. Soc., *Colls., 1869,* 86.

58. John Easton, "A Relacion of the Indyan Warre..." (1675), in Charles H. Lincoln, ed., *Narratives of the Indian Wars, 1675–1699,* Original Narratives of Early American History (New York, 1913), 10.

59. Dec. 1, 1671, Massachusetts Historical Society, *Proceedings,* XVII (1879–1880), 250.

60. Eliot to Commissioners of the United Colonies, Sept. 4, 1671, *ibid.,* 248–249; Eliot, *Brief Narrative,* 6.

61. See chap. 17 below.

of the Bible, joined the hostile forces.[62] How successful, then, were the missions in the long run?

Different standards produce different evaluations. If many or most of the mission Indians took up the hatchet against the Puritans, a certain number of the more faithful converts became indispensable auxiliaries of the colonial troops. By religious standards, judgment depends on what emphasis is given to numbers. Eliot avoided statistics, providing them only under intense pressure from the New England Company in England, and the figures he finally produced need careful analysis. He preferred to dwell upon case studies, and his reports glow—after a fashion—with ponderously rapturous rhetoric about particular individuals.

The rhetoric considerably outran performance, even as depicted by admirers. A hard-nosed, avowedly racist, nineteenth-century historian confessed that "little, if any, credit" was due to the Massachusetts Puritans "for labor spent or for success attained in that work."[63] Even the inner circle of Puritans sometimes blurted out disillusionment. Hugh Peter—a relation by marriage of the Winthrops'; an agent of the Saybrook Company; the pastor who succeeded Roger Williams and then excommunicated him and disciplined the Salem church; and so prominent a Puritan revolutionary in England that he was horribly executed at the Restoration (to the cheers of the multitude)—Peter once let himself remark that the mission work "was but a plain cheat, and that there was no such thing as a gospel conversion amongst the Indians."[64]

Eliot himself reported after a quarter century of missionary activity that his results had been disappointingly meager. Responding to questions from England, he evaded the subject of how many Indians had been admitted to full communion and protested as "too strickt" another question about how many converts were being "daily added."[65] He had good reason for evasion. From his account elsewhere, the number of Indian communicants in 1671 can be calculated at certainly less than one hundred and probably much lower.[66]

Eliot's associate Daniel Gookin remarked in 1674 that "many" of the praying Indians had "not yet come so far as to be able or willing to profess their faith in Christ and yield obedience and subjection to him in his church." Gookin should have said "most" instead of "many." By his own accounting "about" 1,100 Indians had "subjected to the gospel," by which he plainly meant Indians who observed the outward forms of

62. Hubbard, *Narrative*, 96.

63. Ellis, "Indians of Eastern Massachusetts," in Winsor, *Memorial History of Boston*, 257–258.

64. *Dictionary of National Biography*, s.v. "Peters or Peter, Hugh."

65. John Eliot, "An Account of Indian Churches in New-England," Aug. 22, 1673, Mass. Hist. Soc., *Colls.*, 1st Ser., X (Boston, 1809), 126.

66. Eliot, *Brief Narrative*, 6.

worship and lived under the "civil order" or government of the mission towns. Gookin and his editor could find only three towns having Indians in full communion: Natick with 40 to 50, Hassanemesit with 16, and Magunkaquogt with 8—a total of 74 at most. If "baptized" persons are added to those in full communion, Gookin's total comes to 119 souls yielding obedience *in the church*. They were a tiny minority among the 1,100 Indians "subjected" to the gospel government.[67]

That government itself contributed to Indian resistance. Its objective was to impose civilization and repress savagery. Eliot's view was that the Indians "must have visible civility before they can rightly injoy visible sanctitie" in ecclesiastical communion.[68] In practice Massachusetts's missionaries associated the two processes, requiring their praying Indians to alter previous ways of life in a number of rigorously mandated particulars. Eliot believed in "life and zeal in the punishment of Sinners," and he punished such sins as unemployment, long hair, and killing lice between the teeth.[69] In 1684 Eliot attributed the praying Indians' observance of the Puritan Sabbath to "the example of the English churches and the authority of the English laws, which Major Gookin doth declare unto them, together with such mulcts, as are inflicted upon transgressors."[70]

The primary requirement for both civilization and religious instruction was simple and drastic. To be eligible, Indians were first compelled

---

67. The following table is drawn from Gookin, "Historical Collections," Mass. Hist. Soc., *Colls.*, 1st Ser., I. Each number in parentheses refers to a source page number.

Indians in the Massachusetts Mission Towns, 1674

Town	No. Residents	No. Baptized	No. in Communion
Natick	145 (180)	—	40–50 (182)
Punkapaog	60 (184)	—	—
Hassanemesit	60 (185)	30 (185)	16 (185)
Okommakamesit	50 (185)	—	—
Wamessit	75 (186)	—	—
Nashobah	50 (188)	—	—
Magunkaquogt	55 (189)	15 (189)	8 (189)
"New" towns (Nipmuck)			
Manchage	60 (189)	—	—
Chabanakongkomun	45 (189)	—	—
Maanexit	100 (190)	—	—
Quantisset	100 (190)	—	—
Wabquisset	150 (190)	—	—
Pakachoog	100 (192)	—	—
Waeuntag	50 (195)	—	—
Totals	1,100	45	64–74

68. Eliot to Hanmer, July 19, 1652, Eames, ed., *John Eliot and the Indians*, 7.
69. [Wilson], *Day-Breaking*, Mass. Hist. Soc., *Colls.*, 3d Ser., IV, 20–21.
70. Eliot to Robert Boyle, Apr. 22, 1684, *ibid.*, 1st Ser., III (Boston, 1794), 184.

to subject themselves to the government of Massachusetts. In due course the Indians who had so complied were placed under the authority of an English military officer who appointed Indian commissioners to enforce among their people the laws made by the English. All judgments by the Indian officials were subject to review and veto by the English superior, who also sat as a magistrate himself when he pleased. In this scheme native political institutions and customs had no place except that of conduct requiring punishment.[71]

That this self-imposed handicap severely reduced the religious efficacy of Massachusetts's missionaries is demonstrated by the accomplishments of Richard Bourne of Plymouth Colony and the Mayhews of Martha's Vineyard. The regions in which Bourne and the Mayhews worked are all within today's Massachusetts, but they were jealously independent colonies in the mid-seventeenth century. Although their religious doctrines were the same as Eliot's, and therefore of no greater inherent difficulty, and although their respondents were as much or as little savage as Eliot's, Bourne and the Mayhews outperformed Eliot in almost every respect. They made more converts, they founded more churches, and their Indians stayed out of the Second Puritan Conquest except to help the colonists. In 1652, 282 Vineyard Indians united in a covenant drawn up for them by the younger Thomas Mayhew, and in 1659 the elder Thomas Mayhew founded the Vineyard's first Indian church.[72] Eliot's first church at Natick began in 1660. (In fairness, it must be noted that he had been hindered for eight years by his Roxbury congregation's resistance.[73]) By 1673 there were two churches under Eliot in Massachusetts, one under Bourne in New Plymouth, and three under Thomas Mayhew on Martha's Vineyard and Nantucket.[74]

The Second Puritan Conquest worked havoc on Eliot's missions but not on the others. In 1684 Eliot listed the "stated places" of Indian worship in New England (not to be confused with formally organized churches). Four were in Massachusetts, ten in Plymouth, ten on the Vineyard, and five in Nantucket. The Mayhews and Bourne, with their missions based on voluntarism, held a total of twenty-five Christian In-

---

71. Salisbury, "Red Puritans," *WMQ*, 3d Ser., XXXI (1974), 32. The much-touted election of rulers of the mission towns was a meaningless formality. Each successful candidate had to be approved by Gookin, who also approved or vetoed all decisions made by the Indian officials. Eliot intervened in the politics even of "free" Indians when he could. *Ibid.*, 37, and see the discussion of Eliot's convert John Sassamon in chap. 16 below. See also Whitmore, ed., *Colonial Laws of Massachusetts*, (dual paging) 42/162–43/163.

72. Gookin, "Historical Collections," Mass. Hist. Soc., *Colls.*, 1st Ser., I, 203.

73. Salisbury, "Red Puritans," *WMQ*, 3d Ser., XXXI (1974), 51–52.

74. Eliot, "Account of Indian Churches," Mass. Hist. Soc., *Colls.*, 1st Ser., X, 124.

dian communities as compared with Eliot's remnant of four.[75] They all subscribed to the same Puritan theology. The distinction between them lay in Eliot's authoritarian and repressive use of his missions and mission Indians as instruments for political ends.

It remains to be noted that the baneful influence of Massachusetts's missions extended beyond the borders of New England. The praying Indians repeatedly came into conflict with the Mohawks, at whose hands they were beaten badly. Eliot claimed that the mission Indians went forth against his will, but considering his controls over the reservations, this seems at least doubtful. Doubt increases with the knowledge that the arms for these conflicts were provided from mission funds.[76] Later, when refugees from the shambles of the Second Puritan Conquest fled to the Hudson Valley for protection by New York and the Iroquois, they carried with them the memory of the faithful among Eliot's converts hunting them down for Puritan troops to slaughter. Similar memories were preserved by the refugees who fled to Canada and to the Abenaki Indians in Maine, both of which groups willingly received Jesuit missionaries but never forgot their score against the Puritans. Iroquois and Abenaki (supervised by New York and Canada) formed a wall around New England that remained impenetrable for a century.

75. Eliot to Robert Boyle, Apr. 22, 1684, *ibid.*, III, 185.
76. See chap. 16 below.

Chapter 15 ❧ LORDS, SUBJECTS, and SOVEREIGN: A QUARTER CENTURY in TEN SCENES

Prologue

Between the First and Second Puritan Conquests two distinct eras were formed in New England by delayed reflection of events in old England. From the Pequot conquest of 1636–1637 until about 1663 the orthodox Puritan colonies (plus Plymouth) united for conquest through the instrumentality of a confederation. The second era, from 1663 to 1675, was a period of especially great confusion and division, which will be considered in chapter 16 below. During the first era, which is the subject of immediate interest, the United Colonies of New England was dominant.

Consisting of four colonies, only one of which had a legitimate patent, and unsanctioned by either crown or Parliament, the Puritan confederation seized authority by virtue of its regional strength and assumed righteousness and, immediately after its foundation, embarked upon a career of expansionist conquest. As customary in such circumstances, the Puritans represented their combination as a defensive organization necessitated by great perils, but in reality the Puritan confederation never engaged in defensive war, though it was repeatedly involved in conflict. Such a reality was anticipated by the Puritan lords when they subscribed to their compact of association; they took pains to spell out in exact detail the conditions under which the United Colonies might conduct "offensive" war.[1]

During the confederation's effective existence its attention was chiefly devoted to ways of coordinating Puritan efforts for conquest on Narragansett Bay and in the territory of New Netherland. Since both the

1. Text of Articles of Confederation, May 29, 1643, Pulsifer, ed., *Acts of United Colonies*, I, 3–8. A possibly more convenient source is Bradford, *Of Plymouth Plantation*, ed. Morison, 430–437.

coveted areas were occupied by resisting Indians with European allies, the Puritans encountered more complicated problems than they had faced in their first conquest, when the defending Pequot Indians had been isolated. On Narragansett Bay the associates of Samuel Gorton (the so-called Gortonoges[2]) and Roger Williams aided the Indians in defending their territory by political means, and these allies won protection first from Parliament, then from the crown. Puritan expansion into New Netherland achieved results on Long Island and along the mainland coast of Long Island Sound, but in the upper Hudson Valley the Puritans could not penetrate the barrier of the Mohawk Indians backed and armed by the Dutch of Fort Orange and Rensselaerswyck. There was expansion into Maine also, but the peripheries will here be ignored for clarity's sake. Narragansett Bay is this chapter's central interest.

Three of the four members of the United Colonies were interested in the Narragansett region (see map 3, p. 256). Plymouth claimed, by virtue of its protectorate over the Wampanoag Indians, the whole east shore of the bay and an indeterminate quantity of the north shore; but, since much of that territory was also claimed by the Narragansett tribe, Plymouth could only maintain its boundaries by supporting Wampanoag claims against Narragansett claims. Connecticut and Massachusetts, as we shall see, hoped to extend their own jurisdictions into the Narragansett region at the expense of both the Indians and the English colonials already on the scene. Confusion was compounded by the fragmentation and quarrelsomeness of the Rhode Island settlers, who schemed and struggled against each other and who in some cases were willing to conspire with the Puritan colonies. Intrigue was everywhere.

It is not possible here to follow every thread in this tangle. One particular story is our concern—the struggle of the Narragansett Indians to preserve their independence. Regrettably the evidence does not permit that story to be told except by indirection; that is, by describing the varied attacks upon the Narragansetts and the devices used by their allies to thwart the would-be conquerors. The Indians' own attitudes and responses can only be inferred from documents written by passionately partisan Englishmen who wrote to serve their own interests first of all. Yet, without the Indians the history of Narragansett Bay would be *Hamlet* without the prince.

2. The strange name has an interesting origin as explained by Samuel Gorton. "Now our countrey men having given out formerly, amongst the Indians, that we were not English men, to encourage them against us (because the awe of the English, hath been much upon them) and being they could not father the name of any Sectary, or Sect upon us, . . . they then called us Gortoneans, and told the Indians we were such kind of men, not English: now the Indians calling the English in their language Wattaconoges, they now called us Gortonoges." *Simplicities Defence*, 88, in Force, comp., *Tracts*, IV.

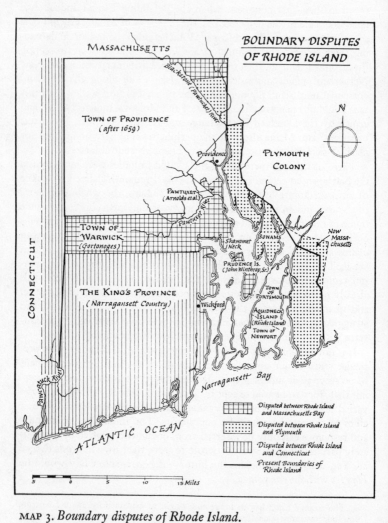

MAP 3. *Boundary disputes of Rhode Island.*
(Drawn by Richard J. Stinely, Williamsburg, Va., from a sketch by the author; adapted from maps in John Hutchins Cady, Rhode Island Boundaries, 1636–1936 [Providence, R.I., 1936]; base map from United States Geological Survey, Department of the Interior, Washington, D.C.)

SCENE I. *The Puritan lords determine to live in peace and love.*

Immediately after the Mystic massacre in 1637, Connecticut dispatched thirty men to the Pequot country "in place convenient to maynteine our right that God by Conquest hath given to us." A month later Connecticut's commissioners parleyed with Boston "about our settinge downe in the Pequoitt Countrey." Massachusetts vetoed this ambitious project; Boston's commanders continued to discuss Pequot territory as one of the spots to be considered for Massachusetts's own expansion.[3]

Besides the Pequot lands, the Pequots' persons became an issue of dispute. Their status was not in question; as captives of war they had become subjects to be disposed of at the will of the conquerors. The problem was one of administration. There were too many prisoners to risk bringing them all into the English settlements as slaves (though a few were distributed in that manner). They had to be kept at a safe distance in their own communities, but they also had to be kept under strong, responsible supervision that would perform two essential functions: it would prevent their organizing for revenge, and it would not fail to extract regular payments of tribute from each and every person. For practical reasons these considerations required the assignment of most of the captives to one or another of the tribes allied to the English. Which one? Uncas's Mohegans were Connecticut's allies, but not Massachusetts's; Miantonomo's Narragansetts had a treaty with Massachusetts, but not with Connecticut. To assign a captive to either tribe would also be to assign his tribute to that tribe's ally, and the colonies were far from agreed as to which should get the lion's share. Similarly they disputed over which should have rights of conquest over the Pequot lands. Massachusetts propounded that a joint conquest had been made and that the Pequot territory should be apportioned between the conquerors, but Connecticut maintained that its troops alone had won the victory and that it alone should have that spoil.

The issue remained undecided for a long while, largely because it was easier to conquer Indians than other Englishmen. Massachusetts did not relinquish claim to Pequot lands, but other places also appeared attractive, particularly Quinnipiac farther west along the coast, where the resident Indians had formerly been Pequot tributaries. After Massachusetts's troops massacred the men and shipped the women and children off to the slave market, the region so conveniently depopulated was

3. Minutes, June 2, 1637, and June 26, 1637, *Recs. of Conn.*, I, 10; Israel Stoughton to Winthrop, Sr., Aug. 9, 1637, *Winthrop Papers*, III, 479. Stoughton esteemed it "a worthy work" to "enlarge the state, and provide for the poor servants of Christ, that are yet unprovided." *ibid.*, 483.

praised without stint by its conquerors; but the fates were whimsical again. Before Massachusetts could organize a subject settlement on the site, a community of recent arrivals from England founded New Haven there as an unsanctioned independent colony a la Connecticut[4] (see map 1, chapter 12).

While the Puritans disputed jurisdictions, Miantonomo requested reward for his Narragansetts' participation in the Pequot conquest. What Miantonomo wanted was a privilege for his men to hunt in the former Pequot lands, and his allies in Massachusetts readily acceded to his wish. But the other English in Connecticut did not much like the notion of Massachusetts dispensing privilege in land that Connecticut claimed as its own—especially since the Narragansetts had indisputably participated in the campaign against Mystic fort. A good lawyer (and John Winthrop, Sr., was certainly that) might talk that participation into a Narragansett claim, which would then become the claim of the Narragansetts' ally in Boston and which would derive additional support from the presence of the Narragansett hunters in the disputed lands—provided that such presence was not challenged.

It was quickly challenged, with force. The force was that of Uncas, but the purpose was that of Connecticut. Uncas's men descended upon the Narragansett hunters in the Pequot lands, and we need not doubt the source of his inspiration. Miantonomo appealed to his ally Massachusetts for permission to redress the injury with his own force. Boston told him to sit still and await developments. Connecticut all the while backed Uncas and winked at his reestablishment of the old Pequot tribe under his new management.[5] Tension increased in the scramble for wampum. One reason for Connecticut's benign attitude toward Uncas was his willingness to pay large quantities of the shell currency for protection. The mathematics of the process were simple and plain: as more Pequots found their way under Uncas's wing, more wampum tribute found its way to Connecticut.

Representatives of the colonies met to discuss the possible formation of a permanent confederation in which such intercolonial issues might be resolved peacefully, but Massachusetts's demand for a dominant role

4. Thomas Hutchinson, *The History of the Colony and Province of Massachusetts-Bay*, ed. Lawrence Shaw Mayo (Cambridge, Mass., 1936), I, 73; Isabel MacBeath Calder, *The New Haven Colony* (New Haven, Conn., 1934), 52. The Indians "freely gave and yeilded up all their right"; the English, "of their owne accord, by way of free and thankefull retribution," gave the Indians "twelve coats of English trucking cloth, twelve alcumy spoones, twelve hatchetts, twelve hoes, two dozen of knives, twelve porengers, and foure cases of French knives and sizers." It looks as though there were 12 Indian families left. Deed, Nov. 24, 1638, Hoadly, ed., *Recs. of New Haven*, I, 1–4.

5. Williams's letters, in *Winthrop Papers*, III, 447–448, IV, 6–7, 16–17, 25, 34–35, 120–121.

in the organization was rejected by the others,[6] and Connecticut men promptly moved on their own initiative to rearrange Indian affairs to their own liking. They issued peremptory orders to Miantonomo to come to Hartford for a treaty. He objected that, in his understanding, he was already bound to all the English by his 1636 treaty with Massachusetts. He was answered that Connecticut made its own alliances. Under pressure, he complied.[7]

At last we are able to examine the actual text of a treaty instead of a retrospective paraphrase. From this text Connecticut's purpose is clear: it was to force the Narragansetts to take Connecticut's orders instead of Massachusetts's. The treaty asserted Connecticut's jurisdiction in certain matters that had already been preempted by Massachusetts's treaty with Miantonomo. Whereas that sachem was bound by the earlier treaty with Boston to gain Massachusetts's approval before making war on other Indians, the new treaty explicitly required him to appeal to "the English Inhabiting the Jurisdiction of the River of Connecticut . . . and they are to decide."

In the same high-handed manner, Connecticut assumed ownership of both the persons and lands of the former Pequots. Eighty persons were allotted to Miantonomo, and to Uncas "his number." For each Pequot thus assigned, Uncas and Miantonomo were to bring wampum tribute "to be paid at Killing time of Corn *at Connecticut* yearly," and no part of the Pequots' territory was to be occupied without Connecticut's permission.[8] The intent of the latter provision was later clarified when Uncas occupied the former Pequot lands. The treaty thus contravened Massachusetts's permission to Miantonomo for the Narragansetts to hunt and fish in the Pequot territory. Its sequel, the establishment of Uncas in possession, constituted a seizure of the lands by proxy.

Massachusetts responded to this *fait accompli* with caution. The unhappy Narragansetts, after their enforced treaty in Connecticut, appealed to their old ally to please "ratifie that promise made to them [by Massachusetts] after the warrs viz: the free use of the Pequt Country for their hunting, etc.," but they did not get much satisfaction. As they reminded John Winthrop: "Since the last yeare at Qunnihticut with Mr. Heynes and the Magistrates, you have not yet pleased to come to Action."[9]

6. *Ibid.*, IV, 36–37, 53, and especially Hooker's long, bitter letter to Winthrop, ca. Dec. 1638, that reviews the history of relationships between the two colonies. *Ibid.*, 75–84.

7. Williams to Winthrop, Sr., Aug. 14, 1638, and Winthrop's summary, Aug. 28, 1638, *ibid.*, IV, 52, 53.

8. Treaty, Sept. 21, 1638, R.–I. Hist. Soc., *Colls.*, III (1835), 177–178 (emphasis added); also printed in Vaughan, *New England Frontier*, 340–341.

9. Williams to Winthrop, Sr., May 9, 1639, *Winthrop Papers*, IV, 120–121.

It was well for the Narragansetts' peace of mind that they did not know what sort of action was in process. Winthrop and Connecticut's Thomas Hooker had exchanged recriminations over many matters in contention between them, including Indian jurisdictions, and Winthrop had had "sadd thoughts about it." What those thoughts came to was that Connecticut and Massachusetts "must live in peace and love, and blessed be God that hath fixt us in one minde in the trueth, which will make the matter the more easy."[10] Nothing was said of honoring any commitment to any Indian. As events would show, Connecticut's hostility for the Narragansetts remained implacable, while Massachusetts's vacillating protection was conditioned on the Narragansetts' acceptance of a subject status that the Indians were unwilling to assume. In five years' time the Puritans settled their own differences and effected a confederation. The heart of that settlement became an agreement on how to dispose of the Narragansetts.

SCENE 2. *Cool heads prefer stratagem to combat.*

The Massachusetts oligarchy seems to have entered into the new association partly to gain some measure of control over Connecticut's explosive expansionism and partly to coordinate all Puritan resources behind Massachusetts's own projects for enlargement. Boston usually moved more slowly and legalistically than the cocky frontiersmen at Hartford. When Connecticut threatened a repetition of a blitzkrieg in the pattern of the Pequot triumph, the larger colony finally was stirred into overt activity.

The agitation for war started in almost exactly the same manner as before. In August 1642 several Indians purportedly approached Connecticut leaders with dire warnings that "the Indians all over the country had combined themselves to cut off all the English" just after the harvest. Connecticut thereupon proposed to Massachusetts that troops of militia should be sent from both colonies to join at Fort Saybrook. Boston's first reaction was panic. The magistrates decided to "strike some terrour into the Indians." All the Indians who could be reached within the jurisdiction were immediately disarmed, and the bewildered Massachuset sachem Cutshamoquin suddenly found himself a resident of Boston's jail.[11]

Further inquiry raised questions, however. The magistrates became convinced that none of the Indians of Massachusetts had been conspiring, and a few days of thought produced a sense of déjà vu. When the General Court assembled on September 8, it counseled caution. "All

10. Winthrop to Hooker, [ca. Mar. 1639], *ibid.*, 99–100.
11. Sept. 1, 1642, Winthrop, *History*, ed. Savage, II, 78–79.

this," John Winthrop remarked, "might come out of the enmity which had been between Miantunnomoh and Onkus, who continually sought to discredit each other with the English." Such reports had been raised "almost every year," Winthrop noted, and had "proved to be but reports raised up by the opposite factions among the Indians."[12]

Massachusetts simply ignored the Hartford treaty of 1638 with its pretensions for Connecticut to have power of decision in Indian disputes. A summons went forth to Miantonomo to come to Boston and give "satisfaction" about rumors of conspiracy and disloyalty. That "very subtile" man arrived in great dignity to demand that he be confronted with his accusers. The magistrates confessed ignorance of who the accusers really were, and they may be believed in this case because Connecticut had refused to provide evidence. Miantonomo had his own ideas. He offered to meet Uncas at Boston for a showdown, demanded that his slanderers be punished, and generally comported himself without betraying any visible sense of guilt. In Boston that was quite a feat. The magistrates were so impressed that they permitted Miantonomo to dine at the lower end of their own table.[13]

In the meantime Connecticut renewed its agitation for war and threatened to begin one before Massachusetts could even reply. Perhaps Connecticut was bluffing; it certainly waited for a reply. Boston responded that to begin war while negotiations were continuing with Miantonomo would be "dishonourable," whereupon Connecticut cooled off, "but (it seemed) unwillingly," commented Winthrop, "and as not well pleased with us." The delay was prolonged and the war forestalled.[14]

This is not to say that Massachusetts had decided to mind its own business and forget about Narragansett Bay. The Boston magistrates had merely adopted a smooth strategy different from the crashing conquest methods of the rough characters at Hartford. Boston preferred a nibbling technique, and Boston preferred also to nibble with its own teeth and to have the tidbits go down its own gullet. While stalling Connecticut the General Court quietly eased into the west shore of Narragansett Bay with a bloodless coup.

SCENE 3. *Boston rumbles and acquires distant clients.*

The Narragansett land at issue was thinly settled by a colony of unchartered squatters, some of whom had made purchase from Miantonomo. In Massachusetts's view these purchasers were undesirables for several reasons. All of them were establishing independent title to land

12. Sept. 8, 1642, *ibid.*, 80.
13. *Ibid.*, 81–82.
14. *Ibid.*, 83, and Savage's note.

that Boston wanted; a majority believed in the anathema of religious toleration; one settler there, Roger Williams, had been exiled for denying the authority of the magistrates; and another, Samuel Gorton, was a raucous, ranting, defiant heretic who might spread the pollution of his doctrines if he were left alone. When a handful of Gorton's neighbors asked Massachusetts to evict the Gortonoges from their vicinity, Boston accepted the complainants as clients or subjects—their precise status was not as clear as a lawyer might desire. Quite clearly, however, Massachusetts's action implied its protection and a claim of jurisdiction over the lands that the complainants claimed as property. While the General Court blocked Connecticut's Narragansett conquest at its session in September 1642, it simultaneously appointed its new clients as local magistrates on Narragansett Bay. Small wonder that Connecticut was "not well pleased." [15]

The settlers at Narragansett quickly learned the full significance of this big foot in their door. The Gortonoges began to fear for their lives as they were warned that Massachusetts intended to take in all of Narragansett Bay.[16] Roger Williams, however, apparently trusted in his personal client-patron relationship with John Winthrop, Sr.; for a while Williams continued to do errands for Winthrop among the Indians.[17] Full enlightenment came at the end of October with a menacing letter from Boston; although a leader of the complainants, William Arnold, delivered it to the Gortonoges, Williams could not mistake its potential applicability to his own settlement.

15. *Ibid.*, 83–84; *Recs. of Mass.*, II, 26. Joshuah Winsor *et al.* to the governor of Massachusetts, Nov. 17, 1641, in Edward Winslow, *Hypocrisie Unmasked: By A true Relation of the Proceedings of the Governour and Company of the Massachusets against Samuel Gorton (and his Accomplices) a notorious disturber of the Peace and quiet of the severall Governments wherein he lived: With the grounds and reasons thereof, examined and allowed by their Generall Court holden at Boston in New-England in November last, 1646* (London, 1646), 56–58; Jan. 1642, Winthrop, *History*, ed. Savage, II, 59.

Massachusetts's client magistrates were Benedict and William Arnold, Robert Coale, and William Carpenter, of whom the Arnolds were the most energetic in persecuting the Gortonoges.

16. Gorton, *Simplicities Defence*, 22, in Force, comp., *Tracts*, IV.

17. Williams to Winthrop, Sr., Oct. 24, [1642]. This letter has been misdated at 1636 because of its references to Pequots, but its contents make that date impossible. The letter refers to questions put by Winthrop to Williams, one of which was, "Is your spirit as even as it was seven years since?" Seven years before 1636 would be 1629, before either Winthrop or Williams was in America. On the other hand, seven years before 1642 would refer to 1635, the year of Williams's exiling, which makes good sense. There was also in 1642 an issue about Pequot captives among the Eastern Niantics, and this apparently was the business that Williams was engaged in when he wrote. The right date is important to the development of relationships between the two men. See texts and editorial comment: "Winthrop Papers," Mass. Hist. Soc., *Colls.*, 4th Ser., VI, 233–238; Bartlett, ed., *Letters of Williams*, Narragansett Club, *Pubs.*, VI, 7–13; *Winthrop Papers*, III, 314–318.

Massachusetts, to our Neighbours of Providence.

Whereas, William Arnald of Pautuxet [a tract adjoining Providence], and Robert Cole, and others, have lately put themselves and their families, lands and estates, under the protection and government of this Jurisdiction, and have since complained to us, that you have since (upon pretence of a late purchase from the Indians) gone about to deprive them of their lawfull interest confirmed by four years possession, and otherwise to molest them: We thought good therefore to write to you on their behalfe, to give you notice, that they and their lands, etc. being under our Jurisdiction, we are to maintain them in their lawfull rights. If therefore you have any just title to any thing they possesse, you may proceed against them in our Court, where you shall have equall justice; But, if you shall proceed to any violence, you must not blame us, if we shall take a like course to right them.

> Jo. Winthrop, *Governor.*
> Tho. Dudley.
> Ri. Bellingham.
> Incr. Nowell.[18]

Reactions to these pressures varied. Samuel Gorton and his associates breathed defiance at the Boston magistrates in a long letter interspersing theology with invective in a bewildering ramble of rhetoric, but they soon decided that the neighborhood of Providence was unsafe. They removed then to a "neck" of land called Shawomet (present-day Warwick) [19] (see map 3, p. 256). Miantonomo continued formally correct behavior as stipulated in his treaty obligations, but he demonstrated his independence by selling Shawomet to the Gortonoges.[20] It would seem that Boston became very angry at that transaction; Benedict Arnold predicted that Miantonomo would lose his head for it.[21] When the full

---

18. Oct. 28, 1642. Gorton, *Simplicities Defence*, 21, in Force, comp., *Tracts*, IV.
19. Letter to "our Neighbours of the Massachusets," Nov. 20, 1642 (written from "Mooshawset," the Indian name for the region of Providence), *ibid.*, 24–44.
20. The deed's proper date is Jan. 12, 1643, New Style. It is given erroneously in Oliver Payson Fuller, *The History of Warwick, Rhode Island, from Its Settlement in 1642 to the Present Time* ... (Providence, R.I., 1875), 10–11. Editor Savage saw a manuscript copy of the deed dated Jan. 12, 1642/43. Winthrop, *History*, ed. Savage, II, 121n. Drake confirms 1643 as the date. *Biography and History of the Indians*, 257. The proper date is essential to the sequence (and implied causes) of the events under discussion here.
21. Randall Holden to "the great and honoured Idol Generall, now set up in the Massachusets," Sept. 15, 1643, in Winslow, *Hypocrisie Unmasked*, 30.
A bibliographic note: Winslow's *Hypocrisie Unmasked*, like everything else he wrote, must be used with great caution. As its full title indicates (see n. 15 above), he wrote this as a spokesman for the Massachusetts General Court, and he slanted it to serve the oligarchy's purposes. Cf. his propaganda for the missions, discussed in chap. 14, above. One of the sectarian hard-liners in Plymouth, Winslow aligned himself with similar spirits in Massachusetts in order to suppress popular agitation for freedom of conscience in Plymouth. For that purpose he did not hesitate even to connive with Boston for the latter's territorial gain at the expense of Plymouth's claims. A Plymouth contemporary (cited by Samuel Gorton without challenge, to my knowledge) denounced *Hypocrisie Unmasked* as having

seriousness of the situation became clear to Roger Williams, he sailed for England to seek protection stronger than rhetoric. Ironically Wiliams, who had served Massachusetts as its indispensable agent in Indian diplomacy, was forced to travel overland to New Amsterdam in order to make his voyage because his sentence of death remained in full force if he should attempt to embark from Boston.[22]

The Gortonoges' removal from their old neighbors delayed Massachusetts's advance only until the magistrates could make terms with the neighbors at the new location. These were two minor sachems named Pumham and Sacononoco. With their cooperation Massachusetts used the same technique (with refinements) to acquire jurisdiction at Shawomet as had earlier been used near Providence. The Indians became Massachusetts's client-subjects. "Without any constraint or persuasion, but of [their] own free motion," they put themselves and their "subjects, lands and estates" under Massachusetts's government. They were the more ready to do this because said lands and estates had already been ceded and sold to the Gortonoges. They gave a nonexistent jurisdictional right to Massachusetts in return for which the magistrates tacitly affirmed a "natural law" property right for the Indians. By a little mutual accommodation, both parties emerged with substantial gain to which neither was entitled.[23]

---

40 recognizable "lies," and my own examination of the book confirms his judgment, although the more accurate terminology would be "deceit by distortion, selection, and omission." Gorton to Morton, June 30, 1669, 16–17, in Force, comp., *Tracts*, IV, 16–17. Cf. *Hypocrisie Unmasked*, 79, with Pulsifer, ed., *Acts of United Colonies*, I, 12, 222. For Winslow's part in repressive politics, see Thomas Aspinwall, "William Vassall no Factionist," Mass. Hist. Soc., *Procs.*, VI (1862–1863), 471–479; Winslow to Winthrop, Nov. 24, 1645, in Hutchinson, comp., *Collection of Papers*, 153–155.

22. Andrews, *Colonial Period*, II, 23–25, gives an alternative interpretation of Williams's departure.

23. Winthrop, *History*, ed. Savage, II, 120–123. For the validity of Winthrop's account, see Andrews, *Colonial Period*, II, 15n, supplemented by Dunn, "Winthrop, Jr., and the Narragansett Country," *WMQ*, 3d Ser., XIII (1956), 68–86. That Pumham's "subjection" to Massachusetts was far from sincere is demonstrated by his leadership of hostile Indian forces in "King Philip's War." Hubbard, *Narrative*, 100.

The clients' case is in Winslow, *Hypocrisie Unmasked*, 2–3. This was directly refuted by Roger Williams, who disliked Gorton. Williams to Massachusetts General Court, [May 12, 1656], in Bartlett, ed., *Letters of Williams*, Narragansett Club, *Pubs.*, VI, 300–301. Williams's version of native custom in land tenure is supported by other sources. (See chap. 8 above.) Gorton's much maligned character is discussed responsibly by editor James Savage in a long note in Winthrop, *History*, ed. Savage, II, 57. See also George A. Brayton, *A Defence of Samuel Gorton and the Settlers of Shawomet*, comprising the whole of *Rhode Island Historical Tracts*, XVII (Providence, R.I., 1883). As a former chief justice of the Supreme Court of Rhode Island, Brayton wrote with authority on legal questions.

In the midst of the Shawomet affair, Winthrop used the Indian purchase device to circumvent the Massachusetts town of Concord in obtaining a large tract of

There remained the problem of convincing Miantonomo that the magistrates knew more than he about Narragansett customary law. He was summoned again to Boston, where he was required to "prove" his rights. Even in Winthrop's report, which is a prosecutor's case, Miantonomo can be seen to have maintained the legitimacy of his acts and powers. (That he had been, in fact, the overlord of Pumham and Sacononoco was to be amply demonstrated by Pumham's subsequent career. As a "subject," that clever rogue gained more from the magistrates than they from him, and he died in arms against them as a chief of the Narragansetts.[24]) Without acknowledging the justice of Massachusetts's usurpation, Miantonomo was compelled to recognize the fact of Massachusetts's power. The magistrates "proved" to their own satisfaction that they had rightfully acquired what they coveted, and they sent him home with orders to keep hands off.[25]

SCENE 4. *A depiction of Puritan justice and prudence:
the case of Miantonomo.*

For clarity's sake our story has moved a little faster than events. Though Boston's aim remained constant, the magistrates took one careful step at a time, and they made certain of the support of other Puritan colonies before committing themselves irrevocably. They negotiated tentatively with Pumham and Sacononoco in the early spring of 1643. Then, in May, they conferred with the other Puritan governments to form the United Colonies of New England, and Massachusetts felt secure enough in its arrangements to concede Connecticut's basic demand of voting parity within the confederation. Plymouth and New Haven—"being all in Church fellowship"—came in also. No war was to be undertaken by any member without the consent of the United Colonies—a provision that effectively brought Connecticut's bellicosity under control but did not in the least hamper Massachusetts's method of protecting clients. Perhaps Connecticut was not fully aware of the implications of what its commissioners ratified on May 19.[26] Massachusetts waited until June 22 to consummate its arrangements on Nar-

land for himself. Rutman, *Winthrop's Boston,* 88; deed, June 20, 1642, *Suffolk Deeds,* I, 34. The purchased land had not been "subdued" by tillage or habitation. Formally, therefore, the Indian landlord had no right recognized by Winthrop in his "General considerations" of 1629. *Winthrop Papers,* II, 120. But in the Concord case, Winthrop bought with the approval of the Massachusetts General Court (against the resistance of Concord town), so that his act was not in the same class as the purchases of Roger Williams and Samuel Gorton.

24. Drake, *Biography and History of the Indians,* 258–260.
25. Winthrop, *History,* ed. Savage, II, 120–123.
26. Pulsifer, ed., *Acts of United Colonies,* I, 5, 7, 8.

ragansett Bay with the formal acceptance of Pumham's and Saconoco's submission.[27]

Their full purpose now disclosed, Boston's magistrates sent notice to Miantonomo and "the English in those parts." If the Gortonoges received such a notice, they disregarded it. Samuel Gorton had a certain flair for the law, and he was ready to argue the validity of his deed against the legitimacy of Massachusetts's jurisdiction. Miantonomo was more tractable. He had ceded the land and had been paid for it; though Massachusetts had denied his right to do so, the magistrates had not demanded that he repay the cession price, and they were not disturbing him in any territory presently in his jurisdiction. Miantonomo simply accepted the secession of Pumham and Saconoco and regarded the affair as a quarrel between Englishmen. He had other problems, very serious ones, with a real challenger, and he needed Massachusetts's approval to restore his authority where it mattered.

The challenger again was Uncas, who attacked a kinsman and tributary of Miantonomo's in the Connecticut Valley. Still moving carefully within the provisions of his treaty, Miantonomo complained to the governors of Connecticut and Massachusetts and asked permission to war against Uncas. Connecticut's Governor Haynes replied noncommittally. Massachusetts's Winthrop replied that "we should leave him to take his own course."[28] The formalities complied with, Miantonomo marched. But he was an ill-fated man whose friends were more dangerous than his enemies. One of the Gortonoges, John Wickes, thought to help by lending Miantonomo heavy armor for the battle, and the armor so encumbered the chief that Uncas's men took him prisoner.[29] The Narragansetts speedily collected a ransom of wampum worth forty pounds, and Miantonomo requested to be delivered to his friends the English. Uncas complied, but the outcome was not what Miantonomo had expected. The English held him prisoner at Hartford, and his case was put at the head of the agenda of the first business meeting of the Commissioners of the United Colonies on September 7, 1643. Setting the tone for their future career, those eminent gentlemen murdered him.[30]

The Commissioners' minutes of this occasion were designed to exculpate the participants in the crime with whatever shreds of reason

---

27. Winthrop, *History*, ed. Savage, II, 123.

28. July 1643, *ibid.*, 129.

29. Winslow, *Hypocrisie Unmasked*, 70–72.

30. "Cold-blooded murder": Andrews, *Colonial Period*, II, 94. "Clerico-judicial murder": George W. Ellis and John E. Morris, *King Philip's War* (New York, 1906), 35. "That Miantonomu whose brutal and cowardly murder the sanctified Commissioners of the United Colonies contrived in 1643": Perry Miller, *Roger Williams: His Contribution to the American Tradition* (Indianapolis, 1953), 51.

could be torn off known or alleged fact. Performing a feat of semantic prestidigitation, they made Miantonomo into a treaty violator. They resurrected the Hartford treaty of 1638 with its provision that neither Uncas nor Miantonomo should war against the other until "they had first complayned, and that the English had heard their greevances." Or so the Commissioners presented it. We may recall that the treaty's actual language was more precise: it said, "The English *of Connecticut* ... and *they* are to decide" (emphasis added). We have seen that Massachusetts had regarded that treaty as null and void and had required Miantonomo to deal with Boston rather than Hartford. Since Miantonomo had in fact consulted John Winthrop, Sr., before attacking Uncas, in accordance with the only obligation that Massachusetts then recognized, and Winthrop had authorized the Indian "to take his own course," the Commissioners of the United Colonies had on their hands a basketful of pretensions, claims, and obligations that none of them wanted to sort out in public discussion. They threw the whole mess up in the air, accused Miantonomo of "plotts" against the "English," and moved the pieces so fast with epithet and tirade that no one noticed the difference between one kind of "English" and another.[31]

The proper explication of the Commissioners' tortuous text was undertaken by John Winthrop. The Commissioners, he wrote, "taking into serious consideration what was safest and best to be done, were all of opinion that it would not be safe to set him at liberty, neither had we sufficient ground for us to put him to death. In this difficulty we called in five of the most judicious elders (it being in the time of the general assembly of the elders) and propounding the case to them, they all agreed that he ought to be put to death." As Winthrop's editor James

31. Pulsifer, ed., *Acts of United Colonies*, I, 10–12, 14–15. Vaughan states that "all available evidence confirms that the Narragansett violated his treaties with Massachusetts and Connecticut as well as the orders of the Commissioners of the United Colonies when he attacked Uncas." *New England Frontier*, 162. He cites the *Acts of United Colonies*, Increase Mather, and Edward Johnson's *Wonder-Working Providence*. Vaughan omits reference to Winthrop's *History* at this point and also omits mention of Miantonomo's having asked permission to war on Uncas. His reference to Mather may be dismissed out of hand; Mather, as a secondary writer, has no evidentiary value against Winthrop the participant. Johnson produced no evidence of his own; he stated only that "the honored Commissioners have had proof of Miantonemo's treachery" (p. 222), being otherwise verbosely inexplicit about which promise. The citation of Johnson is therefore a mere makeweight, and Vaughan's case must rest on the Commissioners of the United Colonies. His finding is the more remarkable because he prints the full text of the Hartford treaty as his Appendix II, *New England Frontier*, 340–341.

Edward Johnson, *Johnson's Wonder-Working Providence, 1628–1651* (1654), ed. J. Franklin Jameson, Original Narratives of Early American History (New York, 1910).

Savage pointed out, only five of fifty elders were consulted; what qualities made them the "most judicious" can easily be inferred.[32]

It is not easy to see why Massachusetts should have turned so violently against its former ally, who appears to have walked carefully within the fences set by treaty. One may speculate that Miantonomo was killed because he had insisted on ceding Narragansett land to persons as heterodox and independent as Roger Williams and Samuel Gorton. Or that he was too intelligent and mature in his diplomacy for Boston's ease of mind. Or that his leadership was so strong that his people could not be divided and weakened by internal conflict. Perhaps it was just that he would not grovel as Uncas did—"savages" have been killed for less than that at other times and places. The precise shade of motivation is not as clear as the deed it brought about.

In the words of the Commissioners' minutes, "Uncus was advised to take away the life of Myantenomo ... according to justice and prudence." Apparently concerned that Uncas might yet yield to native custom and free his ransomed captive, the Commissioners ordered "some discreet and faythfull persons of the English" to "accompany them and see the execucion for our more full satisfaccion." A certain queasiness is evident in these minutes, wedded to dextrous moral agility. Uncas was ordered to refrain from the killing until he had departed from the jurisdiction of the English and arrived in his own territory—a curious kind of "execucion," this—and the Commissioners further decreed "that the English meddle not with the head or body at all." Adroitly they thus made it appear that Uncas was responsible for the crime they had ordered him to perform.[33]

Having found the final solution for the problem of Miantonomo, the Commissioners continued on their agenda. What had moved the Puritan colonies to forget some of their quarrels and thus unite was a com-

---

32. July 5, 1643, Winthrop, *History*, ed. Savage, II, 131–132, and see in addition the valuable long note of editor Savage (another cogent example of the superiority of Savage's editing.) Uncas stated that the ransom agreement was for him to deliver Miantonomo to the English. The Commissioners tried to smother the ransom with words. They wrote that "it appeared not that any Wampom had been payd as A ransom or part of a ransome for Myantinomos life," and they pooh-poohed the "Wampoms and goods sent" as "but smale parcells and scarce considerable for such a purpose." But the purpose was not to ransom Miantonomo from *them*; they were the sachem's treaty allies who had authorized him, per Winthrop, to go to war. He had every proper expectation that delivery to them was delivery to freedom. With good Puritan casuistry they could twist the argument: Uncas had delivered Miantonomo to them in conformity with his agreement, but *they* had made no bargain for Miantonomo's life so they returned him to Uncas. See John Haynes to John Winthrop, Sr., Jan. 17, 1644, *Winthrop Papers*, IV, 506–507, and Pulsifer, ed., *Acts of United Colonies*, I, 52, 28–29.

33. Pulsifer, ed., *Acts of United Colonies*, I, 14–15.

bination of appetite and uneasiness. Their confederation was formed as a means of reconciling interests and coordinating efforts as they expanded. Although it was called the United Colonies of New England, the first thing about the confederation deserving notice is that the members' principles of political alliance were as exclusive as their principles of religion. To call it the "New England Confederation," as has often been done, is therefore somewhat misleading for persons thinking in terms of New England as the region is conceived of now. Roger Williams's Providence Plantations was not invited to join this confederation, and when Providence applied for membership (as it did in 1644), it was rejected. Properly speaking, this was the "Puritan Confederation," but religion was only part of the truth about it. Religion served as a selection device for screening members and as a bond between those admitted; religion served as a sanction for the confederation's policies and activities and as a means for drawing upon substantial support from coreligionists in England; but the other half of the truth about the confederation was that each of its participants benefited from membership in a thoroughly material way.

Connecticut and its satellite New Haven gained support from the other colonies for their continuing encroachments upon New Netherland, both on Long Island and on the mainland (see map 1, chapter 12). New Haven also got from the United Colonies an agreement for the Commissioners to require satisfaction from the Swedes on the Delaware for rough treatment accorded to a New Haven trading and would-be settling expedition.[34] Connecticut's main reward was reaped in the former territory of the Pequots. Since Uncas had been harrying Narragansett hunters out of those lands, the murder of Miantonomo represented the abandonment of Massachusetts's former ally on that scene, and the temporary confirmation, by default of a challenger, of Uncas's possession. In due course the Commissioners would formally recognize Uncas's territory as Connecticut's jurisdiction. But Connecticut also got support in its continuing struggle with the Dutch at the latter's "House of Hope" trading station near Hartford.[35]

Massachusetts and Plymouth were concerned about an apparent detente growing up between Plymouth's client Wampanoags and the

34. *Ibid*. 13. The agreement also pressured other towns to come in under New Haven's wing to make a colony out of what had formerly been only a town. Andrews, *Colonial Period*, II, 164. For New Haven's difficulties in the United Colonies, see Ronald D. Cohen, "The Hartford Treaty of 1650: Anglo-Dutch Cooperation in the Seventeenth Century," *New-York Historical Society Quarterly*, LIII (1969), 311–332.

35. Pulsifer, ed., *Acts of United Colonies*, I, 13, 79, 96–97. A summary of actions in the sustained dispute over the Pequot Country is in *Recs. of Conn.*, I, 570–572, II, 545–547.

Narragansetts. In the wake of the Pequot conquest, Wampanoag sachem Massassoit had promised to sell no land without Plymouth's consent, but he had lately lapsed so far from his promise as to confirm a sale of lands to Rhode Islanders in territory claimed by both Wampanoags and Narragansetts. (Roger Williams had earlier proceeded in the same way, purchasing from both tribes to avoid trouble with either.) Plymouth interpreted such proceedings as an Indian "conspiracy." Since Plymouth had no viable charter, its territorial claims depended largely on the extent of territory of its client tribe, and if Massassoit continued to sell off to Rhode Islanders, Plymouth would be whittled down to nothing. The United Colonies relieved Plymouth men by *ordering* that they "restore" Massassoit "to his full liberties in respect of any encroachments by the Nanohiggansets or any other Natives that so the proprieties of the Indians may be preserved to themselves" and that Massassoit "be reduced to these former termes and agreements betweene Plymouth and him." Translated, this meant that the other colonies would support Plymouth's disciplining of Massassoit so that he would never sell to Rhode Islanders again.[36]

The immediate gain for Massachusetts was legitimation, of a sort, for its enterprise on Narragansett Bay. The Commissioners resolved that "the Majestrats in the Massachusets proceed against" the Gortonoges "according to what they shall fynd just: and the rest of the Jurisdiccions will approve and concurr in what shalbe so warrantably donn, as if their Comissioners had been present at the Conclusions." As blank checks go, it was a little on the wordy side, but cashable.[37]

SCENE 5. *A second depiction of Puritan justice and prudence: the Gortonoges before the bar.*

Massachusetts wasted no time. On September 12, 1643, the magistrates sent a summons to ten of the Gortonoges to appear in court at Boston. Receiving an oral reply that the Gortonoges would acknowledge subjection to no government "but only the state and government of old England," the magistrates wrote again. They were about to send "commissioners," they said, "to receive such satisfaction from you, as shall appear in justice to be due." The commissioners would have a "suf-

36. Pulsifer, ed., *Acts of United Colonies*, I, 15; *Recs. of Plymouth*, I, 133.
37. Pulsifer, ed., *Acts of United Colonies*, I, 12. Plymouth's commissioners hid from their own constituents the full implications of this action. As late as 1646, Edward Winslow was still trying to conceal the situation. In *Hypocrisie Unmasked* (p. 79), he truncated his quotation from the United Colonies minutes, but an opposing Plymouth faction learned the truth and entered a protest at the Commissioners' meeting of Sept. 1651. Pulsifer, ed., *Acts of United Colonies*, I, 222.

ficient guard" for "their safety against any violence." What this self-proclaimed moderate document meant, as the so-called commissioners quickly demonstrated, was that the Gortonoges were to get an ultimatum at the point of a gun. They were to subject themselves to Massachusetts, to depart their lands, to make "satisfaction" about a book in which "were grosse things penned," and to pay a large fine. The commissioners, we may note, were George Cooke, Edward Johnson, and Humphrey Atherton. The name of Atherton will appear prominently in the further dealings between Puritans and Narragansetts.[38]

The approach of Captain Cooke's "guard" alarmed the inhabitants of Providence, who saw it rather as an "army." Some of them expostulated with the commissioners to hold parley with the Gortonoges with themselves as observers; the request was rejected. Then mediators forwarded to Boston an offer from the Gortonoges to have the issue decided peacefully either by appeal to England or by arbitration by "indifferent Judges in this Countrey," and the commissioners stood by till John Winthrop answered. "The wisest and godliest amongst us, assembled in a generall Court," had commanded the operation, he replied, and he neatly twisted the case out of other jurisdictions by revising the charges: the Gortonoges would be judged as "Blasphemers." The troops advanced—on the Sabbath, as Providence noted—and assaulted the Gortonoges. By affidavit of a dozen men of Providence, "the wives and children of our fore-said Countrey-men upon these hostile courses were affrighted and scattered in great extremities, and divers since are dead.... The said Captaine Cooke and his company, carried captive our fore-said Countrey-men through this Towne of Providence, to the Bay of Massachusets.... Their goods, cattle, houses, and plantations were seized upon, by the fore-said Captain, and his company; their cattle were part killed by the souldiers, and the rest by Agents from the Bay disposed of, and driven away to the said Bay of Massachusets."[39]

The Gortonoges stood trial in a court where their prosecutors were also judges and jurors. Gorton, being no man to deny his Lord, fell into the trap laid by the accusation of blasphemy and produced yards of theological disputation with which he was very nearly hanged. His legal instincts served in better stead. Throughout he maintained his rights as an Englishman—a potent phrase in those days—and demanded trial by English law. He did not get it, but instead of death he and his associates received indeterminate sentence to hard labor in chains, and

38. Gorton, *Simplicities Defence*, 46–52, in Force, comp., *Tracts*, IV.
39. *Ibid.*, 53–61.

they were scattered to various towns to perform it.[40] This proved to be a tactical error by the magistrates. The Gortonoges could not be kept quiet even under the harsh terms of their punishment, and their story got around. Such a trial, and particularly the denial of rights under English law, produced disturbance among the people, and murmurings arose. The magistrates gave no ground, but they eliminated the source of the disturbance. Gorton *et al.* were suddenly unchained and exiled; like Roger Williams and others who had been so dealt with, they carried sentence of death for return to Massachusetts.[41]

Meanwhile, time had not stood still; while the Gortonoges defied Massachusetts in its own precincts, Roger Williams had gone to England. After stymying Thomas Weld's attempt to get a charter for Massachusetts embracing all of Narragansett Bay, Williams obtained his own charter for the associated towns on the bay. Williams's charter contained a clause to give thought in Boston when it became known there. The Puritans of Parliament empowered their new colony to make only such laws as were conformable to those of England. The Puritans of New England were observing no such restraint.[42]

SCENE 6. *The Narragansetts become Englishmen at an awkward moment.*

The Gortonoges, of course, were not aware of Williams's charter as they made their way home, but they were keenly conscious that their theology was not what had saved their lives. When the astounded Narragansett Indians asked how these few and feeble Englishmen had escaped the death that had befallen the great and powerful Miantonomo, Gorton answered that the laws of *old* England gave salvation. The Narragansetts promptly asked for the protection of those great laws. They formally submitted themselves and their lands to King Charles I "upon condition of His Majesties royal protection," explaining that they had "just cause of jealousy and suspicion of some of His Majesty's pretended subjects"; and they added, undoubtedly for Puritan perusal, that they would not yield to others "that are subjects themselves . . . having ourselves been the chief Sachems, or Princes successively, of the country, time out of mind." Bearing this prize, Samuel Gorton and Randall Holden hurried off to England to appeal for the restoration of their confiscated property.[43]

Other Gortonoges became advisors and secretaries for the Nar-

40. *Ibid.,* 62–74.
41. *Ibid.,* 83–87.
42. "Patent for Providence Plantations, Nov. 2, 1643," *Recs. of R.I.,* I, 145.
43. Gorton, *Simplicities Defence,* 87–92, in Force, comp., *Tracts,* IV. The deed is also printed in *Recs. of R.I.,* I, 134–136.

ragansett sachems Pessicus and Canonicus. When Boston summoned the sachems it got a tart reply. "Our late brother was willing to stir much abroad," the sachems' letter remarked, "and we see a sad event at the last thereupon." The sachems declined to stir from their own territory and gave notice of their new condition as subjects "unto the same King and State yourselves are." They would no longer accept Massachusetts's intervention in their quarrel with Uncas; in great disputes, they wrote, "neither yourselves, nor we are to be judges; and both of us are to have recourse, and repair unto that honorable and just Government" of England.[44] (Massachusetts refused even its own freemen the right of appeal to the crown.[45]) When two messengers from Boston came to find out what was behind this brave show, Canonicus let them stand in the rain for two hours; and he and Pessicus announced their intention to launch guerrilla war against Uncas.[46]

But an ill star shone upon the Narragansetts—perhaps the same one that hung over Charles I. At just the time when the Indians submitted to that feckless monarch, he had begun the process of losing his head. The Puritans of New England therefore failed to worry long about the menace of a "sharp and princely revenge" from Charles for abusing his Indian subjects.[47] At first they showed a certain caution; the United Colonies confined themselves in 1644 to a warning that they would protect Uncas. As Charles's fortunes deteriorated, however, the Puritan confederation grew bolder.[48] In 1645 it declared war on the Narragansetts.

44. Pessicus and Canonicus to Massachusetts, May 24, 1644, in Gorton, *Simplicities Defence*, 93-94, in Force, comp., *Tracts*, IV; also printed in *Recs. of R.I.*, I, 136-138.

45. John Childe, *New-Englands Jonas Cast up at London* ... (1647), 16, 21, in Force, comp., *Tracts*, IV; Winslow, *Hypocrisie Unmasked*, "Epistle Dedicatory," n.p.; Nov. 4, 1646, Winthrop, *History*, ed. Savage, II, 283; George Cartwright's "Account of Massachusetts" (1665), in "Clarendon Papers," N.-Y. Hist. Soc., *Colls.*, *1869*, 83.

46. May 20, 1644, Winthrop, *History*, ed. Savage, II, 166.

47. Quotation in a letter from Gortonoges to Massachusetts, June 20, 1644, which also tried to frighten the Puritans by claiming that the Mohawks, "furnished with 3700 guns," would aid the Narragansetts. The gun statistic, at least, was fabrication. *Recs. of R.I.*, I, 138-140.

48. Vaughan asserts a "refusal of the Crown to acknowledge the Narragansetts' submission." There was no refusal, and Vaughan's cited sources give no grounds for the assertion. As the couriers carrying the submission explained to the ministry of Charles II at the Restoration, "beinge it was in the midst of those troublous tymes, in the unhapie warrs, we Could not find a way of access unto his majestie [Charles I], only we procured this act don by the Indians to be put in print [in *Simplicities Defence*]." Vaughan, *New England Frontier*, 167-168; Samuel Gorton, John Wickes, and Randall Holden to the Lord Chancellor Hyde, Apr. 4, 1662, in William Greene Roelker, "Samuell Gorton's Master Stroke," *Rhode Island History*, II (1943), long note, 9-10. See also the confirmation in the instructions to royal commissioners, Apr. 23, 1664, *N.Y. Col. Docs.*, III, 55.

SCENE 7.   *Conquest, almost.*

Much attention and acceptance have been given to the Puritan confederation's bill of charges against the Narragansetts, which was concocted, as usual, of a great many highly misleading words. Boiled down, the criminal behavior attributed to these culprits amounted to their insistence upon revenging themselves on Uncas, whether the Puritans liked it or not. Again there was much maundering in the public statement about breaking of treaties, and again it is unsupported by the record. In fact, the Narragansetts had been excessively careful to avoid injuring their fellow subjects of the English crown. Roger Williams was to write in 1654, "I cannot yet learn, that ever it pleased the Lord, to permit the Narragansetts to stain their hands with any English blood, neither in open hostilities nor secret murders."[49] In 1645, however, the Commissioners put words in Williams's mouth that seemed to make him say that the Narragansetts were threatening war against the English.

It took considerable ingenuity to twist Williams about so, and it shows a side of old John Winthrop's character that sorts badly with his reputation for integrity and gentleness. Williams had written to Winthrop— his last letter to him, as it turned out, and no wonder, considering what Winthrop did with it—reporting Indian violence against Indian and advising "loving mediation or prudent neutrality." He stressed that he had been "requested by both parties, yourselves and the Narragansetts, to keep the subscribed league between yourselves and them."[50] When Winthrop and the other commissioners rejected this counsel and decided on war, they used this letter to support their decision! Obviously it required a little improving for their purpose, so they made it seem to say that the Indians "breath out threatenings, provocations and warre against the English themselves." Williams had said, "The flame of war rageth next door unto us. The Narragansetts and Mohegans, with their respective confederates, have deeply implunged themselves in barbarous slaughters." The Commissioners' account changed this to say that Williams had assured them "that the country would suddenly be all on fire, meaneing by warre; that, by strong reasons and arguments, he could convince any man thereof that was of another mind." In this sentence the words before "warre" are distortion; those following it are utter fabrication. To complete their mayhem on Williams's letter, the Commissioners added "that the Narrowgansetts had been with the plantations combined with Providence and had solemnly

49. Williams to Massachusetts General Court, Oct. 5, 1654, in Bartlett, ed., *Letters of Williams*, Narragansett Club, *Pubs.*, VI, 274.
50. June 25, 1645, *ibid.*, 144–145.

treated and settled a neutrality with them, which fully shewes their councells and resolutions for warre." It was true that the Narragansetts had concluded a treaty of peace with the Rhode Islanders, to the latter's great content. To twist this into a seeming declaration by Williams that the treaty evidenced a threat against the English—in the face of his explicit statement of the Narragansetts' desire for peace with all the English—was mendacity extraordinary even among adepts.[51]

Winthrop had in mind an undisclosed consideration when he so mutilated Williams's letter. His brother-in-law Emanuel Downing had suggested a special benefit to be gained from a war with the Narragansetts.

If upon a Just warre the Lord should deliver them into our hands, wee might easily have men woemen and children enough to exchange for Moores, which wilbe more gaynefull pilladge for us then wee conceive, for I doe not see how wee can thrive untill wee get into a stock of slaves sufficient to doe all our buisiness, for our children's children will hardly see this great Continent filled with people, soe that our servants will still desire freedome to plant for themselves, and not stay but for verie great wages. And I suppose you know verie well how wee shall mayneteyne 20 Moores cheaper than one Englishe servant.[52]

Whatever their real motive, the Commissioners declared war, mobilized troops, and issued commissions to officers. In the process they sent for the Narragansett sachems, offering safe conduct for negotiations. Pessicus, Mixan, and some others responded and were astounded at what they had walked into. Although the Commissioners had ordered their messengers to return a Narragansett diplomatic present, thus to signify an end to amity, the agents had failed to obey that instruction. The agents were also "worthy of censure and punishment," according to the Commissioners, because they had resorted to Mr. Williams as interpreter, being unable to get Benedict Arnold as ordered. Williams had softened the Commissioners' message much, and perhaps it was his advice that had caused the retention of the present. The Indians "professed Mr. Williams had not acquainted them with two waignty passages therein, namely that they must give satisfaccion for what is past and good securitie for future peace. And that the English preparacions and direccions for invasive warr might not be stayed or recalled till by treaty some further order were taken."[53]

The overwhelmed Indians were presented with a "treaty" to sign. It made them acknowledge culpability, promise to pay "the full sum of two thousand fathome of good white wampom" in addition to an annual tribute in wampum for each Pequot living amongst them, "resigne and

51. Pulsifer, ed., *Acts of United Colonies*, I, 55.
52. Downing to Winthrop, Sr., [ca. Aug. 1645], *Winthrop Papers*, V, 38–39.
53. Aug. 1645, Pulsifer, ed., *Acts of the United Colonies*, I, 33–43, quotes at 43.

yeild up the whole Peacott Countrey and every part of it to the English Colonies, as due to them by conquest," and give sachems' sons as hostages into the hands of the English. The Indians signed this capitulation, which the Puritans thereafter called a covenant. Since the Puritans and their admirers were to make much in later years about the Indians breaking this "covenant," it may be proper to inquire how the Indians saw it. Pessicus has provided an unambiguous description of why he signed. "He doth say when he made his covenant he did it in feare of the Army that he did see, and though the English kept their covenant with him there and let him goe from them, yet the Army was to goe to Narragansett ymediatly and kill him there, Therefore said the Commissioners, sett to your hands to such and such thinges or els the Army shall goe forth to the Narragansetts."[54] Considering that Indian custom, like English law, prescribed that contracts made under duress were not binding, it does not seem odd that this shotgun covenant settled little.[55]

SCENE 8.   *Roger Williams proves that the long way round is the shortest to the rescue.*

The Puritans could not keep their troops perpetually mobilized, but they maintained pressure on the Narragansetts by other means. Although they had previously shown force, they now avoided attracting unfavorable attention from London, where men in high places had begun to show signs of displeasure. Puritans in England had broader ideas of religious toleration than the Puritans of New England, and the statesmen of the old country had strong ideas about the proper subordination of colonies, whether or not orthodox in religion.[56] Although the Narragansetts had failed to win protection under the laws of old England, Roger Williams's towns had gained a sympathetic hearing and a guarantee of security. Other victims besides Williams and the Gortonoges were complaining in England of the heresy hunts in New England.[57] As we have seen, the defensive reaction in Massachusetts was

54. Aug. 27, 1645, July 31, 1647, *ibid.*, I, 45–49, 86. Pessicus's remark was reported by interpreters Thomas Stanton and Benedict Arnold, both highly hostile to the Narragansetts.

55. See Heckewelder, *Account of Indian Nations*, in Hist. Soc. Pa., *Memoirs*, XII, 57.

56. The English Commonwealth government kept hands off Catholic Maryland so that it should be "an Instrument (as occasion shall require)" to keep Protestant Virginians "in their due obedience to this Commonwealth." "Reasons of State concerninge Maryland in America," C.O. 1/11, 183–184, P.R.O.

57. E.g., Dr. Robert Child, Samuel Maverick, and William Vassall. John Childe, *New-Englands Jonas*, in Force, comp., *Tracts*, IV; Edward Winslow to John Winthrop, Sr., Nov. 24, 1645, *Winthrop Papers*, V, 55–56; Edward Winslow,

to accelerate John Eliot on his missionary career and to drown out the murmurs about mundane matters by trumpeting mightily of the Lord.[58]

Nevertheless the concerns of this vale of tears continued to occupy the minds of the Puritan leaders. Tactics changed, that was all; the long-range strategy of terror and conquest remained intact. Indeed Eliot entered into it with such zeal that the Commissioners of the United Colonies had to caution him to be more prudent: "Wee desire you would bee slow in With Drawing Indian proffessors from paying accustomed Tribute and performing other lawfull servises to theire Sagamores till you have seriously Considered and advised with the Majestrates and Elders of the Massachusetts least the passage and spreading of the Gosspell bee hindered therby."[59]

Roger Williams testified more directly as to Eliot's methods and their effect. "At my last departure for England [1653], I was importuned by the Narragansett Sachems, and especially by Ninigret, to present their petition to the high Sachems of England, that they might not be forced from their religion, and, for not changing their religion, be invaded by war; for they said they were daily visited with threatenings by Indians that came from about the Massachusetts, that if they would not pray, they should be destroyed by war." Williams passed this information on to Oliver Cromwell, then at the peak of power, who was pleased "to grant, amongst other favors to this colony [Rhode Island], some expressly concerning the very Indians, the native inhabitants of this jurisdiction."[60]

Williams need not be doubted. Cromwell was as much nationalist as religionist, and he was discontented with Massachusetts's independent ways. Williams's towns proclaimed unreserved allegiance to Cromwell's government and recognized as their own laws, the laws of England. Massachusetts did neither. For the Lord Protector there was more virtue in obedient heretics than in fractious brothers in faith.[61]

It would appear that the Puritan confederates in New England understood that they should not vex Cromwell too much. Before learning of his personal friendliness to colonists and Indians at Narragansett Bay, the United Colonies had declared another war upon the Indians, in

---

New-Englands Salamander, Discovered by an Irreligious and Scornfull Pamphlet, called New-Englands Jonas Cast up at London... (1647), in Mass. Hist. Soc., *Colls.,* 3d Ser., II (Cambridge, Mass., 1830), 110–145; Thomas Aspinwall, "William Vassall no Factionist," Mass. Hist. Soc., *Procs.,* VI (1862–1863), 471–479. Cf. Langdon, *Pilgrim Colony,* 65; Willison, *Saints and Strangers,* 361–362.

58. See chap. 14.

59. Commissioners to Eliot, Sept. 18, 1654, Pulsifer, ed., *Acts of United Colonies,* II, 123.

60. Williams to Massachusetts General Court, Oct. 5, 1654, *ibid.,* 438–439.

61. See Cromwell's letters to Mass. and R.I., 1653, in Thomas Birch, ed., *A Collection of the State Papers of John Thurloe, Esq.* (London, 1742), II, 1–2.

September 1654. The Indians were ready this time, and the forces sent against them did not like the prospect of venturing into a swamp in pursuit. They decided rather to seek out Indians who "were willing to salve up thinges as well as they could." Great blusters from the English met with cool rejection from sachem Ninigret, and the soldiers returned empty-handed and humiliated. Prior to their expedition the United Colonies had resolved to commit as much additional force as necessary to humble Ninigret; but, in the course of it, Williams informed them of Cromwell's attitude. Angry but wary, the Commissioners let Ninigret win that round. They even gave up the effort to make him pay their expenses.[62]

SCENE 9. *Once more the pen is mightier than the sword, for a while.*

Overt conquest was foregone for a time, but the deed game still remained as means to win by legal stratagem what could not be dared by arms. In this game no colonist was more adroit than the younger John Winthrop. After his father died in 1649, John, Jr., picked up the mantle of leadership, but with a different style and in Connecticut rather than Massachusetts. The younger Winthrop's career had become rather aimless after the Pequot conquest. He had given up the masquerade of governorship at Fort Saybrook and had dabbled in assorted commercial and political projects, none of which absorbed him very long. Nonetheless his unequaled connections with the centers of power in both old and New England made him a magnet for persons wanting a friend at court. What concerns us here is his settling of a "plantation" at Nameaug (what became New London) in the former Pequot territory. Massachusetts and Connecticut acceded to Winthrop's new settlement, and he was empowered to act as Connecticut's magistrate in the locality. His influence in Connecticut grew, and in 1657 he was chosen governor —an honor that may have amused him at first, when he remembered how he had tried to govern from Fort Saybrook. Winthrop's most conspicuous policy carried on the family tradition of aggressive expansion. However, the son avoided the self-righteous confrontations characteristic of his father. His methods of discreet intrigue and urbane maneuver were better suited to New England's new circumstances.[63]

While he was governor, Winthrop, Jr., became a partner in the Atherton Company, a group of land speculators that aimed at acquiring

62. Pulsifer, ed., *Acts of United Colonies*, II, 114-117, 125-126, 144-152, quote at 146.

63. See Dunn, *Puritans and Yankees*, chaps. 3-7, and his "John Winthrop, Jr., and the Narragansett Country," *WMQ*, 3d Ser., XIII (1956), 68-86; Black, *Younger John Winthrop*, chaps. 9-20.

lands from the Narragansett Indians. The company embraced important people from both Massachusetts and Connecticut. It started in business in 1659 with the fraudulent purchase technique, "buying" six thousand acres of the best Narragansett land from sachem Pessicus's feeble-minded younger brother, a man who had no valid power to sell and who was "seduced" by "being made drunk and kept so for some days." To complete the fraud the deed was drawn in terms of gift rather than sale in order to circumvent Rhode Island's law against purchase without the colonial government's consent.[64] (Like John Winthrop, Sr., Roger Williams had switched sides on that issue.)

Perhaps the Restoration of Charles II on the English throne in May 1660 stimulated the Atherton Company Puritans to grab while the getting was good, for in September of that year they contrived to acquire a deed for all the Narragansett Indian lands. In brief, the Commissioners of the United Colonies—John Winthrop, Jr., among them—charged the Narragansetts with sundry crimes and levied a fine upon them of 595 fathoms of wampum. This proved expectedly difficult for the Indians to accumulate within their deadline, so a Mr. Humphrey Atherton obligingly stepped in to pay it for them. He was the Atherton of the Atherton Company, and naturally he took a mortgage to secure his associates against loss, adding a small service charge of additional fathoms of wampum for the six-month loan. Actually this last was a mere makeweight. Although it amounted to an annual interest rate of nearly 50 percent, the extra charge had been thrown in merely to make the debt harder to pay back; Atherton wanted the collateral rather than the return of his money. When, by heroic industry, the Narragansetts manufactured or acquired the needed sum in the allotted time, Atherton refused to accept it. Under sanction of the United Colonies the Atherton Company laid claim instead to ownership of the whole of the remaining Narragansett country—some four hundred square miles.[65]

Despite the smoothness of the coup there was a flaw. Refusing to recognize the Atherton title, Rhode Island claimed jurisdiction over the foreclosed land by virtue of its parliamentary charter. At one time, perhaps, a Puritan expeditionary force might have been sent to discipline Rhode Island, a la the Gortonoges; but in 1660 the ominous

64. "Cartwright's Answer to the Massachusetts Narrative of Transactions with the Royal Commissioners," Jan. 5, 1666, "Clarendon Papers," N.-Y. Hist. Soc., *Colls.,* 1869, 90–91.

65. See Dunn, "Winthrop, Jr., and Narragansett Country," *WMQ,* 3d Ser., XIII (1956), 68–86. See also Sept. 1660, Pulsifer, ed., *Acts of United Colonies,* II, 247–249; Oct. 4, 1660, *Recs. of Conn.,* I, 355; review of documents, *ibid.,* app. VII, II, 541–545. See also the report of Sir Edmund Andros on the claims to the Narragansett country, Aug. 31, 1687, Sainsbury *et al.,* eds., *Calendar of State Papers, Col. Ser., 1685–1688,* doc. 1414, v., pp. 423–424.

shadow of a new Stuart king blighted such notions. Recognizing the need for greater finesse, John Winthrop, Jr., journeyed to England to make things right. To his great disgust, Rhode Island sent a vociferous representative to the same place.

Actually the Atherton mortgage was a relatively minor, though interesting, part of their concerns. Since neither Rhode Island nor Connecticut had a royal charter, and since Charles II was unlikely to feel deferential toward grants made by the Parliament that had cut off his father's head, these colonies were in urgent need of legitimacy. Winthrop, for Connecticut, and Dr. John Clarke, for Rhode Island, petitioned for charters of jurisdiction, and their colonies' entire existence hung on their success.

From the outcome it appears that they saw opportunity as well as necessity in their errands. Both negotiated for charters that would give their colonies more territory than they had formerly governed. Winthrop tried to grasp all of Rhode Island, New Netherland, and New Haven as well as the lands of his Connecticut towns. As fitted his greater experience and larger slush funds, officialdom gave him the more comprehensive charter; but the crown had plans of its own for New Netherland, and Dr. Clarke argued successfully for Rhode Island's independence. Connecticut momentarily contented itself with swallowing up orthodox New Haven, whose leaders had mistakenly trusted Winthrop to represent their own interests.[66]

SCENE 10.   *Peregrinating homage finds its king.*

The crown was now besieged with pleas for redress by colonists who had suffered under Puritan trampling. There were petitions from Maine, from Massachusetts exiles, and finally from the Gortonoges, who were still excluded by force from their lands at Shawomet on Narragansett Bay. Now, at last, the Gortonoges could actually deliver the Narragansetts' deed of submission to the crown, and the crown very sensibly showed interest in this manna.[67]

There was so much clamor, and at the same time so much distraction for the ministry in restoring royal government within England, that no one seemed to know quite what to do about the colonies. Finally a device was hit upon that permitted maximum exertion of royal authority at minimum cost. Taking advantage of the departure of a fleet in 1664 to conquer New Netherland, the crown empowered royal com-

66. Black, *Younger John Winthrop*, chaps. 15–17; Dunn, *Puritans and Yankees*, chap. 6.

67. Sainsbury *et al.*, eds., *Calendar of State Papers, Col. Ser., 1661–1668*, docs. 33, 45, 49–53; Roelker, "Gorton's Master Stroke," *R.I. Hist.*, II (1943), 9–10.

missioners accompanying the fleet to investigate the northern English colonies and tidy things up. Among other missions the commissioners were instructed most specifically to investigate the Narragansett country. "If you have cleare proofe that in truth these territoryes are transferred to us," wrote Charles to his commissioners, "you shall seize upon the same in our Name, and the same tract of land shall bee hereafter called the King's Province."[68]

68. *N.Y. Col. Docs.*, III, 56.

Chapter 16 ?♥ THE DISUNITED COLONIES

The arrival of the royal commissioners inaugu-
rated a brief new era in New England. Although they were but four
persons without any of the paraphernalia of power except the royal seal
on their commissions, they spoke and acted with the confidence of
men who can summon power at need. The voices were those of Colonel
Richard Nicolls, Colonel George Cartwright, Sir Robert Carr, and
Samuel Maverick, but the words were those of the king of England.
These were not men to shiver at a frown from Boston's magistrates or
despair at the trainbands' advance. They strode into the presence of
the colonial great and made demands and gave orders. They stopped
the Puritan juggernaut in its tracks.

But the limit of their authority was precisely marked at the point
where power ceased to be available. While New England contemplated
how quickly an English fleet had conquered New Netherland, the royal
commissioners were deferred to as men who might be able to summon
another fleet to chastise rebellious English colonies. Stubborn Puritans
dragged their heels, equivocated, evaded, quibbled, misinformed, debated, and appealed, but they pretended to be loyal, obedient subjects
acting only within their rights. Others saw new opportunity opening
up and hastened to ingratiate themselves with the commissioners. But
when soundings indicated that the crown was indecisive and not at all
willing to act forcefully—that, in short, it was bluffing—resistance
firmed up, and the commissioners were recalled with their tasks
unfinished.

Nevertheless they had made a difference. The "church fellowship"
of the United Colonies shattered under their impact, and every colony
struggled frantically on its own to stabilize its boundaries against the
claims of all the others. Effects on the Indians varied. Under the
crown's protection the Narragansetts got a decade of reprieve from
Puritan conquest, but the Wampanoags and the inland Nipmucks,
whose bands and lands straddled disputed frontiers, came under intense pressure from many sides. The Wampanoags came under severe

harassment from Plymouth as the leaders of that charterless colony desperately sought to extract from their client's "natural rights" every possible bit of validation for the colony's territorial claims. Ironically it was Plymouth, the weakest and least aggressive member of the Puritan confederation, whose thrashing struggles for political survival precipitated the Second Puritan Conquest.

Almost from the instant of the Restoration of Charles II, complaints had been lodged with his Privy Council against the conduct of Puritan New England. Two themes ran through these charges: that Massachusetts was denying its proper subordination to the crown and that the Puritan governments were trampling upon the rights and liberties of non-Puritans in other colonies as well as in their own. In the eyes of the crown both sorts of accusation evidenced that the Puritans had acquired too much independent power, and the crown's commissioners were instructed to whittle away at that power as much as possible without precipitating outright rebellion. In the nature of the case the royal commissioners became champions not only of royal authority but also of the rights of the multitudes, both English and Indian, whom the Puritan oligarchy had attacked and repressed. Royal concern for popular right need not be interpreted as a sudden accession of democratic humanism in the Stuart dynasty; its motivation, quite clearly, was to achieve enough popular support for the sovereign to break the power of the colonial lords with a minimum of financial and political cost. Regardless of motives, however, the immediate aims of the royal commissioners—and, to some degree, their achievements—included strengthening the "rights of Englishmen" in the colonies because, by so doing, they would strengthen the crown.

New England's historians have tended, by and large, to invert the reality. The commissioners, they have charged, were sent to destroy self-government; indeed, some have been so foolish as to equate the independent Puritan oligarchies with democracy. Especial animosity has been visited upon one commissioner, Samuel Maverick, who is portrayed as a man filled with venom against New England and eager to revenge himself upon it. It is true that Maverick had a score to pay off, for the Massachusetts oligarchy had made him one of their many victims and had driven him away in spite of his status as an Old Planter who had been established before the arrival of the Massachusetts Bay Company.[1] But Maverick's venom is not easy to see in the actual policies he recommended when he got the attention of the crown. Here is his program as he presented it to Lord Chancellor Clarendon at the minister's request:

1. *Dictionary of American Biography*, s.v. "Maverick, Samuel."

That all freeholders may have voats in Election of officers civill and Military.

That all persons inoffencive in life and conversation may be admitted to the sacrament of the Lords supper, and theire childeren to Baptisme.

That such lawes as are now in force there, derrogatinge from the lawes of England, may be repealed.

That the oath of Allegance [to the crown] may be administered in steade of that which they tearme the oath of fidelitie [to the colonial government].

That they goe not beyond their just bounds, even those which for neare twentie years they were content withall.

That they admitt of Appeales [to the crown] on just and reasonable grounds.

That they permitt such as desire it, to use the Common prayer [of the Church of England].

That all writts etc. may be issewed out in his Majesties name.[2]

When Massachusetts later refused to concede a single one of these measures, Maverick proposed coercive pressures directed against the more obstreperous members of the oligarchy, but the acts he suggested do not begin to compare in severity with the sentences inflicted by the oligarchy upon its own opponents.[3]

The crown officially instructed its commissioners to establish royal authority to the extent possible, to secure liberty of conscience in all colonies as had already been guaranteed in Rhode Island, to hear appeals to the king's justice insofar as the issues involved abuse or exceeding of chartered powers, and to treat with Indian "princes." The commissioners were also emphatically instructed to disturb existing institutions and arrangements as little as possible.[4]

Boston met the royal commissioners with adamant refusal in substance, fully visible behind a halfhearted disguise of shuffling evasion in form. As Commissioner Cartwright reported, the magistrates took the position "that they are not obliged to the King, but by civilitie," adding, "they hope to tyre the king, the lord chancelor, and the Secretary too with writing. They can easily spinne 7 yeares out with writing at that distance and before that a change may come."[5] The other colonies distinguished themselves from Massachusetts's intransigence by making haste to submit in due public form, however many reservations they kept in private. Winthrop, Jr., in Connecticut was all smiles, indirection, and amiable pleasantness. Wholly charterless Plymouth humbled itself grudgingly. But Rhode Island jubilated its subjection, and it was there

2. Maverick to earl of Clarendon, n.d. [ca. 1662], "Clarendon Papers," N.-Y. Hist. Soc., *Colls., 1869,* 42–43.

3. Maverick to Clarendon, July 24, 1665, *ibid.,* 74–77.

4. *N.Y. Col. Docs.,* III, 51–61.

5. Cartwright, "Account of Massachusetts," in "Clarendon Papers," N.-Y. Hist. Soc., *Colls., 1869,* 85.

among heretics, democrats, and royalists that the royal commissioners achieved solid accomplishments through unfeigned local cooperation —enough to use as a basis for pregnant constitutional propositions.

At the heart of the issues before the royal commissioners were the powers and status of the United Colonies of New England, and the hearings of inquiry opened to the king's agents a picture much different from the stories that John Winthrop, Jr., had told in London. Winthrop had there cozened the crown into recognizing the Atherton title, even to entrusting the United Colonies with authority to protect Atherton (and his silent partner Winthrop) against "certaine unreasonable and turbulent speritts of Providence Collonie." After an investigation of the whole situation in Rhode Island, the commissioners ordered otherwise. When they called sachem Pessicus to testify, he confirmed the Narragansetts' deed of submission to King Charles I, which had been preserved so long by Samuel Gorton, whereupon the commissioners, as instructed, erected the Narragansett country into "The King's Province" and put it under the administration of the government of Rhode Island[6] (see map 3, chapter 15).

They discovered the fraud of the Atherton mortgage so incontrovertibly that John Winthrop, Jr., did not even attempt to defend it. As the commissioners reported, "Mr. Winthrop governor of Conecticot, Major Wenslo [Winslow] of New Plymoth colony were joyned together with these of the Massachusets" in "a combination (as it was afterwards confesst to be) that the Commissioners of the United Colonies, being always the cheife men of those 3 colonies, and New-haven, (for Rode island was excluded) might alwayes make orders in favour of the purchasers against Rode-island, and so they did." Winthrop, standing by, was so confounded that he could think of nothing but to pretend that his name had been used by the Atherton Company without his consent.[7] This excuse has been disproved by a modern student who concluded that the royal commissioners were "perfectly justified" in their finding.[8]

The commissioners struck down without equivocation the assumed authority of the Puritan confederation to warrant and conduct conquest: "No colony hath any just right to dispose of any lands con-

6. Commissioners' order, Mar. 20, 1665, *Recs. of R.I.*, II, 59–60; John Hutchins Cady, *Rhode Island Boundaries, 1636–1936* ([Providence, R.I.], 1936), 10. Cady's book is a valuable resource in clarifying the confused geography of claims and counterclaims in and around Rhode Island. It contains a set of maps showing sequential changes of boundaries.

7. "Cartwright's Answer," in "Clarendon Papers," N.-Y. Hist. Soc., *Colls.*, *1869*, 91.

8. Dunn, "Winthrop, Jr., and Narragansett Country," *WMQ*, 3d Ser., XIII (1956), 72, and his *Puritans and Yankees*, 159–160.

quered from the natives, unles both the cause of the conquest be just and the land lye within the bounds which the king by his charter hath given it, nor yet to exercise any authority beyond those bounds." They declared void all grants made by "the usurped authority called the United Colonyes," and Commissioner Cartwright explained to the ministry in London that by means of the confederation the Puritan colonies "took more power then was ever given, or entended them."[9]

This was the authentic voice of the national state suppressing all powers save such as derived from itself. The royal commissioners even stepped so far out of their era as to lay down the principle of equality of right among subjects. They tackled Massachusetts's Indian tenure law, with its theological distinctions of superior right for Christians justified by biblical verses. Psalms 115:16 was cited therein: "The heaven, even the heavens, are the LORD's; but the earth hath he given to the children of men." For a brief moment the royal commissioners' comment sounded like a Leveler's. " 'Children of men' comprehends Indians as well as English; and no doubt the country is theirs till they give it or sell it, though it be not improoved."[10] (Suddenly the town of Hingham remembered to purchase from its Indian landlord.[11])

Although the benefit to the Indians was short-lived, New England began to emerge, kicking and screaming, from the politics of feudalism to the modern age. Massachusetts found ways of prolonging the transition and of thwarting the work of Charles's commissioners, and Mr. Winthrop in Connecticut obeyed royal directives by interpreting them to mean what he wanted to do; but the process of implanting royal authority had begun, and its growth was nourished in Rhode Island and in the New York that had been made from New Netherland.

The United Colonies ceased attempts at overt conquest, but it apparently launched an effort at covert conquest with some of the money that it continued to receive from England for distribution to the missions. Arms and ammunition were bought and entrusted to "the care and

9. Commissioners' order, Apr. 4, 1665, *Recs. of Mass.*, IV, Pt. ii, 176; "Cartwright's Answer," in "Clarendon Papers," N.-Y. Hist. Soc., *Colls.*, *1869*, 92.

10. *Recs. of Mass.*, IV, Pt. ii, 213; Whitmore, ed., *Colonial Laws of Massachusetts*, 160.

11. Deed, July 4, 1665, in John D. Long, "Early Settlers" *History of the Town of Hingham, Massachusetts* (Hingham, Mass., 1893), I, Pt. 1, 204–206. The deed states that the town had been settled since 1634 with the Massachuset Indians' "likeing and Consent" but without "any legall conveyance in writing." This is the more interesting because Hingham men had earlier bought from Plymouth's Wampanoags a tract of land 15 miles square. Two points may be noted: (1) The tacit abandonment of the notion that the Massachuset Indians had lost all property right through their uncompensated "grant" of Mar. 8, 1644 (chap. 14, above); (2) the land at Hingham was involved in a jurisdictional dispute between Massachusetts and Plymouth. Deed and confirmations, June 17, 1661, June 2, 1662, and June 8, 1664, *Suffolk Deeds*, VII, 161–163.

prudence of Mr. Eliot" for the praying Indians "upon any occasion." An occasion arose in 1669 when a large force of Indians marched from Massachusetts to attack the Mohawks, by whom they were badly beaten.[12] John Eliot and Daniel Gookin disclaimed responsibility for the march, but the evidence is strong that they must have shared some sort of complicity, possibly under protest. The Indians were led by Josias Wompatuck, "chief ruler" of the mission town of Pakeunit, and they were not chastised upon their return. Besides all this, two governors of New York had been attempting for years to make peace between the Mohawks and all of New England's Indians, and the frustration of their efforts had not been caused by Mohawk intractability. Each time that Governor Richard Nicolls or his successor Francis Lovelace approached John Winthrop, Jr., to arrange a treaty, Winthrop evaded. At one point he came as close to outright refusal as his equivocal temperament permitted, declaring that New England's Indians actually dreaded a peace more than war. Winthrop was, without doubt, the most influential of the Commissioners of the United Colonies, and it is unlikely that he bothered to consult the Indians before he spoke for them. His conduct and language signify that the initiative for the war against the Mohawks came from the Puritan oligarchy, whose motive was to expand into the Hudson Valley by the same conquest-of-Indians techniques they were using openly in Rhode Island. (Both Massachusetts and Connecticut laid claim to territory within New York's jurisdiction.) There is some possibility that Eliot and Gookin may have dissented from a secret decision to launch their praying Indians on a particular campaign against the Mohawks, but they continued to be faithful servants of the agency from which they drew their funds.[13]

12. The Commissioners of the United Colonies represented to the "New England Company" in London that the munitions were provided for defense. The grounds for thinking otherwise cannot be presented here because of restrictions of space and unity of theme. In any case, the 1669 battle was indisputably an invasion of territory in New York's jurisdiction in the manner that the Puritans so often invaded Rhode Island's. The English company took a dim view; it refused to supply money for arms on the reasonable grounds that the protection of the Indians was the responsibility of the colonial governments, "they being now his majesties subjects, and, as wee are informed, all the Collonys by your Asotiation are ingaged to assist in such cases." Commissioners to Boyle, Sept. 10, 1668, and Boyle to Commissioners, Apr. 28, 1669, *Some Correspondence between the Governors and Treasurers of the New England Company in London and the Commissioners of the United Colonies in America* ... (London, 1896), 20, 26; Drake, *Biography and History of Indians*, 109-110.

13. Although Gookin's account pretended there were only five praying Indians in the disaster, Eliot elsewhere involved the whole village of Wamesit. It does not seem likely that the "chief man" of the "sachems of the blood," who was also the "chiefest general" of all the Indians attacking the Mohawks—Josias Wompatuck was all of that—would have been able to attract only four followers on a campaign; nor does it seem likely that they would have marched if deprived

But the Puritan confederation had become a shadow of its former self, and intermural quarrels tore at the fragile fabric of Puritan unity. The charter coup by which Connecticut had seized New Haven aroused so much wrath in the swallowed colony that a contingent of its people sailed off to New Jersey rather than submit. More immediately pertinent to our interests, Plymouth Colony became nervous about its own survival. Plymouth was willing to help the United Colonies spend the "Indian stocke" and attend to "Corporation business"—i.e., the funds and affairs of the missionary society that had made the United Colonies its agent in New England—but Plymouth had been shocked by the New Haven affair. Governor Thomas Prence wrote: "Wee find not our reason seated in sufficient Light to Continew Confeaderation with three Collonies as wee did with foure; because it is against an expresse article that noe two of the said Collonies shall become one (and wee apprehend Grounded upon good reason) except with consent of the rest; which wee doe not nor youer selves for ought wee know nor New haven except Constrained."[14]

The rift was patched up, and the confederation rewrote its articles; but Plymouth's apprehension persisted. The only New England colony still without a royal charter, it was surrounded by border disputes on every side but the ocean. Rhode Island had won royal consent to expand to the east shore of Narragansett Bay, much against Plymouth's protests, and Massachusetts reopened the worrisome issue of its southern line.[15] Plymouth men saw their colony being nibbled away. Who could know certainly that the rest of it might not go down in a gulp?

Somehow Plymouth never did manage to get a valid charter, and it continued to rely heavily for legality upon its protectorate over the Wampanoag Indians. So long as the Wampanoags dealt in land affairs exclusively with Plymouth, the protectorate served to convert Indian rights into colony rights, but the device required constant controls over Indian cessions. Since the Wampanoags were a free tribe, never having subjected themselves in the manner of the Massachuset tribe, and since Plymouth lacked the size and strength of her northern neighbor, controls presented difficulties. Even old sachem Massassoit, subservient

---

of the arms and ammunition in Eliot's custody. Gookin, "Historical Collections," Mass. Hist. Soc., *Colls.*, 1st Ser., I, 166–167; Eliot, *Brief Narrative*, 6, 9; Eliot to Boyle, Sept. 6, 1669, *Some Correspondence of the New England Company*, 28. For Winthrop's role, see Black, *Younger John Winthrop*, 321–322. See also chap. 17, below, for territorial claims.

14. Sept. 1667, Pulsifer, ed., *Acts of United Colonies*, II, 323–324. See Andrews, *Colonial Period*, II, 186–193.

15. Charter, July 8, 1663, *Recs. of R.I.*, II, 18–19; "Clarendon Papers," N.-Y. Hist. Soc., *Colls., 1869*, 98, 108, 151, 155; June 3, 1662, *Recs. of Plymouth*, IV, 24.

though he was, occasionally plucked up courage to sell his own land at his own whim. Indeed Providence Plantations had begun when Massassoit sold off his claim (overlapping the Narragansett claim to the same land) to Roger Williams. When Massassoit died, his successor, Wamsutta, showed considerably more independence than the old chief. Fearful Plymouth learned that Wamsutta was selling territory to outsiders. Plymouth's General Court directed an emissary "to speak to Wamsitta about his estranging land, and not selling it to our collonie." [16]

Wamsutta again asserted independence by selling to Providence after having been "spoken to," [17] upon which defiance Plymouth resorted to more persuasive measures. Major Josiah Winslow, a worthy scion of his sire, Edward, took a small party of armed men to surprise Wamsutta at one of the Indians' hunting stations. Pointing a pistol at the sachem's breast, Winslow told him (as reported by William Hubbard) "that if he stirred or refused to go he was a dead man." [18] It happened that Wamsutta was sick. Hubbard says he became sick on the way to Plymouth town, because of hot weather and choleric pride, but that alibi—so neatly tailored to the myth of the ferocious and irrational savage—fits badly into the circumstances. Wamsutta had lived in the open all his life and was certainly as accustomed as any of Winslow's Englishmen to traveling in hot weather, but he was so badly incapacitated that Winslow became worried and soon turned him loose. [19] Wamsutta died "before he got half way home." Notably, not a word of all this found its way into the official records, although there was considerable indignation even among Englishmen over Winslow's brutality. Years later Hubbard felt obliged to denounce "false reports as if the English had compelled [Wamsutta] to go further or faster than he was able." The proof of

16. Deed and confirmations, June 17, 1661, June 2, 1662, and June 8, 1664, *Suffolk Deeds*, VII, 161–163; deed, Wamsutta to Peter Talman, Jan. 20, 1662, *Rhode Island Land Evidences, Abstracts*, I (Providence, R.I., 1921), 188–189; deed, Wamsutta to Thomas Olney, Sr., *et al.*, Mar. 12, 1662, William R. Staples, ed., *Annals of the Town of Providence from Its First Settlement, to the Organization of City Government* ... (R.-I. Hist. Soc., *Colls.*, V [Providence, R.I., 1843]); Mar. 4, 1662, *Recs. of Plymouth*, IV, 18.

17. The sale to Providence was made on Mar. 12, eight days following Plymouth's decision to "speak to" Wamsutta.

18. Hubbard, *Narrative*, 9–10; Mather, *Early History of New England*, ed. Drake, 229. Hubbard provides the quotation but omits the persuasion of the pistol. Mather completes the picture.

19. Although the route taken and distance covered are not mentioned in the sources, they can be inferred to some extent. Hubbard located Wamsutta's hunting station "within six miles of the English towns." The party marched to Winslow's home at Marshfield (Winslow riding, Wamsutta walking), which would probably be the town referred to since it was only about 10 miles from the Massachusetts border. Distances of that magnitude would not disable a well Indian.

falsity? It was not to be imagined "that a person of so noble a disposition" as Winslow's could be "uncivil to a person allied to them, by his own, as well as his father's league."[20] It would seem that Hubbard included in his definition of admirable civility the threat to shoot Wamsutta on the spot for noncompliance with an ultimatum.

Wamsutta's brother Metacom succeeded to the sachemship. We know him more familiarly as Philip, the name he asked for as a compliment to the English. (But that request was made before the death of his brother, who had also requested an English name and had been dubbed Alexander.[21]) Plymouth lost little time in bringing Philip to terms. Wamsutta's death had occurred sometime after June 8, 1664.[22] Philip was haled to Plymouth town on August 6, on the pretext of "danger of the rising of the Indians against the English." A harried Philip remembered his brother and groveled. He "absolutely" denied conspiring and proffered another brother as hostage "untill the Court could have more sertainty of the truth of his defence." For once Plymouth was totally uninterested in hostages—a fact that implies much about the truth of its charges. What Plymouth did want was a contract that Philip would never again convey lands to any person, by gift, sale, or otherwise, "without our privity, consent, or appointment." Having gained that end, the General Court sent Philip back home.[23]

There is reason to believe that Philip was deceived about what he signed. The document pledged him without limit of time, which was surely not what he understood it to say. Within six months after signing he dictated a letter that reviewed his understanding, and no one at Plymouth corrected him. In his letter he remarked, "Philip would intreat that favor of you, and aney of the majestrats, if aney English or Engians speak about aney land, he preay you to give them no answer at all. This last sumer he maid that promis with you, that he would not sell no land *in 7 years time*, for that he would have *no* English trouble him before that time, he has not forgot that you promis him."[24]

20. Hubbard, *Narrative*, 10.

21. June 13, 1660, *Recs. of Plymouth*, III, 192. It was a general Indian custom to adopt a new name at an especially important moment of one's life. The new name signified a new man. It was also customary to show admiration or respect for someone by assuming his name, and much confusion has been created in records by Indians who adopted the names of living Englishmen, so that two people of the same name sometimes appear at the same time in different places. For Wamsutta and Metacom to ask the Plymouth General Court to rename them was a gesture of respect. The Court's response, with its classical allusions, was derisive. The Indians, of course, were unaware of the mockery.

22. The date is set by his deed in *Suffolk Deeds*, VII, 162.

23. Recitation and treaty in *Recs. of Plymouth*, IV, 25–26.

24. King Philip to Gov. Thomas Prince, n.d., in Mass. Hist. Soc., *Colls.*, 1st Ser., II (Boston, 1793), 40 (my italics). The date (which is crucial to interpretation) was guessed by the editor as "about 1660 or 70." It was assigned by Langdon

It must be stressed that Philip was still a "free" sachem in 1662. His treaty pledged subjection to the king of England, but not to Plymouth. That distinction acquired peculiar force when Rhode Island gained its royal charter in 1663, for the charter put Philip's home village within Rhode Island's boundaries. Called variously Sowams, Pokanoket, and Mount Hope (now Bristol, Rhode Island), this small "neck" of land became the tinder that set all New England in flames (see map 3, chapter 15). By the accepted rules Indian tribes came under the protectorate of the colony whose charter embraced their territory, and Rhode Island claimed that "the native Indians" wanted to be "within this jurisdiction," but Plymouth refused to let go of Philip.[25] Instead Plymouth challenged Rhode Island's charter, and a struggle set in that was only intensified when Charles II wrote, in 1666, to say that the bounds set by his commissioners were to stand until his final royal determination—particularly "the present temporary bound sett by the Commissioners between the Collonies of New Plymouth and Rhode Island, until his Majestie shall find cause to alter the same."[26] Instead of quieting Plymouth, the letter merely aroused hope and desire to provide the indicated cause.

As to what then happened, it is regrettably necessary to omit much detail. In brief, all the New England colonies reopened all their boundary claims, and the competition in the deed game became fiercer than ever. The Narragansett country continued to be a cockpit of struggle as

---

to 1672 because Langdon saw Philip as "concerned by the purchase and settlement of lands belonging to his ally, Awashunks." *Plymouth Colony*, 162. My own finding that the letter was written in fall or winter of 1662 rests on the following reasoning: (1) Philip's "promise" mentioned in the letter would have to have been made at either the treaty of Aug. 6, 1662, or that of Sept. 29, 1671. The letter says the promise was made "this last sumer," a phrase that fits early August better than late September. (2) Neither treaty mentions seven years, and both require Philip to refrain from selling land except with Plymouth's consent; but the 1662 treaty is expressed in terms of mutual obligation—it contains promises by Plymouth as well as by Philip—while the 1671 treaty is wholly unilateral. On the latter occasion, Plymouth promised nothing except to make Philip "smart for it" if he "went on in his refractory way." Thus, Philip's reference in his letter to a promise made by Plymouth accords better with the 1662 treaty than that of 1671. (3) There is a notable lack of sale of lands by Philip after 1662 and a sudden rash of sales seven years later, in 1669, which continues through July 1672, when Philip personally agreed to a sale of land at Assowamsett Pond in the presence of the Plymouth General Court. The latter action is not reconcilable with a 1672 date for the letter to Gov. Prince. See *Recs. of Plymouth*, V, 79, 98.

25. "Clarendon Papers," N.-Y. Hist. Soc., *Colls.*, 1869, 151. The sachem's lands did not necessarily become everywhere coterminous with his protector's. Massachuset sachem Josias Wompatuck sold land within Plymouth as well as in Massachusetts. *Suffolk Deeds*, June 26, 1668, V, 462–463.

26. Charles II to Massachusetts, Apr. 10, 1666, in Robert Noxon Toppan, *Edward Randolph, ... 1676–1703*, Prince Society Publications, XXIV (Boston, 1898–1899), I, 40–41, n. 100 (not printed in *Recs. of Mass.*). Cf. Charles II to Rhode Island, Apr. 10, 1666, *Recs. of R.I.*, II, 149.

Connecticut attempted to enforce its jurisdiction there.[27] And a new area became the scene of active conflict: a three-way struggle commenced in 1668 between Massachusetts, Rhode Island, and Plymouth for the region where their claimed boundaries overlapped[28] (see map 3, chapter 15, and map 1, chapter 12). This was the edge of the Nipmuck Indian territory, and Massachusetts and Connecticut became attentive to the Nipmucks because of still another boundary brawl.[29] The Nipmucks were horribly caught as the client Indians of four colonies claimed tribute from them and fought to enforce it.[30] Eliot's mission Indians heard the voice of God and threw themselves into the same fray, with their governing magistrate and minister in the lead.[31] The sound of the battles reached England in 1671, where the Council for Plantations took alarm. Failure to compromise New England's boundary disputes would lead to civil war, the Council thought, and the crown resolved in 1672 to send a new set of commissioners.[32] But there were delays, and no royal agent was sent until the foreseen war broke out, though not in the foreseen way.

In 1667 Plymouth's General Court established the town of Swansea. Situated at the western edge of Plymouth's claims and straddling the counterclaims of Rhode Island, it also encroached upon sachem Philip's homeland of Sowams. Disregarding Philip's former plea (and Plymouth's promise) to prevent any Englishman from soliciting lands, the Court authorized Indian purchases "within the township of Swansey" early in 1668, providing they would not "too much straiten the Indians."

27. Sainsbury et al., eds., Calendar of State Papers, Col. Ser., 1669–1674, doc. 352; May 12, 1670, Recs. of Conn., II, 135; William Coddington to John Winthrop, Jr., June 15, 1674, "Winthrop Papers," Mass. Hist. Soc., Colls., VII (Boston, 1865), 294–295.

28. Bridgewater grant, July 7, 1668, Recs. of Plymouth, IV, 188; Swansea grant, Oct. 30, 1667, ibid., 169; Inman deeds, R.I. Land Evidences, I, 20–21; Oct. 11, 1670, Recs. of Mass., IV, Pt. ii, 465; report of Jno. Leverett, June 3, 1671, ibid., 497–498; Oct. 29, 1671, Recs. of Plymouth, V, 83; Jan. 2, 1672, Suffolk Deeds, VII, 272–273. See also ibid., V, 462–463, and July 7, 1674, Recs. of Plymouth, V, 151.

29. Recs. of Conn., II, app. XI, 554–556; Allyn to Pynchon, Oct. 28, 1671, Albert C. Bates, ed., The Wyllys Papers (Connecticut Historical Society, Collections, XXI [Hartford, Conn., 1924]), 201–202. The Pequot territory also continued in contention between Massachusetts and Connecticut. Recs. of Conn., II, app. VIII, 545–547.

30. Williams to Massachusetts General Court, May 7, 1668, Bartlett, ed., Letters of Williams, Narragansett Club, Pubs., VI, 326–327; Sept. 5, 1661, Pulsifer, ed., Acts of United Colonies, II, 268–269; Eliot to Endecott, Mar. 28, 1662, Mass. Hist. Soc., Colls., 1st Ser., III (Boston, 1794), 312–313.

31. Gookin, "Historical Collections," Mass. Hist. Soc., Colls., 1st Ser., I, 189–192; Eliot, "Account of Churches," Aug. 22, 1673, ibid., X, 128; Eliot to Commissioners of United Colonies, Sept. 4, 1671, Mass. Hist. Soc., Procs., XVII (1879–1880), 248–249; Eliot, Brief Narrative, 6.

32. Sainsbury et al., eds., Calendar of State Papers, Col. Ser., 1669–1674, 512, 598, 652.

A year later the General Court authorized expansion of Swansea, order-ing "for the accomodateing of more inhabitants in the said township, that all such lands as the Indians can well spare shalbe purchased." The means of determining which lands the Indians could "well spare" do not appear in the records. Certain it is, however, that the Indians were not permitted to make that decision. In 1670 Plymouth mended political fences by resubscribing to the articles of the United Colonies, then turned its attention once more to Philip.[33]

The Wampanoag Indians began to talk angrily and menacingly. Early in 1671 they made a display of armed force before Swansea's settlers, for which Plymouth haled Philip to Taunton on April 10, 1671, for disci-pline. Ordering him to turn in all his people's arms (which was the same as depriving them of essential tools for their livelihood), Plymouth also levied a fine. But the most serious clause in this April treaty demanded that Philip give submission to Plymouth as well as to the English crown. Moreover, the submission was retroactive to bind Philip's dead prede-cessors as well as himself: "My Father, my Brother, and my self, have formerly submitted our selves and our People unto the Kings Majesty of England, and to the Colony of New-Plimouth."[34] Something more than exuberant imagination was behind this, as Plymouth's colonial neighbors instantly recognized. When Philip ran off to Boston to complain of his treatment, the magistrates there "doubted whether the covenants and engagements that Phillip and his predecessors had plighted" meant any-thing more than "a naighborly and frindly correspondency" to Plym-outh. One need not leap to the conclusion that Massachusetts had sud-denly become tender towards Indians. A matter of the validity of land titles can be discerned in the background. If Philip and his father and brother were all acknowledged as having been subject to Plymouth, the titles of lands bought by colonists of other jurisdictions would suddenly become vulnerable to Plymouth's challenge. So would the jurisdiction over those lands. Perhaps Plymouth was aiming the retroactive clause primarily at Rhode Island, but Massachusetts men of the town of Hingham had also bought land from the Wampanoag sachems, and Massachusetts would never recognize a treaty that might carve chunks out of its borders.[35]

Consultation ensued between the Commissioners of the United Colo-nies, and on September 29, 1671, they helped Plymouth bludgeon Philip

---

33. Oct. 30, 1667, Mar. 5, 1668, *Recs. of Plymouth*, IV, 169, 176. July 5, 1669, *ibid.*, V, 24; June 1, 1670, Pulsifer, ed., *Acts of United Colonies*, II, 334–339.

34. Treaty text: Hubbard, *Narrative*, 11–12.

35. Aug. 23 and Sept. 13, 1671, *Recs. of Plymouth*, V, 76–77. Hubbard and Mather omit mention of Massachusetts's action to nullify the Taunton treaty. They give only the treaty, treating it as a continuously valid instrument that was treacherously violated by Philip.

into signing a substitute for the tacitly rescinded Taunton treaty. As far as Philip was concerned, the new treaty was not an improvement. Its abandonment of the retroactive clause helped him not at all, because the first clause of the new treaty made him and his people subject to New Plymouth from that time forward. The treaty once more denied him power to sell his lands except with Plymouth's permission, and, as usual, it levied a large fine.[36]

A modern scholar, usually strongly favorable to Plymouth, has remarked: "This treaty he [Philip] was supposed to have been 'left to accept or reject, as hee should see cause'; that a free choice in fact was his hardly seems possible. The treaty dictated harsh terms, unacceptably harsh for Philip to have signed freely. Such coercion as may have been used to secure his consent, the Secretary of the General Court, Nathaniel Morton, did not choose to record." A year after Philip's capitulation, the General Court put him in charge of all sales of Indian lands within the colony and made him personally responsible to the Court.[37]

On paper Plymouth's triumph was complete. Philip avoided open defiance, and Swansea continued to grow. But rumor traced Philip in conspiratorical journeys to and fro among the tribes, and in January 1675 a praying Indian named John Sassamon traveled to Governor Winslow's house at Marshfield to say that Philip was preparing for war. Whatever the truth of his information, Sassamon's visit guaranteed war, in a manner he would never know, because Sassamon never got home alive. Someone murdered him as he returned from Marshfield and stuffed his body under pond ice.[38]

That became the official version of Sassamon's death, and it was used as a means to put Philip under suspicion of having contrived the murder. There are reasons for doubt, although John Sassamon was indeed an unlovely character in pagan Indian eyes, and one can well imagine him having become the object of someone's lethal hate. A Massachuset Indian in origin, he had joined the English forces in the Pequot conquest. He became an early assistant to John Eliot at the chief mission town of Natick and was sent to Harvard College for at least one term in 1653 to be prepared for teaching at that town.[39] Eliot soon found a more important use for him with Wampanoag sachem Philip. In Eliot's ineffable prose this was accomplished "upon solicitations and means used." The theory was that Sassamon would teach Philip and his men to read, but later history strongly suggests that the function of teacher took second place to those of political agent and spy. Certainly Philip came to think

36. Sept. 24 and 29, 1671, *Recs. of Plymouth*, V, 78–79.
37. Langdon, *Plymouth Colony*, 161; Sept. 20, 1672, *Recs. of Plymouth*, V, 102.
38. Langdon, *Plymouth Colony*, 162.
39. Morison, *Harvard in the Seventeenth Century*, I, 352–353.

so.[40] After several years as amanuensis to Philip, Sassamon left—in a great hurry. As John Easton heard the story in Rhode Island, Sassamon had written Philip's will at the sachem's request but had included a provision that was not Philip's intent: this was a stipulation that much of Philip's land was to become Sassamon's. Apparently Sassamon counted on Philip's illiteracy to keep the provision secret, but Philip learned of it and Sassamon departed. He returned to John Eliot and once more became a Sunday School teacher.[41]

Sassamon's death in 1675 was at first accounted an accident. Months later Plymouth became suspicious, exhumed Sassamon's body, and became convinced of foul play. Thereupon a praying Indian named Patuckson came forward to announce that he had seen the murder. There is, however, a certain difficulty about his testimony. He named three pagan Indians under Philip's government as the killers, and the inference was immediately drawn in Plymouth that Philip had ordered Sassamon's assassination. Few Indians accepted this theory because, as some of them pointed out, in such a case Philip would have had no reason to conceal his role; it was his right as sachem to order an execution. Instead Philip had rushed to Plymouth to disclaim any responsibility. However that may be, Patuckson seems also to have had a personal motive for naming the particular three Indians that he had denounced; he owed them a gambling debt. As John Easton wrote, "The Indians report that the informer had played away his Coate, and these men sent him that coate, and after demanded pay and he not to pay so accused them, and knoing it wold pleas the English so to think him a better Christian."[42]

The three accused were tried in a precedent-shattering court. As Puritan eulogists never fail to point out, Indians were among the jury. But this is not quite right. It is true that the jury foreman made much of the Indians when the trial concluded: "Wee of the jury," he announced, "one and all, both English and Indians doe joyntly and with

40. Sept. 1656, Pulsifer, ed., *Acts of United Colonies*, II, 167; Eliot to Commissioners of the United Colonies, Aug. 25, 1664, *ibid.*, 383–384. Sassamon's service with Philip is sometimes erroneously interpreted as a reversion to paganism. The notion seems to be based on Hubbard's statement that Sassamon "upon some misdemeanour fled from his place [at Natick] to Philip." Eliot's testimony explodes this assertion and the theory based on it. Hubbard obviously was trying to dissemble the political role of Eliot's mission. Leach, *Flintlock and Tomahawk*, 31; Hubbard, *Narrative*, 14.

41. Easton, "Relacion," in Lincoln, ed., *Narratives of Indian Wars*, 7; Drake, *Biography and History of Indians*, 193.

42. Plymouth's "Brief Narrative of the begining and progresse of the present trouble between us and the Indians," Nov. 1675, Pulsifer, ed., *Acts of United Colonies*, II, 362–363; Easton, "Relacion," in Lincoln, ed., *Narratives of Indian Wars*, 7–8. Pro-Puritan David Bushnell thought that "the tardy appearance of such a witness seems somewhat suspicious." "Indians in Plymouth Colony," *NEQ*, XXVI (1953), 96.

one consent agree upon a verdict." The statement is misleading, however, in its implication that the Indians were voting members of the jury. There were only four Indians, who had been added to the full complement of twelve Englishmen, and their function was not to make a decision, but rather "to healp to consult and advice with, of, and concerning the premises." The Indians' agreement with the verdict was precisely defined and delimited: "These [Indians] fully concurred with the jury in theire verdict." It is clear that the Indians sat *with* the jury, but not *of* it. Why, then, were they there? What had made them worthy to be consulted had little to do with their being "indifferentist, gravest and sage"; nor did it signify softening sentiments among Plymouth's hardheaded leadership. It was because these were praying Indians, as the defendants were not. Although the praying Indians' participation was only advisory, their association with the jury seemed to make them as responsible as the colonials for the jury's finding of guilt, and this praying Indian responsibility was strengthened by the testimony of convert Patuckson, who provided the evidence needed to convict. The whole trial procedure was carefully designed to drive a wedge between Philip's pagans and Plymouth's converts, to make reconciliation between them impossible under any circumstances. This was a show trial staged for political purposes from beginning to end.[43]

At the hanging one of the ropes broke (on purpose?), and the reprieved, horribly scared Indian began to babble. Wampapaquan confessed to everything his executioners desired—or almost everything; in return he got a carefully worded stay of execution that seemed to give him a month more of life. Desperately, however, he maintained that he had been only a bystander as the (already hanged) Tobias and Mattashunnamo had killed Sassamon. And he gratified Plymouth by implicating Philip, or so we are told at secondhand. For some reason, Wampapaquan's precise statements, interesting as they must have been, were not preserved, and he was quickly (and this time efficiently) executed before he could confirm or deny what his tormentors attributed to him.[44]

43. Drake, *Biography and History of Indians*, 196; June 1, 1675, *Recs. of Plymouth*, V, 167–168; Chase, "Notes on the Wampanoag Indians," Smithsonian Institution, *Annual Report* (1883), 883.

44. Leach's account is judicious, informative, and troubled: *Flintlock and Tomahawk*, 33. See also June 1, 1675, *Recs. of Plymouth*, V, 167; Hubbard, *Narrative*, 15–16; I. Mather, *Brief History of War with the Indians*, 2; Langdon, *Plymouth Colony*, 162–163. The texts must be given careful attention. It was common in the 17th century, among Puritans and others, to play gallows tricks on criminals, but neither Hubbard nor Mather gives the revealing information about the broken rope. Both make it appear that Wampapaquan's confession had been made before any of the Indians was executed and thus remove the possibility of inference that Wampapaquan confessed guilt only for persons beyond help. Leach and Langdon note the rope episode, Leach giving far more thought to its

The malicious informing of Sassamon, the self-serving testimony of Patuckson, the tortured outcries of Wampapaquan—none of these would carry much weight under modern due process, but they were quite enough for Plymouth. Whatever may have been Philip's intentions earlier, preparations for war were now clearly in order.

A party of Rhode Island Quakers tried to mediate. Headed by Deputy Governor John Easton, they interviewed Philip and apparently departed with some hope of success. But shortly after their conference they "sudingly had leter from Plimoth Governor thay intended in arms to Conforem [conform, subdue] Philip, but no information what that was thay required or what termes. [The governor] refused to have ther quarrell desided [by arbitration]; and in a weckes time after we had bine with the Indians the war thus begun."[45]

No modern account has improved on Easton's, and a good many have only smothered his information. Let him tell the rest of the story in his own words.

Plimoth soldiers were Cum to have ther head quarters within 10 miles of Philip; then most of the English therabout left ther houses and we had leter from Plimoth governor to desier our help with sum boats if thay had such ocation, and for us to looke to our selfs; and from the genarall at the quarters we had leter of the day thay intended to Cum upon the indians, and desier for sum of our boats to atend. So we tooke it to be of nesesety for our Ieslanders [Aquidneck Island] one halef one day and night to atend and the other halef the next, so by turens for our oune safty. In this time sum indians fell a pilfering sum houses that the English had left, and a old man and a lad going to one of those houses did see 3 indians run out therof. The old man bid the young man shoote; so he did, and a indian fell doune but got away againe. It is reported that then sum indians Came to the gareson, asked why thay shot the indian. Thay asked whether he was dead. The indians saide yea. A English lad saied it was no mater. The men indevered to inforem them it was but an idell lad's words, but the indians in hast went away and did not harken to them. The next day, the lad that shot the indian and his father and fief [five] English more wear killed. So the war begun with Philip.[46]

---

implications. Leach hangs Wampapaquan finally. Langdon shoots him, but "a month later." The records say, "Wampapaquan, on some considerations, was reprieved until a month be expired from this present date; But afterwards shott to death *within* the said month" (my emphasis). Hubbard says that the Indian confessed "immediately before his death," which means, I think, that he was shot immediately after he talked.

45. Easton, "Relacion," in Lincoln, ed., *Narratives of Indian Wars*, 8-12.
46. *Ibid.*, 12.

Chapter 17 ❧ OUTRAGE BLOODY and BARBAROUS

> *The war then begun has been misnamed King Philip's War; it was, in fact, the Second Puritan Conquest.* The standard way to characterize this famous event has been to call it a racial showdown. This, too, is wrong. Far from having any unity of contestants, this explosion resembled on a smaller scale and in a shorter span the Thirty Years' War in Europe. It became a congeries of conflicts of which the resistance led by Wampanoag sachem Philip was only one. Different Europeans pursued different interests and fought different conflicts, and so did different Indians. The contestants themselves showed scant evidence of racial objectives as such. Such views were imposed on the phenomena later. As Douglas Edward Leach presents them, "A few intelligent men who lived through King Philip's War, and who later pondered its causes, its development, its outcome, and its effects, sensed the historical significance of that great conflict. *They* realized that the two races had fought a war of extermination."[1]

These few intelligent men were Puritans all, and they were not the only contemporaries to evaluate the war. The colonists of Martha's Vineyard, Rhode Island, and New York held rather different views.

The few intelligent racists' problem was to put a good face on a war of intended conquest by the Puritans that was met with desperate resistance by the Indians. That they concocted elaborate rationalizations to present Puritan aggression as anticipatory defense—to borrow a phrase from the twentieth century—is not strange. Puritans had long known the power of propaganda presented as history. In their scheme of predestination, invention was the mother of necessity. Roger Williams had made the wryly proper assessment of a Puritan justification for aggressive war: "All men of conscience or prudence ply to windward, to maintain their wars to be defensive."[2]

1. Leach, *Flintlock and Tomahawk*, 250 (my emphasis). It will become evident that I owe a debt to Leach's scholarship, though I differ sharply from him in interpretation, and I here acknowledge it explicitly.
2. Williams to Massachusetts General Court, Oct. 5, 1654, Bartlett, ed., *Letters of Williams*, Narragansett Club, *Pubs.*, VI, 271.

Massachusetts's conduct of its attempted second conquest was colossally inept. Disaster after disaster made the magistrates fearful of meeting the same fate as had afflicted the Virginia Company after the Indian uprising of 1622. Virginia had lost its charter then because of the mismanagement disclosed by the shock of war.[3] English colonial statesmen were supposed to know how to handle ignorant wild men. Philip's resistance in 1675 showed plainly enough that the leaders of orthodox New England had lost the knack. Although Plymouth had begun the war, the United Colonies adopted it, and Massachusetts was the great power of that Puritan confederation. Anglicans and royalists gleefully denounced Puritan incompetence, the crown took steps to seize the opportunity, and Massachusetts began a political battle to save its charter.

The old propaganda appeal for Puritan unity against the heathen had been weakened by widespread English disturbance over New England's turmoils, even among English Presbyterians and Independents. A new sort of appeal was needed to touch the emotions of friendly Calvinists as well as hostile Anglicans. It was found in the fear and hatred of alien races as such. In New York and Pennsylvania the word *heathen* continued to be used to identify Indians for half a century to come. Among the New Englanders, however, as among Virginians after 1622, *savage* became the hate-stamped coin in common use.

To say that the war was not one of racial survival or racial extermination is not to say that individual episodes of the conflict lacked the quality of total war. There was carnage and atrocity to surfeit, committed by both sides, but neither the English general populace (apart from its bellicose rulers) nor the Indians in general entered willingly upon the war. Showing no consciousness whatever that racial survival was at stake, militiamen of Massachusetts and Plymouth energetically dodged impressment. To create an adequate military force the authorities had to resort to employment of piratical mercenaries, threats of punishment, and promises of plunder.[4]

On the Indian side the record is quite clear about the bulk of involvement; in spite of the standard rumoring of conspiracies (never supported by substantial evidence), the first mobilizations and the first attacks were made by the Puritans. In spite of intense pressures, a segment of the Niantic-Narragansetts under sachem Ninigret managed to stay neutral throughout the war—a position made possible by the Rhode Islanders' matching desire to stay out of it. Confounding the theory of racial showdown is the fact that some Indians—the Mohegans under Uncas and the convinced converts of Eliot and Mayhew—became indispensable

3. See chap. 5 above.

4. Leach, *Flintlock and Tomahawk*, 94, 123, 137–138, 169, 184–187; Apr. 27, 1676, *Recs. of Conn.*, II, 438; and see n. 39 below.

auxiliaries of Puritan troops, without whom the colonial soldiers refused to march; and the Mohawks under New York's direction assured English victory by striking the decisive blow of the war.

As for the goals of the combatants, the Indians never for a moment aspired to drive out all the English or hoped for mastery over them. Their purpose was to salvage some measure of self-government in secure territory. Nor did any of the colonists worry about being driven into the sea. Even the fervid imagination of the Reverend William Hubbard could conceive only that the "inland plantations," i.e., the isolated backwoods settlements, might have been wholly destroyed, as indeed many of them were.[5] In actuality, the evidence of disunity among the Puritan leadership is overwhelming; massacres and slaughters were for specific ends to serve the interests of specific colonies. Racial bombast has served only too well to disguise the issues that divided even orthodox Connecticut from orthodox Massachusetts, let alone heterodox Rhode Island from both.

As in the Puritan conquest of the Pequots, more historical attention has been given to Massachusetts than to Connecticut, yet much of the war's proceedings cannot be understood without detailed investigation into Connecticut's distinct aims and methods. For present purposes two issues are especially relevant: the long struggle over the Narragansett country and, somewhat surprisingly, a territorial claim of New York. These two became interlinked because of Connecticut's interest in both and because of the mutual interests—it is too strong to say coalition—of Connecticut's opponents. The connection was established immediately upon the outbreak of war, and it governed all of Connecticut's strategy throughout. For essential background we must leave the scene of the war for a moment to take account of New York's connection.

The year 1675 was a critical turning point in the history of the English colonies and their nearby Indians. In the region of the Chesapeake and Delaware bays, outbreaks of violence coincided so closely with the Indian rebellion in New England that English statesmen momentarily feared confederation of all the tribes in a general uprising against all the English. That their fears were not realized is due in some measure to the intelligence and energy of a man who has been freighted with odium by passionately hostile New England historians, but who has never been charged with hesitancy or vacillation.

Edmund Andros was appointed by the duke of York to govern the duke's colony of New York after the second conquest of New Netherland in 1674. His instructions guaranteed that he would instantly become embroiled in conflict with the Puritan colonies of New England over boundary claims in a way that his predecessors had avoided.[6] The claims had existed dormantly ever since the first English conquest of New Netherland in 1664. At that time the duke of York had assumed as his own not only New Netherland's occupied territories but also its territorial claims as well; and he had added claim upon claim by purchasing an old royal grant from the earl of Stirling.[7] Combined, the Dutch claims and the Stirling grant gave theoretical title to a vast territory completely surrounding New England and sharply conflicting with the counterclaims of Connecticut and Massachusetts. The first two governors of New York had not seriously pressed the duke's claims against the Puritan colonies; indeed they had been hoodwinked by Governor John Winthrop, Jr., of Connecticut, into permitting Connecticut to expand at the expense of New York.[8] But when Edmund Andros came in 1674 to take over the administration of New York, he brought the duke of York's instructions to seize effectively all the duke's theoretical claims, and Andros was loyal, intelligent, and bluntly aggressive. (He was also Anglican and authoritarian.)

In modern terms York claimed jurisdiction over Delaware, Pennsylvania, New Jersey, New York, the strip of Connecticut between New York and the Connecticut River, Vermont, New Hampshire, Maine, Nantucket, Martha's Vineyard, and Long Island, but to list these precisely bounded modern units is to create a somewhat misleading impression. In the seventeenth century only the rivers and coasts made sharp boundaries. York was intent on pushing his claims as far as he could make them stretch, and Andros began immediately to establish practical jurisdiction wherever he could muster sufficient power.[9] His first adversary was Connecticut.

When three Long Island towns notified Andros that they were under Connecticut's jurisdiction, he marched a company of troops to "disabuse" them of their idea. Thereafter Long Island remained securely part of New York.[10] Andros then took the strategic offensive against Connecticut. On May 1, 1675, he dispatched a letter to Governor Winthrop and the General Court of Connecticut requesting the delivery into his jurisdiction of all lands within the duke of York's patent, by

6. Andros's commission, July 1, 1674, *N.Y. Col. Docs.*, III, 215.

7. Andrews, *Colonial Period*, III, 58n.

8. Black, *Younger John Winthrop*, 279–282; Dunn, *Puritans and Yankees*, 174–175, and his "John Winthrop, Jr., Connecticut Expansionist: The Failure of His Designs on Long Island, 1663–1675," *NEQ*, XXIX (1956), 3–20.

9. See the "Instructions for Capt. Salisbury," July 2, 1675, N.Y. Col. MSS, Misc. Records, Box 3, 116, N.Y. State Lib., Albany.

10. Dunn, "Connecticut Expansionist," *NEQ*, XXIX (1956), 19–22.

which he meant all the mainland west of the Connecticut River. Compliance would have cost Connecticut half its territory and almost all its towns (see map 4, following). Not strangely, the Connecticut General Court refused to commit suicide, and a wrangle began. It was stiffly polite until a messenger waked Andros at three o'clock in the morning of July 4, 1675, with Connecticut's excited notice of the outbreak of Philip's Indian rebellion.[11]

Regrettably it appears that both Andros and the leaders of Connecticut viewed the war at first in terms of opportunity. In their letter to Andros, Winthrop and his General Court anticipated hostilities with the Narragansett Indians. It would seem that Connecticut had more reason to want such hostilities than to fear them, for the Narragansett country was still very much coveted by Connecticut. With this in the background, the letter to Andros told him explicitly, and falsely, that "the Indyans being in Armes in Plimouth Colony" had killed Englishmen "as neare as Narragansett." At least, that is what Andros recorded as the letter's message. Unaccountably the file copy of the letter itself has disappeared from Connecticut's voluminous archives, and the original in Andros's possession probably burned up in a fire at Albany. Its mutilated enclosures survive to say only that murders had been committed "by Phillip." Burned as they are, the enclosures evidence that Connecticut's assertion of the Narragansetts as belligerents was not a mistake but rather a fabrication to serve policy. One of these documents is a letter from Governor Winthrop's son, Major Wait Winthrop, who had rushed off, before Philip struck a blow, to join Roger Williams at Narragansett Bay. Wait saw nothing of Narragansett hostilities, and the remains of his report say nothing of them. The minutes of Connecticut's council say only that the council had received word of Indian outrages "in Plimouth Pattent." But the message then forwarded by the council to New Haven and other towns (probably in the same phrasing used to Andros) stated that council had been informed of warring Indians "in Plimoth and in the Narragancett Country."[12]

What was the actual situation? Philip's men killed colonists for the first time at Swansea in Plymouth Colony on June 24, 1675. News of this arrived on the morning of June 25 at Wickford, Richard Smith's house on the west shore of Narragansett Bay. Roger Williams and commissioners from Boston were already there and were joined by Wait Winthrop that same morning. They all met with the Narragansett sachems on the same day. In Williams's words, the sachems "professed to hold

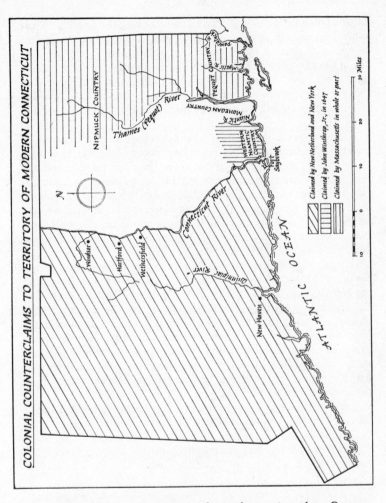

MAP 4. *Colonial counterclaims to the territory of modern Connecticut. (Drawn by Richard J. Stinely, Williamsburg, Va., from a sketch by the author; base map from the Department of Transportation, State of Connecticut, Wethersfield.)*

no agreement with Philip, in this his rising against the English." Their
overriding concern at the time was a "great and vehement desire" to
avenge themselves on the Mohegans for a new murder committed on
one of their people by Uncas's son.[13] The most partisan of propagandists
has admitted that "the good Hand of God was seen in so ordering Things
that the Narhagansets were for the Present restrained from breaking
out into open Hostility against the English at that Time when Philip
began."[14]

This was not enough for the Puritans. Although they professed to be
merely attempting to keep the Narragansetts out of the war, what they
aimed at was the subjugation of that tribe. The chief real issue, so far as
the Puritans were concerned, was whether Massachusetts or Connecticut should take the Narragansett prize; Plymouth was content with the
Wampanoags. On June 21 Plymouth's Governor Josiah Winslow had
offered a deal to Massachusetts. If Boston would let Plymouth have
"fair play" with the Wampanoags, Plymouth would recognize Massachusetts's jurisdiction over the Narragansetts.[15]

Whether Connecticut knew of this arrangement does not appear in
the records. It is clear, however, that Connecticut moved swiftly to win
the Narragansett country for itself. When Wait Winthrop's report of
the opening of hostilities reached Hartford, the Connecticut council
immediately took two steps: besides falsely locating hostilities in the
Narragansett country, the council on the same date, July 1, ordered
troops to march in that direction. The troops were not sent to attack
Philip, who had almost become the forgotten man of the time, or to defend Plymouth. They were sent to Connecticut's border with the Narragansetts, more than fifty miles distant from Swansea.[16]

A race began. Boston gave new instructions to its officers. As Douglas
Edward Leach writes, Massachusetts decided to "force the issue" with
the Narragansetts, and the issue was "an abject surrender."[17] Although
Philip's Wampanoags had escaped from their bottled-up "neck" and
were roaming at will through Plymouth Colony, Massachusetts's troops

13. Bartlett, ed., *Letters of Williams*, Narragansett Club, *Pubs.*, VI, 366–372.

14. Hubbard, *Narrative*, 29.

15. Leach, *Flintlock and Tomahawk*, 37; Richard LeBaron Bowen, *Early Rehoboth: Documented Historical Studies of Families and Events in This Plymouth
Colony Township* (Rehoboth, Mass., 1946), III, 53. Winslow's quid pro quo was
offered with the indirection common to such procedures. He simply supposed the
Narragansetts to be under Massachusetts's jurisdiction. Since nobody else made
such a supposition, the gentlemen in Boston would know how to read him. At
this stage Winslow seems not to have communicated with Connecticut, which
had a very active claim to jurisdiction over the Narragansetts. Connecticut's intervention was on its own initiative.

16. July 1, 1675, *Recs. of Conn.*, II, 331–332.

17. Leach, *Flintlock and Tomahawk*, 57, 58.

departed from Swansea on July 5 to cross into Rhode Island. On July 7 Roger Williams wrote to tell Wait Winthrop that a hundred "privateers" had arrived with Boston's officers at Wickford and were trying to get the Narragansett sachems to a meeting.[18] Winthrop and Connecticut's troops came galloping in two days later.[19]

He and Massachusetts's Captain Hutchinson promptly quarreled over the proper approach to be made to the Indians. Hutchinson was for immediate confrontation; Wait Winthrop counseled delay.[20] The reason for their difference seems to be that Massachusetts was at that moment in the superior position, having arrived earlier on the scene and with a larger force.

Neither party was troubled by its total lack of legality in bringing an army into the territory of Rhode Island unasked and unwanted, and neither intended to let the government of Rhode Island have anything to say. Four witnesses heard a local magistrate protest that "the Indians had given no cause of warre" and that the troops' "coming here Did more hurt than good." Their proper business was to hunt Philip, he added, and they would not find him in Rhode Island if they continued there "this seven year." That magistrate succeeded only in irritating the commanders of the invasion, who arrested him because of his "Mutinous and scurrilous and abusive Carriages towards the Massachuset and Connecticute Government." Connecticut's council ordered him jailed for "retarding and delaying their procedure."[21] Lacking an armed force, Rhode Island's government stood helplessly by. Its leaders knew that the reason for "contention against these Indians" was to invalidate "the king's Determination for Naraganset to be in our Colony."[22] Other forces were gathering, however, that compelled the invaders to improvise hastily and depart without accomplishment. They professed to have made a treaty because they bore away a sheet of paper with some Indian signatures on it, but it could not be a valid instrument under either English or Indian legal sanctions. The reasons for their departure will be described in a moment, after an examination of this so-called treaty.[23]

First, the treaty was imposed under the most extreme and obvious

18. *Ibid.* Williams to Wait Winthrop, July 7, 1675, R.-I. Hist. Soc., *Pubs.*, VIII (1900), 154–155.

19. Leach, *Flintlock and Tomahawk*, 58.

20. *Ibid.*, 59. For the official records, Connecticut's troops had been sent "to Stoneington and New London [both within the colony] to ayd and secure the good people of those townes against the Indians." Winthrop's behavior shows that he had another understanding of his assignment. *Recs. of Conn.*, II, 332, 338n.

21. Testimony and order about Mr. Gold, July 14, 1675, Bates, ed., *Wyllys Papers* (Conn. Hist. Soc., *Colls.*, XXI).

22. Easton, "Relacion," in Lincoln, ed., *Narratives of Indian Wars*, 16–17; Coddington to Andros, July 21, 1675, N.Y. Col. MSS, XXIV, 128.

23. Text in Hubbard, *Narrative*, 21–23.

duress. Second, it was signed, not by Narragansett sachems, but by four subordinate "councellors" of the Narragansetts, who had no authority to act for their people. Besides these fully disqualifying elements there was a third, equally as strong. The Narragansetts were subjects of the crown, protected in their tenure and jurisdiction by royal proclamation, and under the administration of that very government of Rhode Island that was not permitted to participate in the treaty. Recognizing all this, Leach has called the treaty "a waste of time,"[24] and so it would have been if the purpose behind it had genuinely been the preservation of the peace, but there was more.

Ostensibly the treaty was concerned with the Wampanoag war. It obligated the Narragansetts to regard Philip's Wampanoags as enemies and to deny them sanctuary. This provision in itself was especially hypocritical and heartless. Plymouth had already authorized the Narragansetts to receive certain refugee Wampanoags who wanted to remain neutral, but after the "treaty" Plymouth took a different tack; bands who surrendered then, because they had no place to go and did not want to fight, were seized and sold—men, women, and children—into slavery in the West Indies.[25] The "treaty" also promised bounties to the Narragansetts if they would bring in the heads of Wampanoag warriors, and in view of later developments we should notice that the Narragansetts actually did deliver some heads and claim their bounties.[26]

There was, however, another provision, totally unrelated to the war or the prospect of Narragansett-Wampanoag alliance, and it betrays the purpose of the brutal charade. By it the Indians supposedly confirmed *all* previous grants of land to the English—any English—an impossibility in view of the multitude of English claims in direct conflict with one another, and an impossibility that the knowledgeable gentlemen who wrote the provision understood very well. But those gentlemen did not really mean *any* English. They meant the Atherton Company of mixed Massachusetts and Connecticut partners under the patronage of Connecticut's Governor John Winthrop, Jr. The treaty did not spell out its detailed implications in any such crude fashion. It innocently avoided particulars and held to large universal principle, but the Atherton Company fitted snugly into its specifications. The Atherton grant had been made to Englishmen; true, it had been denounced as fraud and invalidated by royal commissioners, but it had been made, and the treaty made no distinctions between validity and

24. Leach, *Flintlock and Tomahawk*, 60–61.

25. Easton, "Relacion," in Lincoln, ed., *Narratives of Indian Wars*, 12–13; Aug. 4 and Sept. 2, 1675, *Recs. of Plymouth*, V, 173, 174. Regarding captives, see also John Winthrop, Jr., to Fitz-John Winthrop, July 9, 1675, Mass. Hist. Soc., *Colls.*, 5th Ser., VIII (Boston, 1882), 170–171.

26. Leach, *Flintlock and Tomahawk*, 113.

invalidity of grants—they were all confirmed. Thus, by a judicious mixture of largesse and threat to lesser claimants, the Atherton Company could pick up all the rest.

This was not especially subtle, and Rhode Island's Governor William Coddington grasped it at once. A former magistrate of Massachusetts (and former Puritan), Coddington had no illusions about the honor of the oligarchs. The invaders' purpose, he wrote, had been "to bring the Indians there to their owne termes, and to call that part of Roade Island theirs." He justified the Narragansetts' defensive posture against the Puritan armies. In stark contrast with the standard Puritan vituperation, Coddington followed the examples of other Rhode Islanders to present the Indians as reasonable, trustworthy people: "Wee doubt not but wee could have prevailed to have brought the Indyans to greater conformity than they have done by their Armes."[27]

Why, then, had the invaders rushed off so precipitately? Why had they not waited at least until they could force the signature of a sachem to their crude pretense? Why were they satisfied with this flimsy unenforceable document, reduced at the last to a mere pretext for argument before some royal agency, when what they really wanted was the kind of control over the Narragansetts and their territory that could only be achieved through a period of occupation? There were two answers to these questions, named respectively Andros and Philip. Andros threw a scare into Connecticut, and Philip struck so bloodily at Massachusetts that he could no longer be ignored.

While Massachusetts and Connecticut had been mobilizing force to seize the Narragansett country, Andros and New York's council had aimed at seizing western Connecticut. On July 4 Andros's council resolved that he should take troops "to protect that part" of the duke of York's "government," thoughtfully adding, "as there may be Opportunity"; and Andros sent notice of his benevolent intentions to Governor Winthrop in Hartford. It was a serious tactical error. Perhaps Andros had thought he could lull Winthrop with talk of assistance, but Winthrop was an old hand at that game. When Andros's notice arrived in Hartford on July 7, the Connecticut council understood at once that they were to be protected right into the jurisdiction of New York. They promptly discovered "a generall conspiracy of the heathen against the English," a revelation that vividly illuminates the uses of heathen conspiracies. Troops were immediately dispatched to Fort Saybrook at the mouth of the Connecticut River, about as far away from the heathen multitudes as was possible to get, but a convenient place to block passage of ships from New York. They arrived a little late, but the local trainband had the situation under control. Andros had sailed in

27. Coddington to Andros, July 21, 1675, N.Y. Col. MSS, XXIV, 128.

on July 8 and demanded capitulation and received armed defiance. When the Hartford troops showed up in their pursuit of heathen conspirators, Andros gave up. In the face of his opponents' numbers and determination, he risked no more than a ceremonial gesture of claim and withdrew. Governor Winthrop sent after him a message suggesting that he should go to relieve the people who were really in danger from the Indians—the people of Plymouth—"for there is the seat of the warr." It was a curious message, considering where Wait Winthrop was.[28]

Andros's politic withdrawal had not been a foregone conclusion to the episode. As the contest of nerves continued, John Winthrop, Jr., thought wistfully of the possible reinforcements that were then off in Rhode Island. He did not panic—such was not the Winthrop way—but he put some urgency into his suggestion that the business there be finished off. In the light of Connecticut's whole history of Indian relations, his letter to Major Thomas Savage made such astonishing admissions that it is worth quotation at length.

The Nahigansetts have hitherto continued in amity with the English, and were voluntarily very helpfull to them in those warrs with the Pequots.... Please to consider whether it be not far better to take up with such ingagements of amity as can be attained freely and willingly, then that the potentest of all our neighboring heathen should be made open, professed enemies because we may have suspicion of them or cannot be so confident or certaine of their continued fidelity:... nor doth it appeare of much consequence to be too strict in inquiry about persons fled to them from Philip, whether old men or soldiers, much lesse women and children (if fled its better then with Philip).... I beleive there is difficulty ynough with that one enemy, and why to stir up an other before an issue with the first.[29]

So much good sense could necessity impart even to a veteran expansionist. The "treaty," as we have seen, did not follow Winthrop's suggestions, very likely in part because the time had passed when "ingagements of amity" could be attained "freely and willingly." The officers in the field took what they could get and returned to bolster Connecticut's defense against the menace of Andros.

So much explains Connecticut's withdrawal from Rhode Island. The explanation for Massachusetts's retreat is simpler. Boston's troops could afford to stay with the Narragansetts only as long as Philip hid and ran from English terror, in keeping with all the old traditions of Indian conflict in New England. But Philip's warriors now put into practice the guerrilla strategy that the Pequots had only proposed in a bygone time. An astounded New England discovered an Indian Menace in

28. N.Y. Council Minutes, MSS, July 4, 1675, III, Pt. ii, 41; *Recs. of Conn.*, II, 579, 333, 334; Dunn, *Puritans and Yankees*, 183–184.
29. John Winthrop, Jr., to Major Savage and other officers, July 12, 1675, Mass. Hist. Soc., *Colls.*, 5th Ser., VIII, 173.

bloody reality—a peasants' war that broke out in sudden flame here, there, and no one knew where next. From Plymouth's Taunton, Rehoboth, Middleborough, and Dartmouth came news of unprecedented and destructive Indian raids, and on July 14 the Nipmucks rose against Massachusetts's town of Mendon, forty miles distant from the troops in Rhode Island who could have defended the place.[30] The hypothetical menace of the Narragansetts was set aside for future attention, the "treaty" with their "councellors" was slapped together, and the troops went off to pursue the real menace of Philip—at last.

The Narragansetts were reprieved for a few months, but they still could not face the grim reality of their predicament. Instead of realizing that their only chance of survival lay in joining Philip at once, they succumbed to their genuine desire to stay clear of the slaughter. Instead of striking their persecutors at advantage, they repeated the Pequots' strategic error and withdrew to a hidden stockade in the fastness of an almost impassable swamp, where they deluded themselves into thinking they could wait out the storm.

Philip's first real allies, as distinct from the conspiratorial multitudes of inspired rumor, came from a startlingly unexpected source—John Eliot's mission towns among the Nipmucks. If more proof is needed that Eliot's proselytizing had been forcible and resented, the rising of the Nipmuck "converts" should be evidence enough.[31]

Present purposes preclude a detailed reporting of the raids and the colonists' countermeasures of that cruel year. It is enough to remark here that the depredations of the Indians on the warpath, bloody as they were, never distracted the Puritan gentry from their concern with the Indians hiding in the swamp. No consideration of morality, gratitude, or humanity deterred these statesmen. Their decisive attack was held up only by policy disagreement among themselves. Connecticut stalled. In the light of proceedings to be described below, Connecticut's declared reasons may be disregarded now as readily as they were dismissed by the other belligerent colonies. The real reason for Connecticut's procrastination was probably fear that Andros would suddenly appear again if the colony's armed forces were committed to a campaign as far off as the Narragansett country. During that tense period Connecticut's soldiers were standing guard against the English enemy as well as the Indian. The allies became impatient. When the resuscitated United Colonies of New England met at Boston on November 2, John Winthrop, Jr., was pressed for decision. He put off,

---

30. Hubbard, *Narrative*, 31.

31. The attack on Massachusetts's Mendon was led by Nipmuck sachem Matoonas, who was constable of the mission town of Pakachoog. Drake, *Biography and History of Indians*, 263–264.

equivocated, and excused in his most expert manner. Boston and Plymouth protested that he was in "absolute violation of the maine ends of the Articles of Confederation,"[32] but Winthrop could not be moved until Connecticut's interests dictated movement. But when a particular message came to him from Hartford, it carried more weight than all the pleadings of his allies, and Winthrop abruptly cast his vote for a blitzkrieg against the Narragansetts.

Once more it becomes necessary to look abroad for a source of motivation. An aggressive and voluble Rhode Islander named William Harris had gained the crown's attention in distant England. Harris complained of disturbances in his possessions, how truthfully is not immediately germane.[33] What is relevant here is his success at court. On August 4, 1675, the crown sent orders to the governors of the New England colonies, commanding them to assemble their representatives to hear Harris's case, "and of your proceedings herein to send Us an account, with all convenient speede." Unlike proceedings before the United Colonies, this one would include Coddington's Rhode Island, and no one could doubt how Rhode Islanders would advantage themselves of such an opportunity to appeal for direct royal intervention. Connecticut's council met on November 2 to consider the royal command "to hear and determine Mr. Harriss his business." Putting the king's letter on file, the council interpreted it for the minutes as having additionally instructed them "to labour to keep off a war with the Narrogancetts." From what happened next, we can infer that the council believed the best way to keep off a "war" would be to destroy the Narragansetts in a peace action. They sent Wait Winthrop to inform his father in Boston, and father and son immediately subscribed Connecticut's cooperation against the Narragansetts.[34]

No sudden violence had been perpetrated by the Narragansetts. Although the United Colonies fulminated that those Indians were "deeply accessory in the present bloody outrages of the Barbarous Natives," its bill of particulars was a flimsy and feeble justification for neglecting a swarm of furious enemies to attack the only peaceful tribe in sight.[35] Naturally the pretense was once more made that the Puritan army had no intention other than to enforce the "actuall performance of theire Covenants," and the fraudulent "treaty" of July 15 was dragged out to serve as the particular "covenant" at issue; but, as Douglas Edward Leach has observed, hostilities began without any further effort at

32. Nov. 5, 1675, Pulsifer, ed., *Acts of United Colonies*, II, 456.

33. Roger Williams testified against Harris, Oct. 18, 1677. Bartlett, ed., *Letters of Williams*, Narragansett Club, *Pubs.*, VI, 387–394.

34. *Recs. of Conn.*, II, 380.

35. Resolution backdated to Nov. 2, 1675, Pulsifer, ed., *Acts of United Colonies*, II, 357.

negotiation. "Indeed," he adds, "the stated purpose of the expedition seems to have dissolved in the general urge to smash the potential foe as quickly as possible."[36] Indeed, indeed.

Rhode Island was notified to expect invasion again in December.[37] Under menace the Rhode Islanders provided water transport for the troops, the advance party of which consisted largely of a company of mercenaries fresh from buccaneering in the West Indies, but Rhode Island drew the line at contributing soldiers of its own.[38] The buccaneers, under Captain John Moseley, had been hired by Massachusetts on their stipulation that they were "not to be bound up in ... marches or executions to particular places," but rather to have full discretion for "destroying the ennemy," and that they were to divide all plunder and captives as their own property.[39] With such large sanction, they did what intelligent buccaneers could be expected to do; wasting no time in parley or palaver, they killed and captured sixty Narragansetts who had been too unwary to flee. After that, naturally enough, there were reprisals from the Indians, and then the hapless Rhode Islanders had to huddle behind the force of their "friends" from the other colonies.[40] Until this moment Rhode Island had been at peace, with colonists and Indians alike going unarmed about their daily business. Venerable

36. Leach, *Flintlock and Tomahawk*, 126. Hubbard justified this sudden decision on the grounds that the Narragansetts had broken "the late League"—the treaty of July 15—"they had all along from the first day when it was confirmed, broken every Article of it, specially in not delivering up the enemies which had sheltered themselves with them all this while." *Narrative*, 48. Unlike Hubbard's usual slanting technique, this statement was a frontal assault on the truth. Within three weeks after the treaty's date, Narragansett sachem Pessicus (Sucqunch) delivered to Richard Smith's house (where all the parleying had been done) the heads of seven of Philip's followers. He delivered also (alive) the Wampanoag "squaw sachem" of Pocasset and a hundred men, women, and children of her followers. On hearing of this the Connecticut council sent word of how well the deed was liked by all the English, and it praised Pessicus for his "good endeavours, and actions against the enemy." He had maintained amity, the council declared, and done good service "according to his professings." The council got its information by letter from Richard Smith, so there can be no question of error. Council to Richard Smith, Aug. 8, 1675, in *Hoadly Memorial*, Conn. Hist. Soc., *Colls.*, XXIV (Hartford, Conn., 1932), 18. This document seems to have been overlooked by students. It requires reinvestigation of the biography of Weetamoo, the "squaw sachem" involved.

37. Pulsifer, ed., *Acts of United Colonies*, II, 457–458.

38. Coddington to Andros, Jan. 19, 1676, N.Y. Col. MSS, XXV, 67.

39. George Madison Bodge, *Soldiers in King Philip's War ...*, 3d ed. (Boston, 1906), chap. 2; Williams to Wait Winthrop, July 7, 1675, R.-I. Hist. Soc., *Pubs.*, VIII (1900), 154–155; I. Mather, *Brief History of the War*, 4; Hutchinson, *History of Mass.*, ed. Mayo, I, 287; May 5, 1676, *Recs. of Mass.*, V, 94–96. It is apparent that the agreement with Moseley preceded the formal date on the document printed in *Recs. of Mass.*

40. Dudley to Leverett, Dec. 15, 1675, in Bodge, *Soldiers in King Philip's War*, 192.

Samuel Gorton had stirred himself in Shawomet neck (now Warwick town) to caution his old adversary John Winthrop, Jr., and his disregarded warning is worth recall: "I remember the time of the warres in Ireland (when I was young, in Queen Elizabeths dayes of famous memory) where much English blood was spilt by a people much like unto these [Indians] ... where many valiant souldiers lost their lives, both horse and foot, by means of woods, bushes, boggs, and quagmires. ... And after these Irish were subdued by force, what treacherous and bloody massacres have they attempted is well knowne."[41] But Gorton is crazy in our histories, and Winthrop is humane.

When the main force of the invaders arrived in Rhode Island, they followed a renegade Indian into the swamp where the Narragansetts' refuge lay hidden, and there on December 19 they committed a massacre.[42] Once more, as in the attack on the Pequots' Mystic fort, the place was set on fire, and once more the noncombatants made up the great bulk of Indian casualties; but this time the English also suffered heavy losses.[43] Most of the Narragansett warriors escaped, enraged, to join the Wampanoags and Nipmucks. Philip's men, showing little consciousness of the conspiratorial relationship purported to exist, fired on the Narragansetts![44] But when the newcomers could explain, they were received with rejoicing. They had arrived just in time to revive drooping spirits. "All faltering and hesitation," writes George Madison Bodge, now turned into "willing and eager adherence."[45] In the most literal sense, the torch was kindled once more, and New England burned.

41. Gorton to Winthrop, Sept. 11, 1675, "Winthrop Papers," Mass. Hist. Soc., Colls., 4th Ser., VII (1865), 629–630. The whole letter (627–631) is interesting and informative.

42. See Welcome Arnold Greene, "The Great Battle of the Narragansetts. Dec. 19, 1675," Narragansett Historical Register, V (1886–1887), 331–343.

43. According to an Englishman who had been with the Narragansetts as a captive in their fort, the Indian casualties were 97 slain and 48 wounded "beside what slaughter was made in the houses and by the burning of the houses." The quoted phrase is apparently the interrogator's (Roger Williams's) delicate way of referring to women and children. As the usual figure mentioned for total casualties at the Narragansett fort is 1,000, the dimension of massacre is easy to see. This figure may easily be excessive, but even if it is scaled down to the lowest estimate reported, of 300 noncombatant casualties, it still makes clear that the English aimed at repeating the successful massacre strategy of the Pequot conquest. The English attackers lost 20 or more dead and about 200 wounded. Williams to Leverett, Jan. 14, 1676, Bartlett, ed., Letters of Williams, Narragansett Club, Pubs., VI, 381; Leach, Flintlock and Tomahawk, 130–133. The Williams letter is a neglected source containing much detail.

44. Drake, Biography and History of Indians, 272–273.

45. Bodge, Soldiers in King Philip's War, 379.

Chapter 18 ᴇ᭬ DEAD END

Philip had not been present to greet the Nar-
ragansett reinforcements. He had so far lost hope of winning the Narragansetts to his aid that while the Puritan forces were mobilizing to
march into Rhode Island he headed in the opposite direction. In
December 1675 Philip and a band of his warriors arrived among the
Mahicans north of Albany, New York, where he excited sympathy and
won recruits. It is likely that he found survivors there, or their descendants, of earlier Puritan massacres during the Pequot conquest.

On January 5, 1676, Governor Andros received word of Philip's
whereabouts and promptly forwarded the information to Connecticut's
Deputy Governor William Leete.[1] (We shall hear no more of John
Winthrop, Jr., who was ailing in Boston and soon to die.) Connecticut's
council responded by urging Andros to send the Mohawks to attack
Philip. "Upon your Honors order," they remarked, the Mohawks might
"with much facility uterly extirpate this bloody generation . . . and soe
the Mohawks will have an opportunity to gratify the English of New
England." Andros professed astonishment. Connecticut had "refused
and slighted" his previous effort at "assistance"—a euphemism for the
frustration of his effort to seize its towns—and he could not see why
he should incur "an extraordinary great charge . . . for bringing heathens
assistance in any part of your Colony."[2]

Nevertheless Andros continued to keep a worried watch on Philip.
Regardless of Connecticut's desires or interests, Philip's activities among
the Hudson Valley Indians might readily create a hazard to New York,
and Andros feared above all other possibilities that a general leaguing

1. Andros to Leete, Jan. 6, 1676, *Recs. of Conn.*, II, 397. On the basis of later
information, Andros stated that Philip and 1,000 men had gone near Albany "in
November and December"; i.e., at exactly the time that Philip was asserted by
the Commissioners of the United Colonies to be "coming in with his forces to
the Narragansetts, makeing one body with them." Andros, "A short account of
the generall concerns of New Yorke from October 1674 to November 1677," in
N.Y. Col. Docs., III, 255; Commissioners to Plymouth, Dec. 25, 1675, *Recs. of
Plymouth*, V, 184; A. J. F. van Laer, trans. and ed., *Minutes of the Court of Albany, Rensselaerswyck and Schenectady, 1668–1685* (Albany, N.Y., 1926–1932),
Dec. 6, 1675, II, 48–49, 56, 65.

2. Letters, Jan. 13 and 20, 1676, *Recs. of Conn.*, II, 397–398, 404.

of the Indians, from Maine to Virginia, might spread devastation on all the colonies. Swallowing his pride, he approached Connecticut once more. Suppose he should engage in "your" Indian war, Andros inquired. Would Connecticut permit either Christians or Iroquois to pursue enemies "unto any part of your Colony?" He asked for a "plaine answer, without delay."[3]

Instead, what came back was full of qualifications and hedges, and no wonder. The Connecticut gentry had every reason to bear in mind their own purpose and conduct in Rhode Island, and they had no reason to think that Andros would deal more altruistically with themselves. The impasse was broken by news from another quarter. A former prisoner of the Indians, one Thomas Warner, came down to New York to report that he had seen "2100 Indyans" with Philip, "all fighting Men," and, worst of all, "5 or 600 French Indyans, with Strawes in their Noses."[4] This was a trigger for Andros's instant propulsion into the conflict. The day after examining Warner, Andros boarded his sloop for Albany, bearing his council's admonition "to settle matters there, It being of very great import." Explicitly, he was to serve only New York's interests, "the other Colonyes . . . not having made us acquainted with their concernes and some of them slighted our friendly tenders, to continue our Endeavours as Christians and the Kings subjects, for the good of this Government without farther application to the said Colonyes."[5]

What Andros did in Albany was briefly shrouded in conspiratorial secrecy that was preserved by historians' bias long after the facts became matter of record. Officially Andros commissioned Lieutenant Gerrit Teunise to find Philip and command him to leave New York "as farr as Caneticut river."[6] According to the Mohawks, however, Andros "did Incourage us, and told how his frindes in New England were Involved in a great warr with Indians and that some of their Enemys were fledd to Hosack, Incourageing us to goe out against them, and killed some and Putt the Rest to the flight."[7] Nobody ever contradicted them, and all the circumstances verify the Mohawks' account. Andros's successor, Thomas Dongan, would one day remark that "New England in

3. Letters, Feb. 4 and 10, 1676, *ibid.*, 406–407.

4. Examination of Thomas Warner, Feb. 25, 1676, in Franklin B. Hough, ed., *A Narrative of the Causes which led to Philip's Indian War . . . With other Documents concerning this Event* (New York, 1858), 145.

5. N.Y. Council minutes, Feb. 26, 1676, *N.Y. Col. Docs.*, XIII, 493–494.

6. Commission, Mar. 4, 1676, *ibid.*, 494.

7. Mohawk speeches: Aug. 1, 1678, *ibid.*, 528; Sept. 23, 1689, in Lawrence H. Leder, ed., *The Livingston Indian Records, 1666–1723* (Gettysburg, Pa., 1956), 155.

their last Warr with the Indians had been ruined, had not Sir Edmund Andros sent some of those [Iroquois] Nations to their assistance."[8]

The Mohawks had their own reasons for plunging into battle. Since 1663 they had been periodically in conflict with confederated Algonquian tribes including the Mahicans of the upper Hudson, the Sokokis (or Squakheags)[9] of the upper Connecticut, and the Pennacooks and Abenakis farther distant. These vaguely known "North Indians" ironically enough had been encouraged and probably instigated against the Mohawks by the Puritans. Now the upheavals of the Second Puritan Conquest had transformed relationships, and now the Mahicans and "North Indians" were enemies to New England, but the Mohawks had not changed. Although they had not become New England's allies, the Mohawks had preserved their own enmity for the tribes that were now New England's enemies. They gladly accepted Governor Andros's "encouragement" to attack, and fell upon their old enemies in a brutally effective surprise attack that shattered and scattered the great force that Philip had collected to ravage New England in the spring. Philip himself fled once more, back toward the coast.[10]

Andros himself acknowledged in 1678 what he had done.

In winter 1675/6 Phillip and other Indians in two partyes armed, his about 500 the other 400 men, tending westward within forty miles of Albany; Connecticutt and Boston refuseing assistance or persueinge [of] them into their Collonys; wee however supplyed our Indyans with ammunicion, armes and all they wanted: and received old Maques Sachems, women and children into our townes and though refused by our neighbours the latter end of February fell upon, killed and tooke severall, and drove said Phillip and other Indians with him quite away, and since kept continuall partyes out to free the coasts towards us and prevent old Indyans recourse to Cannada.[11]

8. Feb. 22, 1687, *N.Y. Col. Docs.*, III, 393.

9. See Gordon M. Day, "The Identity of the Sokokis," *Ethnohistory*, XII (1965), 237–249.

10. The Mohawk strike coincided with an outbreak among the Indians of strange diseases that caused more deaths than combat with colonials. Increase Mather commented that some colonials "dated the turn of Providence towards us" from the time of Mohawk intervention. Mather and Hubbard took no note of Andros's role, and subsequent historians have generally followed their example. The best of modern accounts mentions the Mohawks rather casually and follows Hubbard in slighting their importance; in this connection it omits mention of Andros. Mather, *Brief History of the War*, 29; Hubbard, *Narrative*, 82, 96, 110; Leach, *Flintlock and Tomahawk*, 142, 163.

11. Andros, "Short Account," *N.Y. Col. Docs.*, III, 265. See also Andros to Conn. council, July 5, 1676, *Recs. of Conn.*, II, 461; Andros to governor and council of Massachusetts, May 22, 1676, N.Y. Col. MSS, XXV, 116. This last reference strongly suggests that Hubbard must have known of Andros's role, so that his suppression of it was deliberate. It could not really have been very secret at the time; even the French of Canada were aware of it. Enjalran to ———, Oct. 13, 1676, Thwaites, ed., *Jesuit Relations*, LX, 133.

This was the blow that lost the war for Philip. Until Andros acted Puritan New England was deep in despair over its inability to win a decisive battle. The United Colonies' much-touted massacre of Narragansetts had actually strengthened the uprising by driving recruits into Philip's ranks; but the Mohawks' entry into the war—which is to say, New York's entry—revived Puritan morale while destroying any logistical basis for hope of Philip's success. It was beyond doubt the turning point of the war. The Indians themselves recognized this immediately. Councocling in Massachusetts, they could not agree on future strategy, and the tribal units broke up to return to their home territories, each to find its own way as it could.[12]

This is not to say that the fighting stopped. Although both Massachusetts and Connecticut accepted messengers from the Indians, they demanded unconditional surrender, and their previous disposition of prisoners made that prospect bleak.[13] Campaigns continued on both sides. Regardless of the atrocities perpetrated in particular engagements, the directors of the war never succumbed to the hysterical frenzies that often mark its histories. In Connecticut military operations were carefully dovetailed with certain specific political objectives: to gain undisputed possession of the Narragansett country, to neutralize Andros's pressure on western Connecticut, and to gain absolute mastery over all Indians within Connecticut as well as commanding dominance over others nearby. Attainment of all these objectives depended on the end-game moves in the war. Since the Mohawks' entry had guaranteed Philip's eventual defeat, the question had narrowed to which of the many participants would win.

Like the others Connecticut resolved to come out on top, but an obstacle far more unmanageable than Philip blocked the way. Connecticut could not gain its objectives without coming to terms with Andros, and Andros had objectives of his own. So also had Andros's Mohawks, who continued their raids deep into New England's back country regardless of boundaries and diplomatic protocol. The Mohawks fought their own war, often failing to distinguish between the Puritans' enemies and their own. They had old scores to pay off against Connecticut's Mohegans and Massachusetts's praying Indians as well as Philip's allies. Many a "friend Indian" trudged captive back to the Mohawk villages and was burnt at the torture stake.[14]

Although Andros's mercenary Indians proved vastly more effective in the field than Massachusetts's hired pirates, some time elapsed before the Puritans even became aware of Mohawk entry into the war. Con-

12. Hubbard, *Narrative*, 87, 95–96.
13. *Recs. of Conn.*, May 1, 1676, II, 440.
14. See *N.Y. Col. Docs.*, XIII, 513–514, 516–517, 520–521, 524–525, 528–529.

necticut attempted to approach them directly, to the great annoyance of New York's government. New York's Secretary Matthias Nicolls called it strange that Connecticut wanted to treat "with any branch of this Government apart and upon your own account." Such an attempt was "most mistaken and ineffectuall" because the Mohawks took their orders from the government of New York, "and cannot bee subject to two."[15]

On the face of it, that reply seemed to slam the door to the Mohawk country, but Andros ostentatiously failed to turn the key. Apparently Connecticut had been making interesting secret propositions, to which Andros responded with carrot and club. For the record Secretary Nicolls established the formal position mentioned above. However, Andros replied separately on the same day to encourage Connecticut to keep trying. He was ready, he said, to try to procure an honorable and safe peace, "which if I cannot obtaine by faire meanes, then to use such other as may bee proper for mee." His carrot was an offer to suspend his demands for the disputed territory west of the Connecticut River "till a determination from England."[16] Since the duke of York had already instructed Andros to drop the boundary issue for the time being, this offer was less large than it appeared.[17] Perhaps Connecticut men had their own information of the duke's instruction; at any rate they failed to reach for Andros's bait until cogent reasons emerged from new events.

In another sector, Massachusetts had been fighting a war on many fronts. Its "North Indian" enemies had a vast range of territory in which to maneuver—almost all of Maine, New Hampshire, and Vermont in modern terms. These Abenaki, Pennacook, and Sokoki tribes were able to strike without warning at exposed frontier settlements, then disappear into a wilderness impenetrable to the English. The only effective force against them was the Mohawk tribe, and the Mohawks were uncomfortably out of Massachusetts's control. The only way out of this intolerable situation seemed to be to end the war in the northern sector. Word came to Andros that Massachusetts intended to make a separate peace with the "North Indians." Such a treaty, if consummated, would have had grave implications. We must remember that the duke of York had claimed the territory of the "North Indian" tribes among his other possessions. In that region his claims overlapped those of Massachusetts as they conflicted elsewhere with those of Connecticut. If Massachusetts made peace with the "North Indians" while Andros was still at war with them through the Mohawks, Massachusetts would be able to

15. *Recs. of Conn.*, II, 414, 419–420, 426, 436.
16. *Ibid.*, 437.
17. York to Andros, Jan. 28, 1676, *N.Y. Col. Docs.*, III, 235.

get a grip on the territory and prevent his deputies from entering it. Andros clearly understood these possible developments. In his usual unhesitating manner, he countered Massachusetts's overture to the "North Indians" by taking decisive action of his own.

On May 28, 1676, Andros presented to his council letters from Rhode Island, Martha's Vineyard, and Nantucket reporting the probability of Boston's making peace "on their own Account alone." The council immediately resolved "that Endeavours be made to putt a stop to the Mohawks farther prosecuteing the North Indyans." On May 29 the council ordered "that all North Indyans, that will come in may be protected," and the following day it sent a summons to the Mohawks for a treaty with Andros at Albany and began arrangements "to send word by some good Mahicander Eastward . . . that all Indyans, who will come in and submitt, shall be received to live under the protection of the Government and that the Governor will bee there as afore, where any of them may freely come and speake with him and returne againe, as they see cause without Molestation."[18]

As so often before, the real reason for this delicate political decision was smothered under a justification for diplomatic consumption. Instead of admitting competition with Massachusetts, the Yorkers professed to be competing with French Canada—an always presentable motive. They pointed to the danger of letting "North Indians" seek sanctuary in Canada from the wars in New England, which was indeed happening.[19] There was enough truth in that to explain the desirability of a peace, but not enough to explain why New York should hasten to make the peace before Massachusetts could.

The Yorkers might have moved more leisurely and still preserved competitive advantage, for the substance of what Massachusetts called a peace offer was not likely to lure many Indians. Connecticut proposed an amnesty, but Massachusetts was willing only to offer "hope" for the lives of Indians who surrendered unconditionally.[20] When the

18. N.Y. Council minutes, MSS, May 28, 1676, III, Pt. ii, 97; May 29 and 30, 1676, N.Y. Col. Docs., XIII, 496–497; Instructions to Capt. Thos. Delavall, May 30, 1676, N.Y. Col. MSS, XXV, 121.

19. Enjalran to ———, Oct. 13, 1676, Thwaites, ed., Jesuit Relations, LX, 133–135.

20. Recs. of Conn., II, 425, 440; Rawson to Leete, July 7, 1676, ibid., 466; "Examination of the Messenger of Pessicus," Apr. 29, 1676, in Bates, ed., Wyllys Papers, 240; Hubbard, Narrative, 96–97.

A bibliographic note: In Drake's edition of Hubbard, the editor commented: "The Purport of the Proclamation [by Massachusetts] was an invitation to the Indians to cease their depredations, and to surrender to the authorities. No amnesty was offered, further than in the judgment of the English it might consist with their ideas of justice. All those who had been known to have engaged in the

Indians hesitated to give themselves up to such dubious mercy, the Puritans concluded to force the war more rigorously than ever.[21]

The men of Hadley, Massachusetts, learned simultaneously of the Mohawk intervention and of the absence of warriors from the encampment of enemy Indians (probably Sokokis) at their Turners Falls fishing place up the Connecticut River. "A considerable number, yet most of them old men and women" were an irresistible attraction to Hadley's valor.[22] Over 150 mounted men assembled at Hadley to attack at daybreak of May 19, 1676. By their own report they poked their guns inside the unguarded wigwams and shot sleeping Indians. Of those who waked and fled to the river, many were shot in the water, and others were swept over the falls. When warriors attacked from the opposite shore, the English turned and themselves fled in utter panic, which is the more notable because there probably were no more than 70 warriors on *both* sides of the river to stand up against the 150 Englishmen. In the rout 37 English were killed, whereas only one had died in their dawn attack.[23] It was hardly the stuff of sagas, but it conformed to the Puritan strategy of destroying the warriors' morale by wiping out their kin.

Connecticut pressed forward strongly in that strategy. It organized a new force under Major John Talcott, with instructions to "kill and destroy them, according to the utmost power God shall give you." Missionary James Fitch found that a little hard to swallow. He begged off chaplain duty for Talcott, giving excuses of infirmity and bad health "besides the constant occasions with the Indeans, *especially if they come in according to your instructions given us.*"[24]

war were to expect only such terms as their conquerors might be disposed to award.

For important documents like the one here referred to we look in vain into our published *Colonial Records*, which we are as insultingly as impudently told are *edited!*" (emphasis in original). Hubbard, *History of Indian Wars*, ed. Drake, I, 249n.

21. Massachusetts General Court to Connecticut council, ca. last week of May 1676, *Recs. of Mass.*, V, 96–97.

22. John Russell to Connecticut council, Hadley, May 15, 1676, MSS, Colonial Wars, I, 71a–71b, Connecticut Archives, Hartford.

23. Sylvester Judd, *History of Hadley*... (Northampton, Mass., 1863), 170–172. The English attackers had distrusted their informant's judgment as to the numbers of the Indians, thinking that there might be "many more." Postscript to Russell's letter, May 15, 1676, MSS, Col. Wars, I, 71a–71b, Conn. Archives. In consequence of their fears, "to the great dishonour of the English, a few Indians pursued our Soldiers four or five miles, who were in number near twice as many as the Enemy." I. Mather, *Brief History of the War*, 30. Hubbard pretended that the Indians outnumbered the fleeing English. *Narrative*, 88.

24. Instructions, May 24, 1676, *Recs. of Conn.*, II, 444; Fitch to Ally, May 29, 1676, *ibid.*, 447–448 (emphasis added).

It was no job for a man with a squeamish stomach. Talcott's force of Connecticut troopers and Indian auxiliaries found a former Narragansett peace messenger and his band in a spruce swamp in northern Rhode Island on July 2, 1676, and proceeded according to instructions. The event should be seen in two aspects: the happening itself and the reasons for the participants being there. As to what happened, Major Talcott reported that his men "within 3 hours slew and tooke prisoner 171, of which 45 prisoners being women and children that the Indians saved alive, and the others slayne; in which engagement were slayne 34 men." The report was devious. When analysed, it reveals that Talcott had invaded Rhode Island again and that the Narragansett band consisted of 34 men (ages not given) and 137 women and children—hardly a war party. All the men were killed as well as 92 of the women and children. As in the Pequot conquest, "the Indians saved alive" the women and children taken prisoner.[25]

On the day following Talcott "turned down to Providence and received enformation that the enemye was there to make peace with some of Road Island, upon which enformation, being willing to set our seal to it, posted away and dressed Providence neck; and after that the same daye dressed Warwick neck." At Warwick 18 men and 22 women and children were killed and 27 captives taken.[26] The scenes of "battle," let it be remembered, were in territory to which even omnivorous Connecticut made no claim, and they occurred in defiance of Rhode Island's explicit order that no military forces from other colonies were permitted on Rhode Island territory.[27]

Talcott's two massacres were described by William Hubbard as "the greatest blow given to the Narhagansetts."[28] He might have remarked as truly that it was indirectly, but purposefully, a blow against both Massachusetts and Rhode Island as well. The Indians had been at Samuel Gorton's Warwick awaiting the return of Potuck, their emissary to Massachusetts to negotiate peace. Obviously there was nothing furtive or secret about their presence, which seems to imply that they were there by permission, and such an inference fits well enough into the previous history of the inhabitants of Warwick-Shawomet. Connecticut's forces destroyed these Narragansetts not merely while they were waiting to make peace with Massachusetts, but in order to prevent them from doing so. Although superficially Talcott appears to have acted out of simple bloodlust, second thoughts put his slaughter in a

---

25. Talcott to council, July 4, 1676, *Recs. of Conn.*, II, 458–459.
26. *Ibid.*
27. Leach, *Flintlock and Tomahawk*, 143. Leach's interpretation: "With a familiar gesture of injured pride, Rhode Island was again withdrawing into its own shell."
28. Hubbard, *Narrative*, "A Postscript."

different light. If the peace had been concluded, Massachusetts could have used it to claim that, regardless of Connecticut's participation in the war against the Narragansetts, the Indians had finally surrendered to Boston and therefore the rights of conquest should belong there. The Rhode Islanders had also been aware, it seems, that a peace in Boston would confer a conquest claim, for some of them had stopped Potuck's passage to Massachusetts.[29] Talcott's bloody sword determined Connecticut's future priority as Rhode Island's greatest menace.

Connecticut wasted no time before demonstrating the point. Talcott's massacre took place in July 1676. By October the outraged General Assembly of Rhode Island found it necessary to declare to Connecticut an "absolute dislike of your late proceedings." They protested, "It seems strange that you should, under pretence of subdueinge the Indians, monopolize our privileges by warninge our inhabitants from settlinge upon their own Plantations in said Narragansett, that were forced by reason of the late war with the natives to desert their habitations for the security of their lives."[30]

The war was winding down in different ways on different fronts. While the Puritans mopped up, Andros's peace messengers to the "North Indians" found some attentive ears. In late July a large party of Indians on their way to cross the Hudson River was reported to Connecticut's council. These were "goeinge to seeke another country," the council thought, because the Indians knew that Connecticut planned to destroy their crops "and perpetually to disrest them." The council urged Andros to send the Mohawks against them. Andros replied blandly that he "durst not presume farther" with the Mohawks.[31]

Several weeks later, and apparently still oblivious to Andros's arrangements, the Connecticut council reported another large band of Indians headed toward New York. Urging its "reasonable request" for "the utter extirpation of such as have imbrued their hands in the blood of many of his Majesties good subjects," the council asked permission to send its own soldiers up the Hudson to destroy the In-

29. William Harris to Sir Joseph Williamson, Aug. 12, 1676, in Sainsbury *et al.*, eds., *Calendar of State Papers, Col. Ser., 1675–1676*, doc. 1021, p. 444. Increase Mather's devious reporting of the incident is interesting. Before Talcott's raid, Mather wrote (as of June 30) that "intelligence came to Boston that a chief Narraganset Sachim is now suing to the English for peace." After Talcott's raid Mather noted (as of Aug. 10, 1676), "Whereas Potock a chief Counsellor to the old Squaw-Sachem of Narraganset, was by some of Road Island brought into Boston, and found guilty of promoting the War against the English, he was this day shot to death in the Common at Boston." One would not guess from Mather's disconnected way of telling this story that Potuck had been the sachem suing for peace or that he had been guaranteed safe conduct. Hubbard ignores Potuck and his fate. Mather, *Brief History of the War*, 38, 46.

30. Oct. 25, 1676, *Recs. of R.I.*, II, 556–558.

31. *Recs. of Conn.*, July 1676, II, 466–467.

dians if Andros would not "doe something effectuall yourselfe."[32] Andros replied that he could manage to give "sufficient" orders, and added a sting: "if such barbarous enemyes are to be credited, they would be the most innocent." Much less independence than that had aroused Connecticut to storm into Rhode Island, and the Puritans would dearly have loved to hit the Dutch in Albany, whom they hated almost as much as the fleeing Indians; but New York could not be disregarded in quite the same way as Rhode Island; New York was the special jurisdiction of the king's brother, and New York had the Mohawks. Angry but frustrated, the Connecticut council scaled down its demands to the execution of "the cheife men" among the refugees. This "may do," the council thought; "wee doe not so concerne ourselves for others or women or children, they delivering up themselves to mercy unto your honour there."[33] Andros yawned. Connecticut then switched tactics again and tried to get the Mohawks to Hartford for a treaty "respecting some service done for us against the comon enemie"—and, oh yes, the Mohawks were to bring the refugee Indians along as prisoners. New York's council interposed its own authority with the opinion that it would be "of ill Consequence" for the Mohawks to "treate or to make application to another Government, the which will breede a distraction amongst them."[34]

Meanwhile the Mohawk commotions in New England's back country continued, and the Puritans were helpless to stop or control them. The pride of the Elect was humbled by its fears; after a few preliminaries, Massachusetts and Connecticut sent joint commissioners to Albany where they dealt with the Indians on Andros's terms, through Andros's interpreter, and under Andros's unrelenting censorship. The Puritans made one last gesture at getting their hands on the seven "principle Indians" who had escaped to New York's shelter, but Andros denied them even this remnant of vengeance.[35] What they did get was an organization for preserving their peace with the Indians allied to New York—a "Covenant Chain" that linked the English colonies in perpetual treaty relationships with both the Iroquois tribes and the "River Indians" of the Hudson Valley. In this organization there was a very definite primacy of position for New York. Though the New Englanders later tried to seduce the Mohawks away from Albany for negotiations free of New York's supervision, the Indians remained immovable. "This," they replied invariably, pointing to Albany, "this

32. Council to Andros, Aug. 19, 1676, *ibid.*, 469–470.

33. Aug. 31, 1676, *ibid.*, 477–478.

34. Oct. 6, 1676, *ibid.*, 480; Oct. 11, 1676, *N.Y. Col. Docs.*, XIII, 501–502.

35. Apr. 1676, *Recs. of Conn.*, II, 492–495; Connecticut council to Andros, Sept. 24, 1677, in Bates, ed., *Wyllys Papers* (Conn. Hist. Soc., *Colls.*, XXI), 267–269.

is the prefixed meeting place." The Covenant Chain had its anchor post planted firmly in the soil of Andros's government and those of his successors.[36]

Some of the very Indians whose blood had been demanded by the Puritan governing gentry were links in the great chain. Andros had, in Indian metaphor, planted a tree of peace and welfare for them at Schagticoke on the upper Hudson; i.e., he had appointed that place as their habitation under his direct protection. (Interestingly, Schagticoke was close by Hosick where the Mahicans had formerly entertained King Philip; it also guarded the route from New England.) Andros's protection was real. He disciplined even the Iroquois when some of them ventured to violate his sanctuary by robbing their ancient foes and abducting a Mahican boy. Andros denounced their "Insolence and violence" in a message that shunned ambiguity and got compliance: "I doe expect," he wrote, "that whosoever doth or shall come in and submitt themselves and live quietly with our Indyans, shall be protected from any outrage or force and I shall not suffer them to bee disturbed or harmed, but shall looke upon any violence offered that way, as done to my selfe." Many years later the Schagticoke Indians recalled, as they gratefully renewed their Covenant Chain alliance, that "wee were allmost dead when wee left New England and were first received into this government." Andros's successors had every reason to admire and emulate the stroke of policy by which he had turned New England's destined gallows birds into New York's staunch supporters.[37]

The Puritans took a rather different view, but they had overreached themselves in too many directions. In London the crown saw its own

36. See *N.Y. Col. Docs.*, XIII, 528; Leder, ed., *Livingston Indian Records*, 154; and, with the correction following, Jennings, "Covenant Chain," Am. Phil. Soc., *Procs.*, CXV (1971), 88–96.

Andros later regretted the concession he had made to the Puritans. Although he kept controls, he was obliged to change the principle and protocol of his management of the Mohawks. An unnoticed manuscript in the Public Record Office is important enough to quote at length. In it Andros complained that the Puritan governments' efforts to treat with the Mohawks had "made our [New York] Indians lye if not insolent, which they never were afore, nor did I ever make treaty with, but dealt with them as being under or part of the Government, which I told our Neighbors, and many more arguments against their going to treat, assuring them there soe long as the Indians would hearken to this Government they should not hurt them (but in vaine) and now all my hope is Regulations and Orders from the King, as the only means to keep us well in peace and preserve or defend us if wars." Andros to Blathwait, Oct. 12, 1678, C.O. 5/1111, 43–44 (fol. 24), P.R.O.

37. Indian orator, Aug. 31, 1700, *N.Y. Col. Docs.*, LV, 744; Andros to Albany magistrates, July 12, 1677, *ibid.*, XIII, 509; Oneidas' speech, Dec. 20, 1677, N.Y. Col. MSS, XXVI, 161. See also Randolph to Penn, Nov. 9, 1688, Mass. Hist. Soc., *Colls.*, 4th Ser., VIII (Boston, 1868), 531; Penn to ———, July 30, 1683, *PMHB*, XXXIX (1915), 233–234.

opportunity in the turmoils of the time. The Committee of Trade and Plantations agreed "that this is the Conjuncture to do some thing Effectual for the better Regulation of that [New England] Government, or else all hopes of it may be hereafter lost," and the crown's representative appeared in Boston in June 1676. Besides its political effects, the war against the Indians had drained New England's resources both of manpower and of property. The crown's Edmund Randolph reported, in October 1676, losses of 600 men and £150,000, "there having been about twelve hundred houses burnt, eight thousand head of Cattle great and small, killed, and many thousand bushels of wheat, pease, and other grain burnt . . . and upward of three thousand Indians, men women and children destroyed, who if well managed would have been very serviceable to the English: which makes all manner of labour dear."[38] On Massachusetts's northern frontier, even after the killing of King Philip, Indian raids continued perpetually, and only New York had an organized Indian force capable of relieving that strain. The Puritan commissioners at Albany linked themselves into Andros's Covenant Chain with their former foes in order to cope with their continuing troubles. "Wee doe therefore acknowledge these River Indians our freinds and Neighbours," they stated, with the last spark of old grudge reduced to a reasonable proviso "that you doe not *henceforward* harbour or entertaine any that shall *remain* our enemies."[39]

The New Englanders were never very happy with the alliance and never able to get along entirely independent of it until England conquered Canada and thus eliminated the perpetual source of support for New England's Indian enemies. The Iroquois—more particularly the Mohawks—improved their own situation in the chain by regularly raiding the remaining Indians of New England—allied as well as hostile—in order to subordinate those Indians as Iroquois tributaries. Angry Puritan "protectors" found themselves helpless to act except through New York's intermediation and at a price.[40]

Massachusetts felt its new loss of dominance at once. Shortly after

38. Mar. 20, 1676, Sainsbury *et al.*, eds., *Calendar of State Papers, Col. Ser., 1675–1676*, doc. 848; Randolph's report, Oct. 12, 1676, *N.Y. Col. Docs.*, III, 243–244. The losses should be compared proportionately: the 3,000 Indian casualties occurred in an Indian population of 11,000 whereas the 600 English casualties occurred in an English population over 52,000. Cf. chap. 2 above.

39. Andros to governor of Massachusetts, Mar. 1677, N.Y. Col. MSS, XXVI, 46; commissioners' speech to Salisbury, Apr. 24, 1677, Leder, ed., *Livingston Indian Records*, 39 (my emphasis); Mohawk speech, June 6, 1683, van Laer, ed., *Minutes of Albany*, III, 363.

40. New York's permanent policy was well expressed in the letter of Brockholst to Salisbury, Aug. 2, 1678, *N.Y. Col. Docs.*, XIII, 529–530. An example of New England's treaties is in Leder, ed., *Livingston Indian Records*, 147–158 (Aug.–Sept. 1689).

the Covenant Chain treaty had been signed in April 1677, Andros sent an expeditionary force to Pemaquid, Maine, to pacify the Indians there. Pemaquid was in the territory claimed by both Massachusetts and the duke of York. Andros's men built a fort and remained to occupy it.[41] Unmolested by Massachusetts, the new fort became a barrier to the colony's expansion.

All in all the Second Puritan Conquest was a fiasco for its victors. Instead of easy plunder, the Puritans netted massive debts and smoking ruins, to say nothing of heavy casualties. The "rights of conquest" over the Narragansett country were later nullified by legal action so that there was no gain from that quarter to offset loss of settlements on the Puritan frontiers.[42] Instead of acquiring new territories, Massachusetts lost Maine. Plymouth failed to hold even the territory of King Philip's Sowams, where the war had started; Rhode Island made its town of Bristol out of it. Enfeebled Plymouth Colony limped along for only a dozen years longer before disappearing into Massachusetts's maw by court action as New Haven had earlier been given to Connecticut. Andros summarized the war tartly for a royal board of inquiry: "the advantages thereby were none, the disadvantages very great and like to be more, even in the loss of said Indians."[43] Somehow, incomprehensibly, Jehovah had withdrawn his countenance from his people.

For their own part, the surviving Indians had learned more than they could love about their neighbors' righteous zeal and unrighteous covetousness. Demoralized and dispirited remnants of formerly large Indian communities sank ever deeper into subjection and debauchery. Others, with more will to self-preservation, fled to Canada, to New York, to the Delaware and Susquehanna valleys, and even as far as Virginia to regroup and recuperate and to meditate revenge.[44] Those who went to Canada became willing weapons in the hands of the French. Those who went west were sheltered under the protection of

41. Instructions to Brockles, Knapton, and Nicolls, June 13, 1677, *N.Y. Col. Docs.*, III, 248–249; Andros, "Short Account," Mar. 1678, *ibid.*, 256; Brockholls to governor at Boston, Jan. 7, 1678, N.Y. Col. MSS, XXVII, 5.

42. Order of Privy Council, Dec. 13, 1678, *Recs. of R.I.*, III, 62–63.

43. "Governor Andros' answer to Enquiries of the Council of Trade," Apr. 9, 1678, *N.Y. Col. Docs.*, III, 263.

44. See the Indian tradition in Heckewelder, *Account of the Indian Nations*, ed. Reichel, in Hist. Soc. Pa., *Memoirs*, XII, 77–78.

A bibliographic note: Heckewelder and his informants have been maligned by historians of the Parkman school, who decry Indian tradition as wholly unreliable and disparage Heckewelder as foolishly credulous. Although oral traditions certainly became confused in details, the findings of the present study confirm Heckewelder on substantial issues more often than they support his denigrators. Indian tradition, with all its distortions of transmission, seems like accuracy itself compared to the distortions of both creation and transmission in the Puritan tradition. And Heckewelder was unimpeachably honest.

New York, which enforced western limits for Massachusetts and Connecticut with an effectiveness that New Netherland had never been able to manage. The hitherto most aggressively expansionist colonies in English America became a closed pocket and remained so until the American Revolution. The way to the beckoning West would be found by persons who consciously adopted a strategy of maintaining symbiotic interdependence with the Indians.

Pennsylvania's Governor George Thomas explained that strategy patiently to some proud southern gentlemen:

These Indians by their situation are a Frontier to some of [the English colonies], and from thence, if Friends, are Capable of Defending their Settlements; If Enemies, of making Cruel Ravages upon them; If Neuters, they may deny the French a Passage through their Country, and give us timely Notice of their Designs. These are but some of the Motives for cultivating a good Understanding with them, but from hence the Disadvantages of a Rupture are abundantly evident. Every advantage you gain over them in War will be a Weakning of the Barrier of those Colonies, and Consequently will be in Effect Victories over yourselves and your Fellow-Subjects. Some allowances for their Prejudices and Passions, and a Present now and then for the Relief of their Necessities, which have in some measure been brought upon them by their Intercourse with Us, and by our yearly extending our Settlements, will probably tye them more closely to the British Interest. This has been the Method of Newyork and Pennsylvania, and will not put you to so much Expence in Twenty Years as the carrying on a War against them will do in One.[45]

Such common sense came too late to help the Saints of New England. Perpetually forced to contend with the "cruel ravages" of the Indians they had driven into the embrace of French enemies, the Puritans and their historians have never acknowledged that the victories of Puritan conquest were only defeats for themselves.

45. Gov. George Thomas of Pennsylvania addressing the commissioners of Maryland and Virginia, Lancaster, Pa., June 25, 1744, *Pa. Council Minutes*, IV, 700–701.

APPENDIX ❧

The Formative Period of a Large Society: A Comparative Approach

> *It must be admitted that the word feudalism, which was to have* so great a future, was very ill-chosen, even though at the time the reasons for adopting it appeared sound enough. To Boulainvilliers and Montesquieu, living in an age of absolute monarchy, the most striking characteristic of the Middle Ages was the parcelling out of sovereignty among a host of petty princes, or even lords of villages. It was this characteristic that they meant to denote by the term feudalism, and when they spoke of fiefs they were referring sometimes to territorial principalities, sometimes to manors. But not all the manors were in fact fiefs, nor were all the fiefs principalities or manors. Above all, it may be doubted whether a highly complex type of social organization can be properly designated either by concentrating on its political aspect only, or—if "fief" be understood in its narrowest legal sense—by stressing one particular form of property right among many others. But words, like well-worn coins, in the course of constant circulation lose their clear outline. In the usage of the present day, "feudalism" and "feudal society" cover a whole complex of ideas in which the fief properly so called no longer occupies the foreground. Provided that he treats these expressions merely as labels sanctioned by modern usage for something which he has still to define, the historian may use them without compunction. In this he is like the physicist who, in disregard of Greek, persists in calling an "atom" something which he spends his time in dividing.
>
> It is a question of the deepest interest whether there have been other societies, in other times and in other parts of the world, whose social structures in their fundamental characteristics have sufficiently resembled that of our Western feudalism to justify us in applying the term "feudal" to them as well.
>
> Marc Bloch, *Feudal Society*, I, xvii–xviii.

Theories of American historiography assume or tend toward two kinds of exclusion from the process of formation of American society and culture. In the first place they exclude Amerindians (as also Afro-Americans) from participation, except as foils for Europeans, and thus assume that American civilization was formed by Europeans in a struggle against the savagery or

---

The original paper on which this appendix is based was critiqued by an interdisciplinary panel at the Nineteenth Annual Meeting of the American Society for Ethnohistory, Oct. 15, 1971, at the University of Georgia, Athens. It took a drubbing that compelled reexamination of several chapters in the book as well as this material. For inclusion here the paper has been rewritten from beginning to end, for which the reader should thank (as I do) professors John T. Juricek, Joseph R. Berrigan, Jr., and Raymond Fogelson, as well as Professor Charles Hudson, who arranged the meeting. None of these men has seen or approved the revision, but Professor Edward Peters has read it and suggested some improvements.

barbarism of the nonwhite races. This first conception implies the second—that the civilization so formed is unique. In the second conception uniqueness is thought to have been created through the forms and processes of civilization's struggle on a specifically American frontier. Alternatively, civilization was able to triumph because the people who bore it were unique from the beginning—a Chosen People or a super race. Either way American culture is seen as not only unique but better than all other cultures, precisely because of its differences from them.

This seems like grievous infatuation. Yet it continues to sway minds because no one has offered a comprehensive and consistent alternative. Such an alternative is too great a task to be undertaken here, but some prerequisites for a new theory may be suggested.

The logical counter to a theory of exclusion is one based on inclusion. On the one hand, we must assume that American society and culture are the joint and mutual products of all the peoples resident within the American territory, that the contributing persons were equally members of the human species, that they were of equal moral worth, and that they were (in the average of their groups) of equal inherent capacity. On the other hand, we must assume that American society and culture are unique only in the degree that all societies are individual and that the processes and persons through which this society came into being are strictly and properly comparable with societies and persons elsewhere in the world and in time. Such assumptions, it may be noticed, are democratic without reservation and are irreconcilable with all forms of national and racial elitism. They imply that the processes of American history may not be excepted from the rules and patterns of social development found to be applicable where similar conditions can be identified. They therefore establish an indispensable prerequisite for any history aspiring to be scientific.

Modern theories of historical or cultural evolution, with few exceptions, tend to correlate forward direction in time with upward direction in development. There is no necessity for such correlation. Social development can be and is either progressive or regressive, maturational or degenerative, and it may make quantum leaps or suffer catastrophic setbacks. Lateral diffusion is as possible as internal innovation. In short, although the movement of culture has been cumulative for the world as a whole, it can vary in any given society in any direction, at many rates of speed, and, one is tempted to say, by any means.

Considering the stupendous complexity of variables, it seems best at this stage of knowledge to avoid elaborate conceptual schemes supposedly applicable to all history. However stimulating they may be to speculation, they cannot be put to the true scientific test of independent verification. One scheme becomes as good as another, and taste rather than evidence determines their acceptance. Better progress can be made in a more limited project.

As a science, ethnohistory is still in the stage of gathering and classifying data, and its difficulties are increased by lack of agreement among its professors about the identity and definition of its theoretical objects. Let me suggest that one of those objects should be the processes by which large societies came into being, and let me offer the findings of the present study as a contribution to the description of large society formation.

Anthropologists have long used the comparative method to describe the formation of the small societies normally the subjects of their study. I cannot readily set up criteria for distinguishing between large small societies and small large societies, though certainly the quantity and extent of population would be part of such criteria. For present purposes, however, universal definition is not necessary. It is enough to identify the present society of the United States as a large society, or a major component of such a society embracing all of North America, and to define it as the product of acculturative processes that began when Europeans invaded this continent. The task then becomes to find a comparable large society exhibiting similar processes.

There was a time when Europe went through a complex process of acculturative adaptation between diverse peoples, some of whom had lived in the subcontinent time out of mind and others of whom were recent invaders from Asia. In the sequel to the fall of Rome, a variform Mediterranean society was transmuted on its north shore into modern Europe—not simply and not directly. I think that I see comparable patterns of process in the macrocontact period of European invasion of North America and the much longer macrocontact period of Asiatic invasion of Europe. The comparable large-scale processes include the following: (1) migration and relocation of large numbers of people, establishing massive contact between societies previously separate and culturally disparate; (2) catastrophic depopulation through disease and war, with consequent disturbance and destruction of social and environmental controls; (3) reordering of relations of dominance and dependence on the basis of expedients and local custom; (4) gradual revival of population growth with consequent reordering of the physical environment; (5) establishment of large-scale economic, political, and social institutions through acculturative processes between invading and native peoples; and (6) stabilization of a large society in which all participants have undergone cultural change and in which subcultures continue to maintain vestigial representation of the originating ethnic groups and their cultures.

These headings have purposely been phrased broadly in order to embrace many phenomena that differed much on the two continents; but I do not think that they have been made so vague as to lose meaning. They are ethnically neutral and do not permit absurdities such as the "transit of civilization" or the "frontier between civilization and savagery." Whether they have more positive significance depends upon their subsumed specifications.

The neutrality of language is all important. From time to time in this study particular cultural traits have been discussed in terms of comparison between North America's "colonial" period and Europe's "medieval," or "feudal," period. I have used these terms loosely, in an ordinary colloquial way, knowing full well that they have technical meanings and that historians are far from having arrived at a consensus about them. However, when I attempted theoretical comparison, the semantic problem became too acute to be sloughed over. I thought, at first, to use Marc Bloch's seminal conception of feudalism as framework, but found that European feudalism bore too many birthmarks to be useful as a measure, under that name, for cultures elsewhere; and my initial enthusiasm has changed to mild skepticism about "feudalism" in Japan or ancient Egypt, and so on. There were genuine and significant cultural differences between Europe's Middle Ages and the macrocontact era of Europe in North America. Any theory worth a second glance must take them into account. Categories must be neutral, therefore, in order to permit the inclusion of genuine similarities without connotative corruption. Feudalism and American colonialism were examples of a type; neither was the type.

What most marks the type is similarity of *process*. Overall it is the process of disintegration and reintegration. The situation prevailing in Europe in the latter years of the Roman Empire had little resemblance to America during the early years of its "discovery," for in Rome the "barbarians" were the invaders, and even they had the use of metals and domesticated animals and perhaps some writing as well. The great equalizer was catastrophe. There is no telling which factor preceded the others, but along with the great migrations of Germanic and Asiatic peoples went epidemic and war. Rome's urban civilization, sorely tested by constant combat and pauperizing taxation, neglected to keep its cities in order, and as sanitation facilities deteriorated, disease proliferated. The cities and their interlinking institutions fell apart, and the population suffered an absolute decline of massive proportions. As Europe became rural and local, little survived of the ancient Roman state except the church bureaucracy adopted and fostered by Emperor Constantine. And even the church remained limited in extent and influence until it could find alliance with kings and emperors who enjoyed the substance as well as the form of rule.

At Europe's nadir considerable likeness can be seen between its chaotic forms of social organization and those to be observed in North America's era of disintegration and population decline. Old industries expired, and Europe became dependent upon trade for good cloth and the best metal implements. The distant cities of Byzantium and the Moslem world supplied what Europeans no longer could make for themselves, in return for such crude commodities as could be produced by a technologically inferior society. It is the condition of dependence that counts here; Europeans still spun and wove wool and ate cheese; every village had its smithy, and the greater lords had clerks. In America, where invasion transformed a predominately agricultural Indian economy into one dominated by hunting, the degree of dependence on foreign goods became stronger than in Europe, but the difference was of degree rather than kind. During Europe's era of decline a manor society grew up nearly everywhere, self-sufficient in primitive needs, but only in those. Upon trade's revival, however, Europe created a difference in kind. Indigenous Europeans gained control of their own markets and created complex economic structures that Indians could not even comprehend. Indigenous Americans never secured control of their markets from foreign merchants until the descendants of the invaders became indigenous Euramericans themselves.

In recent years historians have begun to have some respect for the Dark Ages of Rome's decline and fall and to see dimly that in all the confusion something new was being created. Regardless of Saint Augustine's lamentations, human effort was still being directed toward human purpose, not wholly without achievement; the end of the Roman world was not the end of the world. The swarming barbarians could build as well as break. Nevertheless, the first fact was the confusion. Rome became incapable of sending her law and her governors to her own provinces. In the provinces themselves, individual magnates achieved personal power independent of the state's and often greater. Authority became decentralized. Roman law encountered barbarian customs and fell before them, becoming a subject of study rather

Because!

We've got lots more to give you when you register! All registered customers are eligible for technical support, software updates, specially priced upgrades, Claris® product news and special promotions on future purchases of Claris software.

So, take a moment to fill out and mail your product registration card. We're looking forward to hearing from you.

Serial Number

000 0742685

Why bother?

than the director of action. As even the local bureaucracies deteriorated, the state lost its power both to protect persons and to enforce conduct, and that power passed in fragments into thousands of hands. The weak sought protection from the strong, and the strong enforced their wills upon the weak, local despotism being tempered by old custom and the necessity for productive labor. In the place of law emerged custom and contract, both between lord and vassal and between lord and lord. Few sanctions existed for enforcement of contract except custom and personal morality, and morality probably broke down as often then as now. Lord fought lord to gain a manor or a fief or to revenge a wrong; vassals betrayed lords when opportunity offered advantages, and also revenged wrongs; peasants sometimes broke out in desperate insurrection or more often joined gangs of bandits; and robber barons provided the bandits' example.

In formative America old authority also degenerated and fragmented in all components of the population. Europeans recognized subordinate Indian chiefs and protected them against their legitimate superiors in the deliberate strategy of dividing to conquer. Customary authority soon disintegrated, and formerly paramount chiefs were reduced to the level of village bosses with vestiges of ceremonial deference but no real power beyond their immediate followings. As in early medieval Europe, lesser powers sought the protection of the greater; in America this meant that ambitious or fearful local chiefs broke away from their former allegiances and obligations to put themselves under the protection and orders of Europeans. The ties were particularistic and sometimes purely personal: the Mohegan sachem Uncas was Connecticut's man—more especially the man of Captain John Mason, whose descendants were regarded by the Mohegans as their protectors for more than a century; the Western Niantics' Sassious became briefly the man of John Winthrop, Jr., personally, and after the Pequot conquest the Mohegans hostile to Uncas sought protection under Winthrop's wing; the Susquehannocks allied to the Swedes, then to the Maryland English, and then to the New York English; the upper Hudson tribes allied to the Fort Orange and Rensselaerswyck Dutch without commitment to the New Amsterdam Dutch, while the lower Hudson tribes reversed the process; the Mohawks institutionalized their Dutch friend Corlaer; and so on and on.

On the European side the Dutch, Swedes, and English in the Delaware Valley used their Indian alliances and cessions as means of nibbling away at each other's possessions until total conquest could be effected; Maryland attempted to use the Susquehannocks to invade Delaware, and when that failed Maryland used her own troops; Massachusetts made a client out of subsachem Pumham in order to seize the west shore of Narragansett Bay; and New York and New France manipulated the Iroquois and fought each other for the Great Lakes.

The consequence of these separate and conflicting alliances and relationships was kaleidoscopic combat as each tribe or subtribe and each European province or town or individual strove to expand its power and territory and to increase its wealth. This was early feudal Europe all over again.

Fragmentation of political authority implied the weakening of real property rights sanctioned by that authority. As powers came and went in Europe, custom sanctioned allodial right—a property right inherent in the fact of effective occupation and possession "time out of mind." Emperors, kings, and lords might come and go without disturbing the free peasant in his own, so long as he paid his stipulated obligations to whatever lordship happened to be in a position to demand them. This is not to imply that the law of ancient Rome had overlooked provision for sanctioning real property holdings. Rather, when Rome's administrators could no longer function, Rome's sanctions disappeared, and no stable substitute immediately took their place. Allodial right was all that was left. Even when feudal suzerains granted fiefs to their vassals under color of sovereignty, the vassals often felt the force of custom sufficiently to recognize allodial rights—sometimes, of course, for the purpose of negotiating the acquisition of such rights for themselves. Is not this very much the same process that occurred when Indian tribal jurisdictions fragmented? Depending on tribal custom in matters of property, the vestigial councils of the tribe might be left with collective claims, or particular families and individuals might be acknowledged to have rightful claims, because of immemorial possession. "Indian title" and "allodial right" are the same thing—a property right recognized in custom but lacking the formal sanction of an effective sovereignty.

In another respect the fall of Rome created a social parallel with formative America by means of its destruction of the state bureaucracy. When that impersonal arbiter disappeared, "civilized" persons turned to the same resource that the "barbarians" had always used—kinship ties. Among lords and peasants alike, the obligations of kinship provided support and protection, and not least among them was the duty to avenge a wronged kinsman. In a time when justice and strength were almost synonymous, a large and loving family with a reputation for sticking together brought more stability into everyday life than the remote and abstract rules of law.

The Europeans of America's formative era acted as an ethnic aristocracy, stratified within itself but entirely imposed over top of Indian society whenever the two shared the same territory. This is a common feature of lands being invaded by peoples more powerful than the natives. It is plain enough in Frankish Gaul and Norman Britain, not to speak of Magyar Hungary, Teuton East Prussia, Angevin Naples, and so on. In medieval Europe some intergroup mobility was permitted over the centuries, and ethnic caste gradually transformed into social class. So also in America some slight intermarriage and much extramarital mingling have permitted a degree of social mobility; but in the formative eras of both modern Europe and modern America stratification on the order of something very like caste lines followed lines indisputably ethnic.

There seem also to have been parallels in the processes of reintegration as new large societies emerged from the ruins of their predecessors. Basic to all else was the reversal of population decline, with consequent reconversion of the physical environment to human purpose and management. In both Europe and America there came a moment when total population began to grow in spite of continuing disasters in particular localities. No statistics exist except in the form of wildly varying estimates, but Europe's renewed vigor in the twelfth century suggests that growth had begun sometime earlier. In North America renewed growth appears to have begun toward the end of the seventeenth century along the Atlantic coast and river valleys where European migration, added to natural increase, replaced the Indians of a century or more earlier. On both continents renewed numbers implied renewed clearing of forests and the building of urban centers. On both continents the revival showed distinct signs of increased production of crops and goods, and it was linked to commerce with the world market and with technological development. In both reintegrative eras much of the advance of technology was owing to importation of ideas and crafts—in the medieval instance from Asia and Africa, in the American instance from Europe. But techniques were not all imported; native skills and crafts were tested by newcomers and adopted when found useful, with far-reaching effects.

Our eras of comparison seem to show one difference in demographic change, which becomes less of a difference after examination of the sequences of change. Western Europe, except for Spain and Sicily, had been able from the time of the Franks to repel invaders from Asia and Africa, while Eastern Europe was overrun by Mongol and Moslem. In America no part of aboriginal Indian society was able to seal itself off from European intrusion. However, the Franks and Goths who withstood the Moslems had themselves been invaders during the long era of disintegration, expelling or submerging the aboriginal Celts and Britons. Generalizing warily and eschewing specifically any suggestion of inherent ethnic inequality, one may glimpse the same Teutonic ethnic stocks dominating—not creating—the reintegration periods in both Europe and North America. This formulation is not the same as the "germ theory" of Anglo-Saxon supremacist historians, which held that both American and Western European societies "grew out of" social and institutional germs of Teutonic tribes. Rather it is simply to recognize the historical fact that the Teutonic stocks constituted most of the dominant privileged and ruling strata of the reintegrating eras in both Europe and America. Obviously such status did not make them the inventors of "modern democracy," as germ theorists have propounded. Probably they should be credited instead with the rather different invention of the political institutions by which they shared power among themselves while denying it to other ethnic groups. However much the forms changed, that substance persisted throughout both formative periods.

In one respect colonial America and medieval Europe were exactly identical: this was the process of chartered conquest as described earlier. The stages of that process were as follows: (1) a head of state laid claim to distant territories in jurisdictions other than his own; (2) he chartered a person or organized groups to conquer the claimed territory in his name but at private expense; (3) if the conquest was successful, the conquering lord (whether personal or collective) was recognized by the chartering suzerain as the possessor and governor of the territory, and the lord in turn acknowledged the charterer's suzerainty or sovereignty. The charter itself served as the new jurisdiction's legal constitution. More often than not, the conquest was launched ostensibly to reduce heretics or infidels to subjection to a protector or champion of an only true religion, this reason being mentioned prominently in the conquest charter, and clerics of the appropriate orthodoxy preceded, accompanied, or followed the troops. Usually the conquering lord enjoyed considerable independence for a period of time while his nominal sovereign gradually introduced agencies and officers responsible directly to the central state. Often the lord resisted royal encroachments on his independent sway, especially when the crown began to "give law" directly to its subjects without the lord's intermediation, and sometimes the medieval sovereign was obliged to conquer the conqueror when a lord turned insubordinate.

Chartered conquest accompanied by colonization in America did not repeat by mere coincidence the pattern set in Europe; so far as the British colonies were concerned, there was a specific historical link connecting the empire of the Plantagenet kings with the empire begun by Elizabeth Tudor and expanded by the Stuarts. That link was Ireland. Medieval efforts to impose feudal law, church, and land tenure on the Irish tribes resulted in a standoff. Elizabethan conquerors terrorized the Irish "savages" even more ruthlessly than the medieval marcher lords had done, and the methods and propaganda tested in Ireland were transplanted to America. (I do not think that this was quite the same thing as a transit of civilization.) Inexorably, after the marcher lords had beaten the natives into submission, the crown reached out to conform the lords in their turn. Inevitably the crown met resistance, but the struggle's outcome differed in the two lands. Ireland's natives, both the Irish and the Anglo-Irish, went under in the seventeenth century, not to reassert independence until the twentieth century. The American colonies resisted more successfully when their crisis came, but their victory was temporary. Having gained independence from one sovereign, they quickly re-created a new central sovereignty that has acquired ascendancy over "state" lordships as effectively as any crown.

The reduction of lordships to genuine subordination, the establishment of effective law, enforcement of law by appointed judges and officers, administration by bureaucracy, the creation of standing armies and fleets—these are the processes that transform decentralized feudal jurisdictions into the centralized nation-state. The transformation consumed less time in America than in Europe because the processes were already well advanced in Western Europe when the invasion of America began, and the state navy—the existence of which had made the American invasion possible—long prevented the colonizers and conquerors of America from enjoying the full autonomy of the medieval marcher lords. In both continents the central states established effective sovereignty not by a single decisive act but rather by a long process of gradual imposition of power, first upon the natives and then upon the lordships intermediate between the state and the natives.

To some extent the likeness of political process in the two formative periods has been hidden by the emergence of new forms of property in the more recent period. In medieval times the fief combined the functions of jurisdiction and property (though the fief was by no means universal). The seventeenth century recognized the distinctness of these two functions and mentioned both when they were granted in one charter. As chartered proprietaries the Lords Baltimore and the family of Penn were granted both the government and the "soil" of their territories. William Penn once remarked suggestively to his son that "government is a property," and he demonstrated his point in a moment of stress by negotiating to sell his own government, but not his land, to the crown. The distribution of real property in fee simple, or with quitrent satisfaction of vestigial feudal obligations, distinguished most of formative America from much of medieval Europe, but the distinction was neither absolute nor universal. The burghers of medieval times had purchased chartered freedom for their towns from their barons' jurisdictions, and the property held within the free towns seems on its face to be equivalent to the more widely distributed landed property of more modern times. There were no intermediaries except the town government between medieval bourgeois property and the ultimate sanction of the crown.

The state's direct sanctioning, through impersonal agencies, of private property, together with the power of taxation of that property, became the state's bulwark. In such a system kinship ties became irrelevant to maintenance of power. As regards state power and the formal impersonality of property and law, the large society of modern America has been integrated as a structure in the image of the structures of modern European society. As the more powerful component of formative era populations, the Europeans in America imposed their institutions of wealth and rule upon the natives. If such institutions were to be defined as identical with civilization, then indeed American Indians would have to be accounted as aliens to that civilization; although their labors made possible much power and wealth, they have been systematically excluded from its possession. In part this was by their own choice. The kinship principle that dominated tribal custom resisted capital accumulation and bureaucratic government. Indians therefore remained largely separated as an ethnic caste instead of assimilating with the more populous Euramericans in a single structure of social class. (Are there similar peasant minorities in modern Europe?)

The purpose of these remarks, to repeat, is to sketch in some implications of a feasible alternative to present historiographical theories based on assumptions of exceptionalism and elitism. An attempt has been made to provide the basis for the beginning of investigation on new lines. Such an attempt can easily be misunderstood. When comparisons are made systematically, they may be thought to be an effort to prove by analogy—one of the most rudimentary of logical fallacies. Explicitly, then, although I have tried to make a case worth testing I make no claim to "proof," and to underscore that point I have not documented this appendix. My analogies and comparisons are intended as examples to demonstrate meaning—to establish empirical referents for abstract categories. If they stimulate correction, all to the good.

BIBLIOGRAPHY ❧

A Select List of Works Cited

As the bulk of the research for this study has been done in
published materials, manuscripts cited in the notes have not been included
here. Standard reference aids, available in most libraries, are also omitted.
Selections have been made according to various criteria of usefulness respecting the issues discussed in the study.

A few works have been commented upon in "bibliographic notes" scattered
at appropriate places throughout the book. Locations of these notes are added
to the items below.

The list's divisions are as follows: (1) Official records, listed alphabetically
by governments; (2) materials originating before 1800, regardless of the date
of publication; and (3) materials originating since 1800.

Official Records

Connecticut

J. Hammond Trumbull, ed. *The Public Records of the Colony of Connecticut.* 15 vols. Hartford, Conn., 1850–1890.

Great Britain

Sainsbury, W. Noel, ed. *Calendar of State Papers, Colonial Series, 1574–1660.*
London, 1860.
————, et al., eds. *Calendar of State Papers, Colonial Series, America and
West Indies.* London, 1860– .

Maryland

Browne, William Hand, *et al.*, eds. *Archives of Maryland.* 72 vols. to date.
Baltimore, 1883– .

Massachusetts Bay

*The Laws and Liberties of Massachusetts. Reprinted from the Copy of the
1648 Edition in the Henry E. Huntington Library*, with an introduction
by Max Farrand. Cambridge, Mass., 1929.
*Records of the Court of Assistants of the Colony of the Massachusetts Bay,
1630–1692.* 3 vols. Boston, 1901–1908.
Shurtleff, Nathaniel B., ed. *Records of the Governor and Company of the
Massachusetts Bay in New England.* 5 vols. Boston, 1853–1854. See bibliographic notes: chap. 8, n. 24; chap. 18, n. 20.
Suffolk Deeds. 14 vols. Boston, 1880–1906.

Upham, William P., ed. "Town Records of Salem, 1634–1659." Essex Institute, *Historical Collections*, 2d Ser., I (1869), 5–242.

Whitmore, William H., ed. *The Colonial Laws of Massachusetts. Reprinted from the Edition of 1660, with the Supplements to 1672.* Boston, 1889.

New Haven

Hoadly, Charles J., ed. *Records of the Colony and Plantation of New Haven, from 1638 to 1649.* 2 vols. Hartford, Conn., 1857.

New Plymouth

Shurtleff, Nathaniel B., and Pulsifer, David, eds. *Records of the Colony of New Plymouth in New England.* 12 vols. Boston, 1855–1861.

New Sweden

Johnson, Amandus, trans. and ed. *The Instruction for Johan Printz, Governor of New Sweden.* Philadelphia, 1930.

New York

Hastings, Hugh, ed. *Third Annual Report of the State Historian of the State of New York, 1897.* New York and Albany, 1898. See bibliographic note: chap. 5, n. 38.

Leder, Lawrence H., ed. *The Livingston Indian Records, 1666–1723.* Gettysburg, Pa., 1956. Also *Pennsylvania History*, XXIII (January 1956).

O'Callaghan, E. B., ed. *Calendar of Historical Manuscripts in the Office of the Secretary of State, Albany, N.Y.* 2 vols. Albany, N.Y., 1865–1866.

Paltsits, Victor Hugo, ed. *Minutes of the Executive Council of the Province of New York: Administration of Francis Lovelace, 1668–1673.* 2 vols. Albany, N.Y., 1910.

Van Laer, A. J. F., trans. and ed. *Minutes of the Court of Albany, Rensselaerswyck and Schenectady, 1668–1685.* 3 vols. Albany, N.Y., 1926–1932.

Pennsylvania

Hazard, Samuel, ed. *Minutes of the Provincial Council of Pennsylvania. . . .* 16 vols. Harrisburg, Pa., 1838–1853. See bibliographic note: chap. 5, n. 20.

Rhode Island

Bartlett, John Russell, ed. *Records of the Colony of Rhode Island and Providence Plantations, in New England.* 10 vols. Providence, R.I., 1856–1865.

Rhode Island Land Evidences. Abstracts. I. Providence, R.I., 1921.

United Colonies of New England

Pulsifer, David, ed. *Acts of the Commissioners of the United Colonies of New England.* 2 vols. Nathaniel B. Shurtleff and David Pulsifer, eds., *Records of the Colony of New Plymouth in New England*, IX–X. Boston, 1859.

Virginia

Kingsbury, Susan Myra, ed. *The Records of the Virginia Company of London.* 4 vols. Washington, D.C., 1906–1935.

Materials Originating before 1800

Arber, Edward, and Bradley, A. G., eds. *Travels and Works of Captain John Smith, President of Virginia, and Admiral of New England, 1580–1631.* 2 vols. Edinburgh, 1910.

Barbour, Philip, ed. *The Jamestown Voyages under the First Charter, 1606–1609.* Hakluyt Society Publications, 2d Ser., CXXXVI–CXXXVII. 2 vols. Cambridge, 1969.

Bartlett, John Russell, ed. *Letters of Roger Williams, 1632–1682.* Narragansett Club, *Publications*, VI. Providence, R.I., 1874.

Bates, Albert C., ed. *The Wyllys Papers.* Connecticut Historical Society, *Collections*, XXI. Hartford, Conn., 1924.

Bentley, William. "A Description and History of Salem." In Massachusetts Historical Society, *Collections*, 1st Ser., VI, 212–288. Boston, 1800.

Beverley, Robert. *The History and Present State of Virginia* (1705), ed. Louis B. Wright. Chapel Hill, N.C., 1947.

Biggar, H. P., ed. "Jean Ribaut's Discoverye of Terra Florida." *English Historical Review,* XXXII (1917), 253–270.

Boyce, Douglas W., ed. "A Glimpse of Iroquois Culture History through the Eyes of Joseph Brant and John Norton." American Philosophical Society, *Proceedings,* CXVII (1973), 286–294.

Bradford, William. *Of Plymouth Plantation, 1620–1647,* ed. Samuel Eliot Morison. New York, 1952.

Brereton, John. *A Briefe and true Relation of the Discoverie of the North part of Virginia* (1602). March of America Facsimile Series, No. 16. Ann Arbor, Mich., 1966.

Brinley, Francis. "A Briefe Narrative of That Part of New England Called the Nanhiganset Countrey." Rhode Island Historical Society, *Publications,* N.S., VIII (1900), 69–96.

Budd, Thomas. *Good Order Established in Pennsilvania & New-Jersey in America* (1685). March of America Facsimile Series, No. 32. Ann Arbor, Mich., 1966.

Cartier, Jacques. *A Shorte and briefe Narration of the two Navigations and Discoveries to the Northweast partes called Newe Fraunce,* trans. John Florio (1580). March of America Facsimile Series, No. 10. Ann Arbor, Mich., 1966.

Childe, John. *New-Englands Jonas Cast up at London . . .* (1647). In Force, comp., *Tracts,* IV, No. 3 (see entry below).

"The Clarendon Papers." In New-York Historical Society, *Collections,* Publication Fund Series, *1869,* 1–162. New York, 1870.

Cotton, John. *A Reply to Mr. Williams his Examination . . .* (1647), ed. J. Lewis Diman. In Narragansett Club, *Publications,* II, 1–240. Providence, R.I., 1867.

———. *The Way of Congregational Churches Cleared* (1648). In Larzer Ziff, ed., *John Cotton on the Churches of New England.* Cambridge, Mass., 1968.

Davenport, Frances Gardiner, ed. *European Treaties Bearing on the History of the United States and Its Dependencies.* Carnegie Institution of Washington Publication 254. I. Washington, D.C., 1917.

De Vries, David Pietersz. *Short Historical and Journal notes Of several Voyages made in the four parts of the World, namely, Europe, Africa,*

Asia, and America (1655), trans. Henry C. Murphy. In New-York Historical Society, *Collections*, 2d Ser., III, 1–136. New York, 1857.

Eames, Wilberforce, ed. *John Eliot and the Indians, 1652–1657*. New York, 1915.

Eliot, John. "An Account of Indian Churches in New-England" (1673). In Massachusetts Historical Society, *Collections*, 1st Ser., X, 124–129. Boston, 1809.

————. *A Brief Narrative of the Progress of the Gospel amongst the Indians in New-England, in the Year 1670*. London, 1671.

————. *The Christian Commonwealth: or, The Civil Policy of the Rising Kingdom of Jesus Christ* (1660). In Massachusetts Historical Society, *Collections*, 3d Ser., IX, 127–164. Boston, 1846.

————. *A further Accompt of the Progresse of the Gospel amongst the Indians in New-England*. London, 1659.

Force, Peter, comp. *Tracts and Other Papers, Relating Principally to the Origin, Settlement, and Progress of the Colonies in North America, from the Discovery of the Country to the Year 1776*. 4 vols. Washington, D.C., 1836–1846.

Ford, John W., ed. *Some Correspondence between the Governors and Treasurers of the New England Company in London and the Commissioners of the United Colonies in America, the Missionaries of the Company and Others. . . .* London, 1896.

Gardiner, Lion. "Leift. Lion Gardener his relation of the Pequot Warres." In Massachusetts Historical Society, *Collections*, 3d Ser., III, 131–160. Cambridge, Mass., 1833. See bibliographic note: chap. 13, n. 44.

Gookin, Daniel. "Historical Collections of the Indians in New England . . ." (1674). In Massachusetts Historical Society, *Collections*, 1st Ser., I, 141–226. Boston, 1792.

Gorton, Samuel. *Simplicities Defence against Seven-Headed Policy . . .* (1646). In Force, comp., *Tracts*, IV, No. 6 (see entry above).

Hakluyt, Richard. *The Principall Navigations Voiages and Discoveries of the English Nation* (1589), with an introduction by David Beers Quinn and Raleigh Ashlin Skelton. Hakluyt Society Extra Series, XXXIX. 2 vols. Cambridge, 1965.

Hall, Clayton Colman, ed. *Narratives of Early Maryland, 1633–1684*. Original Narratives of Early American History. New York, 1910.

Hoadly Memorial. Connecticut Historical Society, *Collections*, XXIV. Hartford, Conn., 1932.

Hough, Franklin B., ed. *A Narrative of the Causes which led to Philip's Indian War . . . With other Documents concerning this Event*. New York, 1858.

Hubbard, William. *A General History of New England. . . .* Massachusetts Historical Society, *Collections*, 2d Ser., V, VI. Boston, 1815.

————. *The History of the Indian Wars in New England from the First Settlement to the Termination of the War with King Philip, in 1677, from the Original Work by the Rev. William Hubbard* (1677), ed. Samuel G. Drake. 2 vols. Roxbury, Mass., 1865.

————. *The Present State of New-England, Being a Narrative Of the Troubles with the Indians in New-England*. 2d ed. London, 1677. See bibliographic notes: chap. 11, n. 10; chap. 13, n. 55.

Hutchinson, Thomas, comp. *Collection of Original Papers Relative to the History of the Colony of Massachusetts-Bay*. Boston, 1769.

———. *The History of the Colony and Province of Massachusetts-Bay*, ed. Lawrence Shaw Mayo. 3 vols. Cambridge, Mass., 1936.

Jacobs, Wilbur R., ed. *The Appalachian Indian Frontier: The Edmond Atkin Report and Plan of 1755*. Columbia, S.C., 1954.

Johnson, Edward. *Johnson's Wonder-Working Providence, 1628–1651* (1654), ed. J. Franklin Jameson. Original Narratives of Early American History. New York, 1910.

[Johnson, George]. *Nova Britannia: Offering Most Excellent fruites by Planting in Virginia. Exciting all such as be well affected to further the same* (1609). In Force, comp., *Tracts*, I, No. 6 (see entry above).

Lahontan, [Louis-Armand de Lom d'Arce], Baron de. *New Voyages to North-America* (1703), ed. Reuben Gold Thwaites. 2 vols. Chicago, 1905.

Lawson, John. *A New Voyage to Carolina* (1709). March of America Facsimile Series, No. 35. Ann Arbor, Mich., 1966.

Lechford, Thomas. *Plain Dealing; or, News from New-England* (1642), ed. J. Hammond Trumbull (1867). With a new introduction by Darrett B. Rutman. New York, 1969.

Lincoln, Charles H., ed. *Narratives of the Indian Wars, 1675–1699*. Original Narratives of Early American History. New York, 1913.

Lindeström, Peter. *Geographia Americae, with An Account of the Delaware Indians, Based on Surveys and Notes Made in 1654–1656*, trans. and ed. Amandus Johnson. Philadelphia, 1925.

Lorant, Stefan, ed. *The New World: The First Pictures of America*. Rev. ed. New York, 1965.

Mason, John. *A Brief History of the Pequot War* (1736). March of America Facsimile Series, No. 23. Ann Arbor, Mich., 1966. See bibliographic note: chap. 13, n. 44.

Massachusetts Historical Society. *Winthrop Papers*. 5 vols. Boston, 1929–1947.

Mather, Cotton. *The Life and Death of the Renown'd Mr. John Eliot, Who was the First Preacher of the Gospel to the Indians in America*. 2d ed. London, 1691.

Mather, Increase. *A Brief History of the War with the Indians in New-England.* . . . 2d ed. London, 1676.

———. *Diary, March, 1675–December, 1676. Together with Extracts from Another Diary by Him, 1674–1687*, ed. Samuel A. Green. Cambridge, Mass., 1900.

———. *A Relation Of the Troubles which have hapned in New-England, By reason of the Indians there* . . . (1677), ed. Samuel G. Drake as *Early History of New England; Being a Relation of Hostile Passages between the Indians and European Voyagers and First Settlers.* . . . Albany, N.Y., 1864. See bibliographic note: chap. 13, n. 55.

Mayhew, Matthew. *A Brief Narrative of the Success which the Gospel hath had, among the Indians, of Martha's Vineyard (and the Places Adjacent) in New-England.* . . . Boston, 1694.

Morison, Samuel, trans. and ed. *Journals and Other Documents on the Life and Voyages of Christopher Columbus*. New York, 1963.

Morton, Thomas. *New English Canaan; or, New Canaan* . . . (1632). In Force, comp., *Tracts*, II, No. 5 (see entry above).

Myers, Albert Cook, ed. *Narratives of Early Pennsylvania, West New Jersey, and Delaware, 1630–1707.* Original Narratives of Early American History. New York, 1912.

O'Callaghan, E. B., ed. *The Documentary History of the State of New-York.* 4 vols. Albany, N.Y., 1849–1851.

―――, and Fernow, Berthold, eds. *Documents Relative to the Colonial History of the State of New York.* 15 vols. Albany, N.Y., 1856–1887.

Purchas, Samuel. *Hakluytus Posthumus or Purchas His Pilgrimes.* . . . 4 vols. London, 1625. See bibliographic note: chap. 5, n. 62.

―――. *Purchas his Pilgrimage.* 4th ed. London, 1626. See bibliographic note: chap. 5, n. 62.

Quinn, David Beers, ed. *The Roanoke Voyages, 1584–1590.* Hakluyt Society Publications, 2d Ser., CIV–CV. London, 1955.

Ramusio, Giovanni Battista. *Navigationi et Viaggi.* 3 vols. Venice, 1550–1559.

Richardson, Leon Burr, ed. *An Indian Preacher in England.* Dartmouth College Manuscript Series, II. Hanover, N.H., 1933.

Sagard, Gabriel. *The Long Journey to the Country of the Hurons* (1632), ed. George M. Wrong, trans. H. H. Langton. Champlain Society Publications, XXV. Toronto, 1939.

Shepard, Thomas. *The Clear Sun-Shine of the Gospel Breaking Forth upon the Indians in New-England* . . . (1648). In Massachusetts Historical Society, *Collections,* 3d Ser., IV, 25–67. Cambridge, Mass., 1834.

Staples, William R., ed. *Annals of the Town of Providence from Its First Settlement to the Organization of City Government.* . . . Rhode Island Historical Society, *Collections,* V. Providence, R.I., 1843.

Sullivan, James, *et al.*, eds. *The Papers of Sir William Johnson.* 14 vols. Albany, N.Y., 1921–1965.

Taylor, E. G. R., ed. *The Original Writings and Correspondence of the Two Richard Hakluyts.* Hakluyt Society Publications, 2d Ser., LXXVI–LXXVII. London, 1935.

Thwaites, Reuben Gold, ed. *The Jesuit Relations and Allied Documents: Travels and Explorations of the Jesuit Missionaries in New France, 1610–1791.* 73 vols. Cleveland, Ohio, 1896–1901.

Underhill, John. *Newes from America; or, A New and Experimentall Discoverie of New England.* . . . London, 1638.

Van der Donck, Adriaen. *A Description of the New Netherlands* (2d ed., 1656), trans. Jeremiah Johnson. In New-York Historical Society, *Collections,* 2d Ser., I, 125–242. New York, 1841.

Van Laer, A. J. F., trans. and ed. *Documents Relating to New Netherland, 1624–1626, in the Henry E. Huntington Library.* San Marino, Calif., 1924.

―――, trans. and ed. *Van Rensselaer Bowier Manuscripts: Being the Letters of Kiliaen Van Rensselaer, 1630–1643, and Other Documents Relating to the Colony of Rensselaerswyck.* New York State Library, *90th Annual Report,* II. Albany, N.Y., 1908.

Weld, Thomas. "Innocency Cleared" (ca. 1649). *New England Historical and Genealogical Register,* XXXVI (1882), 62–70.

[Weld, Thomas, and Peter, Hugh]. *New England's First Fruits, in respect to the progress of learning, in the Colledge at Cambridge in Massachusetts-bay* . . . (1643). In Massachusetts Historical Society, *Collections,* 1st Ser., I, 242–250. Boston, 1792.

Weslager, C. A. "Susquehannock Indian Religion from an Old Document." *Journal of the Washington Academy of Sciences*, XXXVI (1946), 7–10.

Whitfield, Henry, ed. *The Light appearing more and more towards the perfect Day. Or, a farther Discovery of the present state of the Indians in New-England* ... (1651). In Massachusetts Historical Society, *Collections*, 3d Ser., IV, 100–147. Cambridge, Mass., 1834.

Williams Roger. *Christenings make not Christians, or A Briefe Discourse concerning that name Heathen, commonly given to the Indians. As also concerning that great point of their Conversion* (1645). In *Rhode Island Historical Tracts*, XIV, 1–21. Providence, R.I., 1881.

———. *A Key into the Language of America: Or, An help to the Language of the Natives in that part of America, called New-England* ... (1643), ed. James Hammond Trumbull. In Narragansett Club, *Publications*, I, 61–282. Providence, R.I., 1866.

———. *Mr. Cottons Letter Lately Printed, Examined and Answered* (1644), ed. Reuben Aldridge Guild. In Narragansett Club, *Publications*, I, 285–396. Providence, R.I., 1866.

Williamson, James A., ed. *The Cabot Voyages and Bristol Discovery under Henry VII*. Hakluyt Society Publications, 2d Ser., CXX. Cambridge, 1962.

[Wilson, John]. *The Day-Breaking, If Not The Sun-Rising of the Gospell with the Indians in New-England* (1647). In Massachusetts Historical Society, *Collections*, 3d Ser., IV, 1–23. Cambridge, Mass., 1834.

Winslow, Edward. *The Glorious Progress of the Gospel, Amongst the Indians in New England* ... (1649). In Massachusetts Historical Society, *Collections*, 3d Ser., IV, 69–98. Cambridge, Mass., 1834.

———. *Good Newes from New England* ... (1624). In Alexander Young, ed., *Chronicles of the Pilgrim Fathers of the Colony of Plymouth, from 1602 to 1625*, 269–375. Boston, 1841.

———. *Hypocrisie Unmasked: By A true Relation of the Proceedings of the Governour and Company of the Massachusets against Samuel Gorton (and his Accomplices) a notorious disturber of the Peace and quiet of the severall Governments wherein he lived: With the grounds and reasons thereof, examined and allowed by their Generall Court holden at Boston in New-England in November last, 1646*. London, 1646. See bibliographic note: chap. 15, n. 21.

———. "Letter from Gov. Edward Winslow to Gov. John Winthrop in 1644, in Relation to Early Matters in Connecticut." *New England Historical and Genealogical Register*, XXIX (1875), 237–240.

———. *New-Englands Salamander, Discovered by an Irreligious and Scornfull Pamphlet, called New-Englands Jonas Cast up at London* ... (1647). In Massachusetts Historical Society, *Collections*, 3d Ser., II, 110–145. Cambridge, Mass., 1830.

Winthrop, John. *The History of New England from 1630 to 1649* (1690), ed. James Savage. 2d ed. 2 vols. Boston, 1853. See bibliographic note: chap. 2, n. 45.

———. *Winthrop's Journal, "History of New England," 1630–1649*, ed. James Kendall Hosmer. Original Narratives of Early American History. 2 vols. New York, 1908. See bibliographic note: chap. 2, n. 45.

Wood, William. *New Englands Prospect* (1634). Prince Society Publications, I. Boston, 1865.

Wraxall, Peter. *An Abridgment of the Indian Affairs, Contained in Four Folio Volumes, Transacted in the Colony of New York, from the Year 1678 to the Year 1751,* ed. Charles Howard McIlwain. Harvard Historical Studies, XXI. Cambridge, Mass., 1915.

Materials Originating since 1800

Andrews, Charles M. *The Colonial Background of the American Revolution: Four Essays in American Colonial History.* Rev. ed. New Haven, Conn., 1931.
———. *The Colonial Period of American History.* 4 vols. New Haven, Conn., 1934–1938.
Aspinwall, Thomas. "William Vassall No Factionist." Massachusetts Historical Society, *Proceedings,* VI (1862–1863), 471–479.
Axtell, James. "The Scholastic Philosophy of the Wilderness." *William and Mary Quarterly,* 3d Ser., XXIX (1972), 335–366.
———. "The White Indians of Colonial America." *William and Mary Quarterly,* 3d Ser., XXXII (1975), 55–88.
Bailyn, Bernard. *The Ideological Origins of the American Revolution.* Cambridge, Mass., 1967.
———. *The New England Merchants in the Seventeenth Century.* Cambridge, Mass., 1955.
Banks, Charles Edward. *The History of Martha's Vineyard, Dukes County, Massachusetts.* 3 vols. Edgartown, Mass., 1966; orig. publ. 1911–1925.
Barbour, Philip L. *Pocahontas and Her World.* Boston, 1970.
———. *The Three Worlds of Captain John Smith.* London, 1964.
Belshaw, Cyril S. *Traditional Exchange and Modern Markets.* Modernization of Traditional Societies Series. Englewood Cliffs, N.J., 1965.
Bennett, M. K. "The Food Economy of the New England Indians, 1607–75." *Journal of Political Economy,* LXIII (1955), 369–397.
Benson, Evelyn A. "The Huguenot Le Torts: First Christian Family on the Conestoga." *Journal of the Lancaster County Historical Society,* LXV (1961), 92–103.
Black, Robert C., III. *The Younger John Winthrop.* New York, 1966.
Bloch, Marc. *Feudal Society,* trans. L. A. Manyon. 2 vols. Chicago, 1961.
———. *The Royal Touch: Sacred Monarchy and Scrofula in England and France,* trans. J. E. Anderson. London, 1973.
Blodgett, Harold. *Samson Occom.* Dartmouth College Manuscript Series, III. Hanover, N.H., 1935.
Bodge, George Madison. *Soldiers in King Philip's War....* 3d ed. Boston, 1906.
Borah, Woodrow, and Cook, Sherburne F. "Conquest and Population: A Demographic Approach to Mexican History." American Philosophical Society, *Proceedings,* CXIII (1969), 177–183.
Bowen, Richard LeBaron. *Early Rehoboth: Documented Historical Studies of Families and Events in This Plymouth Colony Township.* 3 vols. Rehoboth, Mass., 1946.
Brayton, George A. *A Defence of Samuel Gorton and the Settlers of Shawomet. Rhode Island Historical Tracts,* XVII. Providence, R.I., 1883.
Brockunier, Samuel Hugh. *The Irrepressible Democrat: Roger Williams.* New York, 1940.

Brodhead, John Romeyn. *History of the State of New York.* 2 vols. New York, 1859–1871.

———. "Memoir on the Early Colonization of New Netherland." In New-York Historical Society, *Collections*, 2d Ser., II. New York, 1849.

Burke, Charles T. *Puritans at Bay.* New York, 1967.

Bushnell, David. "The Treatment of the Indians in Plymouth Colony." *New England Quarterly*, XXVI (1953), 193–218.

Cady, John Hutchins. *Rhode Island Boundaries, 1636–1936.* [Providence, R.I.], 1936.

Calder, Isabel MacBeath. *The New Haven Colony.* New Haven, Conn., 1934.

Canny, Nicholas P. "The Ideology of English Colonization: From Ireland to America." *William and Mary Quarterly*, 3d Ser., XXX (1973), 575–598.

Carneiro, Robert L. "On the Relationship between Size of Population and Complexity of Social Organization." *Southwestern Journal of Anthropology*, XXIII (1967), 234–243.

Caulkins, Frances Manwaring. *History of New London, Connecticut. From the First Survey of the Coast in 1612, to 1852.* New London, Conn., 1852.

Chase, Henry E. "Notes on the Wampanoag Indians." In Smithsonian Institution, *Annual Report.* Washington, D.C., 1883.

Cohen, Ronald D. "The Hartford Treaty of 1650: Anglo-Dutch Cooperation in the Seventeenth Century." *New-York Historical Society Quarterly*, LIII (1969), 311–332.

———. "New England and New France, 1632–1651: External Relations and Internal Disagreements among the Puritans." Essex Institute, *Historical Collections*, CVIII (1972), 252–271.

Collins, Guy N. "Notes on the Agricultural History of Maize." In American Historical Association, *Annual Report for 1919*, I, 409–429. Washington, D.C., 1923.

Cook, Sherburne F. "The Significance of Disease in the Extinction of the New England Indians." *Human Biology*, XLV (1973), 485–508.

———, and Borah, Woodrow. *The Population of the Mixteca Alta, 1520–1960.* Ibero-Americana, L. Berkeley and Los Angeles, 1968.

Cooper, John M. "Is the Algonquian Family Hunting Ground System Pre-Columbian?" *American Anthropologist*, N.S., XLI (1939), 66–90.

———. "Land Tenure among the Indians of Eastern and Northern North America." *Pennsylvania Archaeologist*, VIII (1938), 55–59.

Craven, Wesley Frank. *Dissolution of the Virginia Company: The Failure of a Colonial Experiment.* New York, 1932.

———. "Indian Policy in Early Virginia." *William and Mary Quarterly*, 3d Ser., I (1944), 65–82.

Davitt, Thomas E. *The Basic Values in Law; A Study of the Ethico-legal Implications of Psychology and Anthropology.* American Philosophical Society, *Transactions*, N.S., LVIII, pt. v (1968).

Day, Gordon M. "The Identity of the Sokokis." *Ethnohistory*, XII (1965), 237–249.

———. "The Indian as an Ecological Factor in the Northeastern Forest." *Ecology*, XXXIV (1953), 329–345.

De Forest, John W. *History of the Indians of Connecticut from the Earliest Known Period to 1850.* Hartford, Conn., 1851.

Dobyns, Henry F. "Estimating Aboriginal American Population: An Appraisal of Techniques with a New Hemispheric Estimate." *Current Anthropology*, VII (1966), 395–416.

Drake, Frederick C. "Witchcraft in the American Colonies, 1647–62." *American Quarterly*, XX (1968), 694–725.

Drake, Samuel G. *Biography and History of the Indians of North America from its First Discovery. . . .* 11th ed. Boston, 1856.

Driver, Harold E. *Indians of North America*. Chicago, 1961.

———, and Massey, William C. *Comparative Studies of North American Indians*. American Philosophical Society, *Transactions*, N.S., XLVII, pt. ii (1957).

Dunn, Richard S. "John Winthrop, Jr., and the Narragansett Country." *William and Mary Quarterly*, 3d Ser., XIII (1956), 68–86.

———. "John Winthrop, Jr., Connecticut Expansionist: The Failure of His Designs on Long Island, 1663–1675." *New England Quarterly*, XXIX (1956), 3–26.

———. *Puritans and Yankees: The Winthrop Dynasty of New England, 1630–1717*. Princeton, N.J., 1962.

Eccles, W. J. *The Canadian Frontier, 1534–1760*. Histories of the American Frontier. New York, 1969.

———. *Frontenac: The Courtier Governor*. Toronto, 1959.

Ellis, George Edward. "The Indians of Eastern Massachusetts." In Justin Winsor, ed., *The Memorial History of Boston, Including Suffolk County, Massachusetts, 1630–1880*, I, 241–274. 4 vols. Boston, 1880–1881.

Ellis, George W., and Morris, John E. *King Philip's War*. New York, 1906.

Engels, Frederick. *The Origin of the Family, Private Property, and the State* (1884), trans. Ernest Untermann. Chicago, 1902.

Felt, Joseph B. *Annals of Salem*. 2d ed. 2 vols. Salem, Mass., 1845–1849.

———. "Who was the First Governor of Massachusetts?" Essex Institute, *Historical Collections*, 1st Ser., V (1863), 73–84.

Fenton, William N. "Collecting Materials for a Political History of the Six Nations." American Philosophical Society, *Proceedings*, XCIII (1949), 233–238.

———. "Iroquoian Culture History: A General Evaluation." In William N. Fenton and John Gulick, eds., *Symposium on Cherokee and Iroquois Culture*, 253–277. Smithsonian Institution, Bureau of American Ethnology, Bulletin 180. Washington, D.C., 1961.

———. "Locality as a Basic Factor in the Development of Iroquois Social Structure." In William N. Fenton, ed., *Symposium on Local Diversity in Iroquois Culture*, 35–53. Smithsonian Institution, Bureau of American Ethnology, Bulletin 149. Washington, D.C., 1951.

———. "The New York State Wampum Collection: The Case for the Integrity of Cultural Treasures." American Philosophical Society, *Proceedings*, CXV (1971), 437–461.

Fisher, Raymond H. *The Russian Fur Trade, 1550–1700*. University of California Publications in History, XXXI. Berkeley and Los Angeles, 1943.

Flannery, Regina. *An Analysis of Coastal Algonquian Culture*. Catholic University of America Anthropological Series, VII. Washington, D.C., 1939.

Fontana, Bernard L. "American Indian Oral History: An Anthropologist's Note." *History and Theory: Studies in the Philosophy of History*, VIII (1969), 366–370.

Gibson, James R. *Feeding the Russian Fur Trade: Provisionment of the Okhotsk Seaboard and the Kamchatka Peninsula, 1639–1856.* Madison, Wis., 1969.

Goebel, Julius, Jr. "The Matrix of Empire." Introductory essay in J. H. Smith, *Appeals to the Privy Council from the American Plantations,* xiii–lxi. New York, 1950.

Gonner, E. C. K. *Common Land and Inclosure.* London, 1912.

Gookin, Warner F. "Indian Deeds on the Vineyard." *Bulletin of the Massachusetts Archaeological Society,* XIII (January 1952), 6–7.

Greene, Welcome Arnold. "The Great Battle of the Narragansetts. Dec. 19, 1675." *Narragansett Historical Register,* V (1886–1887), 331–343.

Hadlock, Wendell S. "The Concept of Tribal Separation as Rationalized in Indian Folklore." *Pennsylvania Archaeologist,* XVI (1946), 84–90.

———. "War among the Northeastern Woodland Indians." *American Anthropologist,* N.S., XLIX (1947), 204–221.

Hallett, Leaman F. "Indian Trails and Their Importance to the Early Colonists." *Bulletin of the Massachusetts Archaeological Society,* XVI (April 1956), 41–46.

Hallowell, A. Irving. "The Backwash of the Frontier: The Impact of the Indian on American Culture." In Walker D. Wyman and Clifton B. Kroeber, eds., *The Frontier in Perspective,* 229–258. Madison, Wis., 1957.

———. "The Impact of the American Indian on American Culture." *American Anthropologist,* N.S., LIX (1957), 201–217.

———. *Culture and Experience.* Philadelphia, 1955.

Healy, George R. "The French Jesuits and the Idea of the Noble Savage." *William and Mary Quarterly,* 3d Ser., XV (1958), 153–167.

Heckewelder, John. *An Account of the History, Manners, and Customs of the Indian Nations, Who Once Inhabited Pennsylvania and the Neighbouring States* (1818), ed. William C. Reichel, Historical Society of Pennsylvania, *Memoirs,* XII. Philadelphia, 1871.

Herndon, G. Melvin. "Indian Agriculture in the Southern Colonies." *North Carolina Historical Review,* XLIV (1967), 283–297.

History of the Town of Dorchester, Massachusetts. Boston, 1859.

History of the Town of Hingham, Massachusetts. 3 vols. Hingham, Mass., 1893.

Hodge, Frederick Webb, ed. *Handbook of American Indians North of Mexico.* Smithsonian Institution, Bureau of American Ethnology, Bulletin 30. 2 vols. Washington, D.C., 1907–1910.

Holmes, G. K. "Aboriginal Agriculture—The American Indians." In L. H. Bailey, ed., *Cyclopedia of American Agriculture: A Popular Survey of Agricultural Conditions, Practices, and Ideals in the United States and Canada,* IV, 24–39. 4 vols. New York, 1907–1909.

Hunt, George T. *The Wars of the Iroquois.* Madison, Wis., 1940.

Innis, Harold A. *The Fur Trade in Canada: An Introduction to Canadian Economic History.* New Haven, Conn., 1930. Rev. ed. by S. D. Clark and W. T. Easterbrook. Toronto, 1964.

Jacobs, Wilbur R. *Diplomacy and Indian Gifts: Anglo-French Rivalry Along the Ohio and Northwest Frontiers, 1748–1763.* Stanford, Calif., 1950.

———. *Dispossessing the American Indian: Indians and Whites on the Colonial Frontier.* New York, 1972.

―――. "The Tip of an Iceberg: Pre-Columbian Indian Demography and Some Implications for Revisionism." *William and Mary Quarterly*, 3d Ser., XXXI (1974), 123–132.

Jennings, Francis. "The Constitutional Evolution of the Covenant Chain." American Philosophical Society, *Proceedings*, CXV (1971), 88–96.

―――. "The Delaware Interregnum." *Pennsylvania Magazine of History and Biography*, LXXXIX (1965), 174–198.

―――. "Goals and Functions of Puritan Missions to the Indians." *Ethnohistory*, XVIII (1971), 197–212.

―――. "Glory, Death, and Transfiguration: The Susquehannock Indians in the Seventeenth Century." American Philosophical Society, *Proceedings*, CXII (1968), 15–53.

―――. "Incident at Tulpehocken." *Pennsylvania History*, XXXV (1968), 335–355.

―――. "The Indian Trade of the Susquehanna Valley." American Philosophical Society, *Proceedings*, CX (1966), 406–424.

―――. "Miquon's Passing: Indian-European Relations in Colonial Pennsylvania, 1674 to 1755." Ph.D. dissertation, University of Pennsylvania, 1965.

―――. "The Scandalous Indian Policy of William Penn's Sons: Deeds and Documents of the Walking Purchase." *Pennsylvania History*, XXXVII (1970), 19–39.

―――. "A Vanishing Indian: Francis Parkman versus His Sources." *Pennsylvania Magazine of History and Biography*, LXXXVII (1963), 306–323.

―――. "Virgin Land and Savage People." *American Quarterly*, XXIII (1971), 519–541.

Jennings, Jesse D., and Norbeck, Edward, eds. *Prehistoric Man in the New World*. Chicago, 1964.

Jones, Joseph. "Explorations and Researches Concerning the Destruction of the Aboriginal Inhabitants of America by Various Diseases, as Syphilis, Matlazahuatl, Pestilence, Malarial Fever, and Small-pox." *New Orleans Medical and Surgical Journal*, V (1877–1878), 926–941.

Jones, W. R. "The Image of the Barbarian in Medieval Europe." *Comparative Studies in Society and History*, XIII (1971), 376–407.

Kellaway, William. *The New England Company, 1649–1776: Missionary Society to the American Indians*. London, 1961.

Kellogg, Louise Phelps. "The American Colonial Charter. A Study of English Administration in Relation Thereto, Chiefly After 1688." American Historical Association, *Annual Report*, 191–201. Washington, D.C., 1903.

Kennedy, J. H. *Jesuit and Savage in New France*. Yale Historical Publications, Miscellany, L. New Haven, Conn., 1950.

Knowles, Nathaniel. "The Torture of Captives by the Indians of Eastern North America." American Philosophical Society, *Proceedings*, LXXXII (1940), 151–225.

Kroeber, A. L. *Anthropology*. Rev. ed. New York, 1948.

―――. *Cultural and Natural Areas of Native North America*. University of California Publications in American Archaeology and Ethnology, XXXVIII. Berkeley and Los Angeles, 1939.

―――. "Evolution, History, and Culture." In Theodora Kroeber, ed., *An Anthropologist Looks at History*, 179–199. Berkeley and Los Angeles, 1966.

————. "Native American Population." *American Anthropologist*, N.S., XXXVI (1934), 1–25.

Lanctot, Gustave. *A History of Canada*, trans. Josephine Hambleton and Margaret M. Cameron. 3 vols. Cambridge, Mass., 1963–1965.

Land, Robert Hunt. "Henrico and Its College." *William and Mary Quarterly*, 2d Ser., XVIII (1938), 453–498.

Langdon, George D., Jr. *Pilgrim Colony: A History of New Plymouth, 1620–1691*. Yale Publications in American Studies, XII. New Haven, Conn., 1966.

Leach, Douglas Edward. *Flintlock and Tomahawk: New England in King Philip's War*. New York, 1958.

————. *The Northern Colonial Frontier, 1607–1763*. Histories of the American Frontier. New York, 1966.

Lewis, Theodore B. "Land Speculation and the Dudley Council of 1686." *William and Mary Quarterly*, 3d Ser., XXXI (1974), 255–272.

Lowery, Woodbury. *The Spanish Settlements within the Present Limits of the United States, 1513–1561*. 2 vols. New York, 1959; orig. publ. New York, 1901–1905.

Lurie, Nancy Oestreich. "The World's Oldest On-Going Protest Demonstration: North American Indian Drinking Patterns." *Pacific Historical Review*, XL (1971), 311–332.

Lydon, J. F. *The Lordship of Ireland in the Middle Ages*. Toronto, 1972.

Lynam, Edward, ed. *Richard Hakluyt and His Successors*. Hakluyt Society Publications, 2d Ser., XCIII. London, 1946.

MacLeod, William Christie. "The Family Hunting Territory and Lenápe Political Organization." *American Anthropolgist*, N.S., XXIV (1922), 448–463.

Malone, Patrick M. "Changing Military Technology among the Indians of Southern New England, 1600–1677." *American Quarterly*, XXV (1973), 48–63.

Masselman, George. *The Cradle of Colonialism*. New Haven, Conn., 1963.

Mayhew, Eleanor Ransom. "The Christiantown Story, 1659–1959." *Dukes County Intelligencer*, I, No. 1 (1959).

Mayo, Lawrence Shaw. *John Endecott*. Cambridge, Mass., 1936.

Means, Carroll Alton. "Mohegan-Pequot Relationships as Indicated by the Events Leading to the Pequot Massacre of 1637 and Subsequent Claims in the Mohegan Land Controversy." *Bulletin of the Archaeological Society of Connecticut*, XXI (1947), 26–34.

Mooney, James M. *The Aboriginal Population of America North of Mexico*, ed. John R. Swanton. Smithsonian Miscellaneous Collections, LXXX, No. 7. Washington, D.C., 1928.

Morgan, Edmund S. *The Puritan Dilemma: The Story of John Winthrop*. Boston, 1958.

————. "The Puritans and Sex." *New England Quarterly*, XV (1942), 591–607.

Morgan, Lewis Henry. *Ancient Society, or Researches in the Lines of Human Progress from Savagery through Barbarism to Civilization* (1877), ed. Eleanor Burke Leacock. Cleveland, Ohio, 1963.

————. *League of the Ho-De-No-Sau-Nee, Iroquois*. Rochester, N.Y., 1851.

Nash, Gary B. "The Image of the Indian in the Southern Colonial Mind." *William and Mary Quarterly*, 3d Ser., XXIX (1972), 197–230.

———. "The Quest for the Susquehanna Valley: New York, Pennsylvania, and the Seventeenth-Century Fur Trade." *New York History*, XLVIII (1967), 3–27.

———. *Red, White, and Black: The Peoples of Early America*. History of the American People Series. Englewood Cliffs, N.J., 1974.

Newcomb, W. W., Jr. "A Re-examination of the Causes of Plains Warfare." *American Anthropologist*, N.S., LII (1950), 317–330.

———. "Toward an Understanding of War." In Gertrude E. Dole and Robert L. Carneiro, eds., *Essays in the Science of Culture in Honor of Leslie A. White*, 317–336. New York, 1960.

Otterbein, Keith F. "Why the Iroquois Won: An Analysis of Iroquois Military Tactics." *Ethnohistory*, XI (1964), 56–63.

Palfrey, John Gorham. *History of New England*. 5 vols. Boston, 1858–1890.

Parker, Arthur C. *Parker on the Iroquois*, ed. William N. Fenton. Syracuse, N.Y., 1968.

Parkman, Francis. *The Book of Roses*. Boston, 1866.

———. *The Conspiracy of Pontiac, and the Indian War after the Conquest of Canada* (1851). New Library ed. 2 vols. Boston, 1909.

———. *The Jesuits in North America in the Seventeenth Century* (1867). New Library ed. Boston, 1909.

———. *The Old Regime in Canada* (1874). New Library ed. Boston, 1908.

Parry, J. H. *The Age of Reconnaissance*. Cleveland, Ohio, 1963.

———. *The Spanish Seaborne Empire*. The History of Human Society. New York, 1966.

Pearce, Roy Harvey. "The Metaphysics of Indian-Hating." *Ethnohistory*, IV (1957), 27–40.

———. *The Savages of America: A Study of the Indian and the Idea of Civilization*. Rev. ed. Baltimore, 1965.

Pilling, James Constantine, ed. *Bibliography of the Algonquian Languages*. Smithsonian Institution, Bureau of American Ethnology, Bulletin 13. Washington, D.C., 1891.

Prucha, Francis Paul. *American Indian Policy in the Formative Years: The Indian Trade and Intercourse Acts, 1790–1834*. Cambridge, Mass., 1962.

Rachlin, Carol King. "The Historic Position of the Proto-Cree Textiles in the Eastern Fabric Complex: An Ethnological-Archaeological Correlation." In *Contributions to Anthropology, 1958*, 80–89. National Museum of Canada, Bulletin 167, Anthropological Series, No. 48. Ottawa, 1960.

Rau, Charles. "Ancient Aboriginal Trade in North America." In Smithsonian Institution, *Annual Report, 1872*, 348–394. Washington, D.C., 1873.

———. "Prehistoric Fishing in Europe and North America." In *Smithsonian Contributions to Knowledge*, XXV, 1–342. Washington, D.C., 1885.

Redfield, Margaret Park, ed. *Human Nature and the Study of Society: The Papers of Robert Redfield*. 2 vols. Chicago, 1962–1963.

Redfield, Robert. *Peasant Society and Culture: An Anthropological Approach to Civilization*. Chicago, 1956.

Rich, E. E. "Colonial Settlement and Its Labour Problems." In E. E. Rich and C. H. Wilson, eds., *The Cambridge Economic History of Europe*, IV, 308–373. Cambridge, 1967.

———. *The History of the Hudson's Bay Company, 1670–1870*. 2 vols. London, 1958–1959.

Richards, Cara Elizabeth. "The Role of Iroquois Women: A Study of the Onondaga Reservation." Ph.D. dissertation, Cornell University, 1957.

Roberts, William Iredell. "The Fur Trade of New England." Ph.D. dissertation, University of Pennsylvania, 1958.

Roelker, William Greene. "Samuell Gorton's Master Stroke." *Rhode Island History*, II (1943), 1–10.

Rose-Troup, Frances. *The Massachusetts Bay Company and Its Predecessors.* New York, 1930.

Rotstein, Abraham. "Fur Trade and Empire: An Institutional Analysis." Ph.D. dissertation, University of Toronto, 1967.

Russell, Howard S. "How Aboriginal Planters Stored Food." *Bulletin of the Massachusetts Archaeological Society*, XXIII (April–July 1962), 47–49.

———. "New England Indian Agriculture." *Bulletin of the Massachusetts Archaeological Society*, XXII (April–July 1961), 58–61.

Rutman, Darrett B. *Winthrop's Boston: Portrait of a Puritan Town, 1630–1649.* Chapel Hill, N.C., 1965.

Ruttenber, E. M. *History of the Indian Tribes of Hudson's River* (1872). Empire State Historical Publications Series, No. 95. Port Washington, N.Y., 1971.

Salisbury, Neal Emerson. "Conquest of the 'Savage': Puritans, Puritan Missionaries, and Indians, 1620–1680." Ph.D. dissertation, University of California, Los Angeles, 1972.

———. "Red Puritans: The 'Praying Indians' of Massachusetts Bay and John Eliot." *William and Mary Quarterly*, 3d Ser., XXXI (1974), 27–54.

Sauer, Carl Ortwin. *The Early Spanish Main.* Berkeley and Los Angeles, 1966.

Schaeffer, C. E. "The Grasshopper or Children's War—A Circumboreal Legend?" *Pennsylvania Archaeologist*, XII (1942), 60–61.

Schmitt, Robert C. *Demographic Statistics of Hawaii: 1778–1965.* Honolulu, 1968.

Sheehan, Bernard W. "Indian-White Relations in Early America: A Review Essay." *William and Mary Quarterly*, 3d Ser., XXVI (1969), 267–286.

Slotkin, J. S., and Schmitt, Karl. "Studies of Wampum." *American Anthropologist*, N.S., LI (1949), 223–236.

Smith, Joseph Henry. *Appeals to the Privy Council from the American Plantations.* New York, 1950.

Smith, Marian W. "American Indian Warfare." New York Academy of Sciences, *Transactions*, 2d Ser., XIII (June 1951), 348–365.

Smith, Nicholas N. "The Transition from Wigwams to Frame Houses by the Old Town, Maine, Penobscot and the Woodstock, New Brunswick, Malecite." Paper delivered at the Fourth Conference on Algonquian Studies, Big Moose Lake, N.Y., September 24–26, 1971. Mimeographed.

Snyderman, George S. *Behind the Tree of Peace: A Sociological Analysis of Iroquois Warfare.* Pennsylvania Archaeologist, XVIII, Nos. 3–4 (1948).

———. "The Function of Wampum in Iroquois Religion." American Philosophical Society, *Proceedings*, CV (1961), 571–608.

———. "The Functions of Wampum." American Philosophical Society, *Proceedings*, XCVIII (1954), 469–494.

Speck, Frank G. *Family Hunting Territories and Social Life of Various Algonkian Bands of the Ottawa Valley.* Canada Department of Mines, Geological Survey, Memoir 70. Ottawa, 1915.

————. "The Functions of Wampum among the Eastern Algonkian." American Anthropological Association, *Memoirs*, VI (1919), 3–71.

————. "The Grasshopper War in Pennsylvania: An Indian Myth that Became History." *Pennsylvania Archaeologist*, XII (1942), 31–34.

————, and Eiseley, Loren C. "Significance of Hunting Territory Systems of the Algonkian in Social Theory." *American Anthropologist*, N.S., XLI (1939), 269–280.

————, and Dexter, Ralph W. "Utilization of Marine Life by the Wampanoag Indians of Massachusetts." *Journal of the Washington Academy of Sciences*, XXXVIII (1948), 257–265.

Spicer, Edward H. *Cycles of Conquest: The Impact of Spain, Mexico, and the United States on the Indians of the Southwest, 1533–1960.* Tucson, Ariz., 1962.

Spinden, H. J. "Population of Ancient America." In Smithsonian Institution, *Annual Report*, 451–471. Washington, D.C., 1929.

Stearn, E. Wagner, and Stearn, Allen E. *The Effect of Smallpox on the Destiny of the Amerindian.* Boston, 1945.

Steinberg, Clarence. "Atin, Pyrochles, Cymochles: On Irish Emblems in 'The Faerie Queene.'" *Neuphilologische Mitteilungen*, LXXII (Helsinki, 1971), 749–761.

Swanton, John R. *The Indians of the Southeastern United States.* Smithsonian Institution, Bureau of American Ethnology, Bulletin 137. Washington, D.C., 1946.

Tannahill, Reay. *Food in History.* New York, 1973.

Tate, W. E. *The Enclosure Movement.* New York, 1967.

Taylor, Henry Osborn. *The Mediaeval Mind: A History of the Development of Thought and Emotion in the Middle Ages.* 4th ed. 2 vols. London, 1925.

Thomas, Cyrus. Introduction to Charles C. Royce, comp., *Indian Land Cessions in the United States*, 527–647. In Smithsonian Institution, Bureau of American Ethnology, *Annual Report*, XVIII, pt. ii. Washington, D.C. 1896–1897.

Thompson, Benjamin F. *The History of Long Island.* 2d ed. 2 vols. New York, 1843.

Tooker, Elisabeth. *An Ethnography of the Huron Indians, 1615–1649.* Smithsonian Institution, Bureau of American Ethnology, Bulletin 190. Washington, D.C., 1964.

Trelease, Allen W. *Indian Affairs in Colonial New York: The Seventeenth Century.* Ithaca, N.Y., 1960.

Trigger, Bruce G. "Champlain Judged by His Indian Policy: A Different View of Early Canadian History." *Anthropologica*, N.S., XIII (1971), 85–114.

————. "The Destruction of Huronia: A Study in Economic and Cultural Change, 1609–1650." Royal Canadian Institute, *Transactions*, XXXIII (1960), 14–45.

————. *The Huron: Farmers of the North.* Case Studies in Cultural Anthropology. New York, 1969.

————. "The Jesuits and the Fur Trade." *Ethnohistory*, XII (1965), 30–53.

————. "The Mohawk-Mahican War (1624–28): The Establishment of a Pattern." *Canadian Historical Review*, LII (1971), 276–286.

Vaughan, Alden T. *New England Frontier: Puritans and Indians, 1620–1675.* Boston, 1965.

———. "Pequots and Puritans: The Causes of the War of 1637." *William and Mary Quarterly*, 3d Ser., XXI (1964), 256–269.

———. "A Test of Puritan Justice." *New England Quarterly*, XXXVIII (1965), 331–339.

Vogel, Virgil J. *American Indian Medicine*. Civilization of the American Indian Series, XCV. Norman, Okla., 1970.

Wallace, Anthony F. C. *The Death and Rebirth of the Seneca*. New York, 1970.

———. *King of the Delawares: Teedyuscung, 1700–1763*. Philadelphia, 1949.

———. "Political Organization and Land Tenure among the Northeastern Indians, 1600–1830." *Southwestern Journal of Anthropology*, XIII (1957), 301–321.

———. Review of Albert Cook Myers, ed., *William Penn's Own Account of the Lenni Lenape or Delaware Indians*. In *Pennsylvania History*, XXXVIII (1971), 325.

———. "Woman, Land, and Society: Three Aspects of Aboriginal Delaware Life." *Pennsylvania Archaeologist*, XVII (1947), 1–35.

Walne, Peter. "The Collections for Henrico College, 1616–1618." *Virginia Magazine of History and Biography*, LXXX (1972), 259–266.

Wallace, Paul A. W. *Indian Paths of Pennsylvania*. Harrisburg, Pa., 1965.

Washburn, Wilcomb E. "The Moral and Legal Justifications for Dispossessing the Indians." In James Morton Smith, ed., *Seventeenth-Century America: Essays in Colonial History*, 15–32. Chapel Hill, N.C., 1959.

———. "Philanthropy and the American Indian: The Need for a Model." *Ethnohistory*, XV (1968), 43–56.

———. *Red Man's Land / White Man's Law: A Study of the Past and Present Status of the American Indian*. New York, 1971.

———. "The Writing of American Indian History: A Status Report." *Pacific Historical Review*, XL (1971), 261–281.

Weeden, William B. *Economic and Social History of New England, 1620–1789*. 2 vols. Boston, 1890.

———. *Indian Money as a Factor in New England Civilization*. Johns Hopkins University Studies in Historical and Political Science, 2d Ser., VIII–IX. Baltimore, 1884.

Weslager, C. A. *The English on the Delaware, 1610–1682*. New Brunswick, N.J., 1967.

———, in collaboration with Dunlap, A. R. *Dutch Explorers, Traders and Settlers in the Delaware Valley, 1609–1664*. Philadelphia, 1961.

Willison, George F. *Saints and Strangers. . . .* New York, 1945.

Winship, George Parker. Introduction to *The New England Company of 1649 and John Eliot*, v–lxvi. Prince Society Publications, XXXVI. Boston, 1920.

Witthoft, John. "The Grasshopper War in Lenape Land." *Pennsylvania Archaeologist*, XVI (1946), 91–94.

———, and Kinsey, W. Fred, III, eds. *Susquehannock Miscellany*. Harrisburg, Pa., 1959.

Wolf, Eric R. *Peasants*. Foundations of Modern Anthropology Series. Englewood Cliffs, N.J., 1966.

Wright, Louis B. *Religion and Empire: The Alliance between Piety and Commerce in English Expansion, 1558–1625*. Chapel Hill, N.C., 1943.

Zimmerman, Albright G. "The Indian Trade of Colonial Pennsylvania."
Ph.D. dissertation, University of Delaware, 1966.
————. "James Logan, Proprietary Agent." *Pennsylvania Magazine of History and Biography*, LXXVIII (1954), 143–176.

INDEX ⅊

Francis Jennings is former director of the Center for the History of the American Indian at the Newberry Library, Chicago, Illinois. Before joining the Newberry Library, Mr. Jennings was professor of history at Cedar Crest College, Allentown, Pennsylvania. He is also a past president of the American Society of Ethnohistory.